BAPTIST

CONFESSIONS OF FAITH

BAPTIST
CONFESSIONS OF FAITH

by
WILLIAM L. LUMPKIN

JUDSON PRESS®
VALLEY FORGE

International Standard Book No. 0-8170-0016-X

Library of Congress Catalog Card No. 59-7945

The name JUDSON PRESS is registered as a
trademark in the U.S. Patent Office.

Printed in the United States of America

Foreword

BAPTISTS HAVE PUBLISHED numerous confessions of faith since the early years of the seventeenth century. Many of these documents, intended for local use, are interesting but are not of major significance. Others, however, of a more general nature, mark important developments of the Baptist story and deserve to be remembered and studied.

Two significant collections of Baptist confessions have been made previously. In 1854, Edward Bean Underhill gathered the major seventeenth-century English confessions and prepared a brief introductory editorial comment in connection with them. These confessions, with some other documents, were published by the Hanserd Knollys Society (of London) under the title *Confessions of Faith and other Public Documents Illustrative of the History of the Baptist Churches of England in the Seventeenth Century.* One document included was the *Baptist Catechism* put forth by the Particular Baptist General Assembly of 1693.

In 1910, W. J. McGlothlin, who was Professor of Church History in the Southern Baptist Theological Seminary, Louisville, Ky., prepared a valuable collection of important statements of doctrine of various bodies of Baptists around the world, with historical annotations. His work, entitled *Baptist Confessions of Faith,* published by the American Baptist Publication Society (The Judson Press), was widely read in England as well as in America.

Now a more comprehensive work is called for, especially because of the rising interest in confessionalism and in the Baptist view of the Church. Since 1910 several noteworthy seventeenth-century Baptist documents have been discovered. Documents of Continental

5

Anabaptism and English Separatism are now better known. Also, it is necessary that twentieth-century Baptist confessional developments, particularly in America, be surveyed. Because the entire collection of these materials deserves systematic study, the present work has assumed the form of a confessional history, with the addition of full introductory and editorial matter. The archaic features of many of the early confessions, such as those typified by spelling, punctuation, and grammatical construction, have been maintained. Moreover, since the various confessions, in their original form, do not agree with one another in their orthography and capitalization, this volume may appear to contain many inconsistencies.

The author would acknowledge his indebtedness to the two earlier works. He hopes that this volume will serve as a useful handbook for the study of Baptist history and doctrine. Gratitude for other individual contributions of materials and service in connection with this volume is expressed in the body of the work.

—W. L. LUMPKIN

Norfolk, Va.
June 1, 1959.

Contents

3

4

5

6

1

Backgrounds of the Baptist Movement

THE BAPTIST MOVEMENT appeared in Europe in connection with the left wing of the Protestant Reformation of the sixteenth century. Efforts have often been made to trace the ideological sources of this movement to late medieval evangelical dissent as well as to the Reformation itself. It has not been proven, however, that the Baptist Movement has a genetic connection with any of the pre-Reformation evangelical groups. Leaders of the Swiss Brethren or Anabaptists[1] of sixteenth-century Switzerland and Germany, in many cases having come directly from the priesthood of the Catholic Church, admitted no formal connection with or indebtedness to earlier sects, but declared their only source to be the Scriptures. However, careful study of their teachings leads one to judge that they reflected the outlook and some of the distinctive emphases of such groups as the Waldenses. At the beginning of the sixteenth century there were people in every country of Western Europe who earnestly protested against corruption in the Church and who, therefore, welcomed the protests of Martin Luther and Ulrich Zwingli. Such were the people who came to be called Anabaptists. Having much in common with the churchly reformers, these folk at first were identified with their movements, and they separated from them only when the Reformation seemed to fall short of a full application of principles clearly enunciated by the Reformers.

The English Reformation, in spite of formative influences from the Continent, is generally agreed to have had its roots in native soil. Thus, in its English manifestation, the Baptist Movement

---

[1] Or Re-baptizers, so named by opponents because they baptized on profession of faith those who had been christened in infancy.

reflected, particularly, a heritage from an older native reform spirit as well as a heritage from sixteenth-century Continental Anabaptism and Calvinism. It is consequently to be studied not only against the background of the Protestant Reformation of Europe, but also against that of the Lollards, fourteenth-century co-laborers of John Wyclif, whose movement of evangelical dissent continued in many parts of England until well into the sixteenth century. The Lollards prepared no formal creeds or confessions of faith, their emphasis being rather upon the authority of the Scriptures; however some of their expository tracts are extant. The contents of one such tract, *The Lanterne of Ligt,* written early in the fifteenth century, have been summarized as follows:

> Holy Scripture is the supreme authority in all matters of faith and conduct; therefore all should be allowed to study the Bible in their mother tongue.
> The preaching of God's Word is the chief duty of a priest. Pilgrimage, image-worship, and the costly decoration of churches are unlawful.
> The sale of sacraments, absolutions and indulgences, and the traffic in the benefices of the Church are contrary to God's law.
> The taking of an oath, or swearing in any form, is forbidden by the teaching of Christ.
> The temporal possessions of the clergy are the cause of most of the evils in the Church.
> Holy Church is the company of all faithful souls.
> The Pope is Antichrist: therefore obedience should not be rendered to him or to his servants since they command what is contrary to God's law.[2]

Native religious sources of the Reformation in England, all associated with Lollardy, include Wyclif's writings, the witness of martyrs, a deep anti-clerical feeling, and the circulation of the Scriptures in the vernacular. The work of William Tyndale in translating the Scriptures, early in the sixteenth century, was indispensable to the English Reformation. Because the Scriptures came into the hands of the people, Henry VIII was practically forced to license English Bibles for publication in 1538.

Due largely to lack of strong, passionate leadership after John Wyclif, the native English Reformation failed to develop fully in

---

[2] Swinburn, *The Lanterne of List,* pp. xiv-xv.

its own strength. There was no Luther in England to make the movement articulate. The religious impulse became enveloped in political struggle. It had to be reclaimed and enlarged by influences from outside England.

Early in the reformatory period, Lutheran influences reached England, but they were short-lived. Anabaptism arrived at about the same time, coming by way of the Netherlands. This radical reform movement spread after 1525 with amazing rapidity, from Switzerland throughout many parts of Western Europe. The Anabaptists held that the New Testament Church is a voluntary community of individuals who have been transformed by the working of the Holy Spirit, in an experience of grace, and that baptism is "the symbol and seal of the faith of the regenerated." From these views there followed the doctrines of the brotherhood of baptized believers and the separation of the Church from the State and the world. With the great reformers of the sixteenth century, Church and State were practically coextensive. All citizens of a territory, except those excommunicate, were held to be members of the established Church. The Anabaptists were despised by the reformers for insisting that the Church is composed only of deliberate followers of Christ, that admission to it is by confession and baptism, that it is autonomous, and that it keeps itself pure by discipline.

By 1535, there were many Dutch Anabaptists living in England, and thereafter their numbers increased steadily. The proportion who were Anabaptists is unknown, but in 1562 Dutch people in England numbered 30,000.[3] Gregory records that between 50,000 and 100,000 Dutch refugees came to England in the period of the struggle of the Netherlands against Alva.[4] They came in largest numbers when persecution was greatest in their country and when England offered the most promising refuge, and they congregated in East Coast centers such as London, Norwich (where they were a majority of the population in 1587),[5] Dover, Romeney, Sandwich, Canterbury, Colchester, and Hastings. Not all were to be found in the East, for many went to work in the woolen industry in the West.[6] Few of these immigrants ever repatriated themselves; most of them were assimilated by the English, losing their identity.

---

[3] Walker, *Creeds and Platforms of Congregationalism*, 6.
[4] *Puritanism in the Old World and in the New*, 204.
[5] Walker, *supra*.
[6] Whitley, *Minutes of the General Assembly of Gen. Bapts.*, xl.

In spite of persecution, organized Anabaptist life took shape and continued for a time in numerous English localities. Anabaptists of England sent deputies to the great conference at Buckholt, in Westphalia, in 1536.[7] Years afterward, even when organized life and witness were no longer possible, the spirit and distinctive emphases of Anabaptism survived on the English scene. Heath says, "The more the matter is studied, the more it will be seen that in its interest in Anabaptist teaching England was second only to Germany and the Netherlands."[8] It seems reasonable to suppose that, unconsciously or otherwise, principles of Anabaptism became a part of the thinking of zealous Englishmen who were seeking a more thorough reformation of the Church in their land.

The earliest experiment in congregational separatism took place under the leadership of Robert Browne in Norwich. In other centers in which Anabaptists had settled in large numbers some of the earliest Baptist communities took shape. As Gregory says, "The Anabaptists were Puritans before Puritanism had sprung into recognized existence, and held substantially all that Puritans afterwards contended for. . . ."[9] The Anabaptist principles were never entirely forgotten in England: they leavened both the Established Church and the kingdom; on the basis of them various nonconformist bodies took their rise.

The influence of Anabaptism on the rise of English Baptists was brought to bear more directly than merely in the rise of English Puritanism. By the beginning of the seventeenth century a radical form of Puritanism had developed, called Separatism. The Separatists boldly decided to leave the Church of England in order to set up model churches of the Reformation, to which models they hoped the Church of England would in time conform. Their separation appeared expedient if further reformation of religion was to take place in England, but they hoped the separation was but temporary. They did not forsake the idea of a national Church. Persecution forced numbers of the Separatists into exile in Holland, where Anabaptism still flourished and whence it had come to England. In direct contact with the Dutch Anabaptists, some of the Separatists reached conclusions identified with the Baptist Movement, and an

---

[7] Heath, *Contemporary Review*, 400.
[8] *Ibid.*, 176.
[9] *Ibid.*, 176.

English Baptist Church appeared by 1611 in Amsterdam, but it returned to England the next year.

Calvinism was the dominant theology of the Separatists. Indeed, in the period 1550-1610, it had become the orthodox faith of England, having entered the country especially through associates and pupils of Calvin, teachers in the Universities, and the Genevan Bible (a family Bible with elaborate Calvinistic notes). Calvinism was challenged, however, in 1595, by a Cambridge University student who protested against a lecturer's highly Calvinistic exposition of the Creed. Another lecturer, John Baro, once a pupil of Calvin, supported the challenge. An appeal was made to Archbishop Whitgift, who soon produced nine Calvinistic Articles which were approved in an informal meeting of several bishops at Lambeth. The Articles had no technical authority, but divines at Cambridge almost unanimously subscribed to them. Their acceptance of the Articles is important because it showed that some bishops of the Church of England were not satisfied with the moderate Calvinism of the Thirty-nine Articles of their Church. The first three of the Lambeth Articles stated that:

1. God hath from eternity predestined certain persons to life and hath reprobated certain persons to death.

2. The moving or efficient cause of predestination unto life is not the foresight of faith, or of perseverance, or of good works, or of anything that is in the persons predestined, but the alone will of God's good pleasure.

3. The predestinate are a predetermined and certain number, who can neither be lessened nor increased.[10]

The doctrine of Calvin was challenged in the Netherlands by Arminius, and the Synod of Dort was summoned in 1619, to which were invited representatives of several Reformed Churches. King James sent five divines who accepted, finally, the highly Calvinistic Confession of the Synod. The Church of England was not bound by the decisions at Dort, but its agreement with these conclusions indicates the general Calvinistic position of King and clergy at that time.

Opposition to Calvinism, nevertheless, grew in some circles in England. Arminianism became popular around the court of James I, and the High Church party came to favor it. It was not so with the

---

10 *Cyclopaedia of Biblical, Theological, and Ecclesiastical Literature*, I, 441-442.

Puritan party, which ever favored Calvinism, and, after 1620, adopted the Lambeth Articles as a kind of confession of faith[11] and the "Quinquarticular Formula" of Dort as one of its standards.[12] John Smyth of Lincolnshire became an exception to the Puritan rule. An exile in Holland in 1608, his association with Dutch Anabaptists (Mennonites) encouraged his reaching anti-Calvinistic conclusions. His position, which became approximately that of the first General Baptist Church is, however, not to be considered a thoroughgoing Arminianism so much as a protest against high-Calvinism. His followers were, until the rise of the Quakers, the only important anti-Calvinistic group in English Separatism. Yet, even they were not free from influences of their Calvinistic environment.

The primary streams of English Baptist thought are therefore traceable to the old native evangelicalism, to Anabaptism, and to Calvinism. In one sense, all of the Protestant confessions, beginning with the Lutheran Confession of Augsburg in 1530, stand in the background of the Baptist confessions, but those of Anabaptism and English Separatism are immediate forerunners. Like confessions of the sixteenth and seventeenth centuries generally, the Baptist confessions were sectarian, being intended to differentiate Baptists from other groups of Christians and to justify their separate existence.

The Baptist Movement has traditionally been non-creedal in the sense that it has not erected authoritative confessions of faith as official bases of organization and tests of orthodoxy. An authority which could impose a confession upon individuals, churches, or larger bodies, has been lacking, and the desire to achieve uniformity has never been strong enough to secure adoption of a fixed creed even if the authority for imposing it had existed. Still, Baptists have recognized the valuable uses to which confessions of faith might be put. Their earliest confessions were called forth for apologetic and propaganda purposes in response to criticism from other church groups, State Churches, the Quakers, and groups of Baptists of varying attitudes toward Calvinistic theology. In the seventeenth century, confessions were used both to distinguish Baptist groups from one another and from other Protestants, and to show kinship with one another and other Protestant groups. At the same time

[11] Dorner, *History of Protestant Theology*, 49-50.
[12] Green, *The Christian Creed and the Creeds of Christendom*, 140.

the confessions were employed, as a rule secondarily, as specific summaries for instruction of members, as means of refuting heresy, and as guides to the study of the Bible (rather than as authoritative substitutes for the Bible).

In the American confessions instructional and propaganda purposes have been paramount. Periods of controversy and crisis have been most productive of Baptist confessions, which have appeared in each century since the sixteenth, though in greatest numbers in the seventeenth. Therefore Baptists have freely made, used, and discarded confessions of faith, which have appeared in the name of individuals, of single churches, and of groups of churches or denominations. For them confessions have ever been simply manifestos of prevailing doctrine in particular groups. No confession has ever permanently bound individuals, churches, associations, conventions, or unions among Baptists. Even when issued, the confessions have allowed for individual interpretation and perspective, so that each signatory was made to feel that the statements spoke for him.

Baptist confessions are numerous, but only the more general and important ones are included in this work. Their permanent value is twofold: they define the doctrinal consensus of Baptist groups at particular times and they illustrate Baptist history. In either of these connections, the confessions are indispensable to the student of Baptist history.

2

Forerunner Confessions

---

1. Anabaptist Confessions

The Swiss Brethren or Anabaptists produced no formal creeds. On account of ceaseless persecution and oppression, they had little opportunity to write extensively of their faith. A sense of organizational strength, out of which creedal expression naturally comes, was not permitted to develop. Also, there was entertained by the community a genuine prejudice against authoritative creeds, as inadequate substitutes for the Scriptures, and as dangerous limitations upon the Spirit's leadership in interpreting the Scriptures.

A. *Eighteen Dissertations Concerning the Entire Christian Life and of What It Consists, 1524*

The most scholarly and prolific literary exponent of early Anabaptism was Balthasar Hübmaier, pastor of Waldshut, who embraced Anabaptist views in 1525. Educated at the Universities of Freiburg and Ingolstadt, where he received his doctorate in theology in 1512, his powerful preaching and inspired leadership resulted in the reformation of his church and the turning of a large following in Waldshut to Anabaptist views. While at Waldshut and later at Nickolsburg in Moravia, whither he was forced by persecution to flee in 1526, he acted as spokesman and organizer for a vigorous and growing movement. At least twenty-four of his writings are extant, all having been prepared before July, 1528, when he was arrested by the Austrian authorities and soon burned at the stake in Vienna.

On October 26-28, 1523, Hübmaier engaged in the second religious disputation at Zürich, held by order of the government of Zürich to consider rejection of the mass and of the worship of holy images. In this disputation Hübmaier provided the first public evidence that he had broken with the Roman Catholic Church. He supported Zwingli in opposing the mass and images and, next to Zwingli, he was chiefly prominent in the debate.

Upon his return to Waldshut, Hübmaier zealously set about the task of winning his people to the evangelical faith. Seeking to reproduce the Zürich disputation in Waldshut, he appealed to the city and country clergy of the Deanery of Waldshut to consider eighteen articles or theses which he proposed to debate with them at the next pastoral conference. Vedder[1] doubts that the disputation was actually held, though when the propositions were sent to the printer Hübmaier certainly planned to hold it. Although published prior to the formal organization of the radical party in Zürich in 1525, the propositions included views which were to characterize the Swiss Brethren movement.[2] In 1524, however, Hübmaier had not yet identified himself with the radicals.

The following English translation by G. D. Davidson, Ph.D., of William Jewell College, is in his unpublished collection, *The Writings of Balthasar Hübmaier* (5-9).[3] Hübmaier often used the surname "Friedberger," Friedberg being his native town.

EIGHTEEN DISSERTATIONS CONCERNING THE ENTIRE CHRISTIAN LIFE AND OF WHAT IT CONSISTS. PROPOSITIONS UPHELD AT WALDSHUT BY DR. BALTHASAR FRIEDBERGER, AND OTHERS. 1524

I, Balthasar Friedberger, doctor and pastor at Waldshut, wish for grace and peace in Christ Jesus our Lord, to all the brethren of my chapter, and to the chaplain thereof.

Beloved men and brethren: it is an old custom that comes to us from the times of the apostles, that when evil things befall concerning the faith, all the men who wish to speak the word of God, and are of a Christian way of thinking, should assemble to search the Scriptures. This is done so that in nourishing the Christian flock, according to the word of God, the utmost care might be taken. Such an assembly has been called the synod, or chapter, or brotherhood. And especially, in these recent dangerous times to our Christian believers these assemblies may give honor and good cheer in a not

---

[1] *Balthasar Hübmaier*, 72.

[2] The eighth thesis in particular.

[3] A copy of the original Dissertations may be found in the Staatsbibliothek, Berlin. Davidson has supplied punctuation in the following translation.

unimportant degree. For we should nourish, not our bodies alone but also our souls, with food and drink and thus be more useful to our flocks, and feed them the Word of God in peace and unity. To this end, all contentious and abusive words should be laid aside. Therefore I admonish you, men and brethren, by the bonds of brotherly love, by the holiness of Christian peace, and by the name of our Lord Jesus Christ, that in these dissertations put forth by me in the form of questions and investigations you may perceive a Scriptural foundation, and at the next meeting of the chapter which will be held at Waldshut, you may confer with me fraternally and peaceably. Now in order that we may not consume time unnecessarily with human vanities, and thereby do hurt to our own good reputations, bring your Bibles, or, in case you have none, your mass-books with you, so that we may share one with another, and thoroughly, the God-given words of Christian instruction. To the best of my ability, I shall not send you away from this brotherly meal unnourished by spiritual food and drink. Farewell, in the name of Jesus Christ our Saviour.

1. Faith alone makes us pious before God.

2. This belief is recognition of the mercy of God, since He hath redeemed us by the sacrifice of his only-begotten Son, And this excludes all nominal Christians who have only an historical belief in God.

3. Such a faith must be not idle, but must reach up toward God in thankfulness, and toward men in all good works of brotherly love. And all works of penance must be abandoned, such as the burning of candles, the use of palms and holy water.

4. All works are good which God has commanded us. And all acts which he has forbidden are evil. In this class belong such things as eating of fish on fast days, abstention from meat, the wearing of cowls.

5. The Mass is not a sacrifice but a memorial of the death of Christ. Therefore it may not be offered, either for the quick or for the dead. Thus must perish the counsels of those souls that practice cunning and deceit.

6. As often as such a memorial is celebrated, shall the death of our Lord be preached, as each one of us finds in his heart and on his tongue. This excludes all silent Masses.

7. Images and pictures are of no value. Therefore you should trust no longer in wood and stone, but in the living and suffering God.

8. Since every Christian believes for himself and is baptized for himself, everyone must see and judge by the Scriptures whether he is being properly nourished by his pastor.

9. Since Christ alone has died for our sins and in his name we have all been baptized, therefore he must be for us the only intercessor and mediator. Here perish all pilgrimages.

10. It is far better to read one verse of a Psalm in the speech of one's own land, which can be understood, than to sing five entire songs in a foreign tongue, which cannot be understood by the church. Here perish Matins, Prime, Tercets, Vespers, Complines and Vigils.

11. All teachings that are not of God are in vain and shall be rooted up. Here perish the disciples of Aristotle, as well as the Thomists, the Scotists, Bonaventure and Occam, and all teaching that does not proceed from God's word.

12. The time will come — and now is — when no one will be deemed a true priest save the man who preaches the Word of God. This disposes of Masses, votive offerings, reliquaries, and masses for others.

13. It is the duty of members of the church to support with suitable food and clothing, and to protect those who teach them the Word of God in its purity. Here perish courtiers, pensioners, religious corporations, absentee priests, deceivers, and the tellers of vain dreams.

14. Let him who dreads purgatory and him whose God is his belly seek the grave of Moses, which it will be long ere he finds.

15. That priests and others might hide the sins of their flesh was the reason why Barabas [sic] was set free and Christ was slain.

16. To command virtue in reliance upon human strength, is nothing else than to command one to fly without wings.

17. He who misrepresents the Word of God for temporal gain, or conceals it, sells the grace of God, like red Esau for a mess of pottage and Christ will deny him.

18. He who does not seek, in the sweat of his brow, to earn his bread, is accursed, unworthy of the food that he eats. Here are cursed all idlers, be they who they may.

TRUTH IS IMMORTAL

B. *The Schleitheim Confession, 1527*

The Swiss Brethren were conscious of a larger unity within their movement than is usually credited to it, and on February 24, 1527, at a general conference at the small town of Schleitheim, near Schaffhausen, they addressed themselves to practical problems of their fellowship. The result was a document entitled "Brotherly Union of a Number of Children of God Concerning Seven Articles," otherwise known as the Schleitheim Confession. The Seven Articles were not a complete statement of Christian doctrine, but a defense against the teachings of some "false brethren" who inclined to antinomianism, and a guide for the congregations represented at the conference. The "false brethren" appear to have been certain South German Anabaptists (sometimes called Spiritualist Anabaptists) whose faith was more rationalistic and less biblical than that of the Swiss Brethren. However, the Articles appeared to have all the characteristics of a genuine confession of faith, and they soon gained a wider acceptance and authority.

As the first important Anabaptist declaration of faith to represent a group, the Seven Articles are of supreme importance as a source document for the study of the views of the Swiss Brethren. Indeed, most later confessions and doctrinal summaries of the Anabaptists are founded upon it. After months of controversy with Zwingli on the issues of separation of Church and State and believers' baptism, the little group of radicals in Zürich led by Conrad Grebel had formally organized themselves, in January, 1525, through reinstituting believers' baptism. Persecution of the Brethren at the hands of the authorities had begun at once, and the leaders quickly became fugitives or were imprisoned. Grebel died in the summer of 1526, probably of natural causes. Manz and Blaurock were captured in December of the same year, but not before they had gained a large popular following in the Zürich area. Manz was executed by drowning in January, 1527, while Blaurock was driven from Zürich as a foreigner. Hübmaier was on his way to Moravia in 1526. Reublin, Hetzer, and Michael Sattler escaped or were banished from Zürich in the same year.

Sattler, one of the noblest leaders of the new movement, was a well educated young man, a native of Staufen, near Freiburg. He appears to have been the leader of the Schleitheim Conference, and he must have had much to do with fashioning the Seven Articles.[4] His experience as prior of a monastery had disgusted him with the worldliness of the clergy and monks and, having studied the New Testament, he declared for the reformation. By March, 1525, he was associated with Conrad Grebel. Having been banished from Zürich, he went to Strasburg late in that year and in that city he favorably impressed many. Early in 1527 he left Strasburg and engaged in evangelistic work in the Neckar Valley, gathering a congregation in the small town of Horb. To this period of his life belongs the Schleitheim meeting. Shortly thereafter, he was arrested, imprisoned for eleven weeks in Binsdorf, tried in Rothenburg, and, on May 21, 1527, barbarously executed.

The Seven Articles are also important because of their widespread circulation and use in the Anabaptist Movement. Zwingli, in a refutation of them in 1527, said that there was scarcely an Anabaptist who did not possess a copy of their "so well-grounded commandments," revealing their general acceptance.

The German text of 1533 with epistolary sections by Michael Sattler follows, translated by J. C. Wenger.[5]

BROTHERLY UNION OF A NUMBER OF CHILDREN OF GOD CONCERNING SEVEN ARTICLES

May joy, peace and mercy from our Father through the atonement of the blood of Christ Jesus, together with the gifts of the Spirit — Who is sent from the Father to all believers for their strength and comfort and for their perseverance in all tribulation until the end, Amen — be to all those who love God, who are the children of light, and who are scattered everywhere as it has been ordained of God our Father, where they are with one mind assembled together in one God and Father of us all: Grace and peace of heart be with you all, Amen.

---

[4] Wenger, *Mennonite Quarterly Review*, XIX, 246, in his article on "The Schleitheim Confession of Faith," cites a letter from fifty Swiss Brethren elders to Menno Simons which mentioned that there was a minister at their conference held at Strasburg in 1555-56 in whose house the agreement of Michael Sattler was made.

[5] Perhaps the oldest extant copy of the original German Articles is a manuscript in the Staatsarchive of Bern, Switzerland. Another manuscript copy is in the University Library of Heidelberg, Germany, and another is in the Cathedral Library at Bratislava, Czechoslovakia. Printed copies also exist. One, bearing the date 1533, is in the Staatsbibliothek, Berlin, and another of the same edition is in a private collection. A second print, in two copies, is found in the State Library, Munich. Important translations in other languages include the following: (1) Zwingli's rendering into Latin in his *Elenchus*, 1527, (2) a French translation used by Calvin in his attack on the Anabaptists, 1544, (3) a Dutch translation in the two editions of 1560 and 1565 used by followers of Menno Simons, (4) a modern translation into English (from the Latin) by W. J. McGlothlin in *Baptist Confessions of Faith*. Wenger's translation first appeared in the *Mennonite Qtly. Rev.*, XIX, 247-253.

Beloved brethren and sisters in the Lord: First and supremely we are always concerned for your consolation and the assurance of your conscience (which was previously misled) so that you may not always remain foreigners to us and by right almost completely excluded, but that you may turn again to the true implanted members of Christ, who have been armed through patience and knowledge of themselves, and have therefore again been united with us in the strength of a godly Christian spirit and zeal for God.

It is also apparent with what cunning the devil has turned us aside, so that he might destroy and bring to an end the work of God which in mercy and grace has been partly begun in us. But Christ, the true Shepherd of our souls, Who has begun this in us, will certainly direct the same and teach [us][6] to His honor and our salvation, Amen.

Dear brethren and sisters, we who have been assembled in the Lord at Schleitheim on the Border, make known in points and articles to all who love God that as concerns us we are of one mind to abide in the Lord as God's obedient children, [His] sons and daughters, we who have been and shall be separated from the world in everything, [and] completely at peace. To God alone be praise and glory without the contradiction of any brethren. In this we have perceived the oneness of the Spirit of our Father and of our common Christ with us. For the Lord is the Lord of peace and not of quarreling, as Paul points out. That you may understand in what article this has been formulated you should observe and note [the following].

A very great offense has been introduced by certain false brethren among us, so that some have turned aside from the faith, in the way they intend to practice and observe the freedom of the Spirit and of Christ. But such have missed the truth, and to their condemnation are given over to the lasciviousness and self-indulgence of the flesh. They think faith and love may do and permit everything, and nothing will harm them nor condemn them, since they are believers.

Observe, you who are God's members in Christ Jesus, that faith in the Heavenly Father through Jesus Christ does not take such form. It does not produce and result in such things as these false brethren and sisters do and teach. Guard yourselves and be warned of such people, for they do not serve our Father, but their father, the devil.

---

[6] The words in brackets are inserted by the translator to clarify the text. The words in parentheses are a part of the original text.

But you are not that way. For they that are Christ's have crucified the flesh with its passions and lusts. You understand me well and [know] the brethren whom we mean. Separate yourselves from them for they are perverted. Petition the Lord that they may have the knowledge which leads to repentance, and [pray] for us that we may have constancy to persevere in the way which we have espoused, for the honor of God and of Christ, His Son, Amen.

The articles which we discussed and on which we were of one mind are these 1. Baptism; 2. The Ban [excommunication]; 3. Breaking of Bread; 4. Separation from the Abomination; 5. Pastors in the Church; 6. The Sword; and 7. The Oath.[7]

First. Observe concerning baptism: Baptism shall be given to all those who have learned repentance and amendment of life, and who believe truly that their sins are taken away by Christ, and to all those who walk in the resurrection of Jesus Christ, and wish to be buried with Him in death, so that they may be resurrected with him, and to all those who with this significance request it [baptism] of us and demand it for themselves. This excludes all infant baptism, the highest and chief abominations of the pope. In this you have the foundation and testimony of the apostles. Mt. 28, Mk. 16, Acts 2, 8, 16, 19. This we wish to hold simply, yet firmly and with assurance.

Second. We agree as follows on the ban: The ban shall be employed with all those who have given themselves to the Lord, to walk in His commandments, and with all those who have been baptized into the one body of Christ and who are called brethren and sisters, and yet who slip sometimes and fall into error and sin, being inadvertently overtaken. The same shall be admonished twice in secret and the third time openly disciplined or banned according to the command of Christ. Mt. 18. But this shall be done according to the regulation of the Spirit (Mt. 5) before the breaking of bread, so that we may break and eat one bread, with one mind and in one love, and may drink of one cup.

Third. In the breaking of bread we are of one mind and are agreed [as follows]: All those who wish to break one bread in remembrance of the broken body of Christ, and all who wish to drink of one drink as a remembrance of the shed blood of Christ, shall be united beforehand by baptism in one body of Christ which is the church of God and whose Head is Christ. For as Paul points out we cannot at the same time be partakers of the Lord's table and the table of devils; we cannot at the same time drink the cup of the

---

[7] The distinctive emphasis of The Confession, as of The Anabaptist Movement, is on the nature of the Church.

Lord and the cup of the devil. That is, all those who have fellowship with the dead works of darkness have no part in the light. Therefore all who follow the devil and the world have no part with those who are called unto God out of the world. All who lie in the evil have no part in the good.

Therefore it is and must be [thus] : Whoever has not been called by one God to one faith, to one baptism, to one Spirit, to one body, with all the children of God's church, cannot be made [into] one bread with them, as indeed must be done if one is truly to break bread according to the command of Christ.

Fourth. We are agreed [as follows] on separation:[8] A separation shall be made from the evil and from the wickedness which the devil planted in the world; in this manner, simply that we shall not have fellowship with them [the wicked] and not run with them in the multitude of their abominations. This is the way it is: Since all who do not walk in the obedience of faith, and have not united themselves with God so that they wish to do His will, are a great abomination before God, it is not possible for anything to grow or issue from them except abominable things. For truly all creatures are in but two classes, good and bad, believing and unbelieving, darkness and light, the world and those who [have come] out of the world, God's temple and idols, Christ and Belial; and none can have part with the other.

To us then the command of the Lord is clear when He calls upon us to be separate from the evil and thus He will be our God and we shall be His sons and daughters.

He further admonishes us to withdraw from Babylon and the earthly Egypt that we may not be partakers of the pain and suffering which the Lord will bring upon them.

From all this we should learn that everything which is not united with our God and Christ cannot be other than an abomination which we should shun and flee from. By this is meant all popish and anti-popish works and church services, meetings and church attendance, drinking houses, civic affairs, the commitments [made in] unbelief and other things of that kind, which are highly regarded by the world and yet are carried on in flat contradiction to the command of God, in accordance with all the unrighteousness which is in the world. From all these things we shall be separated and have no part with them for they are nothing but an abomination, and they are the cause

---

[8] The idea of separation is encountered in practically every wing of the Baptist Movement, though understanding of the practical consequences of separation varies among the several branches. The above confessors were striving for a community of saints, without particular regard for the social and economic conditions of their day.

of our being hated before our Christ Jesus, Who has set us free from the slavery of the flesh and fitted us for the service of God through the Spirit Whom He has given us.

Therefore there will also unquestionably fall from us the unchristian, devilish weapons of force—such as sword, armor and the like, and all their use [either] for friends or against one's enemies—by virtue of the word of Christ, Resist not [him that is] evil.

Fifth. We are agreed as follows on pastors in the church of God· The pastor in the church of God shall, as Paul has prescribed, be one who out-and-out has a good report of those who are outside the faith. This office shall be to read, to admonish and teach, to warn, to discipline, to ban in the church, to lead out in prayer for the advancement of all the brethren and sisters, to lift up the bread when it is to be broken, and in all things to see to the care of the body of Christ, in order that it may be built up and developed, and the mouth of the slanderer be stopped.

This one moreover shall be supported of the church which has chosen him, wherein he may be in need, so that he who serves the Gospel may live of the Gospel as the Lord has ordained. But if a pastor should do something requiring discipline, he shall not be dealt with except [on the testimony of] two or three witnesses. And when they sin they shall be disciplined before all in order that the others may fear.

But should it happen that through the cross this pastor should be banished or led to the Lord [through martyrdom] another shall be ordained in his place in the same hour so that God's little flock and people may not be destroyed.

Sixth. We are agreed as follows concerning the sword: The sword is ordained of God outside the perfection of Christ. It punishes and puts to death the wicked, and guards and protects the good. In the Law the sword was ordained for the punishment of the wicked and for their death, and the same [sword] is [now] ordained to be used by the worldy magistrates.

In the perfection of Christ, however, only the ban is used for a warning and for the excommunication of the one who has sinned, without putting the flesh to death,—simply the warning and the command to sin no more.

Now it will be asked by many who do not recognize [this as] the will of Christ for us, whether a Christian may or should employ the sword against the wicked for the defense and protection of the good, or for the sake of love.

Our reply is unanimously as follows: Christ teaches and commands us to learn of Him, for He is meek and lowly in heart and so shall we find rest to our souls. Also Christ says to the heathenish woman who was taken in adultery, not that one should stone her according to the law of His Father (and yet He says, As the Father has commanded me, thus I do), but in mercy and forgiveness and warning, to sin no more. Such [an attitude] we also ought to take completely according to the rule of the ban.

Secondly, it will be asked concerning the sword, whether a Christian shall pass sentence in worldly dispute and strife such as unbelievers have with one another. This is our united answer: Christ did not wish to decide or pass judgment between brother and brother in the case of the inheritance, but refused to do so. Therefore we should do likewise.

Thirdly, it will be asked concerning the sword, Shall one be a magistrate if one should be chosen as such? The answer is as follows: They wished to make Christ king, but He fled and did not view it as the arrangement of His Father. Thus shall we do as He did, and follow Him, and so shall we not walk in darkness. For He Himself says, He who wishes to come after me, let him deny himself and take up his cross and follow me. Also, He Himself forbids [the employment of] the force of the sword saying, The worldly princes lord it over them, etc., but not so shall it be with you. Further, Paul says, Whom God did foreknow He also did predestinate to be conformed to the image of His son, etc. Also Peter says, Christ has suffered (not ruled) and left us an example, that ye should follow His steps.

Finally, it will be observed that it is not appropriate for a Christian to serve as a magistrate because of these points: The government magistracy is according to the flesh, but the Christians' is according to the Spirit; their houses and dwelling remain in this world, but the Christians' citizenship is in heaven; the weapons of their conflict and war are carnal and against the flesh only, but the Christians' weapons are spiritual, against the fornication of the devil. The worldlings are armed with steel and iron, but the Christians are armed with the armor of God, with truth, righteousness, peace, faith, salvation and the Word of God. In brief, as is the mind of Christ toward us, so shall the mind of the members of the body of Christ be through Him in all things, that there may be no schism in the body through which it would be destroyed. For every kingdom divided against itself will be destroyed. Now since Christ is as it is written of Him, His members must also be the same, that His body may remain complete and united to its own advancement and upbuilding.

Seventh. We are agreed as follows concerning the oath: The oath is a confirmation among those who are quarreling or making promises. In the Law it is commanded to be performed in God's Name, but only in truth, not falsely. Christ, who teaches the perfection of the Law, prohibits all swearing to His [followers], whether true or false,—neither by heaven, nor by the earth, nor by Jerusalem, nor by our head,—and that for the reason which He shortly thereafter gives, For you are not able to make one hair white or black. So you see it is for this reason that all swearing is forbidden: we cannot fulfill that which we promise when we swear, for we cannot change [even] the very least thing on us.

Now there are some who do not give credence to the simple command of God, but object with this question: Well now, did not God swear to Abraham by Himself (since He was God) when He promised him that He would be with him and that He would be his God if he would keep His commandments,—why then should I not also swear when I promise to someone? Answer: Hear what the Scripture says: God, since He wished more abundantly to show unto the heirs the immutability of His counsel, inserted an oath, that by two immutable things (in which it is impossible for God to lie) we might have a strong consolation. Observe the meaning of this Scripture: What God forbids you to do, He has power to do, for everything is possible for Him. God swore an oath to Abraham, says the Scripture, so that He might show that His counsel is immutable. That is, no one can withstand nor thwart His will; therefore He can keep His oath. But we can do nothing, as is said above by Christ, to keep or perform [our oaths]: therefore we shall not swear at all [nichts schweren].

Then others further say as follows: It is not forbidden of God to swear in the New Testament, when it is actually commanded in the Old, but it is forbidden to swear by heaven, earth, Jerusalem and our head. Answer: Hear the Scripture, He who swears by heaven swears by God's throne and by Him who sitteth thereon. Observe: It is forbidden to swear by heaven, which is only the throne of God: how much more is it forbidden [to swear] by God Himself! Ye fools and blind, which is greater, the throne or Him that sitteth thereon?

Further some say, Because evil is now [in the world, and] because man needs God for [the establishment of] the truth, so did the apostles Peter and Paul also swear. Answer: Peter and Paul only testify of that which God promised to Abraham with the oath. They themselves promise nothing, as the example indicates clearly. Testifying and swearing are two different things. For when a person swears he is in the first place promising future things, as Christ was promised to Abraham Whom we a long time afterwards received. But when a person bears testimony he is testifying about the present, whether it is good or evil, as Simeon spoke to Mary about Christ and testified, Behold this (child) is set for the fall and rising of man in Israel, and for a sign which shall be spoken against.

Christ also taught us along the same line when He said, Let your communication be Yea, yea; Nay, nay; for whatsoever is more than these cometh of evil. He says, Your speech or word shall be yea and nay. (However) when one does not wish to understand, he remains closed to the meaning. Christ is simply Yea and Nay, and all those who seek Him simply will understand His word. Amen.

* * * * *

Dear brethren and sisters in the Lord: These are the articles of certain brethren who had heretofore been in error and who had failed to agree in the true understanding, so that many weaker consciences were perplexed, causing the Name of God to be greatly slandered. Therefore there has been a great need for us to become of one mind in the Lord, which has come to pass. To God be praise and glory!

Now since you have so well understood the will of God which has been made known by us, it will be necessary for you to achieve perseveringly, without interruption, the known will of God. For you know well what the servant who sinned knowingly heard as his recompense.

Everything which you have unwittingly done and confessed as evil doing is forgiven you through the believing prayer which is offered by us in our meeting for all our shortcomings and guilt. [This state is yours] through the gracious forgiveness of God and through the blood of Jesus Christ. Amen.

Keep watch on all who do not walk according to the simplicity of the divine truth which is stated in this letter from [the decisions of] our meeting, so that everyone among us will be governed by the rule of the ban and henceforth the entry of false brethren and sisters among us may be prevented.

Eliminate from you that which is evil and the Lord will be your God and you will be His sons and daughters.

Dear brethren, keep in mind what Paul admonishes Timothy when he says, The grace of God that bringeth salvation hath appeared to all men, teaching us that, denying ungodliness and worldly lusts, we should live soberly, righteously, and godly, in this present world; looking for that blessed hope, and the glorious appearing of the great God and our Saviour Jesus Christ; Who gave Himself for us, that He might redeem us from all iniquity, and purify unto Himself a people of His own, zealous of good works. Think on this and exercise yourselves therein and the God of peace will be with you.

May the Name of God be hallowed eternally and highly praised, Amen. May the Lord give you His peace, Amen.

The Acts of Schleitheim on the Border [Canton Schaffhausen, Switzerland], on Matthias' [Day], Anno MDXXVII.

C. Discipline of the Church, how a Christian ought to live, 1527

The church of the Anabaptists was unique in that it was a disciplined and regulated church. The discipline was accepted voluntarily by the individual, as it concerned how he should live in the brotherhood; and by the church, as it concerned how the fellowship should be maintained if the principles of the Sermon on the Mount were to be applied practically. A church-order (Gemeinde-Ordnung) or "discipline" thus was called for as a set of rules. The Schleitheim Articles was the first such discipline, and Robert Friedmann[9] has identified another, from the same period, long concealed in the Hutterian chronicle (Geschicht-Buch der Hutterischen Bruder). The section of the Geschicht-Buch containing twelve brief articles seems to have come from the pre-Hutterian period (before 1528, when part of the movement began to practice communism and pacifism in Moravia). It is paralleled in numerous Hutterian codices. Caspar Breitmichel, who wrote the chronicle, does not identify the source of the document, but he lists the articles under the date of 1529.

The manuscript codices present the articles in connection with writings of Hans Schlaffer, and his authorship is strongly suggested. Schlaffer began to witness in the Inn Valley in northern Tyrol about the middle of 1527, and he appears to have been Vorsteher, or pastor, of the Anabaptists at Rattenberg. Since he was arrested in December, 1527, and martyred February 3, 1528, he would have had to draw up the discipline for his people in the early months of 1527.

The brief document gives the impression of being a first or preliminary draft. A finished draft may never have appeared because the Tyrolean government broke up the Anabaptist congregation at

---

[9] Mennonite Quarterly Review, XXIX, 162 ff.

Rattenberg. Many members lost their lives and the others fled to Moravia. The Discipline was carried with the refugees, preserved, and its instructions were observed faithfully.

The Discipline is a typically Anabaptist statement of the first generation of the movement. Its biblicism and spiritualism were prominent characteristics of the brotherhood. Unanimous agreement of the members concerning the *Ordnung* is indicated in the introduction, but the last sentence says in truly liberal spirit that whenever a brother or sister produces a better *Ordnung*, "it will be accepted from him at any time." The articles are eminently practical in tone. The absence of a prohibition against oaths and participation in government is remarkable.

The text given below does not come from the Hutterian chronicle but from a Hutterian codex still extant among the Brethren in Canada. It was translated by Elizabeth Horsch Bender.[10] Passages missing in the codex but present in the *Geschicht-Buch* are added in brackets, and there are other small editorial additions of Mrs. Bender, also in brackets, which give clarity to several statements. The Bible references are from the codex but are not to be found in the chronicle.

DISCIPLINE OF THE BELIEVERS: HOW A CHRISTIAN IS TO LIVE
(*Ordnung der Gemein, wie ein Christ leben soll*)

INTRODUCTION (missing in the *Geschicht-Buch*)

Since the almighty God and heavenly Father is permitting His eternal and all-powerful Word to be proclaimed to all creatures in these most perilous times (Col. 1) and has called us at this time out of pure grace into His marvelous light (I Pet. 3) to one body, one spirit, and one faith, united in the bonds of love (Eph. 4; I Cor. 1) to which we have all agreed, in order that our calling be found worthy, not only with the word of the mouth but in the truth and power (II Thess. 1; I Thess. 1; I Cor. 4; James 1), we have all in one another's presence openly agreed to regulate everything in the best possible way. For the improvement of our brotherhood [*Gemein*, so translated throughout], for the praise and honor of the Lord, and for the service of all the needs, we have unanimously agreed that this *Ordnung* shall be kept among us by all the brethren

---

[10] Published in the *Mennonite Quarterly Review*, XXIX (April, 1955), 162-166.

and sisters. When, however, a brother or sister is able to produce a better *Ordnung* it shall be accepted from him at any time. (I Cor. 14).

FIRST ARTICLE

And beginning: when the brethren are together they shall sincerely ask God for grace that He might reveal His divine will and help to note it (Ps. 86, 118) and when the brethren part they shall thank God and pray for all the brethren and sisters of the entire brotherhood (I Thess. 1 and 5; II Thess. 1 and 2; II Cor. 1; Col. 1,3,4).

SECOND ARTICLE

In the second place: we shall sincerely and in a Christian spirit admonish one another in the Lord to remain constant (Heb. 10:1; Acts 14,15,18; Col. 2). To meet often, at least four or five times, and if possible . . . even at midweek [prayer meetings?] (I Cor. 11, 14; Acts 1,2,9,11,20; Heb. 10; II Cor. 6; Matt. 18).

THIRD ARTICLE

In the third place: when a brother or sister leads a disorderly life it shall be punished: if he does so publicly [He] shall be kindly admonished before all the brethren (Gal. 2,6; I Cor. 5; II Thess. 3); if it is secret it shall be punished in secret, according to the command of Christ (Matt. 18).

FOURTH ARTICLE

In the fourth place: every brother and sister shall yield himself in God to the brotherhood completely with body and life, and hold in common all gifts received of God (Acts 2 and 4; I Cor. 11,12; II Cor. 8 and 9), [and] contribute to the common need so that brethren and sisters will always be helped (Rom. 12); needy members shall receive from the brotherhood as among the Christians at the time of the apostles (Acts 2,4,5; I Cor. 11,12; Eph. 4; Prov. 5; Matt. 8,15,16,17,19; Luke 3,6,8,9,10,12,14,18; I John 1,2,3,4; Mark 3,10,12; Gal. 6; Heb. 12; Dan. 4,8; I Tim. 1; I Cor. 14,16; Rom. 6,18; James 1; Phil. 2).

FIFTH ARTICLE

The elders [*Vorsteher*] and preachers chosen from the brotherhood shall with zeal look after the needs of the poor, and with zeal in the Lord according to the command of the Lord extend what is

C

needed for the sake of and instead of the brotherhood (Gal. 2; II Cor. 8,9; Rom. 15; Acts 6).

SIXTH ARTICLE

In the sixth place: a decent conduct *(ehrbarer Wandel)* shall be kept among them (Rom. 12,13; Phil. 1,2; I Pet. 2,3; I Cor. 1,3; Gal. 5; Eph. 5) before everyone (Titus 3; Matt. 5; I Pet. 3) and no one shall carelessly conduct himself before the brotherhood both with words or deeds (Rom. 1,6; II Tim. 2), nor before those who are "outside" (I Thess. 5; I Pet. 3).

SEVENTH ARTICLE

In the seventh place: in the meeting one is to speak and the others listen and judge what is spoken, and not two or three stand together (I Cor. 14). No one shall curse or swear (Matt. 5; Rom. 3; James 5) nor shall idle gossip be carried on, so that the meek may be spared (I Cor. 15; Eph. 5; Col. 3; II Tim. 2; Psalm 118). [*Geschicht-Buch* here cites only Ecclesiasticus 23.]

EIGHTH ARTICLE

In the eighth place: when the brethren assemble they shall not fill up with eating and drinking, but avoid expenses [reduce expenditures] to the least [eat] a soup and vegetable or whatever God gives (I Cor. 11; I Pet. 4; Gal. 5; Rom. 13; Eph. 5; Eccles. 37; Luke 21), and when they have eaten, all the food and drink shall again be removed [*Geschicht-Buch:* "from the table"] (John 6; Matt. 4; Luke 9; Mark 6), for one should use with thanksgiving and moderation the creatures which God has created, pure and good, for our subsistence.

NINTH ARTICLE

In the ninth place: what is officially done among the brethren and sisters in the brotherhood [*Geschicht-Buch:* "or is judged"] shall not be made public before the world. The good-hearted [an interested but not yet converted or committed] person, before he comes to the brethren in the brotherhood shall be taught [*Geschicht-Buch:* "the Gospel"] (Mark 16; Rom. 1; Col. 1). When he has learned [*Geschicht-Buch:* "understood"] and bears a sincere desire for it, and if he agrees to the content of the Gospel, he shall be received by the Christian brotherhood as a brother or a sister, that is, as a fellow member of Christ (Matt. 7; Prov. 19,29; Col. 4; Rom. 14; II Cor. 6; I Cor. 10; I Tim. 6; Matt. 10). But this shall not be made public before the world to spare the conscience and for the sake of the spouse (I Cor. 9,10; Matt. 15).

TENTH ARTICLE[11]

In the tenth place: all the brethren and sisters after they have committed themselves, shall accept and bear with patience all that He sends us [*Geschicht-Buch:* "accept with gratitude and bear with patience"] (Rom. 6; John 13; Matt. 16; Luke 9; I Pet. 4; II Cor. 12), and [shall] not let themselves be easily frightened by every wind and cry. [The *Geschicht-Buch* adds as a marginal note: "to be ready for cross and suffering."]

ELEVENTH ARTICLE

When brethren and sisters are together, being one body and one bread in the Lord and of one mind, then they shall keep the Lord's Supper as a memorial of the Lord's death (Matt. 26; Mark 14; Luke 22; I Cor. 11), whereby each one shall be admonished to become conformed to the Lord in the obedience of the Father (Phil. 2,3; I Pet. 2,4; Rom. 8; I John 2. — Obedience: Rom. 2; Phil. 2; II Cor. 2,10; II Thess. 1; I Pet. 1).

TWELFTH ARTICLE[12]

In the twelfth place: as we have taught and admonished the brethren and sisters we shall always watch and wait for the Lord that we may be worthy to enter [the kingdom] with Him when He comes, and to escape or flee from the evil that will come to the world. Amen. (Matt. 25; Luke 21; I Thess. 5; I Pet. 5; II Pet. 3; Rom. 2).

God be merciful to me. I commend my spirit and your spirit with our brother in Christ into the hand of the eternal Father. Amen.

D. *Ridemann's Rechenschaft, 1540*

Persecution drove many Swiss and German Anabaptists, in 1525 and afterward, into Moravia, which had long been known as a refuge for dissenters. The great early leader in this region was the scholarly Balthasar Hübmaier. He organized a congregation in 1526 at Nikolsburg under the protection of the tolerant Lords von Lichtenstein, on whose estates the refugees were permitted to settle. Thousands united with this congregation by baptism in a single year, among them being Lord Leonhard von Lichtenstein. Soon, however, there came to Nikolsburg refugees who differed

---

[11] Reveals the threat of persecution standing over the group and challenges members of the brotherhood to claim the attitude of the suffering church.

[12] The eschatological emphasis appeared later in stronger expression in Jacob Hutter.

with Hübmaier on a number of points, including the principle of non-resistance. Differences of opinion centered particularly around questions of the proper relationship of the new church to the political and social order in which it found itself. Jacob Widemann appeared, urging community of goods among Christian brethren as a necessary principle of the gospel. Also, a debate was carried on between Hübmaier and Hans Hut, in 1527, Hut urging views of non-resistance and non-participation in government while Hübmaier took a more positive attitude toward the social order. Leonhard von Lichtenstein called upon the newcomers to unite with the main congregation in Nikolsburg, but they refused and held meetings of their own. At the time of Hübmaier's arrest, around the middle of 1528, the controversy was still unresolved, and afterward differences between the two groups became even more serious. Therefore Lord Lichtenstein informed the non-resistant group that they could not continue in the city, and a company of from two to three hundred people left Nikolsburg in 1528 under the leadership of Jacob Widemann and encamped at a village called Bogenitz. The followers of Widemann refused to participate in the use of force, in courts or government, and in war; hence they came to be called Stäbler (i.e., those who carry a staff instead of a sword). Those who followed in Hübmaier's tradition were called Schwertler (i.e., those who carry a sword). Sword-bearing was a practical issue at the time in view of the threat of invasion by the Turks.

At Bogenitz the Stäbler voluntarily pooled their possessions into a cloak and thus began the practice of community of goods. Moving on to Austerlitz at the invitation of the civil authorities of that place, they built their first community houses. It was not, however, until the arrival of Jakob Hutter that the idea of a perfect community of goods was carried out. Hutter, minister of an Anabaptist group in the Tyrol, appeared among the Stäbler in Austerlitz in 1529, seeking a union between them and his Tyrolean people, who were being badly persecuted. Hutter was fully convinced of the absolute opposition of a Christian society to the existing world social order, and he urged the strategy of radical withdrawal from the world. He returned to the Tyrol and prepared his people to begin their exodus to Moravia.

Meanwhile, a division took place among the Stäbler during the winter of 1530. The Widemann party remained in Austerlitz, while the remainder, led by a co-worker of Hutter, Jorg Zaunring, moved to nearby Auspitz, where they established a community house *(bruderhof)*. Hutter was appealed to by both groups to come again to Moravia to help recover the right discipline and heal the schism. He made three more trips to Moravia for this purpose, and in 1533 he was made bishop of the Stäbler group in Auspitz. He did not succeed in uniting the other congregations with his Auspitz group, but by instituting a strict discipline and a rigorous order of community of goods, he made his congregation the center of Moravian Anabaptism and gave his name permanently to the Hutterite Brethren.[13]

Soon there were numerous thriving communities in Moravia, all under the protection of the nobles. The collective farms were almost entirely self-sufficient; their earnings went into the common treasury and were used according to need in the community. At the head of each *bruderhof* was a bishop or shepherd, elected for life, who kept in touch with business managers and ministers and, along with the elders, maintained oversight over the community. Some ministers were appointed as apostles and sent out to preach and baptize.

One such missioner was Peter Ridemann, who worked in many parts of Germany and Austria for at least ten years. A native of Silesia, he appears to have joined the brotherhood in 1532. While in prison in 1540 in the cities of Marburg and Walkersdorf, he drew up a great doctrinal work, *Rechenschaft unserer Religion, Lehre, und Glaube,*[14] which became "the central document" of the Moravian Anabaptists.

The Austrian authorities raised strenuous objections to the policy of the nobles in tolerating the Hutterites. A Moravian provincial diet ordered the Anabaptists expelled, and they were driven away temporarily. Hutter fled to the Tyrol, where he was captured and brutally murdered in 1536. Around 1540 the brotherhood needed as a measure of self-defense to formulate a confession of their faith which would officially state their tenets. The *Rechenschaft* was the result of the common concern of the Hutterite leadership, though Ridemann was its author.[15] Ridemann was elected co-leader of the

---

[13] *Mennonite Quarterly Review*, XXVI, 25-32.
[14] *Account (or Justification) of our Religion, Teaching, and Faith.*
[15] *Mennonite Quarterly Review*, "The Hutterite Doctrines . . ." by Franz Hermann, XXVI, 24-35.

church in Moravia in 1542, succeeding Hutter, and he continued in that post until his death in 1556.

The *Rechenschaft,* in spite of its length of 110 pages, is not a theological treatise, but a simple confession of faith. Many chapters begin with the clause "We confess," and the author's purpose in writing is confessional. He says that the book was written, first, "because it is good, agreeable and well pleasing to God to confess one's faith," and, second, "because there is so much blasphemy against the truth." The book is divided into two sections of unequal length, the second being a kind of appendix to the first. The basic articles of faith are dealt with in the first half of the first part, while practical regulations and teachings of the community occupy the second half.

This most pretentious Anabaptist document, which enjoyed widespread use among the Hutterites and helped their struggling communities to survive, deserves far more serious study than it can receive here. It shows indebtedness to Hübmaier's writings, especially on the subjects of baptism and the Lord's Supper. While it does not have direct bearing upon the modern Baptist denomination, it did contribute directly to the Anabaptist movement in Western Europe, with segments of which the Hutterites were in communication at various times during the 16th and 17th centuries.

Robert Friedmann has summarized the contents of the book as follows:[16]

ACCOUNT OF OUR RELIGION, TEACHING, AND FAITH

The first part: The Apostolic Creed ("We acknowledge God/[17] the almighty Father/ etc."). What faith is/ Concerning doctrine/ Concerning idolatry/ Why God created man; that God created man in his likeness; what God's likeness is/ Of the likeness of the devil/ How Adam forsook the likeness of God and fell into sin/ What sin is; concerning original sin; what original sin is; the harm wrought by original sin; concerning remorse; concerning repentance/ Man is grafted into Christ/ Concerning God's covenant; concerning the

---

[16] *Ibid.,* XXVI, 35. footnote 16.

[17] Copies of a 1565 reprint of the original book are in the British Museum, the Univ. of Chicago Library, the Staatsbibliothek, Berlin, the Landesmuseum, Brno, Czechoslovakia, and the Rockport-Bruderhof, South Dakota. An English translation appeared in 1950: *Account of our religion, doctrine, and Faith, given by Peter Rideman, of the Brothers whom men call Hutterians* (Hodder and Stoughton, London, and Plough Publishing Co., Salop). The most thorough study of the confession is that of Franz Heimann, *Lehre von der Kirche und Gemeinschaft in der Hutterischen Taufgemeinde,* Univ. Library, Vienna, an English translation of which is in the Goshen College Library, Goshen, Indiana.

old covenant; the law; the Gospel; concerning the New Covenant/ Concerning baptism of children: the reasons of those who baptize children and their refutation; concerning the baptism of Christ and of his Church; how one should baptize who can so baptize and teach?/ Concerning the election of ministers; differences of ministries/ The misuse of the Lord's Supper/ Concerning the Supper of Christ/ Community of goods/ Concerning separation/ Concerning the temple and that we go not therein/ Concerning priests and why we have naught to do with them/ Concerning Marriage; concerning adultery/ concerning governmental authority; why governmental authority hath been ordained; whether rulers can also be Christians?/ Concerning warfare/ Concerning taxation/ Concerning the making of swords; the making of clothes/ Whether a Christian can go to Law (court) or sit in judgment/ Concerning swearing, greeting, giving the hand and embracing, prayer, singing, fasting, celebrating/ Concerning traders, innkeepers, standing drinks, coming together/ Concerning the education of children/ Concerning exclusion (i.e. the Ban); concerning readmission/ Concerning the whole life walk, dress, and adornment of Christians.

This makes a total of ninety articles. Then follows the Second part with seven articles of greater length, and not quite of the character of a "confession" or "account," but rather of the character of doctrinal treatises:

How God desireth to have a people, whom He Himself hath separated from the world and chosen to be His bride/ How the house of the Lord should be built up in Christ/ Concerning the covenant of grace given to His people in Christ/ Concerning the Supper of Christ and how his suffering serveth for our salvation/ Concerning swearing, about which there is much controversy/ Concerning governmental authority and its appointed services and appurtenances/ Conclusion of this book.

Part I comprises (in Engl. and without Bible ref.) 121 pages; Part II (likewise) 85 pages.

McGlothlin, *Baptist Confessions of Faith,* (14-18), explains that it is much more like a treatise on doctrine and practice than a confession, and summarizes the important teachings of the *Rechenschaft* which bear upon Hutterite practice, but it might appear even more profitable to attempt a brief doctrinal summary of the work, following Franz Heimann.[18] Teachings under several important heads are given here.

---

[18] *Lehre von der Kirche und Gemeinschaft in der Hutterischen Taufgemeinde.*

I. DOCTRINE OF THE CHURCH AND OF THE SPIRIT

An assembly of children of God who have separated themselves from all unclean things is the church. It is gathered together, has being, and is kept by the Holy Spirit. Sinners may not be members unless and until they have repented of their sins. The essence of the church is its bearing of the Light; it is a lantern of righteousness in a world of unbelief, darkness, and blindness. It is a pillar and ground of the truth, which is confirmed, ratified, and brought to pass in her by the Holy Spirit. The "power and key" to forgive sins which was received by Christ from the Father is given to the church as a whole and not to individual persons. In its nature the church is spiritual, but concretely it is known as the pure sacred community. Church assembly and community are equated together.

II. DOCTRINE OF REDEMPTION AND ENTRANCE INTO THE CHURCH

Redemption means the working of the Spirit in the individual and his preparation for entrance into the church. It is the Spirit of Christ that leads into the church. ("The Christ of Ridemann is the inwardly experienced and fought-for Christ.") The work of Christ in man means a complete conversion and rebirth. Salvation and redemption consists in the liberation from the dominion of sin. Apart from Christ there is no goodness. Salvation also is a new covenant. God has cast out from our heart evil, sin, and the lust to sin, and we are to seek, love, hear, and keep His Word.

III. DOCTRINE OF FAITH

Faith is a real divine power which renews man and makes him like God in nature, ardent in love and in keeping His commandments.

IV. DOCTRINE OF BAPTISM

Baptism means the entrance into the covenant of grace of God and the incorporation into the Church of Christ. The "right and necessary" sequence is preaching, faith, rebirth, and baptism. Children cannot be baptized in the right way because they are not reborn through preaching, faith, and the Spirit.

V. DOCTRINE OF THE FELLOWSHIP OF THE LORD'S TABLE

The Supper is a sign of the community of Christ's body, in that each member thereby declares himself to be of the one mind, heart, and Spirit of Christ. It is an act of remembrance at which God's children become aware again of the grace which they have received.

Only a true member of Christ may participate. The unity of the fellowship of the Lord's Table must already exist prior to the celebrating.

VI. DOCTRINE OF ORIGINAL SIN

The inheritance that we have from our Father Adam is inclination to sin. Original sin means that all of us have by nature a tendency toward evil and have pleasure in sin. This inheritance removes, devours, and consumes all that is good and of God in man; so that none may attain it again except to be born again.

VII. THE FORMULA FOR BAPTISM

The baptizer first testifies to the baptizand and asks if he believes in God, the Father, the Son, and the Holy Spirit. The baptizand confesses. He then is asked if he desires to yield himself to God to live for Him and His church. If so, he is told to kneel before God and the church, and water is poured upon him. If baptism cannot be performed before the entire church, the baptizer may perform the ordinance alone.

E. The Waterland Confession, 1580

In western Europe the Anabaptist movement spread with incredible speed, winning thousands of converts in Germany and the Netherlands in the ten years following 1525. It grew in spite of severe persecution at the hands of Catholics and Protestants alike. Then around 1530, attachment to the movement on the lower Rhine was made by one, Melchior Hoffmann, a former Lutheran and a native of Swabia. He had little in common with the Swiss Brethren and may never have been baptized as a believer.[19] He embraced Docetic Christology and discarded non-resistance. Many eagerly accepted his view that the millennial kingdom soon would appear in Strasburg, and were not disillusioned when, after he was imprisoned and new leaders arose, Münster was named as the New Jerusalem.

In 1535 Münster was seized by the Hoffmannites who, on being attacked, chose to defend themselves. A long siege followed, during which distorted tales of what was going on within the city were used to bring universal opprobrium upon the name Anabaptist. At length the city was reduced and the surviving defenders tortured and massacred. A year later, at Buckholt, Westphalia, Obbe Philips

---

[19] Horsch, *Mennonites in Europe*, 172-173.

led a general meeting of the Anabaptists of Germany and the Nether-lands. Most had had nothing to do with the Münster episode, and now they reiterated their non-resistant convictions.

A great wave of persecution broke over the people following the Münster affair; but an ex-priest of West Friesland, Menno Simons, being made a bishop in 1537, succeeded in gathering the scattered folk into a fellowship. Until 1553 the *Doopsgezinde*, or Mennonites as they were later to be called, were the largest evangelical group in the Netherlands. Persecution continued throughout the century, the Mennonites compiling an enormous martyrology; yet there was remarkable growth, especially in the northern provinces. The severity of persecution in Flanders caused an extensive exodus of Mennonites to Friesland and other northern provinces. Flemish con-gregations were then established at numerous places in the north.

Divisions began to appear among the followers of Menno during his lifetime, differences occurring especially concerning discipline and the doctrine of the Incarnation. Menno insisted upon an in-creasingly rigid church discipline as he grew older, and his Chris-tology tended toward Hoffmannism. He did not attend a general conference of European Anabaptists at Strasburg in 1555 which discouraged further discussion on the Incarnation as unprofitable. When the conference asked Menno to relax his stern discipline, he wrote *Een Fondament* (Foundation Book) to defend his position.

At the time of Menno's death in 1561, the Netherlands Menno-nites were divided into four groups: the Flemings who rather exag-gerated Menno's discipline, the Frisians and Germans who were in line with Menno's views, and the Waterlanders (living chiefly in a small district between Amsterdam and Purmerend in Holland) who followed the Strasburg decisions. In Amsterdam were the two extreme groups, the rigid Flemings and the liberal Waterlanders. The principal disciplinary difference between them concerned the treatment of members who had been guilty of some serious offense, the Waterland churches holding the original position of Menno that expulsion must be preceded by at least three admonitions with-out repentance. Menno's later position was that immediate excom-munication should follow heinous sin, and this was the view of the Flemings. On this issue the Waterlanders separated from the main body of Mennonites in 1555, but some intercourse continued.

Anabaptists in Poland in the latter part of the sixteenth century came under the influence of Faustus Socinus and adopted unitarian views. In 1574 one of their ministers, Schomann, issued a confession and catechism at Cracow which set forth the new views of the person of Christ. Christology was then a subject widely discussed among the Mennonites. The Socinians, therefore, sent several of their ministers, among them Christopher Osterot, to Holland to visit the liberal wing of the Mennonites, the Waterlanders, urging a union with them. They met with the outstanding Dutch leader of the period, Hans de Ries, who told them that such union was an impossibility. His answer to an offensive letter written by them after their departure was a book entitled, *Clear Proof of the Eternity and Deity of Jesus Christ.* De Ries, a native of Flanders and pastor of the Waterlander Church at Middleburg (and later of churches at Emden and Alkmaar), then, with the help of Lubbert Gerrits, drew up a confession of faith of forty articles which long served the Waterland churches. This confession, published in 1580 or 1581, is reckoned the second Mennonite Confession of Faith, an earlier Waterland confession supposedly having been prepared in 1577.[20] Perhaps the second was a reprint or an elaboration of the first.

Baptist interest in the Confession of de Ries and Gerritz stems from the fact that the Confession was republished in 1610 upon the request of John Smyth, the English Separatist leader out of whose company was formed the first General Baptist Church. In touch with Waterlanders, the Smyth party became convinced of the doctrine of believers' baptism, and it was to the Waterlanders' church in Amsterdam that a majority of the Smyth followers were joined after Smyth's death. The 1580 Confession was employed to test the agreement of the English and the Mennonites; therefore, it should be compared with the confession of thirty-eight articles supplied to Smyth and his people for the same purpose.

The Waterland Confession is a fairly elaborate and complete work. By 1580 the custom of confession-making was well established among the Reformers and there was no lack of models. McGlothlin's[21] translation from the Latin text of Schyn, *Historia Christianorum,* I, 172-220, is given here. No copy of the original confession is known.

---

20 Horsch, *Mennonite History,* I, 246.
21 *Op. cit.,* 26-48.

A BRIEF CONFESSION OF THE PRINCIPAL ARTICLES OF THE CHRISTIAN FAITH.

Prepared by

John de Rys and Lubbert Gerrits, Ministers of the Divine Word among the Protestants who, in the Belgian Confederacy, are called Mennonites.

ARTICLE I.

OF THE UNITY AND ATTRIBUTES OF GOD.

We believe and confess, sacred Scripture preceding and proving it, that there is (a) one God (who is (b) a Spirit or (c) spiritual substance), (d) eternal (e), incomprehensible (f), immense (g), invisible (h), immutable (i), omnipotent (k), merciful (l), just (m), perfect (n), wise (o), wholly good (p), the fountain of life and (q) the spring of all good, (r) Creator and (s) Preserver of heaven and earth, of things visible and invisible.

a. Deut. 6 : 4; 32 : 39. b. John 4 : 24. c. Rom. 1 : 10. d. Gen. 21 : 33. Rom. 16 : 26. e. Ps. 129 : 6; Rom. 11 : 33. f. I Kgs. 8 : 27. Mat. 5 : 34. Act. 7 : 48. g. Col. i : 15. h. James 1 : 17. i. Gen. 17 : 1; 2 Cor. 6 : 18. k. Exod. 34 : 6, 7; Luc. 6 : 36. l. Ps. 11 : 7; Col. 3 : 24, 25. m. Lev. 19 : 2; Mat. 5 : 48. n. Tit. 1 : 17. o. Ps. 103 : 8; Mat. 19 : 17. p. Jer. 2 : 13. q. James 1 : 17. r. Gen. 1 : 1; Exod. 20 : 11; Act. 4 : 24. s. John 5 : 17.

ARTICLE II.

HOW THIS ONE GOD IS DISTINGUISHED IN SACRED SCRIPTURE.

This one God in sacred Scripture is revealed and distinguished into (a) Father, Son and Holy Spirit (b). There are three (and yet) only one God.

a. Mat. 3 : 16-19. b. John 5 : 7.

ARTICLE III.

HOW THE FATHER, SON AND HOLY SPIRIT, ACCORDING TO THIS DISTINCTION, ARE THREE AND ONE.

The Father is (a) the spring and principle of all things, who begat his Son from eternity (b), before all creatures (c), in a manner which the human mind cannot comprehend (d). The Son is the Father's eternal Word and Wisdom (e), through whom are all things (f). The Holy Spirit (g) is God's power, might or virtue (h), proceeding from the Father (i) and the Son (k). These three are neither divided (l) nor distinguished in respect of nature, essence, or essential attributes, such as eternity, omnipotence, invisibility, immortality, glory and similar things.

a. Rom. 11 : 36; I Cor. 8 : 6. b. Mic. 5 : 2. c. Col. 1 : 15; Heb. 7 : 2. d. Ps. 2 : 7. e. John 1 : 1. f. I Cor. 1 : 22; Col. 2 : 3. g. John 14 : 26. h. Luc. 1 : 31. i. John 15 : 26. k. John 16 : 7; Rev. 22 : 1. l. I John 5 : 7.

ARTICLE IV.

OF THE CREATION, FALL AND RESTITUTION OF MAN.

This one God created man, good (a), according to his own image and likeness (b), for salvation or safety, and in him all men for the same happy end (c). The first man fell into sins (d) and became subject to divine wrath, and by God was raised up again through consolatory promises (e) and admitted to eternal life at the same time with all those who had fallen (f); so that none of his posterity, in respect of this restitution, is born guilty of sin or blame (g).

a. Gen. 1 : 31. b. Gen. 1 : 27. c. Rom. 5 : 18. d. Gen. 3 : 6; Rom. 5 : 19. e. Gen. 3 : 15, 21. f. Gen. 12 : 3; 22 : 18; 26 : 4; Rom. 5 : 18. g. Col. 2 : 22.

ARTICLE V.

OF THE FACULTY OF MAN BEFORE AND AFTER THE FALL.

There was in man who was created good (a) and was continuing in goodness, a faculty of hearing, admitting

or rejecting evil which was offered to him by the spirit
of wickedness (b). Now in the same man, fallen and
perverted, was a faculty of hearing, admitting or rejecting good, occurring and offered by God (c). For just
as before the fall (d), hearing and admitting occurring
evil, he manifested the faculty of admitting it, so also
after the fall (e), by hearing and admitting occurring
good, he shows that he has the faculty of accepting it.
But that faculty of accepting or rejecting the grace of
God truly offered, remains, through grace, in all his
posterity (f).

a. Gen. 1 : 31. b. Gen. 3 : 1, 6. c. Gen. 38 : 10, 11, 12, 16, 17.
d. Gen. 3 : 1, 6. e. Gen. 3 : 8, 9, 10, 15. f. Gen. 4 : 6, 7; 6 : 23,
12; Deut. 11 : 26; 30 : 19; Ps. 81 : 14; Isa. 1 : 19, 20; 42 : 18,
19, 20, 21; Jer. 8 : 7; 25 : 4; Mat. 11 : 17; 22 : 3; 23 : 36; Luc.
13 : 32; Jhan 5 : 34, 40.

ARTICLE VI.

OF THE PROVIDENCE OF GOD.

God foresaw and foreknew (a) all things which have
come to pass, are coming to pass, and shall come to pass,
both good and evil, but since he is only perfect good (b)
and the fountain of life, we believe and confess that he
is the sole Author, Origin and Operator of those things
which are good, holy, sincere, pure and which agree with
his nature; but not at all of sins and damnable evils.
For God enjoins that which is good (d); he desires that
we obey him in that which is good (e); he consults for
and admonishes to it (f), and makes great promises to
those who obey (g). On the contrary he forbids evil (h),
exhorts against evil (i), threatens evil doers (k), and
punishes them not rarely in this life (l), and denounces
against them eternal punishment (m). And by this
means shows himself to be an enemy of sinners and that
all iniquity is contrary to his holy nature. And therefore,
not God who is good, but man who is evil, by voluntarily
choosing sin to which the spirit of wickedness leads him,
which is dominant in him, is the author (n), origin and
operator of sins and all wickedness, and for this reason is
worthy of punishment.

a. Job 28 : 24-27; Isa. 14 : 14-16; 48 : 3; Jer. 1 : 5. b. Ps. 103 : 8. Mat. 19 : 17. c. Ps. 36 : 9; Jer. 2 : 13. d. Exod. 20. e. Deut. 5 : 29; 32 : 29; Luc. 19 : 42. f. Rev. 3 : 18. g. Deut. 28; Mat. 24 : 13. h. Gen. 2 : 17. i. Gen. 4 : 6; Deut. 27 : 15; 28 : 15. k. Ps. 7 : 12. l. Gen. 8 : 19, 24. m. Mat. 3 : 12; 25 : 47. n. Hos. 13 : 9; Mich. 9 : 2; Eph. 2 : 1-3.

ARTICLE VII.

OF GOD'S PREDESTINATION, ELECTION AND REPROBATION.

The cause, therefore, to which man owes his misery and condemnation is man's voluntary choice of darkness (a), agreement with sinners (b), and a life which is spent in sins. Perdition, then, has its rise out of man but not at all out of the good Creator. For God, since he is the highest and most perfect good (c), and Love itself, according to the nature of the highest love and goodness, was not able not to have willed that felicity and salvation should fall to the lot of his creatures. He did not, therefore, predestinate, ordain or create any one of them that he should be condemned: nor did he wish nor decree that they should sin or live in sins that he might subject them to condemnation. But inasmuch as this good God, as truly as he lives, does not delight in the destruction of any (f), nor wish that any should perish, but that all men should be saved (g) and attain to eternal salvation, so also he decreed and created all men for salvation (h); and when fallen, through his ineffable love (i) he restored them in Christ and in him ordained and prepared for all a medicine of life (k), if indeed Christ was given (l), offered (m) and died for a propitiation for all. In confirmation of which thing God willed that this universal grace, love and benignity should be announced and offered, through the preaching of the gospel, to all creatures or peoples. All who, being penitent and believing, admit or accept that gracious benefit of God in Christ, (who appeared (o) as a propitiation for the world) (p), and persevere in it (q), are and remain (r) through his mercy the elect, concerning whom God decreed, before the foundation of the world was laid (s), that they should become partakers of the heavenly kingdom and glory. But those who disdain or reject that offered

ACTS 17

VERSE 26

grace (t), love darkness in place of light (v), persevere
in impenitence and unbelief, render (w) themselves
(through that wickedness) unworthy of salvation, and so
on account of their own wickedness are justly rejected by
God (x), and deprived of that end for which they were
created and in Christ destined (y) and called (z), and
therefore do not enjoy forever the Supper of the Lord
to which they were invited and called.

a. John 3 : 19. b. James 1 : 15. c. Mat. 19 : 17. d. I John
4 : 8. e. Eze. 33 : 11. f. 2 Petr. 3 : 9. g. I Tim. 2 : 4. h.
Gen. 1 : 27. i. Gen. 12 : 3; 22 : 18; Rom. 5 : 19. k. Col. 1 : 19,
20; I John 2 : 2; Hebr. 2 : 9. l. John 3 : 16. m. Eph. 5 : 2.
n. Mat. 28 : 19; Marc. 16 : 15; Eph. 1 : 9. o. 1 John 2 : 2.
p. Marc. 16 : 15, 16; John 1 : 12. q. Mat. 24 : 13; Rev. 2 : 10.
r. Mat. 22 : 14; Eph. 1 : 4. s. Mat. 25 : 34. t. Mat. 22 : 5. v.
John 3 : 19. w. Acts 13 : 46. x. 2 Chron. 15 : 2; I Kgs. 15 : 23,
30; 2 Thess. 2 : 10, 11. y. I Pet. 1 : 2. z. Mat. 22; Luc. 14 : 16,
17, 24.

ARTICLE VIII.

OF THE INCARNATION OF THE SON OF GOD.

In the fulness of time God has executed (a) the plan
which was with him before the foundation of the world
was laid, namely, that he would reconcile to himself
the world which he saw would be subjected to divine
wrath, and to this end has sent his eternal word, or
Son (that the promise made by the Father might be
fulfilled (b)) from heaven (c), who in the body of the
virgin Mary was made flesh or man (e) through the ad-
mirable power of God and the incomprehensible operation
of his Holy Spirit. Not indeed in such a manner that the
divine Essence of the Word or any part of it was changed
into visible and mortal flesh and thus ceased to be Spirit,
Deity or God; but so, that, remaining the eternal Son of
God (g), which he was before, namely God (h) and
Spirit (i), he was made (what he was not before)
namely flesh or man (k). And so this same Jesus is our
Emmanuel (l), in the same person true God (m) and true
man (n), born of Mary, visible and invisible, external and
internal, and the true Son of the living God. (o).

a. Gal. 4 : 4. b. Gen. 3 : 15; 22 : 18; 26 : 4; Deut. 18 : 15;
Isa. 7 : 14; 9 : 5; 11 : 1; Jer. 23 : 5. c. John 13 : 3; 16 : 28;

17 : 18. d. Luc. 1 : 27. e. John 1 : 14. f. Luc. 1 : 31. Mat.
1 : 20. g. Hebr. 1 : 10-12. h. Rom. 9 : 5. i. 2 Cor. 3 : 17. k.
John 1 : 14. l. Isa. 7 : 14. m. I John 5 : 20. n. John 8 : 40;
I Tim. 2 : 5. o. Mat. 19 : 16; John 6 : 69; 9 : 35-37.

ARTICLE IX.

OF THE FINAL CAUSE OF THE ADVENT OF CHRIST INTO THE WORLD AND OF HIS THREEFOLD OFFICE.

This person, God (a) and Man (b), Son of the living
God (c), came into this world that he might save sinners
(d), or that he might reconcile the world, polluted by
sins, to God the Father (e). On this account we confess
him to be our only Mediator (f), Prophet (g), Priest
(h), King (i), Lawgiver (k) and Teacher, whose mission into the world (l) God promised, to whom it is
necessary to hearken (m), in whom to believe (n), and
whom to follow (o).

a. I John 5 : 20. b. John 8 : 40. c. Mat. 16 : 16. d. Mat.
9 : 15; I Tim. 1 : 15. e. 2 Cor. 5 : 19; I John 2 : 2. f. I Tim.
2 : 5. g. Deut. 18 : 15. h. Ps. 110 : 4; Hebr. 3 : 1. i. Jer.
33 : 15; Mat. 22 : 5. k. Mat. 17 : 5; 28 : 20; Gal. 6 : 4. l.
Deut. 18 : 15. m. Mat. 17 : 5. n. John 3 : 36. o. John 8 : 12.

ARTICLE X.

OF THE ABROGATION OF THE LAW AND OF LEGAL THINGS.

The intolerable burden of the Mosaic law (a), with
all its shadows and types, was brought to an end in Christ
(b) and removed from the midst of his people; namely,
the sacerdotal office (c) together with temple, altar, sacrifices and whatever was typically connected with the
sacerdotal office; and then the royal office (d) and whatever adhered to that office, as kingdom (e), sword (f),
punishment agreeable to the law (g), war, and, in one
word, all that which typically looked to Christ's person,
function or office and was a shadow and figure of him.

a. Acts 15 : 10; 2 Cor. 3 : 11, 14. b. Col. 2 : 16, 17. c. Hebr.
8 : 4, 5; 10 : 1. d. Luc. 1 : 28, 29; John 18 : 33; Mat. 20 : 25-
27; Marc. 10 : 43-45. e. Isa. 2 : 4; Mich. 4 : 3. f. Mat. 5 : 38.
g. Zech. 9 : 10.

D

ARTICLE XI.

OF THE PROPHETIC OFFICE OF CHRIST.

And so this true promised prophet (a) revealed to us
the will of God and announced all things (b) which God
demands and requires from the people of the New Testament (c). For as God through Moses and other prophets
spoke with the people of the old covenant and declared to
them his will; so in the last days he has spoken to us
through this prophet (Son) (d), and has announced
to us the mystery which had been silent from the times
of ages (e), and has made us certain of those things (f)
which were to be spoken later. He has preached the
promised gospel (g), instituted and ordained sacraments,
functions and offices, prescribed by God to that end and
at the same time, both by life (i) and doctrine (k), has
demonstrated what the law of Christians is (l), what the
rule and norm of life, and what sort of life and (m)
path [leads] to eternal life.

a. Deut. 18 : 15. b. John 17 : 8; Heb. 1 : 2. c. Deut. 18 : 18.
d. Hebr. 1 : 2. e. Mat. 13 : 35. f. Heb. 3 : 5. g. Mat. 1 : 14.
h. Mat. 26 : 25, 26; 28 : 19. i. Matt. 5 : 6, 7. k. John 10 : 25,
28; I Pet. 2 : 21; I John 2 : 6. l. Gal. 6 : 4. m. John 8 : 12.

ARTICLE XII.

OF THE SACERDOTAL OFFICE OF CHRIST.

Moreover, as the only high priest (a) and mediator
of the New Testament (b) he prayed his Heavenly Father
for all believers (c), even for those who affixed him to the
cross and killed him (d). And at last, most obedient to
the Father (e), he underwent the most extreme and
severe passion and offered himself to the Father (f) on
the cross through death as a sacrifice (g) and gift for an
odor of good fragrance, and indeed a universal sacrifice,
which is of perpetual power (h).

a. Heb. 5 : 16, 20. b. 2 Tim. 2 : 5. c. John 17 : 9, 11, 15, 23.
d. Lu. 23 : 33. e. Phil. 2 : 8. f. Matt. 27 : 49; Mark 15 : 39.
g. Eph. 5 : 2. h. Heb. 10 : 12.

ARTICLE XIII.

OF THE EFFICACY AND DIGNITY OF THE OBEDIENCE AND UNIQUE SACRIFICE OF JESUS CHRIST.

We confess that the obedience of the Son of God (a), his bitter passion (b), death (c), effusion of blood (d), and unique sacrifice on the cross, is a reconciliation (e) and satisfaction for us all and for the sins of the whole world: and therefore we, through the blood of his cross, have reconciliation (f) and peace with God (g), and at the same time a firm hope and certitude (h) of entering into eternal life (i) if indeed we persevere in faith, and with unshaken faith place hope in the promise of the gospel.

a. Phil. 2 : 8. b. I Pet. 3 : 18. c. Rom. 4 : 25. d. Heb. 9 : 13, 14, 28. e. 2 Cor. 5 : 19; I John 2 : 2. f. Col. 1 : 14, 19, 20. g. Eph. 1 : 13. h. Heb. 10 : 19. i. Col. 1 : 23.

ARTICLE XIV.

OF THE KINGLY OFFICE OF CHRIST.

Jesus Christ, our prophet (a) and priest (b), as the promised and only spiritual heavenly king of the New Testament, has erected a spiritual kingdom and has collected many spiritual and faithful men, whom he has provided with spiritual and royal laws (e), and whom according to the nature of his kingdom he has clothed with spiritual arms (f). And in it he has ordained law (g), justice, and their ministers. Of this kingdom he is the preserver (i), defender, strong tower (k), firmness and rock (l), and in it he will remain King, ruling unto eternity (m).

a. Deut. 18 : 15. b. Heb. 3 : 1. c. Jer. 23 : 6; Zech. 9 : 9. d. Matt. 18 : 1; 3 : 23. e. Jer. 33 : 15. f. 2 Cor. 10 : 4; Eph. 6 : 13. g. Jer. 23 : 5. h. I Cor. 12 : 28. i. Ps. 121 : 4, 5. k. Ps. 18 : 3; 19 : 2. l. Acts 4 : 11. m. Luke 1 : 19.

ARTICLE XV.

OF THE BURIAL AND RESURRECTION OF CHRIST, AND THEIR UTILITY.

Christ, after he was dead by the office of the cross in the earth, and it had imposed an end on him, was buried (a), a certain indication that he was dead, and on the third day after death he rose again (b). Thus he conquered death and at the same time made it certain that he was Lord of death, and could not be held in its chains (c), which to all believers has been a consolatory certainty (d) that they are to be liberated and so finally raised from the dead.

a. Matt. 27 : 58, 59; I Cor. 15 : 4. b. Matt. 28 : 6; Acts 10 : 40. c. Acts 2 : 24. d. I Cor. 15 : 12, 13, 21.

ARTICLE XVI.

OF CHRIST'S ASCENT INTO THE HEAVENS AND HIS GLORI-FICATION AFTER THE RESURRECTION.

For forty days after the resurrection, he was seen by his disciples (a) and manifested himself to them often, lest anyone should in anywise be doubtful of his resurrection; and at length, being received by a cloud (b), he ascended into the heavens and entered into his glory (c), leading captivity captive (d) and openly making a spectacle of spoiled empires and powers (e), he triumphed over them and sat down at the right hand of the Majesty of God (f), made Lord and Christ (g), glorified in body (h), exalted (i) and crowned with glory and honor (k), and so is priest (l) and king over Mt. Zion forever (m).

a. Acts 1 : 3. b. Mark 16 : 19; Acts 1 : 9. c. Luke 24 : 25. d. Eph. 4 : 8. e. Col. 2 : 15. f. Mark 16 : 19; Heb. 8 : 1. g. Acts 2 : 36. h. John 17 : 5; Phil. 3 : 21. i. Phil. 2 : 9. k. Heb. 2 : 7. l. Ps. 2 : 6. m. Ps. 110 : 2-4. Heb. 7 : 2, 3.

ARTICLE XVII.

WHAT CHRIST, ACCORDING TO HIS SACERDOTAL OFFICE, PERFORMS NOW IN GLORY.

The function or holy office of this glorified priest (a), king (b), Lord (c), and Christ, in that heavenly and glorified state, consists in this, that he directs, rules and guards through his Holy Spirit (d) his holy church in the world through the tempests and billows of the sea of this world. For by virtue of his sacerdotal office, (as minister

(e) of the sanctuary and of that true tabernacle) he is our Intercessor (f), Advocate (g), and Mediator (h) with the Father. He teaches (i), consoles, strengthens and baptizes us with the Holy Spirit and fire (k), with his heavenly gifts and fiery virtues; he sups with faithful souls spiritually (l), and makes them partake of food and drink vitalizing to souls (m), the efficacious fruit and worth of his merits acquired for us through the cross, and also that true and peculiarly necessary good which is shadowed forth through the sacraments.

a. Heb. 8 : 1. b. Rev. 1 : 5. c. Acts 2 : 36. d. Acts 2 : 33. e. Heb. 8 : 2. f. Rom. 8 : 34. g. I John 2 : 1. h. I Tim. 2 : 5. i. John 14 : 26; 16 : 13. k. John 1 : 33; Matt. 3. 11. l. Rev. 3 : 20. m. John 6 : 32-34.

ARTICLE XVIII.

WHAT CHRIST, ACCORDING TO HIS ROYAL OFFICE, PERFORMS NOW IN GLORY.

According to his royal office in that heavenly state (a), he rules the hearts of believers through his Holy Spirit and Word (b). He receives them into his tutelage (c), covers them with the shadow of his wings (d), clothes them with spiritual arms (e) for the spiritual struggle against all their enemies, the spirits of evil under heaven and whatever in earth fights against them. That glorious, omnipotent (f), heavenly king bears to them in anxiety succors, frees them from the hand of enemies (g), helps them (h) that they may overcome and come off victors, and has prepared for them in heaven a crown of righteousness (i). And these are the Lord's freedmen, who dwell in the House of the Lord, and upon the holy Mt. Zion (k), who beat their carnal weapons, their swords (l) into hoes and their spears into pruning hooks, who do not bear the sword, who neither teach the art of war nor give assent to carnal wars.

a. Ps. 2 : 9. b. Rom. 8 : 11, 14. c. John 10 : 28. d. Matt. 23 : 36. e. 2 Cor. 10 : 4; Eph. 6 : 12, 13. f. Matt. 28 : 18. g. Luke 1 : 69. h. 2 Cor. 2 : 16. i. 2 Tim. 4 : 8; Rev. 2 : 10. k. Heb. 12 : 22. l. Isa. 2 : 4; Mich. 4 : 2, 3; 2 Cor. 10 : 4.

ARTICLE XIX.

OF THE KNOWLEDGE OF CHRIST ACCORDING TO THE SPIRIT AND ITS NECESSITY.

From that which has now been said concerning the ascension of Christ into heaven, his glorification, offices and functions in glory, we believe and confess that Christ must be confessed, not only according to the flesh (a), or literally according to history, as his holy incarnation, generation, revelation or appearance in the flesh, passion, death, cross and whatever refers to him; but we must ascend higher (b), know and acknowledge Christ according to the spirit, in his exaltation and glorification (c), according to his holy office in glory (d): what the holy scripture pronounces concerning all these things must be embraced with a faithful heart; and with earnest prayers God must be supplicated, that the knowledge of Christ and his holy office according to the spirit, through his love and kindness, may be consummated in us; *indeed* that the form and image of Christ (e) through him may be born and erected in us, that he may manifest himself to us (f), may live in us (g), may walk (h), teach (i), preach, that miracles done by him according to the flesh, he may consummate in us according to the spirit, heal us from the sickness of souls (k), from deafness, blindness, leprosy, impurity, sin and death; that he may baptize and wash us with the Spirit and fire (m), that he may nourish (n) and restore us (o) with heavenly food and drink and may make us partakers of his divine nature (p); that, indeed through his virtue the old man in us (q) may be crucified with him, so as to have communion with his sufferings and conformity to his death (r); and that through him we may rise and be restored to a new life (s) and may experience the power of his resurrection (t): And all these things for the glory and honor of God, our heavenly Father. This we call knowing Christ according to the spirit; without which knowledge, concerning which our conscience ought to be firmly persuaded, the knowledge of Christ according to the flesh does not at all suffice for obtaining salvation.

a. 2 Cor. 5 : 16. b. Phil. 3 : 20; Col. 3. 1. c. Phil. 2 : 9; John 17 : 5. d. Heb. 8 : 1. e. Matt. 12 : 50; Gal. 4 : 19; James 1 : 18. f. John 14 : 21. g. Eph. 3 : 17; John 14 : 23. h. 2 Cor. 6 : 16. i. Rev. 3 : 20. k. Isa. 35 : 5. l. Matt. 9 : 12; Isa. 53 : 4, 5. m. Matt. 3 : 11. n. Eph. 5 : 30; John 6 : 48-50. o. I Cor. 12 : 13. p. 2 Pet. 3 : 4. q. Rom. 6 : 5. r. Phil. 3 : 10. s. Rom. 6 : 5. t. Phil. 3 : 10. v. 2 Cor. 5 : 16, 17.

ARTICLE XX.

OF TRUE SAVING FAITH.

All goods and benefits which Jesus Christ, through his merits, has acquired for the salvation of sinners we graciously enjoy through true and living faith (a), which operates through love (b). This faith is a most certain cognition or knowledge acquired through the grace of God from the sacred scriptures, concerning God (c), concerning Christ and other heavenly things, the cognition and persuasion of which is necessary to salvation; and these things ought to be accompanied with the love of God (d) and with firm confidence in one God (e), who as a kind loving heavenly Father, will give and donate to us all things which, in respect of body and soul, are useful and effective for salvation (f), on account of Christ and his merits.

a. John 3 : 19, 36; Acts 15 : 2; Rom. 5 : 1, 2. b. Gal. 5 : 6; Rom. 10. c. John 17 : 3. d. Gal. 5 : 6. e. Heb. 11 : 1. f. Matt. 7 : 12; John 16 : 23.

ARTICLE XXI.

OF JUSTIFICATION.

Through living faith (a) of this kind we acquire true righteousness (b), that is (c), pardon or remission of all our past, as well as present, sins (d), on account of the poured out blood of Jesus Christ; as also true righteousness which through Jesus, the Holy Spirit co-operating, is abundantly poured out upon or into us: moreover, as out of evil (g), carnal, avaricious, proud men, we are made good, spiritual, liberal, humble, and even out of unjust men, truly just. And this righteousness has its origin in regeneration.

a. Gal. 5 : 6. b. Rom. 5 : 1. c. Ps. 32 : 1. d. I John 1 : 7. e.
I Cor. 6 : 11; Rom. 4 : 25; I John 3 : 7. f. Tit. 3 : 5, 6. g.
I Cor. 6 : 11.

ARTICLE XXII.

OF REGENERATION.

Regeneration is a certain divine quality in the mind of
a man truly come to himself, an erection of the image of
God in man (a), a renovation of the mind or soul (b),
a true illumination of the mind with the knowledge of
the truth (c), bringing with it a change of will and of
carnal desires and lusts, a sincere mortification of internal
wickedness (d) and of the old man delighting himself in
lust, wickedness and sin: It is, moreover, a vivification
which manifests itself in an honest life according to God,
in true goodness, justice and holiness. It is a removal of
the stony heart (e), full of vanity, stolidity (f), blindness,
ignorance, sin and perverse pleasures, and, on the contrary, is the gracious gift of the promised heart of flesh
(g), replete with the law of God, light (h), sight, wisdom,
understanding, virtue and holy desires. This regeneration has its rise from God (i) through Christ (k). The
medium or instrument through which it is generated
in us, is the Holy Spirit (l) with all his fiery virtues,
apart from any co-operation of any creature. Here concerning the regenerate, we affirm that they are born not
out of anything whatsoever which the creature does, but
from God (m); and by it we become children of God
(n), divine, heavenly and spiritually minded, just and
holy. We believe and teach that this regeneration is
necessary to salvation according to the words of Christ:
(o) "Verily, verily I say to thee, except a man be born
again he cannot see the kingdom of God"; and "Except
a man be born of water and the Spirit, he cannot enter
the kingdom of God."

a. Eph. 4 : 24; Col. 3 : 9, 10. b. Rom. 12 : 2; Eph. 4 : 23. c.
John 8 : 32. d. Eph. 4 : 22-24; Col. 3 : 9, 10. e. Eze. 36 : 26. f.
Eph. 4 : 17, 18. g. Eze. 36 : 26. h. Jer. 31 : 33. Heb. 8 : 10.
i. John 8 : 47; I John 4 : 1, 2, 6, 7. k. I Pet. 1 : 3, 23; James
1 : 18. l. John 3 : 5, 6. m. John 1 : 13; I John 3 : 9. n. John
1 : 12. o. John 3 : 3, 5.

ARTICLE XXIII.

OF GOOD WORKS.

A man, in this way regenerated and justified by God through Christ, lives through love (a) (which is poured out into his heart (b) through the Holy Spirit) with joy and gladness (c), in all good works, according to the laws and precepts and customs enjoined on him by God through Christ. He watches, gives thanks (d) and blesses God (e) with a pure heart and holy life, for all his benefits and especially for those which pertain to the soul. Such are holy plants of the Lord (f), trees of justice who worship God with good works (g) and ardently expect the blessed remuneration promised them by God (h), through his abundant goodness (i).

a. John 14 : 23; Gal. 5. b. Rom. 5. c. Ps. 1 : 2; 10 : 2. d. Ps. 103 : 1. e. Matt. 5 : 8. f. Isa. 61 : 3. g. Matt. 5 : 16. h. Eph. 2 : 7. i. Luke 6 : 23; I Cor. 3 : 14.

ARTICLE XXIV.

OF THE CHURCH.

Such believing and regenerated men, dispersed throughout the whole earth (a), are the true people of God or Church of Jesus Christ in the earth, which he loved (b) and for which he gave himself up that he might sanctify it, which indeed he did sanctify through the laver, in the word of life. Of this church (c) Jesus Christ is the Foundation, Head (d), Shepherd (e), Leader (f), Lord (g), King, and Master (h). This alone is his adored (i) spouse (k), holy body, flock (1), and people and through regeneration (m) his flesh and bones. But even though a huge multitude of deceivers and hypocrites are hidden and live among this church (n), yet those alone who in Christ are regenerated and sanctified are true members of Christ's body (o), and for this reason heirs of his blessed promises of which great benefits the deceivers and hypocrites, on account of their own blame and wickedness, are deprived.

a. Matt. 8 : 11; 24 : 3; Rev. 7 : 9.   b. Eph. 5 : 25.   c. I Cor.
3 : 11.   d. Eph. 5 : 23.   e. John 10 : 11.   f. Phil. 2 : 11.   g. Matt.
21 : 5.   h. John 13 : 15.   i. John 3 : 29; Rev. 21 : 2.   k. Eph.
5 : 23.   l. John 10 : 16.   m. Eph. 5 : 30.   n. Matt. 13 : 24, &c.
o. 2. Cor. 5 : 17.   p. Luke 14 : 24.

ARTICLE XXV.

OF THE MINISTRIES TO BE EXERCISED IN THE CHURCH.

In this his holy church Christ has ordained an evangelical ministry, namely, teaching of the divine word (a),
use of the holy sacraments, and the care of the poor (b),
as also ministers for performing these ministries: and
moreover the exercise of fraternal admonition (c), punishment and finally removal of those who persevere in impenitence: which ordinances, originating in the word of
God, are to be performed only according to the meaning
of the same word (d).

a. Matt. 28 : 19; Mark 16 : 15.   b. Acts 6 : 2, 3, 4.   c. Matt.
18 : 15; Luke 17 : 3.   d. Matt. 17 : 5.

ARTICLE XXVI.

OF THE ORDER WHICH IS TO BE OBSERVED IN THE CHURCH ABOUT MINISTRIES.

Just as the body consists of divers members and each
member performs its own work, for no member is [in
turn] hand, eye or foot; in the same way (a) things are
done in the Church of God.   For although every believer is a member of the body of Christ, not everyone is
for that reason a teacher, bishop or deacon: but those
only who (b) have been set apart to those ministries
according to order.   Wherefore the administrations of
those functions or offices do not pertain to every one,
but to the ordained.

a. Rom. 12 : 4; I Cor. 12 : 12.   b. Heb. 5 : 7.

ARTICLE XXVII.

HOW ELECTION TO THOSE MINISTRIES IS ACCOMPLISHED.

Calling or election to the aforesaid ministries is accomplished through the ministers of the church and its mem-

bers conjointly (a), and by invocation of the name of
God: for God alone knows hearts, walks in the midst of
the believers (b), who are congregated in his name, and
through his Holy Spirit directs their intellects and minds
so that through them he manifests and calls forth such as
he knows will be useful to his church.

a. Acts 1 : 21; 14 : 2. b. Matt. 18 : 19, 20.

ARTICLE XXVIII.

OF CONFIRMATION TO THE AFORESAID MINISTRIES.

But although the election and call aforesaid are accomplished in the method [aforesaid], yet confirmation in
the ministry itself is performed by the elders of the people
in the presence of the church (a) and that for the most
part by the imposition of hands.

a. Acts 6 : 6; 13 : 3; I Tim. 4 : 14; 2 Tim. 1 : 7.

ARTICLE XXIX.

OF THE DOCTRINE AND DOCTRINAL BOOKS OF THE SAME MINISTERS.

The doctrine which ordained ministers propose to the
people ought to be or to agree with that which Jesus
Christ brought from heaven (a), which he taught the
people by word and work, that is, in doctrine and life,
and which the apostles of Christ, at the mandate and according to the spirit of Christ, announced (c). It (as
much as is necessary to us for salvation (d) is contained
in the books of the New Testament to which we join all
that which is found in the canonical books of the Old
Testament and which is consonant with the doctrine of
Christ and his Apostles and in accord with the administration of his spiritual kingdom.

a. Heb. 2 : 3; 12 : 25. b. Acts 1 : 1. c. Matt. 28 : 19; Mark
16 : 15. d. Deut. 4 : 1, 2; 2 Tim. 3 : 16.

ARTICLE XXX.

OF THE SACRAMENTS.

Jesus Christ instituted in his church two sacraments
(whose administration he attached to the teaching office),
namely, Holy Baptism (a) and the Holy Supper (b).
These are external and visible actions, and signs of the
immense goodness of God toward us; placing before our
eyes, on the part of God, the internal and spiritual action which God accomplishes (c) through Christ (the
Holy Spirit co-operating) by regenerating, justifying,
spiritually nourishing and sustaining the souls which
repent and believe (d); we on our part, by the same
means, confess religion, repentance (e), faith (f) and
our obedience (g) by earnestly directing our conscience
to the service (or worship) of God.

a. Matt. 28 : 19; Mark 16 : 15. b. Matt. 26 : 25; Luc. 22 : 19.
c. Tit. 3 : 5. d. Eph. 5 : 29; Rev. 3 : 23. e. Acts 2 : 38. f.
Acts 8 : 36. g. Matt. 3 : 15.

ARTICLE XXXI.

OF EXTERNAL BAPTISM.

Holy Baptism is an external, visible and evangelical
action, in which, according to Christ's precept (a) and
the practice of the apostles (b), for a holy end (c), are
baptized with water in the name of the Father and of
the Son and of the Holy Spirit, those who hear, believe
and freely receive in a penitent heart the doctrine of the
holy gospel (d); for such Christ commanded to be baptized, but by no means infants.

a. I Pet. 3 : 21. b. Matt. 28 : 19; Mark 16 : 15. c. Acts 2 :
38, 41; 8 : 11, 36, 37; 10 : 45, 48; 16 : 15, 32-34; 18 : 8; 19 : 5.
d. Matt. 3 : 15; Acts 2 : 38; Rom. 6 : 3, 4; Col. 2 : 12.

ARTICLE XXXII.

WHAT BAPTISM SIGNIFIES INTERNALLY.

The whole action of external, visible baptism places
before our eyes, testifies and signifies that Jesus Christ

baptizes internally (a) in a laver of regeneration (b) and renewing of the Holy Spirit, the penitent and believing man: washing away, through the virtue and merits of his poured out blood, all the spots and sins of the soul (c) and through the virtue and operation of the Holy Spirit, which is a true, heavenly (d), spiritual and living water, [washing away] the internal wickedness of the soul (e) and renders it heavenly (f), spiritual (g) and living (h) in true righteousness and goodness. Moreover baptism directs us to Christ and his holy office by which in glory he performs that which he places before our eyes, and testifies concerning its consummation in the hearts of believers and admonishes us that we should not cleave to external things, but by holy prayers ascend into heaven and ask from Christ the good indicated through it [baptism] (i): a good which the Lord Jesus graciously concedes and increases in the hearts of those who by true faith become partakers of the sacraments.

a. Matt. 3 : 11; John 1 : 33. b. Eph. 5 : 26; Tit. 3 : 5. c. I John 1 : 7. d. Isa. 44 : 3; Eze. 36 : 27; Joel 2 : 28; John 7 : 38. e. I Cor. 6 : 11; Tit. 3 : 5-7. f. Phil. 3 : 20. g. Rom. 8 : 9. h. Eph. 2 : 4, 5. i. John 7 : 31.

ARTICLE XXXIII.

OF THE HOLY SUPPER.

The Holy Supper (as also Baptism) is an external and visible evangelical action in which, according to the precepts of Christ (a), and the usage of the Apostles (b), for a holy end (c), we partake of bread and wine. The bread is broken, the wine is poured out and by them are sustained those who, believing, are baptized according to the institution of Christ. The bread is eaten by them, the wine is drunk. Thus Christ's death and bitter suffering are proclaimed (d), and all these things are done in commemoration of him. (e).

a. Luke 22 : 19. b. Acts 2 : 42; 20 : 11; I Cor. 11 : 22. c. I Cor. 10 : 15; 11 : 28. d. I Cor. 11 : 25. e. Luke 22 : 19; I Cor. 11 : 24.

ARTICLE XXXIV.

WHAT THE HOLY SUPPER SIGNIFIES.

The whole action of the external and visible supper places before our eyes, testifies and signifies that Christ's holy body was broken on the cross (a) and his holy blood poured out (b), for the remission of our sins; that he is now glorified in heaven, is the living bread, food and drink of our souls (c). It places before our eyes Christ's office or ministry in glory while he sups spiritually with believing souls (d) by nourishing and feeding souls with spiritual food (e). Through it we are taught, in that external action, to elevate our hearts on high with holy supplications (f), and to seek from Christ the true and highest good shadowed forth in this supper; (g) and finally it exhorts us to give thanks to God and to exercise unity and love among ourselves (h).

a. Luke 22 : 19; I Cor. 11 : 23. b. Mark 14 : 24. c. John 6 : 51, 55. d. Rev. 3 : 20. e. Eph. 5 : 29. f. Col. 3 : 1, 2. g. I Cor. 10 : 16. h. I Cor. 10 : 17.

ARTICLE XXXV.

OF EXCOMMUNICATION.

Ecclesiastical discipline or extreme punishment is likewise an external action among believers, by which an impenitent sinner, after Christian conversation (a) and sufficient admonition, is excluded from the communion of God and his saints, on account of sins; and against him the wrath and anger of God (until he comes to himself and amends) is denounced. By which external ecclesiastical exclusion is shown how God has already beforehand dealt with the excluded one on account of his sins, or judged concerning him. With God, therefore, the judgment upon the fallen sinner is antecedent (b), but with the church subsequent judgment. Wherefore special care must be taken, that no one be condemned in the church who has not beforehand been condemned by the word of God.

a. Matt. 18 : 15-18; I Cor. 5 : 2, 12. b. John 5 : 22; 12 : 48.

ARTICLE XXXVI.

OF WITHDRAWAL FROM PERVERSE APOSTATES.

Those excluded from the church are by no means admitted (as long as they persevere in sins) to the communion of the Holy Supper or other ecclesiastical actions, but we deprive them of these and all other privileges by which any communion, fraternity or spiritual participation in sacred things is signified. And since the life and daily conversation of wicked and perverse men offends and is hurtful (a), and not infrequently a stumbling block to the good, and subjects them to calumny; for these reasons, they withdraw themselves from them, nor do they wish to have any communion with them, their actions, words or works, lest their pure mind be polluted and contaminated and the name of God blasphemed: and all this in this manner, in accordance with the word of God as supreme law; the married do not separate themselves nor do they withdraw themselves from marital privileges, and so nothing is done in this matter which is contrary to love, mercy, Christian justice, want, promises and other similar things.

a. I Cor. 5 : 5; 2 Tim. 2 : 10, 17, 18; 2 Tim. 3 : 10; Tit. 3 : 10.

ARTICLE XXXVII.

OF THE OFFICE OF CIVIL MAGISTRATE.

Government or the civil Magistrate is a necessary ordinance of God (a), instituted for the government of common human society and the preservation of natural life and civil good, for the defense of the good and the punishment of the evil. We acknowledge, the word of God obliging us, that it is our duty to reverence magistracy (b) and to show to it honor and obedience in all things which are not contrary to the word of God (c). It is our duty to pray the omnipotent God for them (d), and to give thanks to him for good and just magistrates and without murmuring to pay just tribute and customs (e). This civil government the Lord Jesus did not institute in his spiritual kingdom, the church of the New Testament,

nor did he join it to the offices of his church (f): nor
did he call his disciples or followers to royal, ducal or
other power; nor did he teach that they should seize it
and rule in a lordly manner; much less did he give to the
members of his church the law (g), agreeable to such
office or dominion: but everywhere they are called away
from it (which voice heard from heaven (h) ought to
be heeded) to the imitation of his harmless life (i) and
his footsteps bearing the cross (k), and in which nothing
is less in evidence than an earthly kingdom, power and
sword. When all these things are carefully weighed (and
moreover not a few things are joined with the office of
civil magistracy, as waging war, depriving enemies of
goods and life, etc., which [do not agree with] the lives
of Christians who ought to be dead to the world), they
agree either badly or plainly not at all, hence we withdraw
ourselves from such offices and administrations. And yet
we do not wish that just and moderate power should in
any manner be despised or condemned, but that it should
be truly esteemed, as in the words of Paul (l), the Holy
Spirit dictating, it ought to be esteemed.

a. Rom. 13 : 1, 3, 4, 6. b. Tit. 3 : 1; I Pet. 2 : 13, 17. c. Acts
4 : 19. d. Jer. 29 : 7; I Tim. 2 : 1, 2. e. Matt. 22 : 17; Rom.
13 : 7. f. I Cor. 12 : 28; Eph. 4 : 11. g. Matt. 20 : 25-28;
Luke 22 : 25-27. h. Matt. 17 : 5. i. John 8 : 12; 10 : 27. k.
Heb. 12 : 2, 3; I Pet. 2 : 21-23. l. Rom. 13 : 1-3.

ARTICLE XXXVIII.

OF THE OATH.

Jesus Christ, King and Lawgiver (a) of the New
Testament, has forbidden to Christians every oath (b),
and for this reason all oaths are unlawful to the believers
of the New Testament.

a. Matt. 28 : 20; Gal. 6 : 4. b. Matt. 5 : 34; James 5 : 10.

ARTICLE XXXIX.

OF MARRIAGE.

Marriage we profess to be an ordinance of God which
must be entered into according to the primal institution

(a) ; that each man have his own only wife (b) and each
woman her own and one husband. This marriage cannot
be dissolved except for the cause of adultery (c). Neither
do we think it allowable that any of us should enter into
marriage outside the Church of God, with wicked, unbelieving or carnal men (d), and we condemn that (as
other sins) by the word of God, the state of the time
and the reason of things.

a. Gen. 2 : 22; Matt. 19 : 4. b. I Cor. 7 : 2; Eph. 5 : 31. c.
Matt. 19 : 9. d. Deut. 7 : 3; I Cor. 7 : 39.

ARTICLE XL.

OF CHRIST'S RETURN, OF THE RESURRECTION OF THE DEAD, AND OF THE LAST JUDGMENT.

Lastly, we believe and teach that Jesus Christ, our
glorious King and Lord, visibly just as he ascended (a),
will return from heaven (b) with power and great glory,
and with him all the holy angels (c), that he may be
glorified in his saints (d) and may be admired by all believers, and will manifest himself as the Judge of the
living and the dead (e). At that time (f) all men, just
and unjust, who have lived upon the earth and have
died, will rise from the dead (with incorruption (g)) and
live again, their souls being reunited with their own
bodies in which they had lived evilly or well (h). But
those who are alive in that day and have not died, changed
in a moment and in the twinkling of an eye, will put on
incorruption, (i) and the whole multitude of the human
race will stand before the tribunal of Christ (k) to report
(l) what each one has done in the body according to that
which he has done whether good or evil. Then Jesus
will separate the sheep from the goats as a shepherd
separates the sheep from the goats (m), and will place
the sheep on his right hand but the goats on the left (n),
and will give sentence. The just who have lived here
holily and have exercised all the works of charity and
mercy (o), as the husband (p) of that Christian multitude, he will take to himself. They will enter with him
into eternal life (q) and celestial joy and glory, where all

E

will always be with the Lord (r) and will possess forever
that kingdom (s) which God the Father had prepared for
them from the beginning of the world. But the unrighteous who have not known God (t) nor regarded the
gospel of our Lord Jesus Christ, will be condemned to
eternal fire (v), which was prepared for the Devil and
his angels, and there they will undergo sorrow and eternal
perdition (x), from the face of the Lord and the glory
of his power.

Preserve us, omnipotent God, full of grace and mercy,
from the punishment of the impious; and concede to us
grace and gifts for a holy life and happy death and a
joyous resurrection with all believers. Amen.

a. Acts 1 : 11. b. Matt. 24 : 30; 2 Thess. 1 : 7. c. Matt. 25 :
31. d. 2 Thess. 1 : 10. e. Acts 10 : 42; 2 Tim. 4 : 1. f. Matt.
25 : 32; John 5 : 28. g. I Cor. 15 : 42. h. 2 Cor. 5 : 10. i. I
Cor. 15 : 51, 52. k. Matt. 25 : 32. l. 2 Cor. 5 : 10. m. Matt.
25 : 32. n. Matt. 25 : 47. o. Matt. 25 : 35, 36, 37, 38. p. Matt.
25 : 10. q. John 5 : 29; Matt. 25 : 47. r. I Thess. 4 : 17. s.
Matt. 25 : 34. t. 2 Thess. 1 : 8. v. Matt. 25 : 42. x. Isa. 2 : 10;
2 Thess. 1 : 9.

F. *The Dordrecht Confession, 1632*

The most influential of all Mennonite confessions was adopted
at Dordrecht on April 21, 1632, at a peace conference of Flemish
and Frisian ministers. Representation at this conference was large
enough to draw from the Reformed clergy a protest against "this
extraordinary gathering of Anabaptists from all provinces." The
confession, whose first draft was written by Adrian Cornelis, bishop
of the Flemish Church in Dordrecht, served successfully as a basis
of union for the Frisian and Flemish bodies. Of the fifty-one ministers who signed the confession, two were from Crefeld, Germany,
and two from Central and South Germany ("the upper country").

Alsatian Mennonites adopted the Dordrecht Confession in 1660,
and Palatinate and other German Mennonite churches subsequently
followed their example. Influenced by Dutch Mennonites of Ger-
mantown, the great body of Pennsylvania Mennonites (Swiss in
origin) adopted the Confession in 1725. The Confession is still
owned by the "Mennonite Church" and other conservative Mennonite bodies of America. Its chief significance to American
Mennonites is "its value as a symbol of the Mennonite heritage of
faith and way of life."[22]

---

[22] Wenger, *The Doctrines of the Mennonites,* 75.

The following translation, taken from Wenger, *The Doctrines of the Mennonites* (Appendix II, 76-83), was made by Joseph F. Sohm for his 1938 English edition of the *Martyr's Mirror*.

ARTICLE I

OF GOD AND THE CREATION OF ALL THINGS

Whereas it is declared, that "without faith it is impossible to please God," and that "he that cometh to God must believe that He is, and that He is a rewarder of them that diligently seek Him," therefore we confess with the mouth, and believe with the heart, together with all the pious, according to the Holy Scriptures, that there is one eternal, almighty, and incomprehensible God, Father, Son, and the Holy Ghost, and none more and none other, before whom no God existed, neither will exist after Him. For from Him through Him, and in Him are all things. To Him be blessing, praise, and honor, for ever and ever.

In this one God, who "worketh all in all," we believe. Him we confess as the creator of all things, visible and invisible; who in six days created and prepared "heaven and earth, and the sea, and all things that are therein." And we further believe, that this God still governs and preserves the same, together with all His works, through His wisdom, His might, and the "word of His power."

When He had finished His works and, according to His good pleasure, had ordained and prepared each of them, so that they were right and good according to their nature, being, and quality. He created the first man, Adam, the father of all of us, gave him a body formed "of the dust of the ground, breathed into his nostrils the breath of life," so that he "became a living soul," created by God "in His own image and likeness," in "righteousness and true holiness" unto eternal life. He also gave him a place above all other creatures and endowed him with many high and excellent gifts, put him into the garden of Eden, and gave him a commandment and an interdiction. Thereupon He took a rib from the said Adam, made a woman out of it, brought her to him, and gave her to him as a helpmate and housewife. Consequently He has caused, that from this first man, Adam, all men who "dwell on the face of the earth," have been begotten and have descended.

ARTICLE II

OF THE FALL OF MAN

We believe and confess, that, according to the purport of the Holy Scriptures, our first parents, Adam and Eve, did not long remain in the happy state in which they were created; but did, after being seduced by the deceit and subtilty of the serpent, and envy of the devil, violate the high command of God, and became disobedient to their Creator; through which disobedience "sin entered into the world, and death by sin;" so that "death passed upon all men, for that all have sinned," and thereby incurred the wrath of God and condemnation. For which reason our first parents were, by God, driven out of Paradise, to cultivate the earth, to maintain themselves thereon in sorrow, and to "eat their bread in the sweat of their face," until they "returned to the ground, from which they were taken." And that they did, therefore, through this one sin, so far apostatize, depart, and estrange themselves from God, that they could neither help themselves, nor be helped by any of their descendants, nor by angels, nor by any other creature in heaven or on earth, nor be redeemed, or reconciled to God; but would have had to be lost forever, had not God who pitied His creatures, in mercy, interposed in their behalf and made provision for their restoration.

ARTICLE III
OF THE RESTORATION OF MAN THROUGH THE PROMISE
OF THE COMING OF CHRIST

Regarding the restoration of our first parents and their descendants, we believe and confess: That God, not withstanding their fall, transgression, and sin, and although they had no power to help themselves, He was nevertheless not willing that they should be cast off entirely, or be eternally lost; but again called them unto Him, comforted them, and showed them that there were yet means with Him for their reconciliation; namely, the immaculate Lamb, the Son of God; who "was fore-ordained" to this purpose "before the foundation of the world," and who was promised to them and all their descendants, while they (our first parents) were yet in paradise, for their comfort, redemption, and salvation; yea, who was given to them thenceforward, through faith, as their own; after which all the pious patriarchs, to whom this promise was often renewed, longed and searched, beholding it through faith at a distance, and expecting its fulfillment — expecting that He (the Son of God), would, at His coming, again redeem and deliver the fallen race of man from their sins, their guilt, and unrighteousness.

ARTICLE IV
OF THE ADVENT OF CHRIST INTO THIS WORLD,
AND THE REASON OF HIS COMING

We believe and confess further: That "when the fulness of the time was come," after which all the pious patriarchs so ardently longed, and which they so anxiously awaited — the previously promised Messiah, Redeemer, and Saviour, proceeded from God, being sent by Him, and according to the prediction of the prophets and the testimony of the evangelists, came into the world, yea, into the flesh —, so that the Word itself thus became flesh and man; and that He was conceived by the Virgin Mary (who was espoused to a man named Joseph, of the house of David), and that she bare Him as her first-born son at Bethlehem, "wrapped Him in swaddling clothes, and laid Him in a manger."

Further we believe and confess, that this is the same One, "whose goings forth have been from of old, from everlasting;" who has "neither beginning of days, nor end of life." Of whom it is testified, that He is "Alpha and Omega, the beginning and the end, the first and the last." That this is also He — and none other — who was chosen, promised, and sent; who came into the world; and who is God's only, first, and proper Son; who was before John the Baptist, before Abraham, before the world; yea, who was David's Lord, and who was God of the "whole earth," "the first-born of every creature"; who was sent into the world, and Himself delivered up the body prepared for Him, as "an offering and a sacrifice to God for a sweet smelling savour;" yea, for the comfort, redemption, and salvation of all — of the human race.

But how, or in what manner, this worthy body was prepared, or how the Word became flesh, and He Himself man, we content ourselves with the declaration which the worthy evangelists have given and left in their description thereof; according to which we confess with all the saints that He is the Son of the living God, in whom exist all our hope, comfort, redemption, and salvation, and which we are to seek in no one else.

Further, we believe and confess by authority of scripture, that when He had ended His course, and "finished" the work for which He was sent into the world, He was, by the providence of God, delivered into the hands of the unrighteous; suffered under the judge, Pontius Pilate, was crucified, died, was buried, rose again from the dead on the third day, and ascended into heaven, where He now sits at the right hand of the Majesty of God on high; from whence He will come again to judge the living and dead.

Thus we believe the Son of God died — "tasted death for every man," shed His precious blood, and thereby bruised the head of the serpent, destroyed the works of the devil, "blotted out the handwriting," and purchased redemption for the whole human race; and thus He became the source of eternal salvation to all who from the time of Adam to the end of the world, shall have believed in Him, and obeyed Him.

ARTICLE V

OF THE LAW OF CHRIST, WHICH IS THE HOLY GOSPEL, OR THE NEW TESTAMENT

We also believe and confess, that Christ, before His ascension, established and instituted His New Testament and left it to His followers, to be and remain an everlasting testament, which He confirmed and sealed with His own precious blood; and which He has so highly commended to them, that neither men or angels may change it, neither take therefrom nor add thereto.

And that He has caused this Testament (in which the whole counsel and will of His heavenly Father, so far as these are necessary to the salvation of man, are comprehended), to be proclaimed, in His name, through His beloved apostles, messengers, and servants (whom He chose and sent into all the world for this purpose) — to all nations, people and tongues; these apostles preaching repentance and remission of sins; and that He, in said Testament, caused it to be declared, that all men without distinction, if they are obedient, through faith, follow, fulfill and live according to the precepts of the same, are His children and rightful heirs; having thus excluded none from the precious inheritance of eternal salvation, except the unbelieving and disobedient, the headstrong and unconverted; who despise such salvation; and thus by their own actions incur guilt by refusing the same, and "judge themselves unworthy of everlasting life."

ARTICLE VI

OF REPENTANCE AND AMENDMENT OF LIFE

We believe and confess, that, as the "imagination of man's heart is evil from his youth," and consequently inclined to all unrighteousness, sin, and wickedness, that, therefore, the first doctrine of the precious New Testament of the Son of God is, Repentance and amendment of life.

Therefore those who have ears to hear, and hearts to understand, must "bring forth fruits meet for repentance," amend their lives, believe the Gospel, "depart from evil and do good," desist from wrong and cease from sinning, "put off the old man with his deeds and put on the new man," which after God is created in "righteousness and true holiness." For neither BAPTISM, SUPPER, NOR CHURCH-FELLOWSHIP, nor any other external ceremony, can without faith, the new birth, and a change or renewal of life, help, or qualify us, that we may please God, or receive any consolation or promise of salvation from Him.

But on the contrary, we must go to God "with a sincere heart in full assurance of faith," and believe in Jesus Christ, as the Scriptures speak and testify of Him. Through which faith we obtain the pardon of our sins, become sanctified, justified, and children of God; yea, partakers of His mind, nature and image, as we are born again of God through His incorruptible seed from above.

ARTICLE VII

OF HOLY BAPTISM

Regarding baptism, we confess that all penitent believers, who through faith, the new birth and renewal of the Holy Ghost, have become united with God, and whose names are recorded in heaven, must, on such Scriptural confession of their faith, and renewal of life, according to the command and doctrine of Christ, and the example and custom of the apostles, be baptized with water in the ever adorable name of the Father, and of the Son, and of the Holy Ghost, to the burying of their sins, and thus to become incorporated into the communion of the saints; whereupon they must learn to observe all things whatsoever the Son of God taught, left on record, and commanded His followers to do.

ARTICLE VIII

OF THE CHURCH OF CHRIST

We believe in and confess a visible Church of God, consisting of those, who, as before remarked, have truly repented, and rightly believed; who are rightly baptized, united with God in heaven, and incorporated into the communion of the saints on earth.

And these, we confess, are a "chosen generation, a royal priesthood, an holy nation," who have the testimony that they are the "bride" of Christ; yea, that they are children and heirs of eternal life — a "habitation of God through the Spirit," built on the foundation of the apostles and prophets, of which "Christ Himself is the chief cornerstone" — the foundation on which His church is built.

This church of the living God, which He has purchased and redeemed through His own precious blood, and with which He will be — according to His own promise — for her comfort and protection, "always, even unto the end of the world"; yea, will dwell and walk with her, and preserve her, that no "winds" nor "floods," yea, not even the "gates of hell shall prevail against her" — may be known by her evangelical faith, doctrine, love, and godly conversation; also by her pure walk and practice, and her observance of the true ordinances of Christ, which He has strictly enjoined on His followers.

ARTICLE IX

OF THE ELECTION, AND OFFICES OF TEACHERS, DEACONS AND DEACONESSES, IN THE CHURCH

Regarding the offices, and election of persons to the same, in the church, we believe and confess: That, as the church cannot exist and prosper, nor continue in its structure, without offices and regulations, that therefore the Lord Jesus has Himself (as a father in his house), appointed and prescribed His offices and ordinances, and has given commandments concerning the same, as to how each one should walk therein, give heed to his own work and calling, and do it as it becomes him to do.

For He Himself, as the faithful and great Shepherd, and Bishop of our souls, was sent into the world, not to wound, to break, or destroy the souls of men, but to heal them; to seek that which is lost, and to pull down the hedges and partition wall, so as to make out of many one; thus collecting out of Jews and heathen, yea, out of all nations, a church in His name; for which (so that no one might go astray or be lost) He laid down His own life, and thus procured for them salvation, made them free and redeemed them, to which blessing no one could help them, or be of service in obtaining it.

And that He, besides this, left His church before His departure, provided with faithful ministers, apostles, evangelists, pastors, and teachers, whom He had chosen by prayer and supplication through the Holy Spirit, so that they might govern the church, feed His flock, watch over, maintain, and care for the same: yea, do all things as He left them an example, taught them, and commanded them to do; and likewise to teach the church to observe all things whatsoever He commanded them.

Also that the apostles were afterwards, as faithful followers of Christ and leaders of the church, diligent in these matters, namely, in choosing through prayer and supplication to God, brethren who were to provide all the churches in the cities and circuits, with bishops, pastors, and leaders, and to ordain to these offices such men as took "heed unto themselves and unto the doctrine," and also unto the flock; who were sound in the faith, pious in their life and conversation, and who had — as well within the church as "without" — a good reputation and a good report; so that they might be a light and example in all godliness and good works; might worthily administer the Lord's ordinances — baptism and supper — and that they (the brethren sent by the apostles) might also, at all places, where such were to be had, appoint faithful men as elders, who were able to teach others, confirm them in the name of the Lord "with the laying on of hands," and who (the elders) were to take care of all things of which the church stood in need; so that they, as faithful servants, might well "occupy" their Lord's money, gain thereby, and thus "save themselves and those who hear them."

That they should also take good care (particularly each one of the charge over which he had the oversight), that all the circuits should be well provided with deacons, who should have the care and oversight of the poor, and who were to receive gifts and alms, and again faithfully to distribute them among the poor saints who were in need, and this is in all honesty, as is becoming.

Also that honorable old widows should be chosen as deaconesses, who, besides the deacons are to visit, comfort, and take care of the poor, the weak, afflicted, and the needy, as also to visit, comfort, and take care of the widows and orphans; and further to assist in taking care of any matters in the church that properly come within their sphere, according to their ability.

And as it further regards the deacons, that they (particularly if they are fit persons, and chosen and ordained thereto by the church), may also in aid and relief of the bishops, exhort the church (being, as already remarked, chosen hereto), and thus assist in word and doctrine; so that each one may serve the other from love, with the gift which he has received from the Lord; so that through the common service and assistance of each member, according to his ability, the body of Christ may be edified, and the Lord's vineyard and church be preserved in its growth and structure.

ARTICLE X
OF THE LORD'S SUPPER

We also believe in and observe the breaking of bread, or the Lord's Supper, as the Lord Jesus instituted the same (with bread and wine) before His sufferings, and also observed and ate it with the apostles, and also commanded it to be observed to His remembrance, as also the apostles subsequently taught and observed the same in the church, and commanded it to be observed by believers in commemoration of the death and sufferings of the Lord — the breaking of His worthy body and the shedding of His precious blood — for the whole human race. So is the observance of this sacrament also to remind us of the benefit of the said death and sufferings of Christ, namely, the redemption and eternal salvation which He purchased thereby, and the great love thus shown to sinful man; whereby we are earnestly exhorted also to love one another — to love our neighbor — to forgive and absolve him — even as Christ has done unto us — and also to endeavor to maintain and keep alive the union and communion which we have with God, and amongst one another; which is thus shown and represented to us by the aforesaid breaking of bread.

ARTICLE XI
OF THE WASHING OF THE SAINTS' FEET

We also confess a washing of the feet of the saints, as the Lord Jesus did not only institute and command the same, but did also Himself wash the feet of the apostles, although He was their Lord and Master; thereby giving an example that they also should wash one another's feet, and thus do to one another as He did to them; which they also afterwards taught believers to observe, and all this is a sign of true humiliation; but yet more particularly as a sign to remind us of the true washing — the washing and purification of the soul in the blood of Christ.

ARTICLE XII
OF MATRIMONY

We also confess that there is in the church of God an "honorable" state of matrimony between two believers of the different sexes, as God first instituted the same in paradise between Adam and Eve, and as the Lord Jesus reformed it by removing all abuses which had crept into it, and restoring it to its first order.

In this manner the Apostle Paul also taught and permitted matrimony in the church, leaving it to each one's own choice to enter into matrimony with any person who would unite with him in such state, provided that it was done "in the Lord," according to the primitive order; the words "in the Lord," to be understood, according to our opinion, that just as the patriarchs had to marry amongst their own kindred or generation, so there is also no other liberty allowed to believers under the New Testament dispensation, than to marry among the "chosen generation," or the spiritual kindred of Christ; that is, to such — and none others — as are already, previous to their marriage, united to the church in heart and soul, have received the same baptism, belong to the same church, are of the same faith and doctrine, and lead the same course of life, with themselves.

Such are then, as already remarked, united by God and the church according to the primitive order, and this is then called, "Marrying in the Lord."

ARTICLE XIII

OF THE OFFICE OF CIVIL GOVERNMENT

We also believe and confess, that God has instituted civil government, for the punishment of the wicked and the protection of the pious; and also further, for the purpose of governing the world, countries and cities; and also to preserve its subjects in good order and under good regulations. Wherefore we are not permitted to despise, revile, or resist the same, but are to acknowledge it as a minister of God and be subject and obedient to it, in all things that do not militate against the law, will, and commandments of God; yea, "to be ready to every good work;" also faithfully to pay it custom, tax, and tribute; thus giving it what is its due; as Jesus Christ taught, did Himself, and commanded His followers to do. That we also are to pray to the Lord earnestly for the government and its welfare, and in behalf of our country, so that we may live under its protection, maintain ourselves, and "lead a quiet and peaceable life in all godliness and honesty." And further, that the Lord would recompense them (our rulers), here and in eternity, for all the benefits, liberties, and favors which we enjoy under their laudable administration.

ARTICLE XIV

OF DEFENSE BY FORCE

Regarding revenge, whereby we resist our enemies with the sword, we believe and confess that the Lord Jesus has forbidden His disciples and followers all revenge and resistance, and has thereby commanded them not to "return evil for evil, nor railing for railing;" but to "put up the sword into the sheath," or, as the prophet foretold, "beat them into ploughshares."

From this we see, that, according to the example, life, and doctrine of Christ, we are not to do wrong, or cause offense or vexation to anyone; but to seek the welfare and salvation of all men, also, if necessity should require it, to flee, for the Lord's sake, from one city or country to another, and suffer the "spoiling of our goods," rather than give occasion of offense to anyone; and if we are struck in our "right cheek, rather to turn the other also," than revenge ourselves, or return the blow.

And that we are, besides this, also to pray for our enemies, comfort and feed them, when they are hungry or thirsty, and thus by welldoing convince them and overcome the evil with good.

Finally, that we are to do good in all respects, "commending our-selves to every man's conscience in the sight of God," and according to the law of Christ, do nothing to others that we would not wish them to do unto us.

ARTICLE XV
OF THE SWEARING OF OATHS

Regarding the swearing of oaths, we believe and confess that the Lord Jesus has dissuaded His followers from and forbidden them the same; that is, that He commanded them to "swear not at all;" but that their "Yea" should be "yea," and their "Nay, nay." From which we understand that all oaths, high and low, are forbidden; and that instead of them we are to confirm all our promises and covenants, declarations and testimonies of all matters, merely with "Yea that is yea," and "Nay that is nay;" and that we are to per-form and fulfill at all times, and in all things, to every one, every promise and obligation to which we thus affirm, as faithfully as if we had confirmed it by the most solemn oath. And if we thus do, we have the confidence that no one—not even government itself—will have just cause to require more of us.

ARTICLE XVI
OF THE ECCLESIASTICAL BAN OR EXCOMMUNICATION FROM THE CHURCH

We also believe in and acknowledge the ban, or excommunication, a separation or spiritual correction by the church, for the amend-ment, and not for the destruction, of offenders; so that what is pure may be separated from that which is impure. That is, if a person, after having been enlightened, and received the knowledge of the truth, and has been received into the communion of the saints, does willfully, or out of presumption, sin against God, or commit some other "sin unto death," thereby falling into such unfruitful works of darkness, that he becomes separated from God, and is de-barred from His kingdom—that such an one—when his works are become manifest, and sufficiently known to the church—cannot re-main in the "congregation of the righteous;" but must, as an offensive member and open sinner, be excluded from the church, "rebuked before all," and "purged out as a leaven," and thus remain until his amendment, as an example and warning to others, and also that the church may be kept pure from such "spots" and "blem-ishes"; so that not for the want of this, the name of the Lord be blasphemed, the church dishonored, and a stumblingblock thrown in the way of those "without," and finally, that the offender may not be condemned with the world, but that he may again be convinced of the error of his ways, and brought to repentance and amendment of life.

Regarding the brotherly admonition, as also the instruction of the erring, we are to "give all diligence" to watch over them, and exhort them in all meekness to the amendment of their ways (Jas. 5:19,20) ; and in case any should remain obstinate and unconverted, to reprove them as the case may require. In short, the church must "put away from among herself him that is wicked," whether it be in doctrine or life.

ARTICLE XVII

OF THE SHUNNING OF THOSE WHO ARE EXPELLED

As regards the withdrawing from, or the shunning of, those who are expelled, we believe and confess, that if any one, whether it be through a wicked life or perverse doctrine—is so far fallen as to be separated from God, and consequently rebuked by, and expelled from, the church, he must also, according to the doctrine of Christ and His apostles, be shunned and avoided by all the members of the church (particularly by those to whom his misdeeds are known), whether it be in eating or drinking, or other such like social matters. In short, that we are to have nothing to do with him; so that we may not become defiled by intercourse with him, and partakers of his sins; but that he may be made ashamed, be affected in his mind, convinced in his conscience, and thereby induced to amend his ways.

That nevertheless, as well in shunning as in reproving such offender, such moderation and Christian discretion be used, that such shunning and reproof may not be conducive to his ruin, but be serviceable to his amendment. For should he be in need, hungry, thirsty, naked, sick or visited by some other affliction, we are in duty bound, according to the doctrine and practice of Christ and His apostles, to render him aid and assistance, as necessity may require; otherwise the shunning of him might be rather conducive to his ruin than to his amendment.

Therefore we must not treat such offenders as enemies, but exhort them as brethren, in order thereby to bring them to a knowledge of their sins and to repentance; so that they may again become reconciled to God and the church, and be received and admitted into the same—thus exercising love towards them, as is becoming.

Article XVIII

OF THE RESURRECTION OF THE DEAD AND THE LAST JUDGMENT

Regarding the resurrection of the dead, we confess with the mouth, and believe with the heart, that according to the Scriptures all men who shall have died or "fallen asleep," will, through the incomprehensible power of God, at the day of judgment, be "raised up" and made alive; and that these, together with all those who then remain alive, and who shall be "changed in a moment, in the twinkling of an eye, at the last trump," shall "appear before the judgment seat of Christ," where the good shall be separated from the evil, and where "every one shall receive the things done in his body, according to that he hath done, whether it be good or bad;" and that the good or pious shall then further, as the blessed of their Father, be received by Christ into eternal life, where they shall receive that joy which "eye hath not seen, nor ear heard, nor hath entered into the heart of man." Yea, where they shall reign and triumph with Christ for ever and ever.

And that, on the contrary, the wicked or impious, shall, as the accursed of God, be cast into "outer darkness;" yea, into eternal, hellish torments; "where their worm dieth not, and the fire is not quenched"; and where—according to Holy Scripture—they can expect no comfort nor redemption throughout eternity.

May the Lord through His grace make us all fit and worthy, that no such calamity may befall any of us; but that we may be diligent, and so take heed to ourselves, that we may be found of Him in peace, without spot, and blameless. Amen.

G. Other Mennonite Confessions

After 1580 the Mennonites drew up numerous confessions and other doctrinal statements, usually for the purpose of healing schisms. These do not seem to have had direct influence on Baptist confessions, and so they are only listed here.

(1) The Concept of Cologne, May, 1591, an effort at union of Frisian and Flemish with High German (Swiss Brethren) Mennonites. Signed by representatives of churches in the Rhine country, Alsace, Strasburg, Württemberg, and Holland. Schyn, Historia, II, 79.

(2) The Frisian Confession, 1600. Thirty-three articles drawn up by Peter Janz Twisck. Van Braght, Martyr's Mirror, 373-410.

(3) The Olive Branch, Sept., 1625. Drawn up at Amsterdam with

a view to unite Frisian and Flemish churches. In condensed Latin form in Schyn, *Historia*, II, 85f. In English, translated from Dutch, Van Braght, *supra*, 26-32.

(4) *Confession of some United Frisian and High German churches, 1730*. By John Centsen. Van Braght, *supra*, 27-38.

(5) *A Confession treating only of the one God . . . and of the Incarnation of the Son of God, Oct., 1626*. Accepted by the deputies of Holland as a basis of the policy of toleration of Mennonites. Schyn, *Historia*, I, 79-85.

(6) *A Brief Confession of Faith and of the Principal Articles of the Christian Religion, Oct., 1630*. Used to initiate negotiations between two groups at Amsterdam. In Latin, Schyn, *Historia*, II, 87-114. English from the Dutch, Van Braght, *supra*, 36-38.

(7) *Christian Fundamentals, 1921*. Confession of the Mennonite General Conference (American).

2. PIONEER ENGLISH SEPARATIST-BAPTIST CONFESSIONS

A. *A True Confession, 1596*

The extent of indebtedness of English Separatism to Anabaptism is a much disputed question, but it seems reasonable to conclude that the thinking of the more advanced seekers after reformation in England was in some degree shaped by the thousands of Netherlanders who settled in England, especially along the east coast, during the second half of the sixteenth century. It is now certain that Mennonites thronged to England as a refuge, and that they quietly carried on their religious life for a time in the new land, but evidence is lacking that they made many direct disciples in England. By 1562 Dutch exiles on English soil are said to have numbered 30,000; but the Anabaptist element among these had to lie concealed, for throughout the reign of Elizabeth the death penalty awaited any who were convicted of holding Anabaptist sentiments. These sentiments, however, seem to have penetrated areas of English life where Anabaptists themselves did not appear, and to have become a part of the thought-stream of the people generally, coming into expression in the radical dissent of late sixteenth- and early seventeenth-century England.

It is true that the New Testament could have been understood alike, though independently, by English readers and Dutch Anabaptists, but it is difficult to avoid the conclusion that the interpretation of the Scriptures by certain Englishmen concerning such matters as the doctrine of a pure church, of freedom of conscience, of believers' baptism, of congregational autonomy, and of separation of church and state owed something to the infiltration of Anabaptist ideas. In the case of the pioneer experiment of Robert Browne in congregationalism in 1580, it is significant that Browne went to the county of Norfolk to make his beginning. People there were intent upon establishing religious reforms such as he envisioned; and the county teemed with Dutch artisans. There, in the town of Norwich, he worked out his congregational theories with Robert Harrison, though it must be said that they showed no conscious indebtedness to Anabaptist influences.

The experiment of Browne failed, his people fled to Holland where the group disintegrated, and Browne himself later conformed to the Church of England. Separatist ideas, however, did not cease, and by 1587 or 1588 a Separatist congregation appeared in London. Two leaders of the young church, Henry Barrowe and John Greenwood, were imprisoned in 1586, but in 1589 they sent from prison a simple church creed called *A Trve Description ovt of the Word of God, of the visible Church*. This work was an ideal sketch intended for use in connection with setting up the new church. The authors found the outline for the church in the New Testament, and for them the Bible was the final authority in all matters of doctrine and government. The church itself was defined as a company of believers united in fellowship to Christ and to one another. Church officers to be elected by the congregation were said to be pastor, teacher, elder, deacons, and widows. Administration of the church was put into the hands of elders, who were set above their brethren as a ruling oligarchy. The creed did not concern itself with doctrinal matters since the congregation was already of one mind in holding Calvinistic views.

Severity of persecution prevented the London church from electing appropriate officers until 1592, when Francis Johnson was chosen pastor. John Greenwood, out of prison temporarily, was elected teacher, and two elders and two deacons were chosen.[23] Both Johnson and Greenwood were arrested in December, 1592, and in the spring of 1593 fifty-six members of their church followed them into

---

[23] Walker, W., *The Creeds and Platforms of Congregationalism*, p. 29.

confinement in London prisons. In the summer of that year, however, there was a change of policy on the part of the government toward the Separatists. On observing that most of those imprisoned were politically unimportant folk, the government began to look upon emigration as the best means of getting rid of the Separatists. The way then was made easy for the dissenters to slip over the sea to Holland, except that the leaders were not permitted to go with them, but were kept in prison. Most of the emigrants reached Amsterdam, where the church re-gathered in 1595.[24] Since Johnson was still in prison, Henry Ainsworth was elected pastor.

At this stage a part of the church was yet in London, while its main strength was gathered in Amsterdam. Desiring to make clear its doctrinal position and its ecclesiology, in view of the threat of attacks on both, the church prepared in 1596 a new creed, the shortened title of which is *A Trve Confession*. This document was put forth in the name of both sections of the church and several of the members may have shared in its preparation. The Preface indicates that it was chiefly the work of the Amsterdam group, and Dexter[25] conjectures that Ainsworth was principally responsible for it.

The Preface describes the motives and sufferings of the Separatists. On the basis of biblical standards, the Church of England is found wanting as a true church, and its ministry, liturgy, rites, and membership are impugned.

The forty-five articles of the Confession offer doctrine and polity. Its Calvinism, typical of that of the Puritans, is in no wise novel. Its polity, far more detailed than that of *A True Description,* and marking a real development in appreciation of congregational principles, shows that its authors had worked out many practical questions since 1589.

The seven Particular Baptist Churches of London used this confession as a model when they drew up their earliest confession in 1644. Thus, the Separatist Confession entered Baptist life. The copy of the confession here given is taken from Williston Walker, *The Creeds and Platforms of Congregationalism,* 59-74 ; Charles Scribner's Sons, New York, 1893. Footnotes at the bottom of the pages of this confession are Walker's.

---

[24] It came to be known as the "Ancient Church."
[25] *Ibid.,* p. 43.

F

[xi] A[1] TRVE CONFESSIon OF THE FAITH, AND HVMBLE ACKNOVVLEDGMENT OE THE ALEgeance, vvhich vve hir Maiesties Subjects, falsely called Brovvnists, doo hould tovvards God, and yeild to hir Majestie and all other that are ouer vs in the Lord. Set dovvn in Articles or Positions, for the better & more easie vnderstanding of those that shall read yt: And published for the cleering of our selues from those vnchristian slanders of heresie, schisme, pryde, obstinacie, disloyaltie, sedicion, &c. vvhich by our adversaries are in all places given out against vs.

Wee beleeue with our hearts & confes with our mouths.

THat ther is but[a] one God, one Christ, one Spirit, one Church, one truth, one Faith,[b] one Rule of obedience to all Christians, in all places.

a Deut. 6, 4. Hos. 13, 4. Mark. 12, 29, 32. Eph. 4, 4. 5. 6. 1 Cor. 12, 13. b Rom. 16, 26. 1 Cor. 4, 17. & 16. 1. Gal. 1, 8. 9.

2 That God is a [c]Spirit, whose[d] beeing is of himself, and[e] giveth beeing, moving, and preservation to all other things beeing himself[f] eternall, most holy, every way infinit, in greatnes, vvisdome, povvre, goodnes, justice, truth, &c. And that in this Godhead there bee three[g] distinct persons [h]coeternall, coequall, & [k]coessentiall, beeing every one of thē one & the same God, & therfore not divided but distinguished one frō another by their severall & peculiar propertie: The [l]Father of none, the Sonne[m] begotten of the Father from everlasting, the holy [n]Gost proceding from the Father and the Sonne before all beginnings.

c John. 4, 24. d Exod. 3, 14. Esa. 43, 10, 11. e Rom. 11, 36. Act 17, 28. Gen. 1. f 1 tim. 1, 17. Reu. 4, 18. Esa. 6, 3. and 66. 1. 2. Psal. 145, 3. 8. 9. 17. & 147. 5. Rom. 1, 20. g 1. Joh. 5, 7. Mat. 28, 19. Hag. 2, 5. 6 Heb. 9, 14. h Pro. 8, 22. Joh. 1. 1. Heb. 9, 14. i Phil. 2, 6. Joh. 5, 18. Eph. 4, 4. 5. 6. k Joh. 10, 30. 38. 1 Corint. 2, 11. 12. Heb. 1, 3. l Joh. 5, 26. 1 Cor. 8, 6. m Joh. 1, 14. 18. & 3. 16. Mica. 5, 2. Psal. 2, 7. n Joh. 14, 26. & 1. 16. Gal. 4, 16.

3 That God[o] hath decreed in himself from everlasting touching all things, and the very least circumstances of every thing, effectually to vvork and dispose thē according to the counsell of his ovvn vvill, to the prayse and glorie of his great name. And touching his cheefest Creatures that God hath in[p] Christ[q] before the foundation of the world,[r] according to the good pleasure of his vvill,[s] ordeyned som men and Angells, to eternall lyfe to

[1] The Confession is printed in Roman, with the texts on the margin of the page. I have put the texts after each section for convenience, following in this the Latin edition of 1598.

bee[t] accomplished through Iesus Christ, to the [v]prayse of the
glorie of his grace. And on thother hand hath li*k*evvise [w]before
of old accor*a*ing[x] to his iust purpose[y] ordein*e*d other both Angels
and men, toe ternall condemna-[xii]tion, to bee[z] accomplished
through their o*w*n corruption to the[a] prayse of his iustice.

oEsa. 46, 10. Rō. *z*i, 34. 35. 36. Act. 15, 18. & 2, 22. Gen. 45, 5. 6. 7. 8.
-Mat. 10, 29, 30. and 20. 15. Eph. 1, 11. pEph. 1, 3. 4. 11. qibid & mat. 25,
34. rEph. 1, 5. Rom. 9, 11, 12, 13. Mal. 1, 2. 2, Tim. 1, 9. sAct. 13, 48.
Eph. 1, 4. 5. 1. Tim. 5, 21. Mat. 25, 31. 34. tEphes. 1, 5. 7. 10. Col. 1, 14.
17. 18. 19. & 2. 10. Rom. 8. 19. 30. Rev. 19. 10. veph. 1, 6 to 9, 11. wJud.
ver. 4. xRom. 9, 11. 12. 15. 17. 18. with Mal. 1, 3. Exod. 9. 16. yJud. ver. 4,
& 6. ro 9, 22. Mat. 25, 41. zz. Pet. 2, 12. 2. Cor. 4, 3. 4. 1 pet. 2, 8. joh.
3. 19. & Pro. 16, 4. rom. 2, 5. and 9. 22.

4 T*h*at in the [c]beginning God made all t*h*ings of not*h*ing
*z*ery good: and [d]created man after his o*w*n image and lykenes in
rig*h*teousnes and *h*olines of trut*h*. That[e] streig*h*t *w*ays after by
the subtiltie of the Serpent *w*hich Sathan vsed as his instrument[f]
himself *w*it*h* *h*is Angells *h*auing sinned before and not kept t*h*eir
first estate, but left their own *h*abitation; first [g]E*v*a, t*h*en Adam by
*h*ir meanes, did *w*ittingly & *w*illingly fall into disobedience &
transgression of t*h*e commādement of God. For t*h*e w*h*ich death[h]
reigned over all: yea e*v*en[i] ouer infants also, whic*h* *h*ave not
sinned, after the lyke maner of the transgression of Adam, t*h*at is,
actually: Yet are[k] all since t*h*e fall of Adam begotten in his o*w*n
likenes after *h*is image, beeing conceyued and borne in iniquitie,
and soo by nature the chi*l*dren of *w*rath and servants of sinne,
and subiect to deat*h*, and all ot*h*er calamities due vnto sinne in
this world and for euer.

cGen. 1. Col. 1, 16. Esa. 45, 12. Heb. 11, 3. Revel. 4, 11. dGen. 1,
26. 27. Eph. 4, 24. Eccles. 7, 31. eGen. 3, 1. 4. 5. 2. Cor. 11, 3. Joh. 8,
44. f2. Pet. 2, 4. Joh 8, 44. Jud. 6. gGenes. 3, 1. 2. 3. 6 1. Tim. 2, 14.
Eccles. 7, 31. Gal. 3, 22. hRom. 5, 12. 18. 19. and 6. 23. with Gen. 2, 17.
iRom. 5. 14. and 9, 11. kGen. 5, 3. Psal. 51, 5. Eph. 2, 3.

5 T*h*at all man*k*inde beeing t*h*us fallen and become alto-
get*h*er dead in sinne, & subiect to t*h*e eternall v*v*rat*h* of God both
by origina*l* and actuall corruption: T*h*e [l]elect are redeemed,
quickned, raysed *v*p and saued againe, not of t*h*emselues, neit*h*er
by v*v*orks, lest ani*e* man s*h*ould bost *h*imself; but v*v*h*o*lly and
only by God of *h*is free grace and mercy through faith in Christ
Iesus,[m] v*v*ho of God is made vnto vs v*v*isdome, & righteousnes,
& sanctificatiō, & redemption, that according as it is v*v*ritten, Hee
that reioyceth let him reioyce in the Lord.

1Gen. 3, 15. Eph. 2, 4. 5. Gen. 15. 6. with Rom. 4, 2. 3. 4. 5. and 3. 24. 25. 26. Joh. 3, 16. m1. Cor. 1, 30. 31. Phil. 3, 8. 9. 10. 11. Jir. 23. 5. 6. and 9. 23. 24.

6 That this therfore only is lyfe[n] eternall to knovv the only true God, & vvhom hee hath sent into the vvorld Iesus Crist. And that on the contrarie the [o]Lord vvill rēder vengeance in flaming fire vnto them that knovv not God, & vvhich obey not the Gospell of our Lord Iesus Christ.

n Joh. 17, 3. and 3 36. Jir. 31, 33. 34. o 2. Thes. 1, 8. Eph. 1, 6. joh. 3, 36.

7 That the rule of this knovvledge faith & obedience, concerning the [p]vvorship & service of God & [q]all other christiā dutyes, is not the [r]opinions, devises, lavves, or constitutions of mē, but the vvritten vvord of the everlyving God, conteyned in the canonicall bookes of the old and nevv Testament.

p Exod. 10, 4. 5. 6. Deu. 4, 2. 5. 6. Gen. 6, 22. Exod. 39, 42. 43. 1. Chron. 28. 19. q Psal. 119. 105. r Esa. 29, 13. Mat. 15, 9. Joh. 5, 39. 2. Pet. 16, 19. 2. tim. 3, 16. 17.

8 That in this vvord[s] Iesus Christ hath reveled vvatsoever his father thought needfull for vs to knovv, beleeue & obey as touching his[t] person & Offices, in[v] vvhom all the promises of God are yea, & in vvhom they are Amen to the prayse of God through vs.

s Deut. 18, 18. Joh. 1, 18. & 15, 15. & 4. 25. Act. 3. 22. t the whol Epistle to the Hebr. throughout, & 2. Cor. 1, 28.

[xiii] 9 That touching his person, the Lord Iesus, of vvhō[x] Moses & the Prophets vvrote, & vvhō the Apostles preached, is the [y]everlasting Sonne of God, by eternall generation, the brightnes of his Fathers glorie, & the engrauen forme of his Person; coessentiall, coequall, & coeternall, god vvith him & vvith the holy Gost, by vvhō hee hath made the vvorlds, by vvhom hee vphouldeth and governeth all the works hee hath made; vvho also vvhen the[z] fulnes of tyme vvas come, vvas made man of a vvoman, of [a]the Tribe of Iudah, of the [b]seed of Dauid & Abraham, to vvyt of Mary that blessed Virgin, by the holy Ghost comming vpon hir, & the povvre of the most high ouershadovving hir; & vvas also[c] in all things lyke vnto vs, sinne only excepted.

x Luk. 24, 44. Joh. 5, 46. Act. 10, 41. 43. y Pro. 8, 22, mica. 5, 2. Joh. 1, 1. 2. 3. Heb. 1. Collos. 1, 15. 16. 17. z Gal. 4, 4. Gen. 3, 15. a Heb. 7. 14. Revel. 5, 5. b Rom. 1, 3. Gen. 22, 18. Mat. 1. 1. etc. Luk. 3, 23 etc. Esa. 7, 14. Luk. 1. 26. 27. etc. Hebr. 2, 16. c Heb. 4. 15. Esa. 53, 3. 4. 9. Phil. 2, 7. 8.

10 That touching his Office, hee[d] only is made the Mediator of the nevv Testament, even of the euerlasting Couenant of grace betvveen God & man, to bee perfectly & fully the [e]Prophet, Priest & King of the Church of God for euermore.

d 1. Tim. 2, 5. Heb 9. 15. & 13. 20. Dan. 9 24. 25. e Deut. 18, 15. 18. Psal. 110. 4. Psal. 45, Esa. 9, 6. 7. Act. 5. 31. Esa. 55. 4. Heb. 7, 24. Luk. 1, 32, 33.

11 That hee[f] vvas frō euerlasting, by the iust & sufficient authoritie of the father, & in respect of his manhood frō the womb, called & seperated heervnto, & anoynted also most fully & aboundantly vvith all necessarie gifts, as is [g] vvritten; God hath not measured out the Spirit vnto him.

f Pro. 8, 23. Esa. 42, 6. & 49. 1. 5. and 11, 2. 3. 4. 5. Act. 10. 38. g Joh. 3, 34.

12 That this[h] Office, to bee Mediator, that is, Prophet, Priest and King of the Church of God, is so proper to him, as neither in the whol, nor in anie part therof, it cā be trāsferred frō him to anie other.

h 1. Tim. 2, 5. Heb. 7. 24. Dan. 7. 14. Act. 4, 12. Esa. 43, 11. Luk. 1, 33.

13 That touching his[i] Prophecie, Christ hath perfectly revealed out of the bozome of his father, the vvholl vvord & vvill of God, that is needfull for his seruants, either ioyntly or seuerally to knovv, beleeue & obey : That hee hath spoken & doth speake to his Church in his ovvn[k] ordinance, by his ovvn ministers and instruments only, and not by anie false[l] ministrie at anie tyme.

i Deu. 18, 15. 18. Act. 3, 22. 23. 24. Mat. 3, 17. Joh. 1. 18. & 17. 8. Eph. 1. 8. 9. 2. Tim. 3. 15. 16, 17. k Pro. 9, 3. Joh. 13; 20. Luk. 10. 16. Mat. 10. 40. 41. Deu. 33, 8. 10. l Mat. 7, 15. 16. & 24. 23. 24. 2. Pet. 2. 2. Tim. 4. 3. 4. Rom. 10, 14. 15. ier. 23, 21. 2. ioh. 10.

14 That toching his[m] Priesthood, beein consecrated, hee hath appeered once to put avvay sinne, by offring & sacrificing of himsell ; and to this end hath fully performed aud suffred all those things, by which God through the blood of that his crosse, in an acceptable sacrifice, might bee reconciled to his elect; & having[n] brokē dovvn the partition vvall, & thervvith finished & remoued al those legal rites, shadovves, & ceremonies, is now[o] entred vvithin the vayle into the holy of Holies to the very heauen, and prescnce of God, vvhere hee for euer lyueth, and sitteth at the right hand of Maiestie* appering before the face of his Father, to make intercession for [xiv] such as come vnto the Throne of grace

by that nevv & living vvay; And not that only, but maketh his people a^p spirituall hovvse, an holy Priesthood, to offer up spirituall
sacrifices, acceptable to God through him. Neither doth the
Father accept, or Christ offer anie other sacrifice, vvorship, or
vvorshippers.

m Joh. 17, 19.   Heb. 5, 7. 8. 9. & 91 [9. 26] 1.   Esa. 53,   Ro. 5, 19.   1. Pet.
1, 2.   Collos. 1, 20.   Eph. 5, 2.   n Eph. 2, 1. 4. 15. 16.   Heb. 9, & 10.   o Heb.
4, 14. 16. & 9. 24. and 10. 19. 20.   * Rom. 3, 34.   p 1. Pet. 2, 5.   Rev. 1, 5. 6.
and 8. 3. 4.   Rom. 12, 1.   Mar. 9, 49. 50.   Mal. 1, 14.   Joh. 4 23. 24.   Mat. 7,
6. 7. 8.   Esa. 1, 12. etc.

15 That touching his^q *K*ingdom, beeing risen, ascended, entred into glory, set at the right hand of God, al povvre in Heaven
and earth giuē vnto him; vvhich povvre hee^r novv exerciseth ouer
all Angells and men, good and dad [bad], to the preservation and
saluation of the elect, to the overruling and destruction of the
reprobate;^{s} communicating and app*l*ying the benefits, virtue and
frutes of his prophecy and Priesthood vnto his elect, namely to the
remission, subduing, and takeing avvay of their sinnes, to their ius-
tification, adoption-of-sonnes, regeneration, sanctification, preservation & strēgthning in all their spirituall conflicts against
Sathan, the vvorld & the flesh &c. continually dvvelling in, governing & *k*eeping their hearts in his tue [true] faith and fear by his
holy spirit, vvhich having^t once givē yt, hee never taketh avvay
from them, but by yt still begetteth and nourisheth in them repentance, faith, loue, obedience, comfort, peace, ioy, hope, and all
christian vertues, vnto immortallitie, notvvithstanding that yt be
sometymes throu*g*h sinne and tentation, interrupted, smothered,
and as yt vvere overvvhelmed for the tyme. Againe on the contrary,^{v} ruling in the vvorld over his enimies, *S*athan, and all the vessels of vvrath; limiting, vsing, restrayning them by his mightie
povvre, as seemeth good in diuiue vvisdome and iustice, to the *ex*-
ecution of his determinate counsell, to vvit to their seduction,
hardning & condemnation, delyvering them vp to a reprobate
mynde, to bee *k*ept in darcknes, sinne and sensuallitie vnto iudgment.

q 1. Cor. 15, 4. etc.   1. Pet. 3, 21. 22.   Mat. 28, 18, 20.   r Josh. 5, 14.   Zech.
1, 8. etc.   Mark 1, 27.   Heb. 1. 14.   s Eph. 5, 26, 27.   Ro. 5, and 6. and 7. and
8. Chap.   Rom. 14, 17.   Gal. 5, 22. 23.   1. Joh. 4, 13. etc.   t Psal. 51, 10. 11. 12.
and 89. 30. 31. 32. 33. 34.   Job. 33, 29. 30.   Esa. 54, 8. 9. 10.   Joh. 13, 1. and
16. 31. 32, with Luc. 22, 31. 32. 40.   2. Cor. 12, 7. 8. 9.   Eph. 6, 10. 11. etc.
Rom. 11, 29.   Gal. 5, 17. 22. 23.   v Job. 1, 6. and 2. Chap.   1. King. 22. 19.
Esa. 10, 5. 15.   Rom. 9, 17. 18.   Rom. 1, 21. and 2. 4. 5. 6.   Eph. 4, 17. 18. 19.
2. Pet. 3, 3.   1. Thess. 5, 3. 7.   Esa. 57, 20. 21.   2. Pet. 2, the whol Chapter.

16 *T*hat this Kingdom shall bee then fully perfected vvhen hee shal the˟ second tyme come in glorie vvith his mightie Angells vnto iudgment, to abolish all rule, authoritie and povvre, to put all his enimies vnder his feet, to seperate and free all his chosen from them for ever, to punish the vvicked vvith everlasting perdition from his presence, to gather, ioyne, and carry the godly *w*ith himself into endlesse *g*lory, and 'then to dely*v*er, *v*p the Kingdome to God, e*v*en the Father, that so the *g*lorie of the father may bee full and perfect in the Sonne, the glorie of the Sonne in all his members, and God bee all in all.

x Dan. 12, 2. 3. Joh 5, 22. 28. 29. Mat. 25, 31. 1. Cor. 15. 24. Mat. 13, 41. 49. 2. Thes. 1, 9. 10. 1. Thes. 4, 17. Joh. 17, 22. 23. 1. Cor. 15, 28.

[xv] 17 That in the meane tyme, bisides his absolute rule in the *w*orld, Christ hath here in earth a*ʸ* spirituall *K*ingdome and æ canonicall regiment in his Church ouer his ser*v*ants, which Church hee hath* purchased and redeemed to himself, as a peculiar inheritance (not*w*ithstanding* manie hypocrites do for the tyme lurk emongest thē) *ᵇ*calling and *w*inning them by the po*w*re of his *w*ord *v*nto the faith, *ᵉ*seperating them from emongst *v*nbelee*v*ers, from idolitrie, false *w*orship, superstition, *v*anitie, dissolute lyfe, & *w*orks of darknes, &c; making them a royall Priesthood, an holy Nation, a people set at libertie to she*w* foorth the *v*irtues of him that *h*ath called them out of darknes into his meruelous light, *ᵈ*gathering and *v*niting thē together as members of one body in his faith, loue and holy order, *v*nto all generall and mutuall dutyes,* ins*t*ructing & *g*overning thē by such officers and lawes as hee hath prescribed in his *w*ord; by *w*hich Officers and la*w*es hee governeth his Church, and by*ᶠ* none other.

y Joh. 18. 36. Heb 3, 6. and 10. 21. 1. Tim. 3, 15. Zach. 4, 17. z Act. 20, 28. Tit. 2, 14. a Mat. 13, 47. and 22. 12. Luk. 13, 25. b Mar. 16, 15. 16. Col. 1, 21, 1. Cor. 6 11. Tit. 3, 3. 4. 5. c Esa. 52. 11, Ezr. 6, 21. Act. 2, 40. 2. Cor. 6, 14. Act. 17, 3. 4. and 19. 9.‫ 1. Pet. 2, 4. 5. 9. 25. d Esa. 60, 4. 8. Psal. 110, 3. Act. 2 41. Eph. 4, 16. Col. 2, 5. 6. e Esa. 62, 6. Jer. 3, 15,· Ezek. 34. Zech. 11, 8. Heb. 12, 28. 29. Mat. 28, 20. f Mat. 7, 15. and 24. 23. 24. 2. Tim. 4, 3. 4. Jer. 7, 30. 31. and 23. 21. Deu. 12, 32. Reu. 2, 2. & 22. 18. 19

18 That to this*ᵍ* Church hee hath made the promises, and giuen the seales of his Covenant, presence, loue, blessin*g* and protection:*ʰ* Heere are the holy Oracles as in the side of the Arke, suerly kept & puerly tau*g*ht. Heere are*ⁱ* all the fountaynes and springs of his *g*race continually replenished and flo*w*ing forth. Heere is*ᵏ* hee lyfted *v*p to all Nations, hither hee*ˡ* inuiteth all mē to

his supper, his mariage feast; hither ought^m all men of all estates
and degrees that ac*k*now*l*edg him their Prophet, Priest and
*K*ing to repayre, to beeⁿ enrolled emong*s*t his houshold seruants,
to bee *v*nder his heauenly conduct and government, to leade their
lyues in his *w*alled sheepfold, & *w*atered orchard, to haue communion heere *w*ith the Sainc*t*s, that they may bee made meet to
bee partakers of their inherit*ā*ce in the kin*g*dome of God.

g Lev. 26, 11. 12.   Mat. 28, 19. 20.   Rom. 9, 4.   Ezek. 48. 35,   2. Cor. 6.
18 h Esa. 8, 16.   1. tim. 3, 15. and 4. 16. & 6. 3. 5.   2. Tim. 1, 15.   tit. 1, 9.
Deu. 31. 26.   i Psal. 46, 4. 5.   Ezek. 47, 1. etc.   Joh. 38, 39.   k Isa. 11. 12.
Joh. 3, 14.   Isa. 49, 22.   l Esa. 55. 1.   Mat. 6, 33. & 22. 2.   Pro. 9, 4. 5.   Joh.
7, 37.   m Deu. 12, 5. 11.   Esa. 2, 2. 3.   Zach. 14, 16. 17. 18. 19.   n Esa. 44. 5.
Psal. 87, 5. 6.   Can. 4. 12.   Gal. 6, 10.   Col. 1, 12. 13.   Eph. 2, 19.

19 That as^o all his seruants and subiects are called hither, to
present their bodyes and soules, and to bring the guyfts God hath
gi*v*en them; so beeing come, they are heer by himself besto*w*ed in
their se*v*erall order, peculiar place, due *v*se, beeing fitly compact
and knit together by euery ioynt of help, according to the effect-
uall *w*ork in the measure of euery parte, *v*nto the edification of yt
self in loue; *w*her*v*nto *w*hē hee^p as*c*ended *v*p on high hee gaue
guifts *v*nto men, [xvi] that hee might fill all these things, and hath
distributed these guifts, *v*nto seuerall functions in his Church, hau-
ing instituted and ratified to^q contynue *v*nto the *w*orlds end, only
this publick ordinarie Ministerie of Pastors, Teachers, Elders, Deacons, Helpers to the instruction, government, and seruice of his
Church.

o See the 18. Article before, and Exod. 25. 2. and 35. 5.   1 Cor. 12, 4. 5. 6. 7.
12. 18.   Rom. 12. 4. 5. 6.   1. Pet. 4. 10.   Eph. 4, 16.   Colos. 2, 5.   p Eph. 4, 8.
10. 11. 12. 13.   Rom. 12, 7. 8. & 16. 1.   1. Cor. 12. 4. 5. 6. 7, 8. 11. 14. 15. 16.
17. 18. 28.   1. Tim. 3, & 5. 3. 9. 17. 21.   Act. 6, 2. 3. & 14. 23. and 20. 27. 28.
Phil. 1, 1.   q Rev. 22, 18. 19.   Mat. 28, 20.   1. Tim. 6, 13, 14.

20 That this ministerie is exactly^r described, di*st*inguished,
limited, concerning their office, their calling to their office, ther
administration of their office, and their maintenance in their office,
by most perfect and playne ^sla*w*es in Gods *w*ord, *w*hich la*w*es it is
not la*w*full for these Ministers, or for the *w*holl Church *w*ittinly to
neglect, trans*g*resse, or *v*iolate in anie parte; nor yet to receiue
anie other la*w*es brou*g*ht into the Church by anie person *w*hatso-
e*v*er.

r Pro. 8, 8. 9.   heb. 3. 2. 6.   the first Epistle to Timothy wholly.   Act. 6, 3.
5. 6. & 14. 23. & 20, 17. etc.   1. pet. 5, 2. 3.   1. Cor. 5, 4. 5. 11. 12. 13. etc. and
9. 7. 9. 14.   s Heb. 2. 3. and 3. 3. and 12. 25. etc.   2. Tim 3, 14. 15.   Gal. 1, 8. 9.
1 tim. 6, 13. 14.   Deut. 12, 32. and 4. 2.   Revel. 22, 18. 19.

21 T*h*at[t] none may *v*surp or execute a ministerie but such as are rightly called by the Church *wh*ereof they stand ministers; and that such so called ought to gyve all diligence to[r] fulfill ther ministerie, to bee found faithfull and *v*nblamable in all things.

t Num. 16, 5. 40. & 18. 7. 2. Chron. 26. 18. Joh. 10. 1. 2 and 3. 27. Heb. 5. 4. Act. 6, 3. 5. 6. & 14. 23. Tit. 1, 5. v Act. 2. 28. 1. cor. 4, 1. 2. Col. 4, 17. 1. Tim. 1, 18. 19. & 4. 12. and 5 21 & 6. 11. 12. 13. 14. 2. Tim. 1, 13. 14. and 3. 14. and 4. 5, 1. Pet. 5, 1. 2. 3. 4.

22 That this ministerie is alyke given to euery Christian congregation, *w*ith like po*vv*re and commission to haue and enioy the same, as God offereth fit men and meanes, the same rules gi*v*en to all for the election and execution therof in all places.

Mat. 28, 20. 1. cor 14, 33. 36. 1. Cor. 12, 4. 5. 6. 7. and 4. 17. and 16. 1. eph. 4, 10. 11. 12. 13. 1. cor. 3, 21. 22. 23. Mat. 18. 17. see Article 20.

23 That as e*v*ery christian Con*g*regation[x] hath po*vv*re and commandement to elect and ordeine their ov*v*n ministerie according to the rules prescribed, and[y] *w*hilest they shal faithfully execute their office, to haue them in superaboundant loue for their v*v*orke sake, to pro*v*ide for them, to honour them and reuerence them, according to the dignitie of the o*f*fice they execute. So have they also[z] po*vv*re and commandement *w*hen anie such defalt, either in their lyfe, Doctrine, or administration breaketh out, as by the rule of the word debarreth them from, or depriv*é*th them of their ministerie, by dúe order to depose them from the ministerie they exercised; yea if the case so require, and they remayne obstinate and impenitent, orderly to cut them off by excommunication.

x Act. 6, 3. 5. 6. & 14. 23. 2. Cor. 8. 19. Act. 15. 2, 3. 22. 25. 1. Tim. 3, 10. and 4. 14, & 5. 22. Num. 8, 9. 10. y 1. Thes. 5, 12. 13. 1. Tim. 5, 3. 17. Heb. 13, 17. 1. cor. 9. Gal. 6. 6. z 1. Tim. 3, 10. and 5. 22. Rom. 16, 17. Phyl. 3, 2. 18. 19. 1. Tim. 6, 3. 5. Ezek. 44, 11. 13. Mat. 18, 17.

24 That[a] Christ hath given this po*vv*re to receiue in or to cut off anie member, to the v*v*holl body together of euery Christian Con*g*regation, and not to anie one member aparte, or to moe members sequestred from the *vv*holl, or to anie other Congregation to doo it for thē: yet that[b] ech Congregation ou*g*ht to vse the best help they can heer *v*nto, and the most meet member they haue to pronounce the same in their publick assembly.

a Psal. 122. 3. Act. 1, 47. Rom. 16, 2. Lev. 20, 4. 5. & 24. 14. Num. 5, 3. Deu. 13, 9. Mat. 18, 17. 1. cor. 5, 4. 2. cor. 2, 6. 7. 8. b 1. Cor. 3, 21. 22. 23. Act. 15. 1. cor. 3, 4. 5. & 12. 20.

[xvii] 25 That euery member of ech Christian Congregation, hovv excellent, great, or learned soeu*er*, ought to be subiect to this censure & iudgment of Christ; Yet ought not the Church vvithout great care & due advise to procede against such publick persons.[1]

Lev. 4. Psal. 141, 5. and 2, 10. 11. 12. & 149. 8. 9. 1. Chro 26, 20. Act. 11, 2. 4. 1: Tim. 5, 19. 20. 21.

26 T*h*at for t*h*e °keeping of this. C*h*urch in *h*oly & orderly communion, as Christ *h*at*h* placed some speciall men *o*ver the Church, *w*ho by t*h*eir office are to governe, ouersee, visite, *w*atch, &c. So[d] lykev*v*ise for t*h*e better keeping therof in all places, by all t*h*e members, hee hath giuen aut*h*oritie & layd duty *v*pon thē all to *w*atch one ouer another.

cCant. 3, 3. Esa. 62, 6. Eze. 33. 2. Mat. 14, 45. Luk. 12, 42. Act. 20, 28. Heb. 13, 17. bMar. 13, 34, 37. Luk. 17, 3. 1. Thes. 5, 14. Gal. 6, 1. Jude. 3, 20. Hebr. 10, 24, 25. & 12. 15.

27 That v*v*hilest the Ministers and people t*h*us remayne toget*h*er in this holy order and c*h*ristian communion, ech one endevoring to do the *w*ill of God in t*h*eir calling, & thus to vvalke in t*h*e obedience of fait*h* C*h*rist *h*at*h* promised to bee present *w*ith t*h*em, to blesse & defend them against all adverserie povvre, & that t*h*e gates of Hell s*h*all not prevayle against t*h*em.

Deu. 28, 1. etc. Mat. 28, 20. Luk. 12, 35. 36. 37. 38. Mat. 16. 18. Zach. 2, 5. & 12, 2. 3. 4. Psal. 125, 2. & 132. 12. 13. etc.

28 But *w*hen & vv*h*ere this holy order & diligent vvatch *w*as intermitted, neglected, violated. Antichrist that man of sinne corrupted & altered t*h*e holy ordinances, offices, & administratiōs of the c*h*urch brough*t* in & erected a strange ne*w* forged ministerie, leitourgie and government & the Nations *K*ingdoms & inhabitants of the eart*h*, *w*ere made drunken vvith t*h*is cup of fornications & abhominations, & all people enforced to receiue the Beasts marke and wors*h*ip his image & so brought into confusion & babilonish bondage.

Rev. 9. & 13. & 17. & 18. 1. Thes. 2, 3. 4. 9. 10. 11. 12. psal. 74. Esa. 14. 13. 14. Dan. 7, 25. and 8. 10. 11. 12. & 11. 31. 1. Tim. 4, 1. 2. 1. joh. 2, 18. 22. & 4. 3.

29 T*h*at the present ministerie reteyned & vsed in Englād of Arch. b[bb]. Lo[bb].[2] Deanes, Prebendaries, Canons, Peti-Canons, Arch-

---

[1] An answer to the frequent question what would they do with a sovereign worthy of excommunication.

[2] Lord bishops, the favorite Separatist designation for a diocesan bishop as distinguished from a New Testament bishop.

Deacons, Chancellors, Commissaries, Priests, Deacons, Parsons,
Viccars Curats, Hireling rouing Preachers, Church-wardens,
Parish-clerkes their Doctors, Proctors, & wholl rable of those
Courts with all from & vnder them set ouer these Cathedrall &
Parishionall Assemblies in this confusion, are a strange & Anti-
christian ministerie & offices; & are not that ministerie aboue
named instituted in Christs Testament, or allovved in or ouer his
Church.

Revel. 9, 3. etc. & 13. 15. 16. 17. & 18. 15. 17. compared with Rom. 12, 7.
8. Eph. 4, 11. 12. 1. Tim. 3. 15. & 5. 17. Compare this Art. with the 1. 7. 12.
13. 14. 19. 20. 21. 22. 23. 24. 28. Articles aforesaid.

30 That their ᵉOffices, Entrance, Administration and maintenance, with their ᶠnames, titles, prvileges, & prerogatiues the
povvre & rule they vsurp ouer and in these Ecclesiasticall assemblies ouer the wholl ministerie, wholl ministration and affaires
therof, yea one ouer another by their making Priests, citing, sus-
pending, silencing, deposing, absoluing, excommunicating, &c.
Their confounding of Ecclesiasticall and Civile iurisdiction,
causes & proceedings in ther persons, courts, [xviii] cōmissions,
Visitations, the rest of lesse rule, taking their ministerie frō and
exercising it vnder them by their ᵍprescription and limitation,
swearing Canonicall obedience vnto them, administring by their
devised imposed, stinted popish Leiturgie, &c. are sufficient proofs
of the former assertion, the perticulars therin beeing duly examined by and compared to the Rules of Christs Testament.

e Compare with Articles 1, 7. 12. 13. 14. 19. etc. Rev. 9. 3, etc. & 18. 15. 17.
Joh. 10, 1. Dan. 7, 8. 25. and 8. 10. 11. 12. 2 Thes. 2. 3. 4. 8. 9. rev. 17, 4.
5. 16. f Luk. 22, 25. 26. Rev. 14. 11. & 17. 3. 4. 5. & 13. 15. 16. 17 1. Pet. 5,
3. with Joh. 3, 29. & with Rev. 2. 1. 1. King. 12. 27. zac. 11. 15. 16. g Rev.
13, 15. 16. 17. Esa. 29. 13. Mat. 7, 7. 8. Ga. 1, 10. etc. & 2, 4. 5. Col. 2, 20.
22. 23. Ezek. 8, 5. & 13. 9. 10. 11. 18. 19. Mica 2, 11. mal. 1, 8. 13. 14.

31 That these Ecclesiasticall Assemblies, remayning in confusion and bondage vnder this Antichristian Ministerie, Courts,
Canons, worship, Ordinances. &c. without freedom or povvre to
redresse anie enormitie, have not in this confusion and subiection,
Christ their Prophet, Priest, and King, neither can bee in this
estate, (whilest wee iudge them by the rules of Gods word) esteemed the true, orderly gathered, or cōstituted churches of
Christ, wherof the faithfull ought to beecome or stand Members,
or to haueʰ anie Spirituall communion vvith them in their publick
vvorship and Administration.

Rev. 18, 2. 1. Cor. 14, 33. Jir. 15, 19. Mal. 1, 4. 6. 8. Hos. 4, 14. etc. Rom. 6, 16. 2. Pet 2, 19. compare with. Art. 1. 7. 11. 12. 13. 14. 15. 17. 18. 19. 20. 24. 28. 29. 30. aforesaid. h Levit. 17, Hos. 4, 15, 1. Cor. 10. 18. 19. 20. 2. Cor. 6, 14. 15, 16. Rev. 18, 4. Cant. 1, 6. 7.

32 That[i] by Gods Commandement all that will bee saued, must vvith speed come forth of this Antichristian estate,[k] leauing the suppression of it vnto the Magistrate to vvhom it belongeth.[1] And that both all such as haue receyued or exercised anie of these false Offices or anie pretended function or Ministerie in or to this false and Antichristian constitution, are vvillingly in Gods feare, to giue ouer and leaue those vnlavvfull Offices, and no longer to minister in this maner to these Assemblies in this estate   And that[1] none also, of what sort or condition soeuer, doo giue anie part of their Goods, Lands, Money, or money vvorth to the maintenance of this false Ministerie and vvorship vpon anie Commandement, or vnder anie colour vvhatsoeuer.

i Reu. 18, 4. Esa. 48, 20. and 52. 11. Jir. 50, 8. & 51. 6. 45. Zech. 2, 6. k 2. Chro. 15, and 27. 6. 2. King. 23, 5. etc. Rom. 13, 4. Mat. 22, 21. rev. 17, 16. l Zech. 13, 2. 4. 5. 6. Jir. 51, 26. Psal. 119, 59. 60. 128. Prov. 5, 20. Esa. 8, 11. 12. and 35. 8. Zach. 14, 21. Prov. 3, 9. 10. compared with Exod. 20. 4, 5. Judg. 17. 3. 4. 5. Ezek. 16. 17. 18. 19. 1. Cor. 10. 19. 20. 21. 22. compared with Heb. 13, 10. & with 2. Cor. 8. 3. 4. 5. 1. Tim. 5, 17.

33 That beeing come forth of this antichristian estate vnto the freedom and true profession of Christ, besides the[m] instructing and [xix] vvell guyding of their ovvn Families, they are[n] vvillingly to ioyne together in christian communion and orderly couenant, and by confession of Faith and obedience of Christ, to[o] vnite themselues into peculiar Congregatiōs; vvherin, as members of one body vvherof Christ is the only head, they are to vvorship and serue God according to his vvord, remembring[p] to keep holy the Lords day.

m Gen. 18. 19. Exod. 13, 8. 14. Pro. 31, 26. 27. Eph. 6, 4. Deut. 6, 7. Psal. 78, 3. 4   n Luk. 17, 37. Psal. 110, 3. Mat. 6, Esa. 44. 5. Act. 2, 41, 42. Jir. 50, 4. 5. Neh. 9, 38. Act. 2, 41. 42. o 1. Cor. 1, 2. and 12. 14. Rev. 1, 20 and 2. 1. 8. 12. 18. & 3. 1. 7. 14. Eph. 2, 19. Col. 2, 19. p Exod. 20, 8. Rev. 1, 10. Act. 20, 7. 1. Cor. 16, 2.

34 That such as[q] God hath giuen guiftes to enterpret the Scriptures, tryed in the exercise of Prophecie, giuing attendance to studie and learning, may and ought by the appointment of the Congregation, to teach publickly the vvord, vntill the people bee meet or, and God manifest men vvith able guifts and fitnes to such Of-

_____

1 See ante, p. 46.

fice or Offices as Christ hath appointed to the publick ministerie of his church; but 'no Sacraments to bee administred *v*ntill the Pastors or Teachers bee chosen and ordeyned into their Office.

q 1. Cor. 14, rom. 12. 6. 1. Cor. 12, 7. 1. Pet. 4, 10. Act. 13. 15. 1. Thes. 5, 20. r Num. 16, 10. 39. 40. Rom. 12. 7. Heb. 5, 4. Joh. 1, 23. 25.

35 That* *vv*heras ther shalbee a people fit, and men furnished *w*ith meet and necessarie *g*uifts, they doo not only still continue the exercise of Prophecie aforesayd, but doo also vpon due tryall, proceed vnto choyce and ordination of Officiers for the ministerie and ser*v*ise of the Church, according to the rule of *G*ods *vv*ord; And that soe they* hold on still to *vv*alke forward in the *w*ayes of Christ for their mutuall edification and comfort, as it shall please God to giue knowledge and grace thervnto. And perticularly, that^v such as bee of the seed,[1] or vnder the government of anie of the Church, bee euen jn their infancie receiued to Baptisme, ond made perta*k*ers of the signe of Gods Couenant made with the faithfull and their seed thro*v*ghout all Generations. And that* all of the Church that *a*re of yeeres, and able to examine themselues, doo communicate also in the Lords Supper both men^y and *vv*omen, and in* both kindes bread and *vv*yne in *w*hich* Elements, as also in the *vv*ater of baptisme, euen after their are consecrate, there is neyt*h*er transubstantiation into, nor Consubstantiation with t*h*e bodye and bloode of *I*esus Christ; *vv*home ᵇthe *H*eauens must conteyne; *v*ntill the tyme [xx] that al things bee restored. ᵉBut they are in the ordinance of God signes and seales of Gods euerlasting couenant, representing and offring to all the receiuers, but exhibiting only to the true beleevers the Lord Iesus Christ and all his benefits vnto righteousnes, sanctification and eternall lyfe, through faith in his name to the glorie and prayse of God.

s Lev. 8. Act. 6, 3. 5. 6. & 14. 21. 22. 23. Tit~ 1, 5. etc. 1. Cor. 12, 7. 8. 14. 15. 1. Tim. 3. t Col. 2, 5. 6. 7. 2. Thes. 2. 15. Jud. 3, etc. Mat. 28, 20. v Act. 2, 38, 39. 1. Cor. 7, 14. Rom. 11, 16, Gen. 17, 7. 12. 27. 1. cor. 10, 2. Psal. 22, 30. Exod. 12, 48. 49. Act. 16, 15. 33. 1. Cor. 1, 16. Mar. 10, 13, 14. 15. 16. Gal. 3, 29. x Mat. 26, 26. 27. 1. Cor. 11. 28. and 10. 3. 4. 16. 17. act. 2, 42, & 20. 7. 8. y Gal. 3, 28. Act. 2. 42. with 1. 1 4. 1. Cor. 12, 13. z Mat. 26, 26. 27. 1. Cor. 10, 3. 4. 16. & 11. 23. 24. 25. 26. 27. 28. 29. a 1. Cor. 10, 16. 17. & 11. 23. 24. 25. 26. etc. Mat. 26, 26. 27. 29. & 15. 17. Joh. 12, 8. b Act. 3, 21. & 7. 56. c Gen. 17, 11. rom. 4, 11. Exod. 12, 13. with Heb. 13, 20. d 1. Cor. 11, 26. 27. 28. 29. & 10. 3. 4. 5. Rom. 2. 28. 29. Act. 15. 9. Rom. 5, & 6. 7. & 8. Chapt.

---

[1] *I. e.*, Children of those who are members of the local church, thus in covenant relation with God.

36   That thus* beeing righly gathered, established, and still proceeding in christian communion & obedience of the Gospell of Christ, none is to seperate for falts and corruptions which may and so long as the Church consisteth of mortall men, will fall out & arise emong them, even in à true constituted Church, but by due' order to seeke redresse therof.

e Lev. 4. 13. etc.   2. Chro. 15, 9. 17. and 30. 18. 19.   rev. 2, and 3.   1. Cor. 1. 10.   Phil. 2, 1. 2. 3. 4. 5. 6. and 3. 15. 16.   heb. 10. 25.   ind [Jude] 19.   f 2. Cor. 13. 1. 2.   rev. 2. and 3.   1. Thes. 5. 14.   2. Thes. 3, 6. 14.   Mat. 18, 17.   1. Cor. 5, 4. 5.   Act. 15. 1. 2.

37   That⁵ such as yet see not the truth, may heare the pùblik doctrine and prayers of the church, and with al meeknes are to bee sought by all meanes: Yet ʰnone who are growne in yeeres to bee received into their communion as members, but such as doo make confession of their faith, publickly desiring to bee receiued as members, and promising to walke in the obedience of Christ. Neither anieᶦ Infants, but such as are the seed of the faithfull by one of the parents, or vnder their education and gouernment. And further not anieᵏ from one Congregation to bee receiued members in another, without bringing certificate of their former estate and present purpose.

g 1. cor. 14, 24. 25.   Psal. 18. 49.   rom. 15, 9. 10.   1. Tim. 2, 4.   2. Tim. 2, 25.   h 2. Cor. 6, 14. 15. 16.   Ezra. 4, 3.   Exod. 12, 43.   Lev. 22. 25.   Exod. 34. 12.   Deu. 7,   Esa. 44. 5.   Act. 19, 18.   i Exod. 20, 5. 6.   1. Cor. 7, 14.   Gen. 17, 7. 12. 27.   Exod. 12, 48. 49.   Act. 16. 15, 33.   k Act. 9, 26. 27.   rom. 16, 1. 2. 2. Cor. 3, 23.   Col. 4, 10

38   That though Congregations bee thus distinct and severall bodyes, every one as a compact Citie in it self, yet are they all to walke by one and the same rule, & by all meanes convenient to haue the counsell and help one of another in all needfull affayres of the Church, as members of one body in the common Faith, vnder Christ their head.

Look Articles 1. 22. 23.   Psal. 122 3.   Cant. 8. 8. 9.   1. cor. 4, 17. and 16. 1.

39   That it is the Office and duty of Princes and Magestrates, ᶦwho by the ordinance of God are supreme Governers vnder him over all persons and causes within their Realmes and Dominions, toᵐ suppress and root out by their authoritie all false ministeries, voluntarie Relligions and counterfeyt worship of God, to abolish and destroy the Idoll Temples, Images, Altares, Vestments, and all other monuments of Idolatrie and superstition and to take and convert to their own civile vses not only the benefit of all such

idolitrous buyldings & monuments, but also the Revenues, Demeanes, Lordships, Possessions, Gleabes and maintenance of anie false ministeries and vnlawfull Ecclesiasticall functions whatsoever within their Dominions. [xxi] And on the other hand[n] to establish & mayntein by their lawes every part of Gods word his pure Relligion and true ministerie to cherish and protect all such as are carefull to worship God according to his word, and to leade a godly lyfe in all peace and loyalltie; yea to enforce al their Subiects whether Ecclesiasticall or civile, to do their dutyes to God and men, protecting & mainteyning the good, punishing and restreyning the evill according as God hath commanded, vvhose Lieuetenants they are heer on earth.

1 Rom. 13, 3. 4. 1. Pet. 2. 3, 14. 2. Chro. 19, 4. etc. and. 29. and 34. Chap. Judg. 17, 5. 6. Math. 22. 21. Tit. 3, 1. m 2. King. 23, 5, etc. Psal. 110. Deu. 12, 2. 3. with 17. 14. 18. 19. 20. 2 King. 10. 26. 27. 28. 2. Chro. 17, 6. Pro. 16, 12. and 25. 2. 3. 4. 5. Act. 19, 27. Rev. 17. 16. n Deut. 17. 14, 18. 19. 20. Josua. 1, 7. 8. 2 Chro. 17, 4. 7. 8. 9. & 19. 4. etc. & 29. & 30. Dan. 6, 25. 26. Psal. 2, 10. 11. 12. & 72. 1. etc. Esa. 49, 23. Rev. 21. 24. Ezra. 7. 26.

40 That therfore the[o] protection & commandement of the Princes and Magistrats maketh it much more peaceable, though[p] no whit at all more lavvfull, to vvalke in the vvayes and ordinances of Iesus Christ vvhich hee hath commanded his church to keep vvithout spot and vnrebukeable vntill his appeering in the end of the vvorld. ¶And that in this behalf the brethren thus mynded and proceeding as is beforesaid, doo both contynually supplicate to God, and as they may, to their Princes and Gouernours that thus and vnder them they may leade a quiet and peaceable lyfe in all godlynes and honestie.

o Pro. 16, 15. Ezr. 5. aud 6. Act. 9, 31. 1. Tim. 2, 2. Dan. 6, 25. 26. Rev. 21, 24. p Act. 4, 18. 19. and 5. 28. 29. Dan. 6, 7. 8. 9. 10. 22. Luk. 21, 12. 13. Mat. 28, 20. 1. tim. 5, 21. and 6. 13. 14. q Psal. 72, 1. etc. 1. tim. 2, 2. 2 chro. 15, 1. 2. Hag. 1. 4. 14. and 2. 5.

41 That if God encline the Magistrates hearts to the allovvance & protection of them therin they accompt it a happie blessing of God who granteth such nourcing Fathers and nourcing Mothers to his Church, & be carefull to walke vvorthie so great a mercy of God in all thankfulnes and obedience.

Psal. 126, 1. etc. Esa. 49, 13. and 60 16. Psal. 72, 1. etc. Rom. 13, 3. 1. Tim. 2, 2. 3. 4.

42 That if God vvithold the Magistrates allovvance and furtherāce heerin, they[r] yet proceed together in christian coue-

nant & communion thus to vvalke in the obedience of Christ evē
through the middest of all tryalls and afflictions, not accompting
their goods, Lands VVyves, Children, Fathers, Mothers, brethren,
Sisters, no nor their ovvn lyues dear vnto thē, so as they may
finish their course with ioy, remembring alvvayes that wee •ought
to obey God rather thē mā, & grounding⁺ vpon the commandement, commission and promise of our Saviour Christ, vvho as hee
hath all povvre in heauē & in earth, so hath also promised if they
keep his commandements vvhich hee hath giuē without limitatiō
of tyme, place, Magistrates allovvance or disallowance, to bee
with them vnto tbe end of the world and vvhen they haue finished
their course and kept the faith, to giue them the crovvn of righteousnes vvhich is layd vp for all them that loue his appeering.

r Act. 2, 40. 41. 42. and 4. 19. and 5. 28. 29. 41. and 16. 20. etc. and 17. 6. 7.
and 20. 23. 24.   1. Thes. 3. 3.   Phil. 1. 27. 28. 29.   Dan. 3, 16. 17. 18. and 6. 7.
10. 22. 23. 24.   Luk. 1 4, 26. 27. & 21. 12. 13, 14.   2. tim. 2, 12. and 3, 12.   heb
10, 32. etc.   1. Pet. 4.   Rev. 2, 10. 25. 26. and. 6. 9. and 12. 11   •Act. 5, 29. and
17. 6. 7.   t Mat. 28. 18. 19. 20.   1. Tim. 6, 13. 14. 15. 16.   2. Tim. 4, 7. 8.   Rev.
2, 10. and 14. 12. 13. and 22. 16. 17. 18. 19. 20.

43 That they doo also vvillingly and orderly pay and performe all maner of lavvfull and accustomed dutyes vnto all men,
submitting [xxii] in the Lord themselues, their bodyes, Landes,
Goods and lyves to the Magistrates pleasure.   And that euery
vvay they acknovvledge, reverence and obey them according to
godlynes, not because of vvrath only but also for conscience sake.

Rom. 13, 1. 5. 6. 7.   Mat. 22, 21.   2. chro 27, Ezr 7, 26.   Tit. 3, 1.   1.
Pet. 2, 13 etc.

44 And thus doo vvee the Subiects of God and hir Matie
falsely called Brovvnists labour to giue vnto God that vvhich is
Gods, & vnto Cæsar that vvhich is Cæsars, endevoring our selues
to haue alvvayes a cleere conscience tovvards God and tovvards
men: And if anie take this to be heresie, then doo vvee vvith the
ᵛApostle freely confesse that after the vvay vvhich they call
heresie vve vvorship Cod the Father of our Lord Iesus Christ;
beleeving all things that are vvritten in the Lavv, and in the
Prophets & Apostostles: And vvhatsoeuer is according to this
vvord of truth published by this State or holden by anie reformed
churches abrode in the vvorld.

v Act. 24, 14.

45 Finally, vvheras vvee are much slandered, as if vve
denyed or misliked that forme of prayer commonly called the

Lords Prayer vvee thought it needfull heere also concerning it to make knovvn that *vv*ee beleeue and acknovvledg it to bee a most absolute & most excellent forme of prayer sush [such] as no men or Angells can set do*w*ne the like And that it was taught & appointed by our Lord Iesus C*h*rist, not that vvee should bee tyed to the *v*se of those very *w*ords, but *t*hat vvee should according to that rule mak*e* all our requests & *t*hanksgyuing *v*nto God, forasmuch as i*t* is a perfect forme and patterne conteyning in it playne & sufficient directions of prayer for all occasions and necessities that haue been, are, or shalbee to the church of God, or anie member therof to the end of the world.

Mat. 6, 9. etc. Luk. 11, 2. etc. compared with Mat. 14, 30. and 26. 39. 42. Act. 1. 24. 25. and 4. 24. etc. Rom. 8, 26. 27. Rev. 8, 3, 4. Eph. 6. 18, 19. Phyl. 4, 6. Heb. 11, 18. 19. 20. 21. Jude vers. 24, 25.

Now vnto him that is ahle [able] to keep vs that wee fall not, & to present us faltlesse before the presence of his glorie with joy ; that is to God only wise our Sauiour, bee glory, & Majestie & dominion, & powre both now & for ever. Amen.

B. *Short Confession of Faith in XX Articles by John Smyth, 1609*

Very early in the seventeenth century there were numbers of Puritans in and near the diocese of Lincoln who regarded the Church of England as being unscriptural, corrupt, and incapable of reform. These Puritans began to meet for worship separately from the National Church, although, for a time, they retained their membership in the parent Church of England. Notwithstanding this retention of membership, they were persecuted because of their views. In the light of this persecution they decided to terminate all relationship with the Established Church, and organize separatist churches of their own. Thus, a new communion was organized by 1606 or 1607,[28] on the basis of a covenant which bound the congregation to walk in all of God's ways "made known, or to be made known unto them, according to their best endeavors, whatsoever it should cost them, the Lord assisting them." For purposes of convenience and safety the church divided into two groups which met separately. One group met at Scrooby under the leadership of Richard Clifton, and later of John Robinson. The other met at Gainsborough, having

[28] It has been held that the covenanting took place in 1602, but Gov. Bradford's version of the event puts it around the beginning of the year 1606/07, and this appears correct. Vid. Burrage, *Early English Dissenters*, I, 230-231.

G

as its pastor John Smyth, former Church of England city lecturer (preacher) at Lincoln. When severe persecution threatened the church, there was consultation between the two groups as to whither they might flee, and a decision was made to go to the Netherlands. The Separatists may have tried to leave England late in 1607, but they did not succeed in leaving for the Netherlands until the spring of 1608.

When they arrived in Amsterdam, they found that the "Ancient Church" of Johnson was already there. Nevertheless, it is apparent that the group led by John Smyth did not become united with this existing church, but maintained its own identity. The company under Clifton may have joined the Johnson Church for a short while, but around the end of April, 1609, most of this company moved on to Leyden under the leadership of John Robinson. In 1620 a part of this group came to America in the *Mayflower,* and are known as the Pilgrim Fathers of America.

Controversy developed among the several groups of Englishmen, especially when Smyth urged that, though the "Ancient Church" had made considerable progress toward determining the constitution of the primitive churches, the work of reconstruction was not yet complete, and that he differed from the Johnsonian Church on some important matters. Smyth already held that the visible church consists only of believers and that the seat of authority in a church is the congregation itself. To these conclusions the former London Church had not progressed. Moreover, Smyth next criticized the baptism of the Separatists. Since he and his followers resided in property belonging to a Waterland Mennonite, it was natural that they should early become acquainted with the Mennonites. It is possible that these new friends raised questions about baptism, persuaded the English that in the primitive church infants were not baptized, and helped them to conclude that they ought to be baptized as believers. It seems more likely, however, that Smyth, who was known to be an independent thinker, made this discovery of the truth of believers' baptism by means of his own research and processes of logic.

Having decided to be baptized, Smyth and his people now faced the problem of finding a suitable person to baptize them. The Mennonites were excluded on account of certain erroneous opinions which they were said to hold concerning free will, the incarnation, oaths, and other matters. Beyond them there was no qualified person to administer the ordinance. So, Smyth baptized himself and his followers late in 1608 or early in 1609. By thus rejecting the Church of England's baptism and undergoing rebaptism, Smyth cut his church off from his fellow Separatists. Within a year, however, he began to have doubts about the propriety of his initiating baptism anew. Better acquaintance with the Mennonites led him to conclude that some of his earlier opinions of them were false, that they were a true church of Christ, and that he should have received the ordinance at their hands. Had there been no true church at hand, his baptism had been justified as a new beginning, but he now felt that he had acted too hastily in view of the presence of the Mennonites.

He attempted to lead his church, therefore, to apply for admission to the Mennonite communion. A petition, written in Latin, confessed the error of the group and asked for membership in the Dutch Church. But, not all of the English members followed Smyth in this action of 1610. Thomas Helwys and about eight others insisted upon the validity of their baptism at Smyth's hands and refused to seek membership with the Mennonites. Still other individuals separated from Smyth on account of new views of the incarnation, opinions probably learned from some of the Anabaptists.[29] Thirty-two of the Smyth party at first applied for membership with the Waterland Mennonites; later, there were additions to this number.

As evidence of the doctrinal soundness of his party, Smyth seems to have written in his own hand a twenty-article Confession of Faith for perusal by the Mennonites and probably sent it along with the application for admission to the Waterland church of Amsterdam. The Confession, which was never printed, may be reckoned a private Confession, but it was intended to represent the entire party of Smyth's followers. It shows some accommodation to Mennonite views, but there is no mention of oath-taking, of bearing arms, or of participation in government. The theology is more Anabaptistic than Calvinistic. Indeed, the Confession is unique among English Separatist confessions prior to 1610 in two respects: it was anti-Calvinistic and anti-pedobaptist.

The English translation of Müller in Evans, *The Early English Baptists*, (I, 253-254) is followed here.

---

[29] Burrage, *Early English Dissenters*, I, 243-244.

SHORT CONFESSION OF FAITH
IN XX ARTICLES BY JOHN SMYTH[30]

WE BELIEVE WITH THE HEART AND WITH THE MOUTH CONFESS:

(1.) That there is one God, the best, the highest, and most glorious Creator and Preserver of all; who is Father, Son, and Holy Spirit.

(2.) That God has created and redeemed the human race to his own image, and has ordained all men (no one being reprobated) to life.

(3.) That God imposes no necessity of sinning on any one; but man freely, by Satanic instigation, departs from God.

(4.) That the law of life was originally placed by God in the keeping of the law; then, by reason of the weakness of the flesh, was, by the good pleasure of God, through the redemption of Christ, changed into justification of faith; on which account, no one ought justly to blame God, but rather, with his inmost heart, to revere, adore, and praise his mercy, that God should have rendered that possible to man, by his grace, which before, since man had fallen, was impossible by nature.

(5.) That there is no original sin (lit., *no sin of origin or descent*), but all sin is actual and voluntary, viz., a word, a deed, or a design against the law of God; and therefore, infants are without sin.

(6.) That Jesus Christ is true God and true man; viz., the Son of God taking to himself, in addition, the true and pure nature of a man, out of a true rational soul, and existing in a true human body.

(7.) That Jesus Christ, as pertaining to the flesh, was conceived by the Holy Spirit in the womb of the Virgin Mary, afterwards was born, circumcised, baptized, tempted; also that he hungered, thirsted, ate, drank, increased both in stature and in knowledge; he was wearied, he slept, at last was crucified, dead, buried, he rose again, ascended into heaven; and that to himself as only King, Priest, and Prophet of the church, all power both in heaven and earth is given.

(8.) That the grace of God, through the finished redemption of Christ, was to be prepared and offered to all without distinction, and that not feignedly but in good faith, partly by things made, which declare the invisible things of God, and partly by the preaching of the Gospel.

(9.) That men, of the grace of God through the redemption of

---

[30] The original manuscript confession is preserved in the Mennonite Archives, Amsterdam.

Christ, are able (the Holy Spirit, by grace, being before unto them *grace prevemènt*) to repent, to believe, to turn to God, and to attain to eternal life; so on the other hand, they are able themselves to resist the Holy Spirit, to depart from God, and to perish for ever.

(10.) That the justification of man before the Divine tribunal (which is both the throne of justice and of mercy), consists partly of the imputation of the righteousness of Christ apprehended by faith, and partly of inherent righteousness, in the holy themselves, by the operation of the Holy Spirit, which is called regeneration or sanctification; since any one is righteous, who doeth righteousness.

(11.) That faith, destitute of good works, is vain; but true and living faith is distinguished by good works.

(12.) That the church of Christ is a company of the faithful; baptized after confession of sin and of faith, endowed with the power of Christ.

(13.) That the church of Christ has power delegated to themselves of announcing the word, administering the sacraments, appointing ministers, disclaiming them, and also excommunicating; but the last appeal is to the brethren or body of the church.

(14.) That baptism is the external sign of the remission of sins, of dying and of being made alive, and therefore does not belong to infants.

(15.) That the Lord's Supper is the external sign of the communion of Christ, and of the faithful amongst themselves by faith and love.

(16.) That the ministers of the church are, not only bishops ("Episcopos"), to whom the power is given of dispensing both the word and the sacraments, but also deacons, men and widows, who attend to the affairs of the poor and sick brethren.

(17.) That brethren who persevere in sins known to themselves, after the third admonition, are to be excluded from the fellowship of the saints by excommunication.

(18.) That those who are excommunicated are not to be avoided in what pertains to worldly business (*civile commercium*).

(19.) That the dead (the living being instantly changed) will rise again with the same bodies; not the substance but the qualities being changed.

(20.) That after the resurrection, all will be borne to the tribunal of Christ, the Judge, to be judged according to their works; the pious, after sentence of absolution, will enjoy eternal life with Christ in heaven; the wicked, condemned, will be punished with eternal torments in hell with the devil and his angels.

C. *A Short Confession of Faith, 1610*

Early in 1610 the Helwys party, also desirous of maintaining friendly relations with the Waterlanders, sent the Dutch a letter, written in Latin, urging them not to accept the English into their church. To receive them, Helwys said, would be but to encourage the erroneous belief of Smyth in a succession in spiritual things. With the letter went a confession of faith, also in Latin, consisting of nineteen articles in which the group described itself as the "true Christian English church."[31] The confession was intended to enable the Dutch to distinguish its authors from the Smyth congregation, rather than to argue for admission of the Helwys party to the Mennonite fellowship. The Helwys party did not intend to seek such admission.

Some of the Waterlanders, in spite of Helwys' protest, were favorably disposed toward the Smyth application, and they suggested that a closer study of doctrinal positions be undertaken. Would the English examine the popular confession of de Ries and Gerrits of 1580 and afterwards indicate their agreement or disagreement? The Smyth people being willing, an English translation in somewhat shortened form was drawn up by de Ries and submitted to them. Soon the names of forty-three English people, John Smyth's standing first, were affixed to the document.

The confession is practically a reproduction of that of Gerrits and de Ries of 1580, with articles XIX and XXII omitted. The English now were willing to accept Menno's views of oaths, war, and civil magistracy. The Dutch original is in the Mennonite Archives, Amsterdam, and the translation of Müller is given below. [32]

A SHORT CONFESSION OF FAITH.

Article 1. We believe, through the power and instruction of the Holy Scriptures that there is one only God, who is a Spirit, eternal, incomprehensible, infinite, almighty, merciful, righteous, perfectly wise, only good, and only fountain of life and all goodness, the Creator of heaven and earth, things visible and invisible.

---

[31] *Synopsis fides, verae Christianae Ecclesiae Anglicanae, Amsterdamiae,* q.v., in Burrage, *Early English Dissenters,* II, 182-184.

[32] McGlothlin, *Bapt. Confessions of Faith,* 54-65.

2. This only God in the Holy Scriptures is manifested and revealed in Father, Son, and Holy Ghost, being three, and nevertheless but one God.

3. The Father is the original and the beginning of all things who hath begotten his Son from everlasting before all creation. That Son is the everlasting Word of the Father, and his wisdom. The Holy Ghost is his virtue, power, and might, proceeding from the Father and the Son. These three are not divided, nor separated in essence, nature, property, eternity, power, glory or excellency.

4. This only God hath created man good, according to his image and likeness, to a good and happy estate, and in him all men to the same blessed end. The first man was* fallen into sin and wrath and was again by God, through a sweet comfortable promise, restored and affirmed to everlasting life, with all those that were guilty through him so that none of his posterity (by reason of this institution) are guilty, sinful, or born in original sin.

5. Man being created good, and continuing in goodness, had the ability, the spirit of wickedness tempting him, freely to obey, assent, or reject the propounded evil: man being fallen and consisting (*sic*) in evil, had the ability, the T—himself moving freely to obey, assent or reject the propounded good; for as he through free power to the choice of evil, obeyed and affirmed that evil; so did he through free power to the choice of good, obey and reassent that propounded good. This last power or ability remaineth in all his posterity.

6. God hath before all time foreseen and foreknown all things, both good and evil, whether past, present, or to come. Now, as he is the only perfect goodness, and the very fountain of life itself, so is he the only author, original, and maker of such good things as are good, holy, pure, and of nature like unto him; but not of sin, or damnable uncleanness. He forbiddeth the evil, he forewarneth to obey evil, and threateneth the evil doer: he is the permitter and punisher. But evil men, through free choice of all sin and wickedness, together with the spirit of wickedness which ruleth in them, are the authors,

* Interlined.

originals, and makers of all sin, and so worthy the punishment.

7. The causes and ground, therefore, of man's destruction and damnation, are the man's free choice of darkness or sin, and living therein. Destruction, therefore, cometh out of himself, but not from the good Creator. For being perfect goodness and love itself (following the nature of love and perfect goodness) he willeth the health, good, and happiness of his creatures; therefore hath he predestinated that none of them should be condemned, nor ordained, or will the sinner, or means whereby they should be brought to damnation: yea, much more (seeing he hath no delight in any man's destruction, nor willing that any man perish, but that all men should be saved or blessed) hath he created them all to a happy end in Christ, hath foreseen and ordained in him a medicine of life for all their sins, and hath willed that all people or creatures, through the preaching of the gospel, should have these tidings published and declared unto them; now all they that with penitence and faithful hearts receive and embrace the gracious benefits of God, manifested in Christ, for the reconciliation of the world, they are and continue the elect which God hath ordained before the foundation of the world, to make partakers of his kingdom and glory. But they which despise and contemn this proffered grace of God, which love the darkness more than the light, persevere in impenitence and unbelief, they make themselves unworthy of blessedness, and are rejected, excluded from the end whereto they were created and ordained in Christ, and shall not taste forever of the Supper of the Lord, to which they were invited.

8. The purpose which God, before the foundation of the world, had for the reconciliation of the world (which he saw would fall into wrath and want of grace), he hath in the fulness of time accomplished; and for this purpose hath sent out of heaven his everlasting Word, or Son, for the fulfilling of the promises made unto the fathers and hath caused him to become flesh * .. in the womb of the holy virgin (called Mary) by his word, and power,

* Word wanting.

and the working of the Holy Ghost. Not that the essence of God, the eternal Word, or any part thereof, is changed into a visible mortal flesh or man, ceasing to be Spirit, God, or God's essence; but that he, the everlasting Son of God, continuing that he was before, namely, God or Spirit, became what he was not, that is, flesh or man; and he is one person true God and man, born of Mary, being visibly and invisibly, inwardly and outwardly, the true Son of the living God.

9. This Person, God and Man, the Son of the living God, is come into the world to save sinners, or to reconcile the sinful world to God the Father: therefore now acknowledge him to be the only Mediator, King, Priest and Prophet, Lawgiver and Teacher, which God hath promised to send into the world, whom we must trust, believe, and follow.

10. In him is fulfilled, and by him is taken away, an intolerable burden of the law of Moses, even all the shadows and figures; as, namely, the priesthood, temple, altar, sacrifice; also the kingly office, kingdom, sword, revenge appointed by the law, battle and whatsoever was a figure of his person or office, so thereof a shadow or representation.

11. And as the true promised Prophet he hath manifested and revealed unto us whatsoever God asketh or requireth of the people of the New Testament; for as God, by Moses and the other prophets, hath spoken and declared his will to the people of the Old Testament; so hath he in those last days, by his Prophet spoken unto us, and revealed unto us the mystery (concealed from the beginning of the world), and hath now manifested to us whatsoever yet remained to be manifested. He hath preached the promised glad tidings, appointed and ordained the sacraments, the offices and ministries, by God thereto destinated; and hath showed by doctrine and life, the law of Christians, a rule of their life, the path and way of everlasting life.

12. Moreover, as a High Priest and Mediator of the New Testament, after that he hath accomplished the will of his Father in the foresaid works, he hath finally given himself obediently (for the reconciliation of the sins of

the world) to all outward suffering, and hath offered up himself in death upon the cross unto the Father, for a sweet savor and common oblation.

13. We acknowledge that the obedience of the Son of God, his suffering, dying, bloodshed, bitter passion, death, and only sacrifice upon the cross, is a perfect reconciliation and satisfaction for our sins and the sins of the world; so that men thereby are reconciled to God, are brought into power, and have a sure hope and certainty to the entrance into everlasting life.

14. Christ, our Prophet and Priest, being also the promised, only spiritual, heavenly King of the New Testament, hath erected, or built, a spiritual kingdom, and united a company of faithful, spiritual men; these persons hath he endowed with spiritual, kingly laws, after the nature of the heavenly kingdom, and hath established therein justice, righteousness, and the ministers thereof.

15. Having accomplished and performed here upon the earth, by dying the death, his office of the cross he was afterwards buried, thereby declaring that he was truly dead; the third day he rose again, and stood up from the dead, abolishing death, and testifying that he was Lord over death, and he could not possibly be detained by the hands of death, thereby comfortably assuring all the faithful of their resurrection and standing up from death.

16. Afterwards, forty days spent, he conversed amongst his disciples, and ofttimes showed himself unto them that there might no doubt be had concerning his resurrection; after that, being compassed by a cloud, he was carried up into heaven, and entered into his glory, leading captivity captive, and making a show of his enemies, hath gloriously triumphed over them, and is sat at the right hand of the Majesty of God, and is become a Lord, and Christ, glorified in body, advanced, lifted up, and crowned with praise and glory, and remaineth over Mount Sion a Priest, and King for everlasting.

17. The holy office of this glorified Priest, King, Lord and Christ, in the heavenly glorious being is to help, govern, and preserve, by his Holy Spirit, his holy church

and people in the world, through the storm, wind, and troubles of the sea; for, according to his priestly office, as an overseer or steward of the true tabernacle, is he our Intercessor, Advocate, and Mediator by the Father. He teacheth, comforteth, strengtheneth, and baptizeth us with the Holy Ghost, his heavenly gifts and fiery victims, and keepeth his spiritual supper with the faithful soul, making it partaker of the life giving food and drink of the soul, the fruit, virtue, and worth of his merits obtained upon the cross; the only and necessary good signified in the sacraments.

18. And according to his kingly office, in his heavenly* being he governeth the hearts of the faithful by his Holy Spirit and Word; he taketh them into his protection, he covereth them under the shadow of his wings, he armeth them with spiritual weapons for the spiritual warfare against all their enemies, namely, the Spirit of wickedness, under heaven, and whatsoever dependeth on them in this earth. He, their most Glorious, Almighty, Heavenly King, standeth by them, delivereth and freeth them from the hands of their enemies, giveth them victory and the winning of the field, and hath prepared for them a crown of righteousness in heaven. And they being the redeemed of the Lord, who dwell in the house of the Lord, upon the Mount Sion, do change their fleshly weapons, namely, their swords into shares, and their spears into scythes, do lift up no sword, neither hath nor consent to fleshly battle.

19. All these spiritual good things and beneficial, which Christ, by his merits, hath obtained for the saving of sinners, we do graciously enjoy through a true, living, working faith. Which faith is an assured understanding and knowledge of the heart, obtained out of the Word of God, concerning God, Christ, and other heavenly things which are necessary for us to know, and to believe to salvation, together with a hearty confidence in the only God, that he, as a gracious and heavenly Father, will give and bestow upon us, through Christ, and for his merits, whatsoever is helpful and profitable for body and soul for salvation.

* Interlined.

20. Through such a faith we obtain true righteousness, forgiveness, absolution from sin through the bloodshed of Christ, and through righteousness, which through the Christ Jesus, by the co-operation of the Holy Ghost, is plentifully shed and poured into us, so that we truly are made, of evil men, good; of fleshly, spiritual; of covetous, liberal; of proud, humble; and through regeneration are made pure in heart, and the children of God.

21. Man being thus justified by faith, liveth and worketh by love (which the Holy Ghost sheddeth into the heart) in all good works, in the laws, precepts, ordinances given them by God through Christ; he praiseth and blesseth God, by a holy life, for every benefit, especially of the soul; and so are all such plants of the Lord trees of righteousness, who honor God through good works, and expect a blessed reward.

22. Such faithful, righteous people, scattered in several parts of the world, being the true congregations of God, or the Church of Christ, whom he saved, and for whom he gave himself, that he might sanctify them, ye whom he hath cleansed by the washing of water in the word of life: of all such is Jesus the Head, the Shepherd, the Leader, the Lord, the King, and Master. Now although among these there may be mingled a company of seeming holy ones, or hypocrites; yet, nevertheless, they are and remain only the righteous, true members of the body of Christ, according to the spirit and the truth, the heirs of the promises, truly saved from the hypocrites the dissemblers.

23. In this holy church hath God ordained the ministers of the Gospel, the doctrines of the holy Word, the use of the holy sacraments, the oversight of the poor, and the ministers of the same offices; furthermore, the exercise of brotherly admonition and correction, and, finally, the separating of the impenitent; which holy ordinances, contained in the Word of God, are to be administered according to the contents thereof.

24. And like as a body consisteth of divers parts, and every part hath its own proper work, seeing every part is not a hand, eye, or foot; so is it also the church of God: for although every believer is a member of the body of

Christ, yet is not every one therefore a teacher, elder, or deacon, but only such as are orderly appointed to such offices. Therefore, also, the administration of the said offices or duties partaineth only to those who are ordained thereto, and not to every particular common person.

25. The vocation or election of the said officers is performed by the church, with fasting, and prayer to God; for God knoweth the heart; he is amongst the faithful who are gathered together in his name; and by his Holy Spirit doth so govern the minds and hearts of his people, that he by them bringeth to light and propoundeth whom he knoweth to be profitable to his church.

26. And although the election and vocation to the said offices is performed by the aforesaid means, yet, nevertheless, the investing into the said service is accomplished by the elders of the church through the laying on of hands.

27. The doctrine which by the foresaid ministers must be proposed to the people, is even the same which Christ brought out of heaven, which he, by word and work, that is, by doctrine and life, hath taught, which was preached by the apostles of Christ, by the commandment of Christ and the Spirit, which we find written (so much as is needful for us to salvation) in the Scripture of the New Testament, whereto we apply whatsoever we find in the canonical book of the Old Testament, which hath affinity and verity, which by doctrine of Christ and his apostles, and consent and agreement, with the government of his Spiritual Kingdom.

28. There are two sacraments appointed by Christ, in his holy church, the administration whereof he hath assigned to the ministry of teaching, namely, the Holy Baptism and the Holy Supper. These are outward visible handlings and tokens, setting before our eyes, on God's side, the inward spiritual handling which God, through Christ, by the cooperation of the Holy Ghost, setteth forth i the justification in the penitent faithful soul; and which, on our behalf, witnesseth our religion, experience, faith, and obedience, through the obtaining of a good conscience to the service of God.

29. The Holy Baptism is given unto these in the name

of the Father, the Son, and the Holy Ghost, which hear, believe, and with penitent heart receive the doctrines of the Holy Gospel. For such hath the Lord Jesus commanded to be baptized, and no unspeaking children.

30. The whole dealing in the outward visible baptism of water, setteth before the eyes, witnesseth and signifieth, the Lord Jesus doth inwardly baptize the repentant, faithful man, in the laver of regeneration and renewing of the Holy Ghost, washing the soul from all pollution and sin, by the virtue and merit of his bloodshed; and by the power and working of the Holy Ghost, the true, heavenly, spiritual, living Water, cleanseth the inward evil of the soul, and maketh it heavenly, spiritual, and living, in true righteousness or goodness. Therefore, the baptism of water leadeth us to Christ, to his holy office in glory and majesty; and admonisheth us not to hang only upon the outward, but with holy prayer to mount upward, and to beg of Christ the good thing signified.

31. The Holy Supper, according to the institution of Christ, is to be administered to the baptized; as the Lord Jesus hath commanded that whatsoever he hath appointed should be taught to be observed.

32. The whole dealing in the outward visible supper, setteth before the eye, witnesseth and signifyeth, that Christ's body was broken upon the cross and his holy blood spilt for the remission of our sins. That the being glorified in his heavenly Being, is the alive-making bread, meat, and drink of our souls: it setteth before our eyes Christ's office and ministry in glory and majesty, by holding his spiritual supper, which the believing soul, feeding and* . . the soul with spiritual food: it teacheth us by the outward handling to mount upwards with the heart in holy prayer, to beg at Christ's hands the true signified food; and it admonisheth us of thankfulness to God, and of verity and love one with another.

33. The church discipline, or external censures, is also an outward handling among the believers, whereby the impenitent sinner, after Christian admonition and reproof, is severed, by reason of his sins, from the communion of the saints for his future good; and the wrath

* Word wanting.

of God is denounced against him until the time of his contrition and reformation; and there is also, by this outward separation of the church, manifested what God before had judged and fore-handled, concerning this secret sinner, by reason of his sin. Therefore, first before the Lord, the prejudging and predetermining of the matter must pass* . . in respect of the sinner* . . and the after-judging and handling by the church. Therefore the church must carefully regard that none in the church be condemned with it, and be condemned in the Word of God.

34. The person separated from the church may not at all be admitted (so long as he proceedeth in sin) to the use of the holy supper or any other* . . handling, but he must be avoided therein, as also in all other things betokening the communion of saints or brotherhood. And as the rebellious life, conversation, or daily company of the godless and perverse, or anything with them, is dangerous and hurtful, and oftentimes promoteth scandal and slander to the godly, so must they withdraw themselves from the same rebels, avoiding them in all works and ends whereby their pure souls might be polluted and defiled: yet so that always the Word of God take place, and that nothing take place or be performed that is contrary to love, mercy, Christian discretion, promise, or any other like matter.

35. Worldly authority or magistry is a necessary ordinance of God, appointed and established for the preservation of the common estate, and of a good, natural, politic life, for the reward of the good and the punishing of the evil; we acknowledge ourselves obnoxious, and bound by the Word of God to fear, honor, and show obedience to the magistrates in all causes not contrary to the Word of the Lord. We are obliged to pray God Almighty for them, and to thank the Lord for good reasonable magistrates, and to yield unto them, without murmuring, beseeming tribute, toll and tax. This office of the worldly authority the Lord Jesus hath not ordained in his spiritual kingdom, the church of the New Testament, nor adjoined to the offices of his church.

* Cannot decipher the word.

Neither hath he called his disciples or followers to be worldly kings, princes, potentates, or magistrates; neither hath he burdened or charged them to assume such offices, or to govern the world in such a worldly manner; much less hath he given a law to the members of his church which is agreeable to such office or government. Yea, rather they are called of him (whom they are commanded to obey by a voice heard from heaven) to the following of his unarmed and unweaponed life, and of his cross-bearing footsteps. In whom approved nothing less than a worldly government, power, and sword. This then considered (as also further, that upon the office of the worldly authority many other things depend, as wars* . . to hurt his enemies in body or good* . . which evilly or not at all will fit or consort with the Christ, and the crucified life of the Christians), so hold we that it beseemeth not Christians to administer these offices; therefore we avoid such offices and administrations, notwithstanding by no means thereby willing to despise or condemn reasonable discreet magistrates, nor to place him in less estimation than he is described by the Holy Ghost, of Paul.

36. Christ, the King and Lawgiver of the New Testament, hath prohibited Christians the swearing of oaths · therefore it is not permitted that the faithful of the Ne Testament should swear at all.

37. The married estate, or matrimony, hold we for an ordinance of God, which, according to the first institution, shall be observed. Every man shall have his one only wife, and every woman shall have her one only husband; those may not be separated but for adultery. We permit none of our communion to marry godless, unbelieving, fleshly persons out of the church; but we censure such (as other sinners) according to the disposition and desert of the cause.

38. Lastly, we believe and teach the resurrection of the dead, both of the just and the unjust, as Paul (1 Cor. 15) soundly teacheth and witnesseth: The soul shall be united to the body, every one shall be presented before the judgment seat of Christ Jesus, to receive in his own body

* Cannot decipher the word.

wages according to his works. And the righteous,
whosoever hath lived holily, and through faith brought
forth the works of love and mercy, shall enter into everlasting life with Christ Jesus, the Bridegroom of the
Christian host. But the unsanctified, which have not
known God, and have not obeyed the Gospel of Jesus
Christ, shall go into everlasting fire. The Almighty,
gracious, merciful God, preserve us from the punishment
of the ungodly, and grant us grace and gifts helpful to
a holy life, saving death, and joyful resurrection with all
the righteous. Amen.

We subscribe to the truth of these Articles, desiring
further information. [Forty-two names are attached to
this document. We cannot decipher the whole, but the
following are plain. A line is drawn through some of
them. The * marks them. † Uncertain.]

*John Smyth,
Hugh Broomhead,
*John Grindall,
*Samuel Halton,
Thomas Piggott,
John Hardie,
*Edward Hawkins,
Thomas Jessopp,
Robert Staveley,
*Alexander Fleming,
John Arnfeld,
Hannah Piggott,
Thomas Solphin,
Solomon Thomson,
Alexander Hodgin,
Ursula Bywater,
Dorothea Oakland,
John ——,
Fylis ——,
*—— ——,

*Matthew Pigott,
Mary Smyth,
Janus ——,,
Margarett Staveley,
†Isabella Thomson,
*Jane Argan,
Mary Dickens,
Bettriss Dickens,
Dorothe Hamand,
*Elnh. Buywater,
Ann Broomhead,
Alexander Parsons,
*Joan Haughton,
*Joane Brigge,
Alexander Pigott,
Margaret Pigott,
Alexander Armfield,
Elnh. White,
Dorothe Thomson,
Margaret Morris.

[We judge the whole of these signatures autograph.]

H

D. *A Declaration of Faith of English People Remaining at Amsterdam in Holland, 1611*

When the Smyth party sought admission to the Amsterdam Waterlander Church in 1610, some resistance was encountered inside the Mennonite fellowship. Some Waterlanders discouraged haste in the matter, suggesting that Mennonites in parts of Holland beyond Amsterdam and even in Prussia and Germany should be consulted to forestall possible later disharmony and disunity. The English could wait; therefore the Dutch should proceed with caution. As a source of information for congregations outside of Amsterdam a Dutch translation of the "Epistle to the Reader" of Smyth's work, *Character of the Beast,* seems to have been prepared and was sent with letters to churches of several areas. After many groups of Mennonites considered this Epistle and the prospect of admitting the English, some of the answers advised caution, and so action on the application was deferred indefinitely.

Moreover, Smyth's followers were not in unanimous agreement. Regarding the question of their baptism, Smyth, Gerrits, and others of Smyth's close followers stood in a position near that of the Mennonites, for they now believed their own baptism to have been unscriptural. These did not resign the hope that the English believers might still be received into the fellowship of the Amsterdam Waterlander Church.[33] On the other hand, there were those of Smyth's group who disagreed with their pastor on this point, and found an able leader in Thomas Helwys. These were not desirous of being unfriendly with the Mennonites, but they continued to assert the validity of their own baptism, and believed it best to preserve their independent organization and identity.

Meanwhile, Thomas Helwys was busily writing in 1610 and 1611, and in the latter year he published, in the name of his church, a confession of faith of twenty-seven articles. It repudiated the conciliatory views of the Latin articles which he had earlier submitted to the Waterlanders, particularly renouncing Arminian views of sin and the will. The purpose of publishing was declared to be to defend the "Truth of God" professed by its owners, to give enlightenment to their own number because of the "fearful falls of some that hath been of us," and to clear those represented of unjust

---

[33] Burrage, *op. cit.,* I, 249-250.

charges.[34] The confession is noteworthy as a composition of laymen; Helwys indicated that he had had the help as well as the consent of his little flock in preparing the confession.

Mennonite influence is readily seen in the confession for it shows a departure from the hitherto markedly consistent Calvinism of the Separatist movement. But it shows also decided signs of its authors' Calvinistic background. It is anti-Calvinistic on the doctrine of the atonement and anti-Arminian in its views of sin and the will. Obviously it owed much to John Smyth, though it goes beyond his confessions at a number of points: in urging the independence and autonomy of the local church ("though in respect of CHRIST, the Church bee one"), in denying a succession in church life, and in rejecting the Mennonite prohibitions against oaths, the bearing of arms, participation in government, and having dealings with excommunicants. It aimed, indeed, to distinguish its authors from the Mennonites. The confession shows considerable independence of thought and is rightly judged the first English Baptist Confession of Faith. Reflection upon some of its principles led Helwys to conclude that the primary duty of a church of Christ is to bear witness to the truth, and that his church was divinely called to return to England to make known in the homeland the new insights which were theirs. Late in 1611 or early in 1612, the church of perhaps ten members returned to England, to face persecution and to plant the General Baptist denomination.

Article 24 reproduces part of a passage from Smyth's *Character of the Beast.* But Helwys added the sentence on the propriety of a church member serving as magistrate. The Mennonites regarded the holding of magisterial office as incompatible with membership in the church.

Article 26 should be compared with sections 19-20 of Smyth's twenty-article personal Confession (Burgess, *op. cit.*), and with Acts 26-27.

When republishing it in 1738, Crosby (Vol. II, 389 ff.) accidentally combined articles 24 and 25, thus reducing the total number of articles to twenty-six. The transcript which follows was made by W. T. Whitley and was included in McGlothlin's *Baptist Confessions of Faith.* The only copy of the original publication (printed in Amsterdam in English) is in the York Minster Library.

---

[34] Burgess, *John Smyth,* 205.

A

DECLARATION OF | FAITH

of

ENGLISH | PEOPLE

REMAINING AT AM | STERDAM IN HOLLAND. |

Heb. 11 . 6.
Without Faith it is impossible to please | GOD. Heb. 11.
Rom. 14 . 23.
Whatsoever is not off Faith is sin.

Prynted . 1611 .

To Al The Humble mynded | which love the truth in simplicitie Grace and | peace.

[This is followed by two pages of preface.]

A DECLARATION, ETC.

WEE BELEEVE AND | CONFESSE |

I.

That there are THREE which beare record in heaven, the FATHER, the WORD, and the SPIRIT; and these THREE are one GOD, in all equalitie, I Jno. 5.7; Phil. 2.5, 6. By whome all thinges are created and preserved, in Heaven and in Earth. Gen. I Chap.

2.

That this GOD in the begining created al things off nothinge, Gen. I. I. and made man off the dust off the earth, Chap. 2.7, in his owne ymage, Chap. 1.27, in righteousnes and true Holines. Ephes. 4.24: yet being tempted, fel by disobedience. Chap. 3.1-7. Through whose disobedience, all men sinned. Rom. 5.12-19. His sinn being imputed vnto all; and so death went over all men.

3.

That by the promised seed off the woman, IESVS CHRIST, [and by] his obedience, al are made righteous. Rom. 5.19. Al are made alive, I Cor. 15.22. His righteousness being imputed vnto all.

4.

That notwithstanding this Men are by nature the Children off wrath, Ephes. 2.3. borne in iniquitie and in sin conceived. Psal. 51.5. Wise to all evill, but to good they have no knowledg. Jer. 4.22. *The natural ma perceiveth not the thinges off the Spirit off God.* I Cor. 2.14. And therefore man is not restored vnto his former estate, but that as man, in his estate off innocency, haveing in himselff all disposition vnto good, & no disposition vnto evill, yet being tempted might yeild, or might resist:

even so now being fallen, and haveing all disposition
vnto evill, and no disposition or will vnto anie good, yet
GOD giveing grace, man may receave grace, or my
reject grace, according to that saying; Deut. 30.19. *I call
Heaven and Earth to record. This day against you, that
I have set before you life and death, blessing and cursing:
Therefore chuse life, that both thou and thy seed may live.*

5.

That GOD before the Foundatiō off the World hath
Predestinated that all that beleeve in him shall-be saved,
Ephes. 1.4, 12; Mark 16.16. and al that beleeve not shalbee
damned. Mark 16.16. all which he knewe before. Rom.
8.29. And this is the Election and reprobacion spoken
of in the Scripturs, concerning salvacion, and condem-
nacion, and not that GOD hath Predestinated men to bee
wicked, and so to bee damned, but that men being
wicked shallbee damned, for GOD would have all men
saved, and come to the knowledg off the truth, 1 Tim.
2.4. and would have no man to perish, but would have
all men come to repentance. 2 Pet. 3.9. and willeth not
the death of him that deith. Ezec. 18.32. And therefore
GOD is the author off no mens comdemnacion, according
to the saieing off the Prophet. Osæa. 13. Thy distruction
O Israel, is off thy selfe, but thy helpe is off mee.

6.

That man is justified onely by the righteousness off
CHRIST, apprehended by faith, Roman. 3.28. Gal. 2.16.
yet faith without works is dead. Jam. 2.17.

7.

That men may fall away from the grace off GOD,
Heb. 12.15. and from the truth, which they have received
& acknowledged, Chap. 10.26. after they have taisted off
the heavēly gift, and were made pertakers off the HOLY
GHOST, and have taisted off the good word off GOD,
& off the powers off the world to come. Chap. 6.4, 5.
And after they have escaped from the filthines off the
World, may bee taugled againe therein & overcome. 2

Pet. 2.20. That a righteous man may forsake his righteousnes and perish Ezec. 18.24, 26. And therefore let no man presume to thinke that because he hath, or had once grace, therefore he shall alwaies have grace: But let all men have assurance, that iff they continew vnto the end, they shalbee saved: Let no man then presume; but let all worke out their salvacion with feare and trembling.

8.

That IESVS CHRIST, the Sonne off GOD the second Person, or subsistance in the Trinity, in the Fulnes off time was manifested in the Flesh, being the seed off David, and off the Isralits, according to the Flesh. Roman. 1.3 and 8.5. the Sonne off Marie the Virgine, made of hir substance, Gal. 4.4. By the power off the HOLIE GHOST overshadowing hir, Luk. 1.35. and being thus true Man was like vnto us in all thing, sin onely excepted. Heb. 4.15. being one person in two distinct natures, TRVE GOD, and TRVE MAN.

9.

That IESVS CHRIST is Mediator off the New Testament betweene GOD and Man, 1 Tim. 2.5, haveing all power in Heaven and in Earth given vnto him. Mat. 28.18. Being the onely KING, Luke 1.33, PREIST, Heb. 7.24, and PROPHET, Act. 3.22. Off his church, he also being the onely Law-giver, hath in his Testament set downe an absolute, and perfect rule off direction, for all persons, at all times, to bee observed; Which no Prince, nor anie whosoever, may add to, or diminish from as they will avoid the fearefull judgments denounced against them that shal so do. Revel. 22.18, 19.

10.

That the church off CHRIST is a compainy off faithful people 1 Cor. 1.2. Eph. 1.1. seperated frō the world by the word & Spirit off GOD. 2 Cor. 6, 17. being kint vnto the LORD, & one vnto another, by Baptisme. 1 Cor. 12.13. Vpon their owne confessiō of the faith. Act. 8.37. and sinnes. Mat. 3.6.

II.

That though in respect off CHRIST, the Church bee one, Ephes. 4.4. yet it consisteth off divers particuler congregacions, even so manie as there shallbee in the World, every off which congregacion, though they be but two or three, have CHRIST given them, with all the meanes off their salvacion. Mat. 18.20. Roman. 8.32. 1. Corin. 3.22. Are the Bodie off CHRIST. 1. Cor. 12.27. and a whole Church. 1. Cor. 14.23. And therefore may, and ought, when they are come together, to Pray, Prophecie, breake bread, and administer in all the holy ordinances, although as yet they have no Officers, or that their Officers should bee in Prison, sick, or by anie other meanes hindered from the Church. 1 : Pet. 4.10 & 2.5.

12.

That as one congregacion hath CHRIST, so hath all, 2. Cor. 10.7. And that the Word off GOD cometh not out from anie one, neither to anie one congregacion in particuler. 1. Cor. 14.36. But vnto everie particuler Church, as it doth vnto al the world. Coll. 1.5. 6. And therefore no church ought to challeng anie prerogative over anie other.

13.

That everie Church is to receive in all their members by Baptisme vpon the Confession off their faith and sinnes wrought by the preaching off the Gospel, according to the primitive Institucion. Mat. 28.19. And practice, Act. 2.41. And therefore Churches constituted after anie other manner, or off anie other persons are not according to CHRISTS Testament.

14.

That Baptisme or washing with Water, is the outward manifestacion off dieing vnto sinn, and walkeing in newnes off life. Roman. 6.2, 3, 4. And therefore in no wise apperteyneth to infants.

15.

That the LORDS Supper is the outward manifestacion off the Spiritual communion betwene CHRIST and the

faithful mutuallie. 1. Cor. 10.16, 17. to declare his death
vntil he come. 1 Cor. 11.26.

16.

That the members off everie Church or Congregacion
ought to knowe one another, that so they may performe
all the duties off love one towards another both to soule
and bodie. Mat. 18.15. 1 Thes. 5.14. 1 Cor. 12.25. And
especiallie the Elders ought to knowe the whole flock,
whereoff the HOLIE GHOST hath made them overseers.
Acts 20.28; 1 Pet. 5.2, 3. And therefore a Church ought
not to consist off such a multitude as cannot have particuler knowledg one off another.

17.

That Brethren impenitent in one sin after the admonition off the Church, are to bee excluded the cōmunion off
the Sainets. Mat. 18.17. 1 Cor. 5.4, 13. & therfore not
the cōmitting off sin doth cut off anie from the Church,
but refusing to heare the Church to reformacion.

18.

That Excommunicants in respect of civil societie are
not to bee avoided, 2. Thess. 3.15. Mat. 18.17.

19.

That everie Church ought (according to the exāple off
CHRISTS Disciples and primitive Churches) vpon
everie first day off the weeke, being the LORDS day, to
assemble together to pray Prophecie, praise GOD, and
breake Bread, and performe all other partes off Spirituall
communiō for the worship off GOD, their owne mutuall
edificacion, and the preservacion off true Religion, &
pietie in the church Io 20.19. Act. 2.42 and 20.7, 1. Cor.
16.2. and that ought not to labor in their callings according to the equitie off the moral law, which CHRIST came
not to abolish, but to fulfill. Exod. 20.8, &c.

20.

That the Officers off everie Church or congregation
are either Elders, who by their office do especially feed
the flock concerning their soules, Act. 20.28,   Pet. 5.2,
3. or Deacons Men, and Women who by their office re-

leave the necessities off the poore and impotent brethrē
concerning their bodies, Acts. 6.1-4.

21.

That these Officers are to bee chosen when there are
persons qualified according to the rules in Christs Testament, 1. Tim. 3.2-7. Tit. 1.6-9. Act. 6.3. 4. By Election
and approbacion off that Church or congregacion
whereoff they are members, Act. 6.3. 4 and 14.23, with
Fasting, Prayer, and Laying on off hands, Act. 13.3.
and 14.23. And there being but one rule for Elders,
therefore but one sort off Elders.

22.

That the Officers off everie Church or congregacion
are tied by Office onely to that particuler congregacion
whereoff they are chosen, Act. 14.23, and 20.17. Tit. 1.5.
And therefore they cannot challeng by office anie aucthor-
itie in anie other congregation whatsoever except they
would have an Apostleship.

23.

That the scriptures off the Old and New Testament are
written for our instruction, 2. Tim. 3.16 & that wee ought
to search them for they testifie off CHRIST, Io. 5.39.
And therefore to bee vsed withall reverence, as conteyning
the Holie Word off GOD, which onelie is our direction
in al thinges whatsoever.

24.

That Magistracie is a Holie ordinance off GOD, that
every soule ought to bee subject to it not for feare onelie,
but for conscience sake. Magistraets are the ministers off
GOD for our wealth, they beare not the sword for nought.
They are the ministers off GOD to take vengance on them
that doe evil, Rom. 13. Chap. That it is a fearefull
sin to speake evill off them that are in dignitie, and to
dispise Government. 2. Pet. 2.10. Wee ought to pay
tribute, custome and all other duties. That wee are to
pray for thē, for GOD would have them saved and come
to the knowledg off his truth. 1 Tim. 2.1. 4. And therefore they may bee members off the Church off CHRIST,

reteining their Magistracie, for no Holie Ordinance off GOD debarreth anie from being a member off CHRISTS Church. They beare the sword off GOD,—which sword in all Lawful administracions is to bee defended and supported by the servants off GOD that are vnder their Goverment with their lyves and al that they have according as in the first Institucion off that Holie Ordinance. And whosoever holds otherwise must hold, (iff they vnderstād themselves) that they are the ministers of the devill, and therefore not to bee praied for nor approved in anie off their administracions,—seing all things they do (as punishing offenders and defending their countries, state, and persons by the sword) is vnlawful.

25.

That it is Lawful in a just cause for the deciding off strife to take an oath by the Name off the Lord. Heb. 6.16. 2. Cor. 1.23. Phil. 1.8.

26.

That the dead shall rise againe, and the liveingh being changed in a moment,—haveing the same bodies in substance though divers in qualities. 1. Cor. 15. 52 and 38. Job 19. 15-28. Luk 24.30.

27.

That after the resurrection all men shall appeare before the judgment seat off CHRIST to bee judged according to their workes, that the Godlie shall enioy life Eternall, the wickeed being condemned shallbee tormented everlastinglie in Hell. Mat. 25.46.

FINIS

E. *Propositions and Conclusions concerning True Christian Religion, 1612-1614*

After Smyth's death in August, 1612, his party, now abandoned by the Helwys party, continued to wait for admission into the Amsterdam Waterlander Church. By this time Helwys had written not only his Confession of 1611, but also some additional works. Smyth's followers responded by issuing a confession consisting of one hundred, two articles. This may have been a modification of a confession written in the Dutch language by Smyth. It was an elaboration of the articles of John de Ries and Lubbert Gerrits. The first draft, made by Smyth himself, may have been in the English language, but a copy in the Dutch language was promptly drawn up for submission to the Dutch Mennonites.

There are two Dutch language copies of the Confession, written in manuscript, in the Mennonite Archives in Amsterdam. One of these consists of one hundred, one, and the other of one hundred, two articles. The latter copy is in folio and is beautifully executed. The Confession probably reached its final form in one hundred articles written in the English language. This edition was published along with Smyth's so-called "Retraction of His Errors" and an account of his death. The second Dutch copy and the final English copy agree with each other, excepting slight differences in wording, numbering, and arrangement of articles.[35] This Confession has appeared not only with variations and modifications, but also under at least one other title, for John Robinson (*Works*, III, 237, Ashton, ed.) calls it "The Confession of Faith Published in Certain Conclusions by the Remainders of Mr. Smyth's Company after his death."

The Confession may have been instrumental in finally accomplishing union with the Mennonites, which occurred on Jan. 20, 1615. It is principally notable, however, as perhaps the first confession of faith of modern times to demand freedom of conscience and separation of church and state. In these respects it was the pioneer for later Baptist confessions which almost always contained similar views. This Confession found its way into John Cotton's hands in America,[36] and it appears to have been referred to by English General Baptists as late as 1651. Thus, it is regarded as an important landmark. The only existing original English copy is in the York Minster Library. Barclay includes a reprint of the Confession in *Inner Life of the Religious Societies of the Commonwealth*, Appendix to Chap. VI, and McGlothlin (66-84) offers a copy.

> Propositions and Conclusions concerning True Christian Religion, containing a Confession of Faith of certain English people, living at Amsterdam.

> 1. We believe that there is a God (Heb. xi. 6) against all Epicures and Atheists, which either say in their hearts or utter with their mouths, that there is no God (Psal. xiv. 1; Isaiah xxii. 13.)

---

[35] Burrage, *op. cit.*, I, 247-248.
[36] Burgess, *John Smyth*, 237.

2. That this God is one in number (1 Cor. viii, 4, 6) against the Pagans or any other that hold a plurality of gods.

3. That God is incomprehensible and ineffable, in regard of His substance or essence that is God's essence can neither be comprehended in the mind, nor uttered by the words of men or angels (Exod. iii. 13-15, and xxxiii. 18-21).

4. That the creatures and Holy Scriptures do not intend to teach us what God is in substance or essence, but what He is in effect and property (Rom. i. 19, 22; Exod. xxxiii. 23).

5. That these terms, Father, Son, and Holy Spirit, do not teach God's substance, but only the hinder parts of God: that which may be known of God (Rom. i., Exod. xxxiii).

6. That God may be known by His titles, properties, effects, imprinted, and expressed in the creatures, and Scriptures (John xvii. 3).

7. That to understand and conceive of God in the mind is not the saving knowledge of God, but to be like to God in His effects and properties; to be made conformable to His divine and heavenly attributes. That is the true saving knowledge of God (2 Cor. iii. 18; Matt. v. 48; 2 Peter i. 4), whereunto we ought to give all diligence.

8. That this God manifested in Father, Son, and Holy Ghost (Matt. iii. 16, 17) is most merciful, most mighty, most holy, most just, most wise, most true, most glorious, eternal and infinite (Exod. xxxiv. 6, 7; Psalm xc. 2 and cii. 27).

9. That God before the foundation of the world did foresee, and determine the issue and event of all His works (Acts xv. 18), and that actually in time He worketh all things by His providence, according to the good pleasure of His will (Eph. i. 11), and therefore we abhor the opinion of them, that avouch, that all things happen by fortune or chance (Acts. iv. 27, 28; Matt. x. 29, 30).

10. That God is not the Author or worker of sin (Psal. v. 4; James i. 13), but that God only did foresee and determine what evil the free will of men and angels

would do; but He gave no influence, instinct, motion or inclination to the least sin.

11. That God in the beginning created the world viz., the heavens, and the earth and all things that are therein (Gen. i.; Acts xvii. 24). So that the things that are seen, were not of things which did appear (Heb. xi. 3).

12. That God created man to blessedness, according to His image, in an estate of innocency, free without corruption of sin (Gen. i. 27; ii. 17, 25); He created them male and female (to wit) one man and one woman (Gen. i. 27); He framed man of the dust of the earth, and breathed into him the breath of life, so the man was a living soul (Gen. ii. 7; 1 Cor. xv. 45). But the woman He made of a rib, taken out of the side of the man (Gen. ii. 21, 22). That God blessed them, and commanded them to increase, and multiply, and to fill the earth, and to rule over it and all creatures therein (Gen. i. 28; ix. 1, 2; Psal. viii. 6).

13. That therefore marriage is an estate honorable amongst all men, and the bed undefiled: viz. betwixt one man and one woman (Heb. xiii. 4; 1 Cor. vii. 2), but whoremongers and adulterers God will judge.

14. That God created man with freedom of will, so that he had ability to choose the good, and eschew the evil, or to choose the evil, and refuse the good, and that this freedom of will was a natural faculty or power, created by God in the soul of man (Gen. ii. 16, 17; iii. 6, 7; Eccles. vii. 29).

15. That Adam sinning was not moved or inclined thereto by God, or by any decree of God but that he fell from his innocency, and died the death alone, by the temptation of Satan, his free will assenting thereunto freely (Gen. iii. 6).

16. That the same day that Adam sinned, he died the death (Gen. ii. 17), for the reward of sin is death (Rom. vi. 23), and this is that which the Apostle saith, dead in trespasses and sins (Eph. ii. 1), which is loss of innocency, of the peace of conscience and comfortable presence of God (Gen. iii. 7, 11).

17. That Adam being fallen did not lose any natural power or faculty, which God created in his soul, for the

work of the devil, which is (sin), cannot abolish God's work or creatures: and therefore being fallen he still retained freedom of will (Gen. iii. 23, 24).

18. That original sin is an idle term, and that there is no such thing as men intend by the word (Ezek. xviii. 20), because God threatened death only to Adam (Gen. ii. 17) not to his posterity, and because God created the soul (Heb. xii. 9).

19. That if original sin might have passed from Adam to his posterity, Christ's death, which was effectual before Cain and Abel's birth, He being the lamb slain from the beginning of the world, stopped the issue and passage thereof (Rev. xiii. 8).

20. That infants are conceived and born in innocency without sin, and that so dying are undoubtedly saved, and that this is to be understood of all infants, under heaven (Gen. v. 2; i. 27 compared with 1 Cor. xv. 49) for where there is no law there is no transgression, sin is not imputed while there is no law (Rom. iv. 15 and v. 13), but the law was not given to infants, but to them that could understand (Rom. v. 13; Matt. xiii. 9; Neh. viii. 3).

21. That all actual sinners bear the image of the first Adam, in his innocency, fall, and restitution in the offer of grace (1 Cor. xv. 49), and so pass under these three conditions, or threefold estate.

22. That Adam being fallen God did not hate him, but loved him still, and sought his good (Gen. iii. 8-15), neither doth he hate any man that falleth with Adam; but that He loveth mankind, and from His love sent His only begotten Son into the world, to save that which was lost, and to seek the sheep that went astray (John iii. 16).

23. That God never forsaketh the creature until there be no remedy, neither doth He cast away His innocent creature from all eternity; but casteth away men irrecoverable in sin (Isa. v. 4; Ezek. xviii. 23, 32, and xxxiii. 11; Luke xiii. 6, 9).

24. That as there is in all creatures a natural inclination to their young ones, to do them good, so there is in the Lord toward man; for every spark of goodness in

the creature is infinitely good in God (Rom. i. 20; Psal.
xix. 4; Rom. x. 18).

25. That as no man begetteth his child to the gallows,
nor no potter maketh a pot to break it; so God doth not
create or predestinate any man to destruction (Ezek.
xxxiii. 11; Gen. i. 27; 1 Cor. xv. 49; Gen. v. 3).

26. That God before the foundation of the world hath
determined the way of life and salvation to consist in
Christ, and that He hath foreseen who would follow it
(Eph. i. 5; 2 Tim. i. 9), and on the contrary hath determined the way of perdition to consist in infidelity, and in
impenitency, and that He hath foreseen who would follow
after it (Jude, 4th verse).

27. That as God created all men according to His image, so hath He redeemed all that fall by actual sin, to the
same end; and that God in His redemption hath not
swerved from His mercy, which He manifested in His
creation (John i. 3, 16; 2 Cor. v. 19; 1 Tim. ii. 5, 6; Ezek.
xxxiii. 11).

28. That Jesus Christ came into the world to save sin-
ners, and that God in His love to His enemies did send
Him (John iii. 16); that Christ died for His enemies
(Rom. v. 10); that He bought them that deny Him (2
Peter ii. 1), thereby teaching us to love our enemies
(Matt. v. 44, 45).

29. That Jesus Christ after His baptism by a voice out
of heaven from the Father, and by the anointing of the
Holy Ghost, which appeared on His head in the form of
a dove, is appointed the prophet of the church, whom all
men must hear (Matt. iii.; Heb. iii. 1, 2); and that both
by His doctrine and life, which He led here in the earth,
by all His doings and sufferings, He hath declared and
published, as the only prophet and lawgiver of His
Church, the way of peace and life, the glad tidings of the
gospel (Acts iii. 23, 24).

30. That Jesus Christ is the brightness of the glory
and the engraven form of the Father's substance, supporting all things by His mighty power (Heb. i. 3); and
that He is become the mediator of the New Testament
(to wit) the King, Priest, and Prophet of the Church, and
that the faithful through Him are thus made spiritual

Kings, Priests, and Prophets (Rev. i. 6; 1 John ii. 20;
Rev. xix. 10).

31. That Jesus Christ is He which in the beginning did
lay the foundation of the heavens and earth which shall
perish (Heb. i. 10; Psalm cii. 26); that He is Alpha and
Omega, the beginning and the end, the first and the last,
He is the wisdom of God, which was begotten from everlasting before all creatures (Micah v. 2; Prov. viii. 24;
Luke xi. 49); He was in the form of God, and thought
it no robbery to be equal with God; yet He took to Him
the shape of a servant, the Word became flesh (John i.
14), wonderfully by the power of God in the womb of the
Virgin Mary; He was of the seed of David according to
the flesh (Phil. ii. 7; Heb. 10.; Rom. i. 3); and that He
made Himself of no reputation, humbled Himself, and became obedient unto the death of the cross, redeeming us
from our vain conversation, not with silver or gold, but
with the precious blood of Himself, as of a lamb without
spot and undefiled (1 Peter i. 18, 19).

32. That although the sacrifice of Christ's body and
blood offered up unto God His Father upon the cross,
be a sacrifice of a sweet smelling savour, and that God in
Him is well pleased, yet it doth not reconcile God unto us,
which did never hate us, nor was our enemy, but recon-
cileth us unto God (2 Cor. v. 19), and slayeth the enmity
and hatred, which is in us against God (Eph. I. 14, 17;
Rom. I. 30).

33. That Christ was delivered to death for our sins
(Rom. iv. 25), and that by His death we have the remission of our sins (Eph. ii. 7), for He cancelled the handwriting of ordinances, the hatred, the law of commandments in ordinances (Eph. ii. 15; Colos. ii. 14) which was
against us (Deut. xxxi. 26); He spoiled principalities and
powers, made a shew of them openly, and triumphed
over them on the cross (Colos. ii. 15); by death He destroyed him that had the power of death, that is the devil
(Heb. ii. 14).

34. That the enemies of our salvation, which Christ
vanquished on His cross, are the gates of hell, the power
of darkness, Satan, sin, death, the grave, the curse or
condemnation, wicked men, and persecutors (Eph. vi. 12;

I

1 Cor. xv. 26, 54, 57; Matt. xvi. 18; Rev. xx. 10, 14, 15),
which enemies we must overcome no otherwise than
Christ hath done (John xxi. 22; 1 Peter ii. 21; Rev. xiv.
4).

35. That the efficacy of Christ's death is only derived to
them, which do mortify their sins, which are grafted with
Him to the similitude of His death (Rom. vi. 3-6), which
are circumcised with circumcision made without hands,
by putting off the sinful body of the flesh, through the
circumcision which Christ worketh (Colos. ii. 11) who is
the minister of the circumcision for the truth of God, to
confirm the promises made to the fathers (Rom. xv. 8
compared with Deut. xxx. 6).

36. That there are three which bear witness in the
earth, the spirit, water and blood, and these three are one
in testimony, witnessing that Christ truly died (1 John v.
8) for He gave up the ghost (John xix. 30); and out of
His side pierced with a spear came water and blood (verse
34, 35), the cover of the heart being pierced, where there
is water contained.

37. That every mortified person hath this witness in
himself (1 John v. 10), for the spirit blood, and water of
sin is gone, that is the life of sin with the nourishment
and cherishment thereof (1 Pet. iv. 1; Rom. vi. 7; 1
John iii. 6).

38. That Christ Jesus being truly dead was also buried
(John xix. 39, 42), and that he lay in the grave the whole
Sabbath of the Jews; but in the grave He saw no corrup-
tion (Psal. xvi. 10; Acts ii. 31).

39. That all mortified persons are also buried with
Christ, by the baptism, which is unto His death (Rom. vi.
4; Colos. ii. 12); keeping their Sabbath with Christ in the
grave (that is) resting from their own works as God did
from His (Heb. iv. 10), waiting there in hope for a
resurrection (Psal. xvi. 9).

40. That Christ Jesus early in the morning, the first
day of the week, rose again after His death and burial
(Matt. xxviii. 6) for our justification (Rom. iv. 25), being mightily declared to be the Son of God, by the Spirit
of sanctification, in the resurrection from the dead (Rom.
i. 4).

41. That these that are grafted with Christ to the similitude of His death and burial shall also be to the similitude of His resurrection (Rom. vi. 4, 5.); for He doth quicken or give life unto them, together with Himself (Colos. ii. 13; Eph. ii. 5, 6); for that is their salvation, and it is by grace (Eph. ii. 5; 1 John v. 11, 12, 13; Titus iii. 5, 6, 7).

42. That this quickening or reviving of Christ, this laver of regeneration, this renewing of the Holy Ghost, is our justification and salvation (Titus iii. 6, 7). This is that pure river of water of life clear as crystal, which proceedeth out of the throne of God, and of the Lamb (Rev. xxii. 1); which also floweth out of the belly of him that believeth in Christ (John vii. 38); this is those precious promises whereby we are made partakers of the divine nature, by flying the corruptions that are in the world through lust (2 Pet. i. 4); this is the fruit of the tree of life which is in the midst of the paradise of God; this is the white stone wherein there is a name written, which no man knoweth, save he that receiveth it. This is the morning star, this is the new name, the name of God, the name of the City of God; the new Jerusalem which descendeth from God out of heaven; this is the hidden manna, that white clothing, eye salve and gold, and that heavenly supper which Christ promises to them, that overcome (Rev. ii. 7, 17, 18, and iii. 5, 12, 18, 20).

43. That there are three which bear record in heaven, the Father, the Word, and the Holy Spirit; and that these three are one in testimony, witnessing the resurrection of Christ. The Father saith thou art my Son, this day have I begotten thee (Acts xiii. 33-35). The Son testifieth of his own resurrection being forty days with His disciples (Act. i. 3). The Holy Ghost testifieth the same whom Christ sent to His disciples upon the day of Pentecost (Acts. ii).

44. That every person that is regenerate and risen again with Christ hath these three aforesaid witnesses in himself (1 John v. 10); for Christ doth dwell in his heart by faith (Eph. iii. 17); and the Father dwelleth with the Son (Joh. xiv. 23); and the Holy Ghost likewise (1 Cor. iii. 16); and that the grace of our Lord Jesus Christ,

and the love of God, and the fellowship of the Holy
Ghost is with them (2 Cor. xiii. 13).

45. That Christ having forty days after His resurrection conversed with his disciples (Acts i. 3), ascended
locally into the heavens (Acts i. 9), which must contain
Him unto the time that all things be restored (Acts iii.
21).

That they which are risen with Christ, ascend up spiritually with Him, seeking those things which are above,
where Christ sitteth at the right hand of God, and that
they set their affections on heavenly things, and not on
earthly things (Col. iii. 1-5).

46. That Christ now being received into Heaven, sitteth
at the right hand of God (Mark xvi. 9), having led captivity captive, and given gifts unto men (Eph. iv. 8); that
God hath now highly exalted Him, and given Him a
name above every name; that at the name of Jesus every
knee should bow, of things in heaven, in earth and under
the earth (Phil. ii. 9, 10), that He hath obtained all power
both in heaven and in earth (Matt. xxviii. 18), and hath
made all things subject under His feet, and hath appointed
Him over all things to be the head to the church, that is
His body, the fulness of Him that filleth all in all things
(Eph. i. 2-23).

47. That the regenerate do sit together with Christ
Jesus in heavenly places (Eph. ii. 6), that they sit with
Him in His throne as He sitteth with the Father in His
throne (Rev. iii. 21), that they have power over nations
and rule them with a rod of iron, and as a potter's vessel
they are broken in pieces (Rev. ii. 26, 27); and that sit-
ting on twelve thrones, they do judge the twelve tribes of
Israel (Matt. xix. 28), which spiritually is to put all their
enemies in subjection under their feet, so that the evil
one doth not touch them (1 John v. 18), nor the gates of
hell prevail against them (Matt. xvi. 28), and that they
are become pillars in the house of God, and go no more
out (Rev. iii. 12).

48. That Christ Jesus being exalted at the right hand
of God the Father, far above all principalities and powers,
might, and domination, and every name that is named, not
only in this world, but in the world to come (Eph. i. 21),

hath received of His Father the promise of the Holy Ghost, which He also shed forth upon His disciples on the Day of Pentecost (Act ii. 33).

49. That Christ Jesus, in His resurrection, ascension, and exaltation, is more and rather Lord and Christ, Saviour, anointed, and King, than in His humiliation, sufferings and death (Acts. ii. 36; Phil. ii. 7, 11), for the end is more excellent than the means, and His sufferings were the way by the which He entered into His glory (Luke xxiv. 16), and so by consequent the efficacy of His resurrection in the new creature, is more noble and excellent, than the efficacy of His death in the mortification and remission of sins.

50. That the knowledge of Christ according to the flesh is of small profit (2 Cor. v. 16, 17), and the knowledge of Christ's genealogy and history, is no other but that which the Devil hath as well if not better than any man living; but the knowledge of Christ according to the spirit is effectual to salvation, which is spiritually to be grafted to the similitude of Christ's birth, life, miracles, doings, sufferings, death, burial, resurrection, ascension, and exaltation (Rom. vi. 3, 6).

51. That Christ Jesus, according to the flesh and history in His doings and suffering, is a great mystery, and divine sacrament of Himself, and of His ministry in the spirit, and of those spiritual things which He worketh in those which are to be heirs of salvation (Rom. vi. 3, 6; Eph. ii. 5, 6), and that spiritually He performeth all those miracles in the regenerate which He wrought in His flesh; He healeth their leprosy, bloody issue, blindness, dumbness, deafness, lameness, palsy, fever, He casteth out the devils and unclean spirits, He raiseth the dead, rebuketh the winds and the sea, and it is calm; He feedeth thousands with the barley loaves and fishes (Matt. viii. 16, 17, compared with Isaiah liii. 4, John vi. 26, 27).

52. That the Holy Ghost proceedeth from the Father and the Son (John xiv. 26, and xvi. 7); that He is the eternal spirit, whereby Christ offered Himself without spot to God (Heb. ix. 14); and He is that other comforter, which Christ asketh, obtaineth, and sendeth from the Father (John xiv. 16), which dwelleth in the regener-

ate (1 Cor. iii. 16), which leadeth them into all truth
(John xvi. 13), He is that anointing which teacheth them
all things, and that they have no need that any man teach
them, but as the same anointing teacheth (1 John ii. 20,
27).

53. That although there be divers gifts of the Spirit
yet there is but one Spirit, which distributeth to every
one as He will (2 Cor. xii. 4, 11; Eph. iv. 4), that the
outward gifts of the spirit which the Holy Ghost poureth
forth, upon the Day of Pentecost upon the disciples, in
tongues and prophesy, and gifts, and healing, and miracles, which is called the Baptism of the Holy Ghost and
fire (Acts. i. 5) were only a figure of and an hand
leading to better things, even the most proper gifts of the
spirit of sanctification, which is the new creature; which
is the one baptism (Eph. iv. 4, compared with Acts ii. 33,
38, and with Luke x. 17, 20).

54. That John Baptist and Christ are two persons,
their ministries are two ministries several, and their baptisms are two baptisms, distinct the one from the other
(John i. 20; Acts xiii. 25; Acts i. 4, 5; Matt. iii. 11).

55. That John taught the baptism of repentance for the
remission of sins, baptizing with water to amendment of
life (Matt. iii. 11), thus preparing a way for Christ and
His baptism (Luke iii. 3, 6), by bringing men to repentance and faith in the Messias, whom he pointed
out with the finger (saying), behold the Lamb of God
that taketh away the sins of the world (John i. 31, 29;
Acts xix. 4).

56. That Christ is stronger, and hath a more excellent
office and ministry than John (Matt. iii. 11); that He
baptiseth with the Holy Ghost and fire; that He
cometh and walketh in the way which John hath prepared; and that the new creature followeth repentance
(Luke iii. 6).

57. That repentance and faith in the Messias, are the
conditions to be performed on our behalf, for the obtaining of the promises (Acts ii. 38; John i. 12); that the
circumcision of the heart, mortification and the promise
of the spirit, that is, the new creature, are the promises
which are made to the aforesaid conditions (Deut. xxx. 6;

Acts ii. 38; Gal. iii. 14; 2 Pet. i. 4, 5), which promises are all yea and Amen in Christ Jesus (2 Cor. i. 20), and that in the regenerate (Gal. iii. 16).

58. That repentance and faith are wrought in the hearts of men, by the preaching of the word, outwardly in the Scriptures, and creatures, the grace of God preventing us by the motions and instinct of the spirit, which a man hath power to receive or reject (Matt. xxiii. 37; Acts vii. 51; Acts vi. 10; Rom. x. 14, 18), that our justification before God consisteth not in the performance of the conditions which God requireth of us, but in partaking of the promises, the possessing of Christ, remission of sins, and the new creature.

59. That God, the Father, of His own good will doth beget us, by the word of truth (James i. 18), which is an immortal seed (1 Pet. i. 23), not the doctrine of repentance and faith which may be lost (Luke viii. 13); and that God the Father, in our regeneration, neither needeth nor useth the help of any creature, but that the Father, the Word, and the Holy Ghost, immediately worketh that work in the soul, where the free will of men can do nothing (John ii. 13).

60. That such as have not attained the new creature, have need of the scriptures, creatures and ordinances of the Church, to instruct them, to comfort them, to stir them up the better to perform the condition of repentance to the remission of sins (2 Pet. i. 19; 1 Cor. xi. 26; Eph. iv. 12-23).

61. That the new creature which is begotten of God, needeth not the outward scriptures, creatures, or ordinances of the Church, to support or help them (2 Cor. xiii. 10, 12; 1 Joh. ii. 27; 1 Cor. i. 15, 16; Rev. xxi. 23), seeing he hath three witnesses in himself, the Father, the Word, and the Holy Ghost: which are better than all scriptures, or creatures whatsoever.

62. That as Christ who was above the law notwithstanding was made under the law, for our cause: so the regenerate in love to others, can and will do no other, than use the outward things of the church, for the gaining and supporting of others: and so the outward church and ordinances are always necessary, for all sorts of per-

sons whatsoever (Matt. iii. 15; xxviii. 19, 20; 1 Cor. viii. 9).

63. That the new creature although he be above the law and scriptures, yet he can do nothing against the law or scriptures, but rather all his doings shall serve to the confirming and establishing of the law (Rom. iii. 31). Therefore he cannot lie, nor steal, nor commit adultery, nor kill, nor hate any man, or do any other fleshly action, and therefore all fleshly libertinism is contrary to regeneration, detestable, and damnable (John viii. 34; Rom. vi. 15, 16, 18; 2 Pet. ii. 18, 19; 1 John v. 18).

64. That the outward church visible, consists of penitent persons only, and of such as believing in Christ, bring forth fruits worthy amendment of life (1 Tim. vi. 3, 5; 2 Tim. iii. 1, 5; Acts xix. 4).

65. That the visible church is a mystical figure outwardly, of the true, spiritual invisible church; which consisteth of the spirits of just and perfect men only, that is of the regenerate (Rev. i. 20, compared with Rev. xxi. 2, 23, 27).

66. That repentance is the change of mind from evil to that which is good (Matt. iii. 2), a sorrow for sin committed, with a humble heart for the same; and a resolution to amend for time to come; with an unfeigned endeavor therein (2 Cor. vii. 8, 11; Isaiah i. 16, 17; Jer. xxxi. 18, 19).

67. That when we have done all that we can we are unprofitable servants, and all our righteousness is as a stained cloth (Luke xvii. 20), and that we can only suppress and lop off the branches of sin, but the root of sin we cannot pluck up out of our hearts (Jer. iv. 4, compared with Deut. xxx. 6, 8).

68. That faith is a knowledge in the mind of the doctrine of the law and gospel contained in the prophetical, and apostolical scriptures of the Old and New Testament: accompanying repentance with an assurance that God, through Christ, will perform unto us His promises of remission of sins, and mortification, upon the condition of our unfeigned repentance, and amendment of life (Rom. x. 13, 14, 15; Acts v. 30-32; and Acts ii. 38, 39; Heb. xi. 1; Mark i. 15).

69. That all penitent and faithful Christians are brethren in the communion of the outward church, wheresoever they live, by what name soever they are known, which in truth and zeal, follow repentance and faith, though compassed with never so many ignorances and infirmities; and we salute them all with a holy kiss, being heartily grieved that we which follow after one faith, and one spirit, one Lord, and one God, one body, and one baptism, should be rent into so many sects and schisms: and that only for matters of less moment.

70. That the outward baptism of water, is to be administered only upon such penitent and faithful persons as are (aforesaid), and not upon innocent infants, or wicked persons (Matt. iii. 2, 3, compared with Matt. xxviii. 19, 20, and John iv. 1).

71. That in Baptism to the penitent person, and believer, there is presented, and figured, the spiritual baptism of Christ, (that is) the baptism of the Holy Ghost, and fire: the baptism into the death and resurrection of Christ: even the promise of the Spirit, which he shall assuredly be made partaker of, if he continue to the end (Gal. iii. 14; Matt. iii. 11; 1 Cor. xii. 13; Rom. vi. 3, 6; Col. ii. 10).

72. That in the outward supper which only baptised persons must partake, there is presented and figured before the eyes of the penitent and faithful, that spiritual supper, which Christ maketh of His flesh and blood: which is crucified and shed for the remission of sins (as the bread is broken and the wine poured forth), and which is eaten and drunken (as is the bread and wine bodily) only by those which are flesh, of His flesh, and bone of His bone: in the communion of the same spirit (1 Cor. xii. 13; Rev. iii. 20, compared with 1 Cor. xi. 23, 26; John vi. 53, 58).

73. That the outward baptism and supper do not confer, and convey grace and regeneration to the participants or communicants: but as the word preached, they serve only to support and stir up the repentance and faith of the communicants till Christ come, till the day dawn, and the day-star arise in their hearts (1 Cor. xi. 26; 2 Peter i. 19; 1 Cor. 1. 5-8).

74. That the sacraments have the same use that the word hath; that they are a visible word, and that they teach to the eye of them that understand as the word teacheth the ears of them that have ears to hear (Prov. x. 12), and therefore as the word pertaineth not to infants, no more do the sacraments.

75. That the preaching of the word, and the ministry of the sacraments, representeth the ministry of Christ in the spirit; who teacheth, baptiseth, and feedeth the regenerate, by the Holy Spirit inwardly and invisibly.

76. That Christ hath set in His outward church two sorts of ministers: viz., some who are called pastors, teachers or elders, who administer in the word and sacraments, and others who are called Deacons, men and women: whose ministry is, to serve tables and wash the saints' feet (Acts vi. 2-4; Phil. i. 1; 1 Tim. iii. 2, 3, 8, 11, and chap. v.).

77. That the separating of the impenitent, from the outward communion of the church, is a figure of the eternal rejection, and reprobation of them that persist impenitent in sin (Rev. xxi. 27, and xxii. 14-45; Matt. xvi. 18 and xviii. 18; John xx. 23, compared with Rev. iii. 12).

78. That none are to be separated from the outward communion of the Church but such as forsake repentance, which deny the power of Godliness (2 Tim. iii. 5), and namely that sufficient admonition go before, according to the rule (Matt. xviii. 15-18), and that none are to be rejected for ignorance or errors, or infirmities as long as they retain repentance and faith in Christ (Rom. xiv., and 1 Thess. v. 14; Rom. xvi. 17, 18), but they are to be instructed with meekness; and the strong are to bear the infirmities of the weak; and that we are to support one another through love.

79. That a man may speak a word against the Son, and be pardoned (that is), a man may err in the knowledge of Christ's history, and in matters of the outward church, and be forgiven, doing it in an ignorant zeal; but he that speaketh a word against the Holy Ghost (that is) that after illumination forsaketh repentance and faith in Christ, persecuting them, trampling under

foot the blood of the covenant: returning with the dog to the vomit; that such shall never be pardoned, neither in this world, nor in the world to come (Matt. xii. 31, 32, compared with Heb. vi. 4, and chap. x. 26-29; 2 Pet. ii. 20, 22).

80. That persons separated from the communion of the church, are to be accounted as heathens and publicans (Matt. xviii.), and that they are so far to be shunned, as they may pollute: notwithstanding being ready to instruct them, and to relieve them in their wants: seeking by all lawful means to win them: considering that excommunication is only for the destruction of the flesh, that the spirit may be saved in the day of the Lord (1 Cor. v. 5, 11; Matt. xi. 19; Luke xv. 1, 2).

81. That there is no succession in the outward church, but that all succession is from heaven, and that the new creature only, hath the thing signified, and substance, whereof the outward church and ordinances are shadows (Col. ii. 16, 17), and therefore he alone hath power, and knoweth aright, how to administer in the outward church, for the benefit of others (John. vi. 45): yet God is not the God of confusion but of order, and therefore we are in the outward church, to draw as near the first institution as may be, in all things (1 Cor. xiv. 33); therefore it is not lawful for every brother to administer the word and sacraments (Eph. iv. 11, 12, compared with 1 Cor. xii. 4, 5, 6, 28, 29).

82. That Christ hath set in his outward church the vocation of master and servant, parents and children, husband and wife (Eph. v. 22-25, chap. vi. 1, 4, 5, 9), and hath commanded every soul to be subject to the higher powers (Rom. xiii. 1), not because of wrath only, but for conscience sake (verse 5) that we are to give them their duty, as tribute, and custom, honour, and fear, not speaking evil of them that are in authority (Jude, verse 8), but praying and giving thanks for them (1 Tim. ii. 1, 2), for that is acceptable in the sight of God, even our Saviour.

83. That the office of the magistrate, is a disposition or permissive ordinance of God for the good of mankind: that one man like the brute beasts devour not another

(Rom. xiii.), and that justice and civility, may be preserved among men: and that a magistrate may so please
God in his calling, in doing that which is righteous and
just in the eyes of the Lord, that he may bring an outward blessing upon himself, his posterity and subjects (2
Kings, x. 30, 31).

84. That the magistrate is not by virtue of his office
to meddle with religion, or matters of conscience, to force
or compel men to this or that form of religion, or doctrine: but to leave Christian religion free, to every man's
conscience, and to handle only civil transgressions (Rom.
xiii), injuries and wrongs of man against man, in murder,
adultery, theft, etc., for Christ only is the king, and law-
giver of the church and conscience (James iv. 12).

85. That if the magistrate will follow Christ, and be
His disciple, he must deny himself, take up his cross, and
follow Christ; he must love his enemies and not kill them,
he must pray for them, and not punish them, he must
feed them and give them drink, not imprison them, banish
them, dismember them, and spoil their goods; he must
suffer persecution and affliction with Christ, and be slandered, reviled, blasphemed, scourged, buffeted, spit upon,
imprisoned and killed with Christ; and that by the authority of magistrates, which things he cannot possibly
do, and retain the revenge of the sword.

86. That the Disciples of Christ, the members of the
outward church, are to judge all their causes of difference, among themselves, and they are not to go to law,
before the magistrates (1 Cor. vi. 1, 7), and that all their
differences must be ended by (yea) and (nay) without
an oath (Matt. v. 33-37; James v. 12).

87. That the Disciples of Christ, the members of the
outward church, may not marry any of the profane, or
wicked, godless people of the world, but that every one is
to marry in the Lord (1 Cor. vii. 39), every man one only
wife, and every woman one only husband (1 Cor. vii. 2).

88. That parents are bound to bring up their children in
instruction and information of the Lord (Eph. vi. 4), and
that they are to provide for their family: otherwise they
deny the faith, and are worse than infidels (1 Tim. v. 8).

89. That notwithstanding if the Lord shall give a man

any special calling, as Simon, and Andrew, James, and John, then they must leave all, father, ship, nets, wife, children, yea, and life also to follow Christ (Luke xiv. 26; Matt. iv. 18-20).

90. That in the necessities of the church, and poor brethren, all things are to be common (Acts iv. 32), yea and that one church is to administer to another in time of need (Gal. ii. 10; Acts xi. 30; 1 Cor. iv. 8, and chap. ix.).

91. That all the bodies of all men that are dead, shall by the power of Christ, be raised up, out of his own proper seed, as corn out of the seed rotting in the earth (1 Cor. xv.).

92. That these which live in the last day shall not die, but shall be changed in a moment: in the twinkling of an eye, at the last trumpet (1 Cor. xv. 52), for the trump shall blow, and the dead shall be raised up incorruptible, and we shall be changed, not in substance but in qualities; for the bodies shall rise in honour, in power, in incorruption, and spiritual: being sown in dishonour, in weakness, in corruption, and natural (1 Cor. xv. 42, 44).

93. That the bodies, being raised up, shall be joined to the souls, whereto formerly they were united; which to that time were preserved in the hands of the Lord (Rev. vi. 9, Job xix. 25-27).

94. That it is appointed to all men that they shall once die, and then cometh the judgment (Heb. ix. 27), and that the change of them that live on earth at the last day, shall be as it were a death unto them (1 Cor. xv. 52; 1 Thes. iv. 15-17).

95. That there shall be a general, and universal day of judgment, when every one shall receive according to the things that are done in the flesh, whether they be good or evil (1 Cor. v. 10, Acts xvii. 31).

96. That of the day and hour knoweth no man; no, not the Angels in heaven, neither the Son Himself, but the Father only. (Mark xiii. 32).

97. That Christ Jesus that man, shall judge in that day (Acts xvii. 31), that he shall come in the clouds with glory: and all His holy angels with Him (Matt. xxv.), with a shout, and with the voice of the Archangel, and with the trump of God (1 Thes. iv. 16), and He shall

sit upon the throne of His glory; and all nations shall be gathered before Him, and He shall separate them one from another, as a shepherd separateth the sheep from the goats, setting the sheep on His right hand and the goats on the left (Matt. xxv.).

98. That the king shall say to the sheep, the regenerate, which are on His right hand, " Come, ye blessed of my Father, inherit the kingdom prepared for you before the foundation of the world; " and it shall be performed accordingly (Matt. xxv.).

99. That the king shall say to them on His left hand, the goats, the wicked ones, " Depart from me, ye cursed, into everlasting fire prepared for the Devil and his angels," and it shall be accomplished accordingly (Matt. xxv.).

100. That after the judgment ended and accomplished, and the last enemy that is death being put under the feet of Christ, then the Son himself shall deliver up the kingdom into the hands of the Father, and be subject unto Him, that subdued all things unto Him, that God may be all in all (I Cor. xv. 24-28).

KOLASIS

CUTTING OF OR PRUNING
OF A TREE

3

Early English Baptist Associational Confessions

THE PARTICULAR BAPTISTS (so called for their belief in the Calvinistic doctrine of a particular election) arose in England in the decade 1630-1640. These Baptists came out of the Separatist movement. They first appeared in the church which Henry Jacob organized in 1616 in London following his return from exile in Holland. This church was "gathered" on the basis of a confession of individual faith and of a covenant. It contained both Independent Puritans and radical Separatists. The former honored the National Church and sought its further reformation, although separated from it; the latter called the Established Church false and rejected all connection with it.

Varying attitudes toward the Establishment soon led to divisions of the church, beginning about 1630. There was difference of opinion in 1633 as to the validity of baptism administered by a parish clergyman, and a group, including some who had anti-pedobaptist convictions, withdrew under the leadership of Samuel Eaton. The parent church amicably dismissed another group in 1638 whose members held that only regenerated believers should be baptized. This group, coming under the leadership of John Spilsbery, who meanwhile had become pastor of Eaton's mixed church, is looked upon as the first Particular Baptist Church. Further study convinced a portion of Spilsbery's and perhaps some of the mother church, during 1640, that baptism "ought to be by dipping the Body into the Water, resembling Burial and rising again." The problem now confronting them concerned the best means of beginning scriptural baptism anew. No English Christians were known to practice believers' baptism by immersion, but the Rhynsburgers or Collegiants, a liberal sect of Mennonite background, practiced it in the Netherlands. So

143

Richard Blunt, who could speak Dutch and who probably initiated the discussion, was sent to Holland, where he may have been baptized by the Collegiants. At least, his views on the mode of baptism were confirmed by them, and he returned home to baptize those who were in agreement with him. If Blunt was looking for a succession in baptism, he did not carry the main body of the Baptists with him in this quest. Crosby remarks:

> But the greatest number of the English Baptists, and the more judicious, looked upon all this as needless trouble, and what proceeded from the old Popish Doctrine of right to administer sacraments by an uninterrupted succession, which neither the Church of Rome, nor the Church of England, much less the modern dissenters, could prove to be with them. They affirmed, therefore, and practiced accordingly, that after a general corruption of baptism, an unbaptized person might warrantably baptize, and so begin a reformation.[1]

The baptism of Blunt's followers occurred not later than 1641, and in 1642 other baptismal services were held involving numbers of the radical Separatists.

A. *The London Confession, 1644*   No REPROBATION

By 1644 there were seven Particular Baptist churches in London, who soon discovered that their life had begun in the midst of times of great excitement and of great opportunity for their views. In England the royal pretensions were being destroyed; parliamentary government was becoming a reality. A product of this revolutionary time was the dethronement of ecclesiastical tyranny and, temporarily at least, the realization of religious freedom. Dissenters dared work more openly; pastors had freedom to itinerate and evangelize. The Baptists were especially active, and they began to gain important converts from various religious parties. The theology of Particular Baptists was of a piece with the prevalent Calvinism of the nation, and so it offered no obstacle to the mass of Englishmen. By 1644, however, the rapid growth of Baptist views called forth serious opposition to the Baptists and their program. The most serious accusations levelled against them by their enemies were of Pelagianism and anarchy, both of which were associated in the popular mind with the radical wing of the Anabaptist movement of the Continent.

---

[1] *History of the English Baptists*, I, 101-103.

It has been suggested that the publication of the scurrilous work, *A Short History of the Anabaptists of High and Low Germany* (1642), gave rise to the Confession of 1644;[2] but, *A Warning for England especially for London* . . . appearing in the same year, was equally provoking. Moreover, it is likely that the appearance in 1644 of *A Confutation of the Anabaptists and of All others who affect not Civill Government*, furnished the final provocation to issuing the Confession. In order to distinguish themselves from both the General Baptists and the Anabaptists, the Calvinistic Baptists of London determined to prepare and publish a statement of their views. The seven London churches, already informally associated together by 1644, evidently pushed aside their prejudice against the use of confessions and prepared their own statement for apologetic purposes.

Some of the signatories had been connected with the older Separatist movement, and so the Separatist Confession of 1596 was known among them. This Confession served as their model, as they prepared a longer and more comprehensive document. Other models also may have been before them. For example, John Spilsbery, a signatory, had published the year before a confession of his faith consisting of ten articles in connection with a longer treatise on baptism.[3] Spilsbery was known as "the great Patriarch of the Anabaptist Confession,"[4] and he must have played a prominent part in its preparation. Some of the order and phrasing of the Confession is like that of the Spilsbery document.

Another probable source of doctrinal expressions of the Confession has been suggested. Robert B. Hannen[5] has noted the remarkable similarity of large sections with corresponding sections in the Aberdeen Confession (a document authorized for the Church of Scotland by the Episcopal Assembly in 1616) and has shown that this similarity goes beyond the assertion in both documents that the authors are open to correction if their tenets can be shown to be unscriptural and beyond some stock phrases of Calvinism drawn from the *Institutes*. Daniel Featley's work, *The Dippers dipt.* (1645), reveals that there was an unknown Scot identified with

[2] A note in the front of this pamphlet in the Angus Library, Regent's Park College, Oxford, probably by Dr. Jos. Angus, dated 1854, says, "This scurrilous history originated the first confession of 1644."

[3] *A Treatise Concerning the Lawful Subject of Baptism*, p. 43.

[4] Underwood, *A History of English Baptists*, 60.

[5] *Baptist Quarterly*, XII (1946-49), 389-399.

K

London Particular Baptists in 1642, and Hannen conjectures that this man brought the little-known confession to the attention of the leaders of the seven churches. He further concludes that this Scot could have been one William Gardin of Aberdeenshire, who was accused of "Brownism" in 1643 and was called by a contemporary an Anabaptist.

Still, the structure of the London Confession is more like that of "A True Confession" of 1596; both Confessions are notable for their Christological emphasis. To be sure, the large section of the 1596 document dealing with the means of reforming the Church of England along Separatist lines is absent from the London Confession, for the Baptists did not think of reforming the National Church but of building an entirely new structure on the New Testament pattern.

If the Confession was the product of joint authorship, Spilsbery probably had the assistance of William Kiffin and Samuel Richardson. The signatories included two men from each church represented, except that Spilsbery's church had three. None of them had been trained formally for the ministry.

The Calvinism of the Confession is of a moderate type. The doctrine of election is balanced by the statement that the Gospel is to be preached to all men, and there is no teaching of reprobation. The twelve articles dealing with Christology are an indirect denial of Arminianism. The definition of the church is novel, though not unlike that of the Helwys church of 1611. It includes the concept of the invisible Church. This is the first Baptist Confession to pronounce in favor of immersion as the proper mode of baptism. Article CI is an outline of conduct to be followed in case of civil persecution. There is a strong emphasis throughout the Confession on preaching, in substantiation of the widespread Baptist practice of lay-preaching. The Confession, in spite of its incompleteness and its infelicity of wording at points, is one of the noblest of all Baptist confessions. Essentially independent in statement, it largely anticipates the Westminster Confession, "but with more rhetorical expansion and greater tenderness of tone."[6]

It appears that the Confession was received with enthusiasm by London Particular Baptists as a worthy doctrinal standard and as a basis for church co-operation. Some London General Baptists

---

[6] Green, *The Christian Creed and the Creeds of Christendom,* 150.

FREEDOM OF THE WILL ·
BONDAGE OF THE WILL

GOD DID NOT CREATE SOME TO BE DAMNED ETERNALLY
ROMAN CATHOLIC LUTHERAN CALVINIST DOGMATICIANS
OF AUGUSTINE - "DEPRAVED MAN IS FREE ENOUGH TO
MAKE RESPONSIBLE CHOICES BY HIS OWN WILL AND THUS
INCUR GUILT BUT NOT FREE ENOUGH TO MAKE GOOD
CHOICES AND THUS AVOID GUILT."

seem to have responded to it in 1645 with a pamphlet called *The Fountaine of Free Grace Opened,* in which they defended their distinctive doctrine of a general atonement but distinguished themselves from "The Arminians" and denounced "scandalous aspersions" that they held to freedom of the will and denied a free election of grace. Outside the Baptist fellowship the Confession was received with unequalled surprise. People generally were amazed at the moderation and sanity of its articles.

Some refused to believe that it fairly represented Baptist views. The strongest attack came from Dr. Daniel Featley, brilliant liberal clergyman of the Church of England, who devoted to it the last chapter of his book. *The Dippers dipt. or, The Anabaptists duck't and plunged Over Head and Eares, at a Disputation in Southwark* (1645). Featley had been a member of the Westminster Assembly; but, like others of his party, he had come under suspicion of disloyalty and had been imprisoned at the behest of the Parliament. In prison he had worked over some notes on a disputation he had had with William Kiffin and some others in 1642.[7] These he included in the above scurrilous work, in which he devoted several chapters to the errors and extravagances of the continental Anabaptists of the previous century. This book was to go through six editions.[8] The English Anabaptists, it said, inherited all the evils of continental Anabaptism, and these evils would soon burst in full fury upon England. Featley named six articles of the Confession as heretical.

In consequence of the attack by so famous a man as Featley, and especially because his book had been dedicated to Parliament, which was then the ruling body of the country, the Baptists felt compelled to reply. Samuel Richardson published a small volume, *Some Brief Considerations on Doctor Featley His book entitled The Dipper Dipt.* . . . However, the attitude of Parliament being the chief concern, it was decided to work over the Confession, changing as far as possible the language to which Featley objected, and to submit the resulting document to the House of Commons. The revision was carefully and thoroughly made, so thoroughly indeed, that much of the distinctively Baptist emphasis was removed from some of the

[7] A. S. Langley, "17th Century Baptist Disputations," Transactions B.H.S. VI (1918-19), 216-243. McGlothlin (*Baptist Confessions of Faith,* 190) says it was with "the General Baptists."

[8] Whitley, *A Baptist Bibliography,* 19.

articles. After the middle of 1645, in response to Presbyterian agitation for uniformity, the principle of religious freedom was stated even more clearly. Article 38 became Article 48, as follows:

> So it is the magistrates duty to tender the liberty of men's consciences . . . and we believe it to be our express duty, especially in matters of religion, to be fully persuaded in our minds of the lawfulness (sic) of what we do . . . and as we cannot do anything contrary to our understandings and consciences, so neither can we forbid the doing of that which our understandings and consciences bind us to do; and if the magistrate should require us to do otherwise, we are to yield our persons in a positive way to their power. . . .[9]

The articles on magistracy (XLVIII to LII) were condensed and altered. The two following articles were added:

> L. It is lawfull for a Christian to be a Magistrate or Civill Officer; and also it is lawfull to take an Oath, so it be in truth, and in judgement, and in righteousnesse, for confirmation of truth, and ending of all strife; and that by rash and vain oaths the Lord is provoked, and this Land mournes. Acts 8.38 & 10.1,2,35,44. Rom. 16.23. Deut. 6.13. Rom. 1.9. 2 Cor. 10.11. Jer. 4.2. Heb. 6.16.
> LII. There shall be a resurrection of the dead, both of the just and the unjust, and everyone shall give an account of himselfe to God, that every one may receive the things done in his body, according to that he hath done, whether it be good or bad. Acts 24.15. Rom. 14.12.

Changes in the new edition apart from those directly occasioned by Featley's criticism included statements denying free will, communalism, and falling from grace, a stronger declaration in favor of election, and a statement of the doctrine of original sin. This strengthening of the Calvinism of the Confession was due probably to the efforts of two ex-clergymen, Benjamin Cox and Hanserd Knollys, who had recently become identified with the London Baptists. In addition to representatives of the seven congregations, the second edition was signed by two ministers of a French (Huguenot) congregation of London. A straightforward Epistle Dedicatory[10] was placed before the preface and addressed to the Parliament (late

---

[9] Underhill, *Confessions of Faith*, 45.
[10] Given in full in Underhill, *ibid.*, 13 f.

in 1646). The following noble conclusion was also attached to it:

THE CONCLUSION

"Thus we desire to give unto Christ that which is his, and unto all lawfull Authority that which is their due, and to owe nothing to any man but love, to live quietly and peaceably, as it becometh Saints, endeavouring in all things to keep a good conscience, and to doe unto every man (of what judgement soever) as we would they should doe unto us, that as our practice is, so it may prove us to be a conscionable, quiet, and harmless people, (no ways dangerous or troublesome to human Society) and to labour and work with our hands, that we may not be chargeable to any, but to give to him that needeth both friends and enemies, accounting it more excellent to give than to receive. Also we confesse that we know but in part, and that we are ignorant of many things which we desire and seek to know: and if any shall doe us that friendly part to shew us from the word of God that we see not, we shall have cause to be thankfull to God and them. But if any man shall impose upon us anything that we see not to be commanded by our Lord Jesus Christ, we should in his strength, rather embrace all reproaches and tortures of men, to be stript of all outward comforts, and if it were possible, to die a thousand deaths, rather than to doe any thing against the least tittle of the truth of God, or against the light of our own consciences. And if any shall call what we have said Heresie, then doe we with the Apostle acknowledge, that after the way they call heresie, worship we the God of our Fathers, disclaiming all Heresie (rightly so called) because they are against Christ, and to be steadfast and immovable, always abounding in obedience to Christ, as knowing our labour shall not be in vain in the Lord.

Psalm 74.21,22.

Arise, O God, plead mine own cause. Remember how the foolish man blasphemeth thee daily.

O let not the oppressed returne ashamed, but let the poore and needy praise thy Name.

Come, Lord Jesus, come quickly.

FINIS

At length, on March 4, 1647, Parliament seems to have given a favorable reply to the appeal of the Baptists; legal toleration was granted them.[11]

11 Cramp. *Baptist History*, 276-277.

Shortly after the publication of the Second Edition, on November 30, 1646, Benjamin Cox published twenty-two articles in elaboration on some points of the Confession, or, as he called it, *An Appendix to a Confession of Faith.* These articles are characterized by an even higher Calvinism than the Second Edition. These Articles may never have been published with the Confession, but they found some immediate use.

Before a third and fourth edition of the Confession appeared in 1651 and 1652, respectively, the position of the Baptists as compared with that of 1646, was greatly altered. In the Army of Cromwell, Baptists had distinguished themselves and had risen to positions of leadership. Overnight they became a principal source of Cromwell's strength; and they found their new position in the military service greatly to their advantage. The Army proved to be an excellent medium for the spread of their principles. When the brief wars were over, Baptists were everywhere in prominent positions, and no longer lived in fear of King and Parliament. The Westminster Confession had appeared in 1646, and by comparing the London Confession with it men could see that Baptists indeed belonged to the mainstream of Reformed life.

There was by 1651 little danger of persecution by the State, but there had appeared a new kind of danger. George Fox had found the "Inward Light" in 1647, and Baptists at Mansfield were the first to share his experience and join in initiating the Quaker movement.[12] Quakerism had gathered its earliest following in North Lancashire, Westmoreland, and Cumberland, and from among Baptist churches. Some of its more ardent apostles were formerly Baptist pastors. Indeed, between the Baptist and the Quaker movements there was a most intimate kinship. While the General Baptists suffered more from inroads of the Quakers than did their Calvinistic brethren, the latter also were very conscious of the new danger which they faced. Moreover, rumor was flying about the provinces to the effect that all the Baptist churches of London had fallen away to Quakerism, though, as a matter of fact, Quakerism had made little impression on London by 1651. To correct this false impression and to reaffirm their faith to the world, London Particular Baptists prepared two new editions of their Confession which they termed "the third Impression corrected" and "the fourth

---

[12] Whitley, *History British Baptists*, p. 85.

Impression corrected." While these were substantially reprints of the 1646 Edition, the "Epistle Dedicatory" and the "Preface" were replaced by an "Epistle to the Reader." The Calvinism of Articles III and XXI was somewhat softened and the article on ministerial support was omitted, in deference to Quaker criticism. Also, indicating more directly the specific purpose of the new editions, there were appended eight pages addressed to:

> all the Churches of God sanctified in Jesus Christ, called to be saints, with all that in every place profess the name of Christ Jesus our Lord, both theirs and ours.

This was called *Heart-bleedings for Professors' Abominations.* Fox, in emphasizing the authority of the "Inner Light," appeared to have been depreciating the authority of the Scriptures, the atoning work of Christ, and the ordinances. In him liberty seemed to be running into license, and by his movement historical Christianity was being challenged. In "Heart-bleedings" the Baptists, therefore, made an earnest and powerful plea for biblical Christianity and against the views of the Quakers and Ranters. They denied that the Baptist movement naturally runs to such extremes, as some had been saying, and opposed the view that Baptists had indeed "gone up to a further attainment and light." The address closed with an urgent call to steadfastness in the faith. The fact that one edition was not enough to meet the need would indicate that the Confession found wide use over the country, and that it had important influence in the troubled times. The Preface shows that the new editions were called for by churches from many parts of the nation.

It was not at all uncommon for Baptist churches to be organized in the Army. Such a church appeared at Leith in Scotland in 1650, and it soon had some civilian members. Baptists in the Army in Scotland were both numerous and important, but they experienced a sense of isolation from the great body of their brethren in England. Therefore, to show their unity with London Baptists and to advertise their beliefs, they issued in Leith in March, 1653, a new edition of the Confession of 1644. It was a reprint of the 1651-52 editions, and it was called "The Fourth Impression, corrected." The Edition was introduced by a short letter "To the impartiall Reader," in which the errors and prejudices of the time were named as the provocation for publishing. "Quaker teachings" may have been chiefly in mind, as

McGlothlin[13] says, but some of the "prejudices of the time" against Baptists were probably more generally entertained in Scotland. Thomas Spencer, Abra. Holmes, Thomas Powell, and John Brady signed the Edition "in the name and by the appointment of the Church of Christ, usually meeting at Leith and Edinburgh."

In 1653 a "Fifth Impression Corrected" was issued by Henry Hills, London. Possibly there were yet other editions; certainly there were reprints, one in 1802 and another by the British Tract Society in 1847.

Perhaps no Confession of Faith has had so formative an influence on Baptist life as this one. Vedder calls it one of the chief landmarks of Baptist history. Harold Brown well says, "This significant document of 1644 embodies practically every doctrine that present-day Baptists hold dear, and is, therefore vastly important in Baptist history. . . ."[14] Its immediate value to Baptist life can hardly be overstated. Though issued in the name of London Baptists, it served Baptists all over the country at a time when the Particular Baptist stream was becoming the major stream of Baptist life. It certainly was one of the most effective bits of propaganda both for winning a toleration for Baptists and for winning converts to the Baptist position. By 1688, however, it had fallen into disuse, the Assembly of that year reporting that copies of it were exceedingly rare; but by that time it had entered the life stream of the Baptist movement.

Original copies of the 1644 version of the Confession may be found at the following places: Baptist College, Bristol; the Gould Collection, Oxford; the British Museum; the Bodleian Library, Oxford; Baptist College, Manchester; and Trinity College, Dublin. Copies of the 1646 Edition of this Confession may be found in the Gould Collection, the British Museum, the Bodleian Library, and Trinity College; one copy of the 1651 Edition is in the Gould Collection. One copy of the 1652 Edition is in the Midland Baptist College, Nottingham (Whitley, *A Baptist Bibliography*, 17). McGlothlin included the 1644 Edition, which appears below, in *Baptist Confessions of Faith*, and Underhill included the 1646 Edition in his work, *Confessions of Faith . . . of the Baptist Churches of England*.

---

[13] *Baptist Confessions of Faith*, 200.

[14] "The History of the Baptists in England to 1644," *The Chronicle*, Jan., 1945, p. 14.

* The

CONFESSION

OF FAITH,

Of those CHURCHES which are commonly (though falsly) cal led ANABAPTISTS;

Presented to the view of all that feare
GOD, to examine by the touchstone of the Word
of Truth: As likewise for the taking off those
aspersions which are frequently both in Pulpit and
Print, (although unjustly) cast upon them.

Acts 4. 20.

*Wee can not but speake the things which wee have seene
and heard.*

Isai. 8. 20.

*To the Law and to the testimony, if they speake not
according to | this Rule, it is because there is no light
in them.*

2 Cor. 1. 9, 10.

*But wee had the sentence of death in our selves, that
wee should not | trust in our selves, but in the living
God, which raiseth the dead; | who delivered us from so
great a death, and doth deliver, in whom | wee trust that
he will yet deliver.*

LONDON

Printed by *Matthew Simmons* in *Aldersgate-street.*

1644.

---

* Title page of edition of 1646 reads, "A Confession of Faith of † seven Congregations or Churches of Christ in London, which are commonly (but unjustly) called
Anabaptists. Published for the vindication of the Truth, and Information of the
ignorant; likewise for the taking off of those Aspersions which are frequently both
in Pulpit and Print unjustly cast upon them. The second Impression corrected and
enlarged. Published according to Order, 1646."

† For "seven," subsequent editions have "the severall."

To

ALL THAT DESIRE

The lifting up of the Name of the | Lord Jesus in sinceritie, the poore despi- | sed Churches of God in *London* send greeting, | with prayers for their farther increase in the | knowledge of Christ Jesus.

Wee question not but that it will seeme strange to many men, | that such as wee are frequently termed to be, lying under that | calumny and black brand of Heretickes, and sowers of di | vision as wee doo, should presume to appear so publickly as | now wee have done: But yet notwithstanding wee may well | say, to give answer to such, what David *said to his brother,|when the* Lords *battell was a fighting,* 1 Sam. 29. 30. *Is there not a cause? | Surely, if ever people had cause to speake for the vindication of the truth of |* Christ *in their hands, wee have, that being indeed the maine wheele at this | time that sets us aworke; for had any thing by men been transacted against | our persons onely, wee could quietly have sitten still, and committed our Cause to | him who is a righteous Judge, who will in the great day judge the secrets of | all mens hearts by Jesus Christ: But being it is not only us, but the truth pro | fessed by us, wee cannot, wee dare not but speake; it is no strange thing to any | observing man, what sad charges are laid, not onely by the world, that know | not God, but also by those that thinke themselves much wronged, if they be not | looked upon as the chiefe Worthies of the Church of God, and Watchmen of the | Citie: But it hath fared with us from them, as from the poor Spouse seeking | her Beloved,* Cant. 5. 6, 7. *They finding us out of that common road-way | themselves walke, have smote us and taken away our vaile, that so wee may by | them be recommended odious in the eyes of all that behold us, and in the hearts | of all that thinke upon us, which they have done both in Pulpit and Print, | charging us with*

holding *Free-will, Falling away from grace, denying
Origi | nall sinne, disclaiming of Magistracy, denying to
assist them either in persons | or purse in any of their
lawfull Commands, doing acts unseemly in the dispen |
sing the Ordinance of Baptism, not to be named amongst
Christians: All | which Charges wee disclaime as notor-
iously untrue, though by reason of these | calumnies cast
upon us, many that feare God are discouraged and fore-
stalled | in harbouring a good thought, either of us or
what wee professe; and many that | know not God
incouraged, if they can finde the place of our meeting, to
get | together in Clusters to stone us, as looking upon us
as a people holding such | things, as that wee are not
worthy to live: Wee have therefore for the cleering | of
the truth we professe, that it may be at libertie, though
wee be in bonds, | briefly published a Confession of our
Faith, as desiring all that feare God, seri | ously to con-
sider whether (if they compare what wee here say and
confesse in the | presence of the Lord Jesus and his
Saints) men have not with their tongues in | Pulpit, and
pens in Print, both spoken and written things that are
contrary to | truth; but wee know our God in his owne
time will cleere our Cause, and lift | up his Sonne to
make him the chiefe cornerstone, though he has been (or
now | should be) rejected of Master Builders. And be-
cause it may be conceived, that | what is here published,
may be but the Judgement of some one particular Con |
gregation, more refined then the rest; We doe therefore
here subscribe it, some | of each body in the name, and
by the appointment of seven Congregations, | who though
wee be distinct in respect of our particular bodies, for con-
veniency | sake, being as many as can well meete together
in one place, yet are all one in | Communion, holding
Jesus Christ to be our head and Lord; under whose go |
vernment wee desire alone to walke, in following the
Lambe wheresoever he | goeth; and wee beleeve the
Lord will daily cause truth more to appeare in the |
hearts of his Saints, and make them ashamed of their
folly in the Land of | their Nativitie, that so they may
with one shoulder, more studie to lift up the | Name of
the Lord Jesus, and stand for his appointments and*

Lawes; which | is the desires and prayers of the con-temned Churches of Christ in London *| for all Saints.*
Subscribed in the Names of seven Churches in *London.*

William Kiffin.
Thomas Patience.

John Mabbatt.

John Spilsbery.
George Tipping.
Samuel Richardson.

John Webb.
Thomas Killcop.

Thomas Skippard.
Thomas Munday.

Paul Hobson.
Thomas Goare.

Thomas Gunne.

Joseph Phelpes.
Edward Heath.

The
CONFESSION
Of FAITH, of those Churches
which are commonly (though falsly)
called ANABAPTISTS.

I.

THat GOD as he is in himselfe, cannot | be comprehended of any but himselfe, [1] dwelling in that inaccessible light, that no eye can attaine unto, whom never man saw, nor can see; that there is but [2] one God, one Christ, one Spirit, one Faith,| one Baptisme; [3] one Rule of holinesse and obedience for | all Saints, at all times, in all places to be observed.

[1] 1 Tim. 6 . 16.
[2] 1 Tim. 2 . 5.
Eph. 4 . 4, 5, 6.
1 Cor. 12 . 4, 5, 6, 13.
John 14. chap.
[3] 1 Tim. 6 . 3.
13, 14.
Gal. 1 . 8, 9.
2 Tim. 3 . 15.

II.

That God is [1] of himselfe, that is, neither from ano- | ther, nor of another, nor by another, nor for another: | [2] But is a Spirit, who as his being is of himselfe, so he | gives [3] being, moving, and preservation to all other | things, being in him-selfe eternall, most holy, every way | infinite in [4] greatnesse, wisdome, power, justice, goodnesse, | truth, &c. In this God-head, there is the Father, the | Sonne, and the Spirit; being every one of them one and | the same God; and therefore not

[1] Esa. 44 . 67
& 43 . 11.
& 46 . 9.
[2] John 4 . 24.
[3] Exod. 3 . 14.
[4] Rom. 11 . 36.
Act. 17 . 28

divided, but distingui- | shed one from another by their severall properties; the | [5] Father being from himselfe, the [6] Sonne of the Father | from everlasting, the holy [7] Spirit proceeding from the | Father and the Sonne.

[5] 1 Cor. 8 . 6.
[6] Pro. 8 . 22, 23
Heb. 1 . 3
John 1 . 18
[7] Joh. 15 . 16.
Gal. 4 . 6.

[Page 2]

III.

1 Esa. 46 . 10
Rom. 11 . 34,
35, 36
Mat. 10 . 29, 30
2 Eph. 1 , 11.

3 Col. 2 . 3.
4 Num. 23 . 19,
20.

5 Jere. 10 . 10.
Rom. 3 . 4.

That God hath [1] decreed in himselfe from everlasting | touching all things, effectually to work and dispose them | [2] according to the counsell of his owne will, to the glory | of his Name; in which decree appeareth his wisdome, con- | stancy, truth, and faithfulnesse; [3] Wisdome is that where- | by he contrives all things; [4] Constancy is that whereby | the decree of God remaines alwayes immutable; [5] Truth | is that whereby he declares that alone which he hath de- | creed, and though his sayings may seeme to sound some- | times another thing, yet the sense of them doth always | agree with the decree; [6] Faithfulnesse is that whereby he | effects that he hath decreed, as he hath decreed. And | touching his creature man, [7] God had in Christ before | the foundation of the world, according to the good plea- | sure of his will, foreordained some men to eternall life | through Jesus Christ, to the praise and glory of his | grace, [8] leaving the rest in their sinne to their just con- | demnation, to the praise of his Justice.

6 Esa. 44 . 10.
7 Eph. 1, 3, 4, 5,
6, 7.
2 Tim. 1 . 9.
Acts 13 . 48.
Rom. 8 . 29, 30.
8 Jude ver. 4.
& 6.
Rom. 9 . 11,
12, 13.
Prov. 16 . 4.

IV.

1 Gen. 1, chap.
Col. 1 . 16.
Heb. 11 . 3.
Esa. 45 . 12.
2 Gen. 1 . 26.
1 Cor. 15 . 45,
46
Eccles. 7 . 31.
3 Psal. 49 . 20.
4 Gen. 3 . 1 4, 5.)
2 Cor. 11 . 3.
5 2 Pet. 2 . 4.
Jude ver. 6.
Joh. 8 . 44
6 Gen. 3 . 1, 2, 6.
1 Tim. 2 . 14.
Eccles. 7 . 31.
Gal. 3 . 22.

[1] In the beginning God made all things very good, | created man after his own [2] Image and likenesse, filling | him with all perfection of all naturall excellency and up- | rightnesse, free from all sinne. [3] But long he abode not in | this honour, but by the [4] subtiltie of the Serpent, which | Satan used as his instrument, himselfe with his Angels | having sinned before, and not [5] kept their first estate, but | left their owne habitation; first [6] Eve, then Adam being | seduced did wittingly and willingly fall into disobedience | and transgression of the Commandement of their great | Creator, for the which death came upon all, and reigned | over all, so that all since the Fall are conceived in sinne, | and brought forth in iniquitie, and so by nature children | of wrath, and servants of sinne, subjects of [7] death, and all [Page 3] other calamities due to sinne in this world and for ever, | being considered in the state of nature, without relation | to Christ.

7 Rom. 5 . 12,
18, 19
& 6 . 23.
Eph. 2 . 3.
Rom. 5 . 12.

V.

All mankind being thus fallen, and become altogether | dead in sinnes and trespasses, and subject to the eternall | wrath of the great God by transgression; yet the elect, | which God hath [1] loved with an everlasting love, are [2] re- | deemed, quickened, and saved, not by themselves, neither | by their own workes, | lest any man should boast himselfe, | but wholly and onely by God of [3] his free grace and mer- | cie through Jesus Christ, who of God is made unto us | wisdome, righteousnesse, sanctification and re- | dempti | on, that as it is written, Hee that re- | joyceth, let him re- | joyce in the Lord.

[1] Jer. 31 . 2
[2] Gen. 3 . 15.
Eph. 1 . 3, 7.
& 2 . 4, 9.
1 Thess. 5 . 9.
[3] Acts 13 . 38
1 Cor. 1 . 30, 31.
2 Cor. 5 . 21.
Jer. 9 . 23, 24.

VI.

[1] This therefore is life eternall, to know the onely true | God, and whom he hath sent Jesus Christ. [2] And on the | contrary, the Lord will render vengeance in flaming fire | to them that know not God, and obey not the Gospel of | our Lord Jesus Christ.

[1] Joh. 17 . 3.
Heb. 5 . 9.
Jer. 23 . 5, 6.
[2] 2 Thess. 1 . 8.
Joh. 3 . 36.

VII.

The Rule of this Knowledge, Faith, and Obedi- | ence, | concerning the worship and service of God, and all other | Christian duties, is not mans inventions, opinions, devi- | ces, lawes, constitu- tions, or traditions unwritten whatso- | ever, but onely the word of God contained in the Cano- | nicall Scriptures.

Joh. 5 . 39
2 Tim. 3 . 15.
16, 17.
Col. 21 . 18, 23.
Matth. 15 . 9.

VIII.

In this written Word God hath plainly re- | vealed | whatsoever he hath thought needfull for us to know, be- | leeve, and acknowledge, touch- ing the Nature and Office | of Christ, in whom all the promises are Yea and Amen | to the praise of God.

Acts 3 . 22, 23
Heb. 1 . 1, 2
2 Tim. 3 , 15,
16, 17.
2 Cor. 1 . 20.

[Page 4]

IX.

[1] Gen. 3 . 15
& 22 . 18 &
49 . 10
Dan. 7 . 13 &
9 . 24, 25, 26
[2] Prov. 8 . 23
Joh. 1 . 1, 2, 3.
Col. 1 . 1, 15,
16, 17.
[3] Gal. 4 . 4
[4] Heb. 7 . 14
Rev. 5 . 5 with
Gen. 49 . 9, 10.

Touching the Lord Jesus, of whom [1] *Moses* and the | Prophets wrote, and whom the Apostles preached, is the | [2] Sonne of God the Father, the brightnesse of his glory, | the ingraven forme of his being, God with him and with | his holy Spirit, by whom he made the world, by whom | he upholds and governes all the workes hee hath made, | who also [3] when the fulnesse of time was come, was made | man of a [4] woman, of the Tribe of [5] *Judah,* of the seed of | *Abraham* and David,

Rom. 1 . 3. &
9 . 5
Mat. 1 . 16 with
Luke 3 . 23, 26.
Heb. 2 . 16
⁶ Esa. 53 . 3, 4, 5.
Phil. 2 . 8.

to wit, of *Mary* that blessed Vir- | gin, by the
holy Spirit comming upon her, and the power |
of the most High overshadowing her, and was
also in ⁶ all | things like unto us, sinne only
excepted.

X.

¹ 2 Tim. 2 . 15
Heb. 9 . 15.
Joh. 14 . 6

² Heb. 1 . 2. & 3.
1, 2 & 7 . 24.
Esa. 9 . 6, 7.
Acts 5 . 31.

Touching his Office, ¹ Jesus Christ onely is
made the | Mediator of the new Covenant, even
the everlasting Co- | venant of grace between
God and Man, to ² be perfectly | and fully the
Prophet, Priest and King of the Church of | God
for evermore.

XI.

¹ Prov. 8 . 23
Esa. 42 . 6 &
49 . 1, 5
² Esa. 11 . 2, 3,
4, 5, & 61 . 1, 2,
3 with Luk. 4.
17, 22.
Joh. 1 . 14, 16.
& 3 . 34.

Unto this Office hee was fore-ordained from
everla- | sting, by the ¹ authority of the Father,
and in respect of | his Manhood, from the womb
called and separated, and | ² anointed also most
fully and abundantly with all gifts | necessary,
God having without measure poured the Spi- |
rit upon him.

XII.

¹ Heb. 5 . 4, 5, 6.

² Esa. 53 . 10.

In this Call the Scripture holds forth two
speciall | things considerable; first, the call to
the Office; secondly, | the Office it self. First,
that ¹ none takes this honour but | he that is
called of God, as was *Aaron,* so also Christ, it |
being an action especially of God the Father,
whereby a | speciall covenant being made, hee
ordaines his Sonne to | this office: which Cove-
nant is, that ² Christ should be [Page 5] made a
Sacrifice for sinne, that hee shall see his seed, and
| prolong his dayes, and the pleasure of the Lord
shall | prosper in his hand; which calling there-
fore contains in | it selfe ³ chusing, ⁴ fore-ordain-
ing, ⁵ sending. Chusing re- | spects the end, fore-
ordaining the means, sending the ex- | ecution
it self, ⁶ all of meere grace, without any condi-
tion | fore-seen either in men, or in Christ him-
selfe.

³ Esa. 42 . 13
⁴ 1 Pet. 1 . 20
⁵ Joh. 3 . 17 &
9 . 27 & 10 . 36
Esa. 61 . 1.
⁶ Joh. 3 . 16
Rom. 8 . 32.

XIII.

So that this Office to be Mediator, that is, to be
Pro- | phet, Priest, and King of the Church of
God, is so proper | to Christ, as neither in the
whole, nor in any part there- | of, it can be trans-
ferred from him to any other.

1 Tim. 2 . 5.
Heb. 7 . 24
Dan. 5 . 14
Act. 4 . 12.
Luke 1 . 33.
Joh. 14 . 6.

XIV.

This Office it self to which Christ was called, is three- | fold, of [1] a Prophet, of [2] Priest, & of [3] a King: this num- | ber and order of Offices is shewed; first, by mens neeessi- | ties grievously labouring [4] under ignorance, by reason | whereof they stand in infinit necessity of the Prophetical | office of Christ to relieve them. Secondly, alien- ation from | God, wherein they stand in need of the Priestly Office to | reconcile them: Thirdly, our [6] utter disability to return | to him, by which they stand in need of the power of Christ | in his Kingly Office to assist and govern them.

[1] Deut. 18 . 15 with Acts 3 . 22, 23.
[2] Psal. 110 . 3.
Heb. 3 . 1. & 4 . 14. 15. & 5 . 6.
[3] Psal. 2 . 6.
[4] Acts 26 . 18.
Col. 1 . 3.
[5] Col. 1 . 21.
Eph. 2 . 12.
[6] Cant. 1 . 3.
Joh. 6 . 44.

XV.

Touching the Prophesie of Christ, it is that whereby | he hath [1] perfectly revealed the whole will of God out of | the bosome of the Father, that is needful for his servants [Page 6] to know, beleeve, and obey; and therefore is called not | onely a Prophet and [2] a Doctor, and the [3] Apostle of our profession, and the [4] Angel of the Covenant; but also the | very [5] wisdome of God, and [6] the treasures of wisdome | and understanding.

[1] Joh. 1 . 18 & 12 . 49, 50 & 15 & 17 . 8.
Deut. 18 . 15.

[2] Matth. 23 . 10.
[3] Heb. 3 . 1.
[4] Mal. 3 . 1.
[5] 1 Cor. 1 . 24.
[6] Col. 2 . 3.

XVI.

That he might be such a Prophet as thereby to be every | way compleat, it was necessary that he should bee [1] God, | and withall also that he should be man; for unlesse hee | had been God, he could never have perfectly understood | the will of God, [2] neither had he been able to reveale it | throughout all ages; and unlesse hee had been man, hee | could not fitly have unfolded it in his [3] own person to | man.*

[1] Joh. 1 . 18 & 3 . 13.

[2] 1 Cor. 2 . 11, 16.

[3] Acts 3 . 22 with Deut. 18 . 15.
Heb. 1 . 1.

XVII.

Touching his Priesthood, Christ [1] being consecrated, | hath appeared once to put away sinne by the offering and | sacrifice of himself, and to this end hath fully performed | and suffered all those things by which God, through the | blood of that his Crosse in an acceptable sacrifice, might | reconcile his elect onely; [2] and having broken downe the | partition wall, and therewith finished & removed all those | Rites, Shadowes, and Ceremonies, is now entred within | the Vaile,

[1] Joh. 17 . 19.
Heb. 5 . 7, 8, 9 & 9 . 26.
Rom. 5 . 19.
Eph. 5 . 12.
Col. 1 . 20.

[2] Eph. 2 . 14, 15, 16.
Rom. 8 . 34.

* Many additional Scriptural proofs of Christ's deity and his humanity were added to this article in subsequent editions.

into the Holy of Holiest, that is, to the very |
Heavens, and presence of God, where he for ever
liveth | and sitteth at the right hand of Majesty,
appearing before | the face of his Father to make
intercession for such as | come to the Throne of
Grace by that new and living way; | and not that
1 Pet. 2 . 5. onely, but [3] makes his people a spirituall | House,
Joh. 4 . 23, 24. an holy Priesthood, to offer up spirituall sacri-
[Page 7] fice acceptable to God through him; |
neither doth the | Father accept, or Christ offer
to the Father any other | worship or worship-
pers.

XVIII.

This Priesthood was not legall, or temporary,
but ac- | cording to the order [1] of *Melchi-* **1 Heb. 7 . 17.**
sedec; [2] not by a carnall | commandement, but by **2 Heb. 7 . 16.**
the power of an endlesse life; | [3] not by an order **3 Heb. 7 . 18, 19,**
that is weak and lame, but stable and per- | fect, **20, 21.**
not for a [4] time, but for ever, admitting no suc- **4 Heb. 7 . 24, 25**
cessor, | but perpetuall and proper to Christ, and
of him that ever | liveth. Christ himselfe was
the Priest, Sacrifice and Al- | tar: he was [5] Priest, **5 Heb. 5 . 6.**
according to both natures, hee was a | sacrifice
most properly according to his humane nature: |
[6] whence in the Scripture it is wont to be at- **6 Heb. 10 . 10.**
tributed to his | body, to his blood; yet the **1 Pet. 1 . 18, 19**
chiefe force whereby this sa- | crifice was made **Col. 1 . 20, 22.**
effectuall, did depend upon his [7] divine | nature, **Esa. 53 . 10.**
namely, that the Sonne of God did offer him- **Matth. 20 . 28.**
selfe | for us: he was the [8] Altar properly ac- **7 Act. 20 . 28.**
cording to his di- | vine nature, it belonging to **Rom. 8 . 3.**
the Altar to sanctifie that | which is offered upon **8 Heb. 9 . 14 &**
it, and so it ought to be of greater | dignity then **13 . 10, 12, 15,**
the Sacrifice it selfe. **Matth. 23 . 17**
Joh. 17 . 19.

XIX.

1 1 Cor. 15 . 4.
1 Pet. 3 . 21, 22,
Touching his Kingdome, [1] Christ being risen **Matth. 28 . 18, 19,**
from the | dead, ascended into heaven, sat on the **20.**
right hand of God | the Father, having all power **Luke 24 . 51.**
in heaven and earth, given | unto him, he doth **Acts 1 . 11 & 5 .**
spiritually govern his Church, exerci- | sing his **30, 31.**
power [2] over all Angels and Men, good and bad, | **John 19 . 36.**
to the preservation and salvation of the elect, **Rom. 14 . 17.**
to the over- | ruling and destruction of his ene- **2 Mark 1 . 27.**
3 John 5 . 26, 27. mies, which are Re- [Page 8] probates, [3] commu- **Heb. 1 . 14.**
Rom. 5 . 6, 7, 8 & nicating and applying the benefits, | vertue, and **Joh. 16 . 7, 15.**
14 . 17. fruit of his Prophesie and Priesthood to his |
Gal. 5 . 22, 23. elect, namely, to the subduing and taking away of
John 1 . 4, 13. their | sinnes, to their justification and adoption
of Sonnes, re- | generation, sanctification, preser-

L

vation and strengthe- | ning in all their conflicts against Satan, the World, the | Flesh, and the temptations of them, continually dwelling | in, governing and keeping their hearts in faith and

[4] John 13 . 1 &
10 . 28, 29 & 14.
16, 17.
Rom. 11 . 29.
Psal. 51 . 10, 11.
Job 33 . 29, 30.
2 Cor. 12 . 7, 9.

filiall | feare by his Spirit, which having [4] given it, he never takes | away from them, but by it still begets and nourisheth in | them faith, repentance, love, joy, hope, and all heaven- | ly light in the soule unto immortality, notwithstanding | through our own unbeliefe, and the temptations of Satan, | the sensible sight of this light and love be clouded and | overwhelmed for the time.

[5] Job 1. and 2. chap.
Rom. 1 . 21 &
2 . 4, 5, 6 & 9.
17, 18.
Eph. 4 . 17, 18.
2 Pet. 2. chap.

[5] And on the contrary, ruling | in the world over his enemies, Satan, and all the vessels of | wrath, limiting, using, restraining them by his mighty po- | wer, as seems good in his divine wisdome & justice to the | execution of his determinate counsell, delivering them | up to a reprobate mind, to be kept through their own de- | serts, in darknesse and sensuality unto judgement.*

'XX.

1 Cor. 15 . 24, 28.
Heb. 9 . 28
2 Thess. 1 . 9, 10.
1 Thess. 4 . 15, 16, 17.
John 17 . 21, 26.

This Kingdome shall be then fully perfected when hee | shall the second time come in glory to reigne amongst | his Saints, and to be admired of all them which doe be- | leeve, when he shall put downe all rule and authority un- | der his feet, that the glory of the Father may be full and | perfectly manifested in his Sonne, and the glory of the | Father and the Sonne in all his members.

[Page 9]
XXI.

That Christ Jesus by his death did bring forth salva- | tion and reconciliation onely for the [1] elect, which were | those which [2] God the Father gave him; & that the Gospel | which is to be preached to all men as the ground of faith, | is, that [3] Jesus is the Christ, the Sonne of the ever-blessed | God, filled with the perfection of all heavenly and spi- | rituall excellencies, and that salvation is onely and alone | to be had through the beleeving in his Name.

1 John 15 . 13.
Rom. 8 . 32, 33, 34.
Rom. 5 . 11 & 3 . 25.
[2] Job 17 . 2 with 6, 37.
[3] Matth. 16 . 16.
Luke 2 . 26.
Joh. 6 . 9 & 7, 3. & 20 . 31.
1 John 5 . 11.

XXII.

That Faith is the [1] gift of God wrought in the hearts | of the elect by the Spirit of God, whereby they come to | see, know, and beleeve the truth

1 Eph. 2 . 8.
Joh. 6 . 29 & 4. 10.
Phil. 1 . 29.
Gal. 5 . 22.

* This article was considerably shortened in subsequent editions.

of [2]the Scriptures, & not | onely so, but the
excellencie of them above all other wri- | tings
and things in the world, as they hold forth the
glory | of God in his attributes, the excellency
of Christ in his | nature and offices, and the
power of the fulnesse of the | Spirit in its work-
ings and operations; and thereupon | are inabled
to cast the weight of their soules upon this |
truth thus beleeved.

[2] Joh. 17 . 17.
Heb. 4 . 11, 12.
Joh. 6 . 63.

XXIII.

Those that have this pretious faith wrought
in them | by the Spirit, can never finally nor
totally fall away; and | though many stormes
and floods do arise and beat against | them, yet
they shall never be able to take them off that |
foundation and rock which by faith they are
fastened up- | on, but shall be kept by the power
of God to salvation, [Page 10] where they shall
enjoy their purchased possession, they | being
formerly engraven upon the palms of Gods hands.

Matth. 7 . 24, 25
John 13 . 1.
1 Pet. 1 . 4, 5, 6.
Esa. 49 . 13, 14,
15, 16.

XXIV.

That faith is ordinarily [1]begot by the preaching
of the | Gospel, or word of Christ, without re-
spect to [2]any | power or capacitie in the creature,
but it is wholly [3]pas- | sive, being dead in sinnes
and trespasses, doth beleeve, and | is converted
by no lesse power, [4]then that which raised |
Christ from the dead.

[1] Rom. 10 . 17.
1 Cor. 1 . 21.
[2] Rom. 9 . 16.
[3] Rom. 2 . 1, 2.
Ezek. 16 . 6.
Rom. 3 . 12.
[4] Rom. 1 . 16.
Eph. 1 . 19.
Col. 2 . 12.

XXV.

That the tenders of the Gospel to the conver-
sion of | sinners, [1]is absolutely free, no way
requiring, as absolute- | ly necessary, any quali-
fications, preparations, terrors of | the Law, or
preceding Ministry of the Law, but onely | and
alone the naked soule, as a [2]sinner and ungodly
to re- | ceive Christ, as crucified, dead, and
buried, and risen a- | gaine, being made [3]a Prince
and a Saviour for such sin- | ners.

[1] Joh. 3 . 14, 15|
& 1 . 12.
Esa. 55 . 1.
Joh. 7 . 37.
[2] 1 Tim. 1 . 15.
Rom. 4 . 5.
& 5 . 8.
[3] Act. 5 . 30, 31
& 2 . 36.
1 Cor. 1 . 22,
23, 24.

XXVI.

That the same power that converts to faith in
Christ, | the same power carries on the [1]soule
still through all du- | ties, temptations, conflicts,
sufferings, and continually | what ever a Chris-
tian is, he is by [2]grace, and by a con- | stant
renewed [3]operation from God, without which he |
cannot performe any dutie to God, or undergoe
any | temptations from Satan, the world, or men.

[1] 1 Pet. 1 . 5.
2 Cor. 12 . 9.
[2] 1 Cor. 15 . 10.
[3] Phil. 2 . 12, 13.
Joh. 15 . 5.
Gal. 19, 20.

XXVII.

That God the Father, and Sonne, and Spirit, is one [Page 11] with [1] all beleevers, in their [2] ful- | nesse, in [3] relations, [4] as | head and members, [5] as house and inhabitants, as [6] hus- | band and wife, one with him, as [7] light and love, and one | with him in his inheritance, and in all his [8] glory; and | that all beleevers by vertue of this union and one- | nesse | with God, are the adopted sonnes of God, and heires | with Christ, co-heires and joynt | heires with him of the | inheritance of all the promises of this life, and that which | is to come.*

[1] Thess. 1 . 1.
Joh. 14 . 10, 20.
　　& 17 . 21.
[2] Col. 2 . 9, 10.
　　& 1 . 19.
[3] Joh. 1 . 17.
Joh. 20 . 17.
Heb. 2 . 11.
[4] Col. 1 . 18
[5] Eph. 5 . 30.
Eph. 2 . 22
1 Cor. 3 . 16, 17.
[6] Esa. 16 . 5.
2 Cor. 11 . 3.
[7] Gal. 3 . 26.
[8] Joh. 17 . 24

XXVIII.

That those which have union with Christ, are justified | from all their sinnes, past, [1] present, and to come, by the | bloud of Christ; which justification wee conceive to be | a gracious and free [2] acquittance of a guiltie, sinfull crea- | ture, from all sin by God, through the satisfaction that | Christ hath made by his death; and this applyed in the | manifestation of it through faith.

[1] Joh. 1 . 7.
Heb. 10 . 14
　　& 9 . 26.
[2] Cor. 5 . 19.
Rom. 3 . 23.
[2] Acts 13 . 38,
　　39.
Rom. 5 . 1
　　& 3 . 25, 30.

XXIX.

That all beleevers are a holy and [1] sanctified people, | and that sanctification is a spirituall grace of the [2] new | Covenant, and effect of the [3] love of God, manifested | to the soule, whereby the beleever is in [4] truth and rea- | litie sepa- rated, both in soule and body, from all sinne and | dead workes, through the [5] bloud of the everlasting Co- | venant, whereby he also pres- seth after a heavenly and | Evangelicall perfec- tion, in obedience to all the Com- | mands, [6] which Christ as head and King in this new Co- | venant has prescribed to him.

[1] 1 Cor. 1 . 1
1 Pet. 2 . 9
[2] Eph. 1 . 4
[3] 1 Joh. 4 . 16.
[4] Eph. 4 . 24
[5] Phil. 3 . 15.
[6] Mat. 28 . 20.

XXX.

All beleevers through the knowledge of [1] that Justi- [Page 12] tification of life given by the Father, and brought forth | by the bloud of Christ, have this as their great privi- | ledge of that new [2] Covenant, peace with God, and re- | conciliation, whereby they that were afarre off, were | brought nigh by [3] that bloud, and have (as the Scripture | speaks) peace [4] passing all under-

[1] 2 Cor. 5 . 19.
Rom. 5 . 9, 10.
[2] Esa. 54 . 10
　　& 26 . 12.
[3] Eph. 2 . 13, 14.
[4] Phil. 4. 7.

* Considerably shortened in subsequent editions.

standing, yea, joy in God, | through our Lord
Jesus Christ, by [6] whom wee have re- | ceived the
Atonement.

[6] Rom. 5. 10, 11.

XXXI.

That all beleevers in the time of this life, are
in a con- | tinuall warfare, combate, and oppo-
sition against sinne, | selfe, the world, and the
Devill, and liable to all manner | of afflictions,
tribulations, and persecutions, and so | shall con-
tinue untill Christ comes in his Kingdome, | be-
ing predestinated and appointed thereunto; and
what- | soever the Saints, any of them doe
possesse or enjoy of | God in this life, is onely by
faith.*

Eph. 6. 10, 11, 12, 13,
2 Cor. 10. 3.
Rev. 2. 9, 10.

XXXII.

That the onely strength by which the Saints
are ina- | bled to incounter with all opposition,
and to overcome | all afflictions, temptations, per-
secutions, and tryalls, is | onely by Jesus Christ,
who is the Captain of their salva- | tion, being
made perfect through sufferings, who hath | in-
gaged his strength to assist them in all their
afflictions, | and to uphold them under all their
temptations, and to | preserve them by his power
to his ever- | lasting Kingdome.

Joh. 16. 33.

Heb. 2. 9, 10.

John 15. 5.

XXXIII.

That Christ hath here on earth a spirituall
Kingdome, [Page 13] which is the Church, which
he hath purchased and re- | deemed to himselfe,
as a peculiar inheritance: which | Church, as
it is visible to us, is a company of visible |
[1] Saints, [2] called & separated from the world, by
the word | and [3] Spirit of God, to the visible pro-
fession of the faith | of the Gospel, being bap-
tized into that faith, and joyned | to the Lord, and
each other, by mutuall agreement, in | the prac-
tical injoyment of the [4] Ordinances, commanded |
by Christ their head and King.

[1] Cor. 1. 1.
Eph. 1. 1.
[2] Rom. 1. 7.
Act. 26. 18
1 Thes. 1. 9.
2 Cor. 6. 17.
Rev. 18. 18.
[3] Acts 2. 37 with
Acts 10. 37.
[4] Rom. 10. 10.
Act. 20. 21.
Mat. 18. 19, 20.
Act. 2. 42.
1 Pet. 2. 5.

XXXIV.

To this Church he hath [1] made his promises,
and gi- | ven the signes of his Covenant, pres-
ence, love, blessing, | and protection: here are the
fountains and springs of his | heavenly grace

[1] Mat. 28. 18, 19, 20.
[2] Cor. 6. 18.

* Featley criticised this article as denying real ownership to any but
believers. The criticism was recognized in subsequent editions by adding
these words: " Outward and temporall things are lawfully enjoyed by a
civill right by them who have no faith."

continually flowing forth; [2] thither ought | all men
to come, of all estates, that acknowledge him to |
be their Prophet, Priest, and King, to be in-
rolled amongst | his houshold servants, to be
under his heavenly conduct | and government,
to lead their lives in his walled sheep- | fold,
and watered garden, to have communion here
with | the Saints, that they may be made to be
partakers of their | inheritance in the Kingdome
of God.

[2] Esa. 8 . 16.
1 Tim. 3 . 15.
    & 4 . 16.
    & 6 . 3, 5.
Acts 2 . 41, 47
Song. 4 . 12.
Gal. 6 . 10.
Eph. 2 . 19.

XXXV.

And all his servants are called thither, to
present their | bodies and soules, and to bring
their gifts God hath gi- | ven them; so being
come, they are here by himselfe be- | stowed in
their severall order, peculiar place, due use, be- |
ing fitly compact and knit together, according to
the ef- | fectuall working of every part, to the
edification of it | selfe in love.

1 Cor. 12 . 6, 7,
   12, 18.
Rom. 12 . 4, 5, 6.
1 Pet. 4 . 10.
Eph. 4 . 16.
Col. 2 . 5, 6, 19.
1 Cor. 12 . 12
  to the end.

[Page 14]

XXXVI.

That being thus joyned, every Church has
[1] power gi- | ven them from Christ for their
better well-being, to | choose to themselves meet
persons into the office of | [2] Pastors, Teachers(a),
Elders, Deacons, being qualified ac- | cording to
the Word, as those which Christ has appoin- |
ted in his Testament, for the feeding, governing,
serving, | and building up of his Church, and that
none other have | power to impose them, either
these or any other.

[1] Acts 1 . 2.
   & 6 . 3.
  with 15. 22,25
1 Cor. 16 . 3.
[2] Rom. 12 . 7, 8
   & 16 . 1.
1 Cor. 12 . 8, 28
1 Tim. 3. chap.
Heb. 13 . 7.
1 Pet. 5 . 1, 2, 3.

XXXVII.

That the Ministers aforesaid, lawfully called
by the | Church, where they are to administer,
ought to conti- | nue in their calling, according
to Gods Ordinance, and | carefully to feed the
flock of Christ committed to them, | not for
filthy lucre, but of a ready mind.

Heb. 5 . 4.
Acts 4 . 23.
1 Tim. 4 . 14.
Joh. 10 . 3, 4.
Acts 20 . 28.
Rom. 12 . 7, 8.
Heb. 13 . 7, 17.

(b)XXXVIII.

That the due maintenance of the Officers afore-
said, | should be the free and voluntary com-
munication of the | Church, that according to
Christs Ordinance, they that | preach the Gospel,
should live on the Gospel and not by | con-

1 Cor. 9 . 7, 14.
Gal. 6 . 6.
1 Thes. 5 . 13.
1 Tim. 5 . 17,
  18.

(a) " Pastors " and " teachers " are omitted in later editions.
(b) The final clause, beginning "and not by constraint," was criticised
by Featley and consequently omitted in the edition of 1646. The entire
article was omitted from the editions of 1651 and 1652, probably owing to
Quaker influence.

Phil. 4 . 15, 16.   straint to be compelled from the people by a
forced | Law.

XXXIX.

Mat. 28 . 18, 19.   That Baptisme is an Ordinance of the new
Mark 16 . 16.   Testament, | given by Christ, to be dispensed(a)
onely upon persons pro- [Page 15] fessing faith, Acts 2 . 37, 38
or that are Disciples, or taught, who upon | a   & 8 . 36, 37, 38
[1] profession of faith, ought to be baptized.(b)   & 18 . 8.

XL.

The way and manner of the [1] dispensing of this   The word
Ordi- | nance (c) the Scripture holds out to be   *Baptizo*, signi-
dipping or plung- | ing the whole body under   under water,
water: it being a signe, must an- | swer the thing   yet so as with
signified, which are these: first, the [2] wash- | ing   convenient
the whole soule in the bloud of Christ: Second-   upon the ad-
ly, | that interest the Saints have in the [3] death,   ministrator
buriall, and re- | surrection; thirdly, together   with all mo-
with a [4] confirmation of our | faith, that as cer-   destie. (d)
tainly as the body is buried under water, | and [1] Mat. 3 , 16.
riseth againe, so certainly shall the bodies of the | Joh. 3 . 23.
Saints be raised by the power of Christ, in the [2] Rev. 1 . 5
day of the | resurrection, to reigne with Christ.   & 7 . 14.
                                          with Heb. 10,
                                          22.
XLI.   [3] Rom. 6 . 3, 4, 5,
                                       [4] 1 Cor. 15 .
The persons designed by Christ, to dispense   28, 29.
this Or- | dinance, the [1] Scriptures hold forth to [1] Esa. 8 . 16.
be a(e) preaching | Disciple, it being no where   Mat. 28 . 16, 17,
tyed to a particular Church, | Officer, or person   18, 19.
extraordinarily sent, the Commission | injoyning   Acts 20 . 7.
the administration, being given to them under | Mat. 26 . 26.
no other consideration, but as considered Dis-
ciples.

(a) Featley declared this article would not be objectionable if the word
only were omitted, and again strangely enough it was omitted in subsequent editions.

(b) Later editions added, " and after to partake of the Lord's Supper."

(c) In criticising this article, Doctor Featley denied that the Scripture defines baptism as an immersion, and in subsequent editions the phrase, " the
Scripture holds out to be," is omitted, as well as the words " first, the
washing the whole soule in the bloud of Christ." To the words " death,
buriall, and resurrection " are added " of Christ " in later editions.

(d) Editions 1651 and 1652 add " which is also our practice, as many eye
witnesses can testifie."

(e) Doctor Featley ridiculed the expression " preaching Disciple," and in
later editions " preaching " is omitted, and the words " being men able to
preach the Gospel " are added at the end of the article. " Church, Officer "
is changed into " Church-officer " in later editions, as it appears in Doctor
Featley.

XLII.

Christ has likewise given power to his whole Church | to receive in and cast out, by way of Excommunication, | any member; and this power is given to every particular | Congregation, and not one particular person, either | member or Officer, but the whole.

Acts 2 . 47.
Rom. 16 . 2.
Math. 18 . 17.
1 Cor. 5 . 4
2 Cor. 2 . 6, 7, 8.

[Page 16]

XLIII.

Mat. 18 . 16,
17, 18.
Act. 11 . 2, 3.
1 Tim. 5 . 19,
20, 21.

And every particular member of each Church, how | excellent, great, or learned soever, ought to be subject to | this censure and judgement of Christ; and the Church | ought with great care and tendernesse, with due advice | to proceed against her members.

XLIV.

1 Acts 20 . 27,
28.
Heb. 13 . 17, 24.
Mat. 24 . 25.
1 Thes. 5 . 14.
2 Mark 13.
34, 37.
Gal. 6 . 1.
1 Thes. 5 . 11.
Jude ver. 3, 20.
Heb. 10 . 34, 35.
& 12 . 15.

And as Christ for the [1]keeping of this Church in holy | and orderly Communion, placeth some speciall men | over the Church, who by their office are to governe, o- | versee, visit, watch; so likewise for the better keeping | thereof in all places, by the members, he hath given [2]au- | thoritie, and laid dutie upon all, to watch over one ano | ther.

XLV.

1 Cor. 14. cha.
Rom. 12 . 6.
1 Pet. 4 . 10, 11.
1 Cor. 12 . 7.
1 Thes. 5 . 17,
18, 19.

That also such to whom God hath given gifts, being | tryed in the Church, may and ought by the appointment | of the Congregation, to pro- | phesie, according to the pro- | portion of faith, and so teach publickly the Word of | God, for the edification, exhortation, and comfort of | the Church.

XLVI.

Rev. 2. & 3,
Chapters
Acts 15 . 12.
1 Cor. 1 . 10.
Ephef. 2 . 16.
& 3 . 15, 16.
Heb. 10 . 25.
Jude ver. 15.
Matth. 18 . 17.
1 Cor. 5 . 4, 5.

Thus being rightly gathered, established, and still pro- | ceeding in Christian communion, and obedience of the | Gospel of Christ, none ought to separate for faults and | corruptions, which may, and as long as the Church con- | sists of men subject to failings, will fall out and arise a- | mongst them, even in true constituted Churches, untill | they have in due order sought redresse thereof.

[Page 17]

XLVII.

And although the particular Congregations be distinct | and severall Bodies, every one a compact and knit Ci- | tie in it selfe; yet are they

1 Cor. 4 . 17,
& 14 . 33, 36.
& 16 . 1.
Matth. 28 . 20.

all to walk by one and the same | Rule, and by
all meanes convenient to have the counsell | and
help one of another in all needfull affaires of the |
Church, as members of one body in the common
faith | under Christ their onely head.

1 Tim. 3 . 15.
& 6 . 13, 14.
Rev. 22 . 18, 19.
Col. 2 . 6, 19,
& 4 . 16.

XLVIII.

That a civill Magistracie is an ordinance of
God set up | by God for the punishment of
evill doers, and for the | praise of them that doe
well; and that in all lawfull things | commanded
by them, subjection ought to be given by us |
in the Lord: and that we are to make supplica-
tion and | prayer for Kings, and all that are in
authority, that under | them we may live a peace-
able and quiet life in all godliness | and honesty.

Rom. 13 . 1, 2, 3, 4.
1 Pet. 2 . 13, 14.
1 Tim. 2 . 2.

*XLIX.

The supreme Magistracie of this Kingdome we
beleeve | to be the King and Parliament freely
chosen by the King- | dome, and that in all those
civill Lawes which have been | acted by them, or
for the present is or shall be ordained, | we are
bound to yeeld subjection and obedience unto in |
the Lord, as conceiving our selves bound to de-
fend both | the persons of those thus chosen, and
all civill Lawes | made by them, with our per-
sons, liberties, and estates, with | all that is
called ours, although we should suffer never so |
much from them in not actively submitting to
some Ec- | clesiasticall Lawes, which might be
conceived by them to [Page 18] be their duties to
establish which we for the present could | not
see, nor our consciences could submit unto; yet
are | we bound to yeeld our persons to their
pleasures.

L.

And if God should provide such a mercie for
us, as to | incline the Magistrates hearts so far
to tender our con- | sciences, as that we might
bee protected by them from | wrong, injury, op-
pression and molestation, which long we | for-
merly have groaned under by the tyranny and op-

1 Tim. 1 . 2, 3, 4.
Psal. 126 . 1.
Acts 9 . 31.

* Articles XLIX and L, somewhat modified, are in the second edition
added as a note to Art. XLVIII. Art. LI then becomes XLIX. An Art. L
is added, expressing the lawfulness of oaths and of a Christian's holding
civil office; Art. LII becomes LI, and a final Art. LII on the resurrection is
added. All references to the king and Parliament are omitted from editions of 1651 and 1652 when Cromwell was in control of affairs.

pres- | sion of the Prelaticall Hierarchy, which God through | mercy hath made this present King and Parliament won- | derfull honourable, as an instrument in his hand, to throw | downe; and we thereby have had some breathing time, | we shall, we hope, look at it as a mercy beyond our expe- | ctation, and conceive our selves further engaged for ever | to blesse God for it.

LI.

[1] Acts 2 . 40, 41. & 4 . 19, & 5 . 28, 29, 41. & 20 . 23. 1 Thess. 3 . 3. Phil. 1 . 27, 28, 29. Dan. 3 . 16, 17. & 6 . 7, 10, 22, 23.

But if God with-hold the Magistrates allow- ance and | furtherance herein; [1] yet we must notwithstanding pro- | ceed together in Christian communion, not daring to give | place to suspend our practice, but to walk in obedience to | Christ in the profession and holding forth this faith be- | fore mentioned, even in the midst of all trialls and affli- | ctions, not accounting our goods,

[2] Matth. 28 . 18, 19, 20. 1 Tim. 6 . 13, 14, 15. Rom. 12 . 1, 8. 1 Cor. 14 . 37. 2 Tim. 4 . 7, 8. Rev. 2 . 10. Gal. 2 . 4, 5.

lands, wives, children, | fathers, mothers, brethren, sisters, yea, and our own lives | dear unto us, so we mag finish our course with joy: re- | membering alwayes we ought to [2] obey God rather then | men, and grounding upon the commandement, commissi- | on and promise of our Lord and master Jesus Christ, who [Page 19] as he hath all power in heaven and earth, so also hath pro- |mised, if we keep his commandements which he hath gi- | ven us, to be with us to the end of the world: and when we | have finished our course, and kept the faith, to give us the | crowne of righteousnesse, which is laid up for all that | love his appearing, and to whom we must give an account | of all our actions, no man being able to discharge us of | the same.

LII.

And likewise unto all men is to be given whatsoever is | their due; tributes, customes, and all such lawful duties, | ought willingly to bee by us paid and performed, our | lands, goods, and bodies, to submit to the Magistrate in | the Lord, and the Magistrate every way to bee acknow- | ledged, reverenced, and obeyed, according to godlinesse; | not because of wrath onely but for conscience sake. And | finally, all men so to be esteemed and regarded, as is due | and meet for their place, age, estate and condition.

Rom. 13 . 5, 6. 7. Matth. 22 . 21. Titus 3. 1 Pet. 2 . 13. Ephes. 5 . 21, 22. & 6 . 1, 9. 1 Pet. 5 . 5.

LII [sic].

And thus wee desire to give unto God that which is | Gods, and unto *Cesar* that which is

Matth. 22 . 21. Acts 24 . 14, 15, 16.

Cesars, and unto all | men that which belongeth John 5.28.
unto them, endevouring our | selves to have al- 2 Cor. 4.17.
wayes a cleare conscience void of offence | 1 Tim. 6.3, 4, 5.
towards God, and towards man. And if any take 1 Cor. 15.58, 59.
this that | we have said, to be heresie, then doe
wee with the Apostle | freely confesse, that after
the way which they call heresie, | worship we the
God of our Fathers, beleeving all things | which
are written in the Law and in the Prophets and
A- | postles, desiring from our soules to dis-
claime all heresies [Page 20] and opinions which
are not after Christ, and to be sted- | fast, unmo-
veable, alwayes abounding in the worke of the |
Lord, as knowing our labour shall not be in vain
in the | Lord.

1 Cor. 1. 24.

*Not that we have dominion over your faith, but
are helpers of | your joy: for by faith we stand.*

FINIS

Regarding one of the notable signers of the London Confession,
Isaac Backus says:

> Mr. Hanserd Knollys was a minister in the church of England
> for nine years, and then he was so cruelly persecuted therein,
> that he came over to Boston in the spring of 1638; but their
> rulers called him an Antinomian, and would not suffer him
> there; therefore he went to Dover on Piscataqua river, where
> he preached near four years, and then returned to England, and
> arrived in London in December, 1641. As the war broke out
> there the next year, liberty for various opinions was caused
> thereby, and he became a Baptist, and gathered a church in
> London, where he often had a thousand hearers. He baptized
> Mr. Henry Jessy, an eminent minister in that city, and was one
> who signed the Baptist confession of faith in 1643 [1644?]. . . .
> Mr. Knollys continued a faithful pastor of his church in London,
> through great changes and sufferings, until he died in peace,
> September 19, 1691, aged 93 years.

[Isaac Backus, *Church History of New England from 1620 to 1804.*
Baptist Tract Depository. Philadelphia, 1839.]

B. The Faith and Practice of Thirty Congregations, 1651

The Baptist confessions of faith which appeared during the period
of the Commonwealth (1650-59) were closely connected with the

association movement, and they often served as its unifying instruments. The period was more productive of Confessions than any similar period of Baptist history. Formal associationalism was primarily the result of a native Baptist connectional instinct (for Baptists were never independents, strictly speaking) and of expediency in view of the tasks to be undertaken. Political events hastened the development; military and political organization followed associational patterns. A new sense of liberty challenged the nation early in the sixth decade, and the churches, for the first time, had full freedom to associate. Before 1660 permanent Associations had become typical Baptist institutions.

In the Commonwealth Period, the Midlands was a principal area of Baptist strength. As far as General Baptists are concerned, Lincolnshire seems to have been their leading county, with Leicestershire close behind. It is not surprising, then, that the first General Baptist Association should gather about Leicester because of its central location in the Midlands. An associational meeting was held in 1651, probably at Leicester, but it is not certain that this was the first such meeting of the churches. Messengers for both special and constant work were appointed and there was agreement on sharing the needs of the poor. Thirty churches from an area one hundred miles long and twenty-four miles wide were represented at the meeting, each by two messengers or delegates.[15]

Probably the most important thing done in the meeting of 1651 was the adoption of a Confession called *The Faith and Practice of Thirty Congregations, Gathered According to the Primitive Pattern*. The introductory statement implies that local opponents were active, but who they were is not specified. One would expect the usual Church of England and Calvinistic Separatist critics to be involved, and in addition the Quakers and Seekers. There is no direct evidence that any of the early Quaker leaders labored among these particular churches. However, George Fox had gathered his first followers among Nottinghamshire General Baptists in 1647, and soon after he was preaching with great success in a General Baptist church at Broughton, on the borders of Leicestershire and Nottinghamshire.[16] From that time his preaching attracted much attention, and Quakers began to multiply in the North Midlands.

---

[15]Whitley, *History British Baptists*, 89.

The Confession is important because it is the first General Baptist statement representing the views of more than one church, rather than because of the prominence of its author or signatories. It shows essential agreement with the first General Baptist Confession (1611). The first forty-five articles concern the doctrines of the churches; the remaining thirty demonstrate their practices. No consistently Arminian system is revealed; rather, some traditional emphases of Calvinism are set forth. Article 21 seems to follow the statement in John Smyth's one hundred *Propositions and Conclusions*. The doctrine of free will is repudiated in Article 25. Articles 4 through 16 present a pioneer statement of the Baptist doctrine of soul competency. Though deficient in polish, the statement is unmistakable in meaning.

Article 48 contains an evident reference to immersion, though the term is not used. Articles 45 and 75 appear to be directed at the Quakers, while the emphasis in Articles 60 and 61 on the ministry may be credited, partly, to the cavils of the Quakers. The "Postscript," having to do with the "Magistratical power," may have been suggested by the statement of the London Confession on that subject, but there may have been some feeling that an article on magistracy was out of place in a confession of faith and practice.

Adoption of the Confession drew the churches closer together, giving them a greater sense of unity and strength. The confession was soon known beyond the Midlands. A group of London Baptists mentioned it in a petition of 1651 to Parliament asking that an ordinance of 1648 for punishing blasphemies and heresies be declared null and void.[16] The Midland churches were commended in the petition upon putting out their Confession. Two original copies of the Confession of 1651 are known to be extant: one in the Angus Library, Regent's Park College, Oxford, and the other in the Gould Collection. McGlothlin offers a copy in *Baptist Confessions of Faith*, 95-109, which follows a facsimile reprint of the original made by John Taylor of Northampton. This copy is reproduced here.

[16] Emmott, *A Short History of Quakerism*, 86.

[17] *The Petition of divers gathered churches . . . about the city of London, for declaring the ordinance of the Lords & Commons, for publishing blasphemies and heresies, null and void*, 3-4.

THE

FAITH

AND

PRACTISE

OF THIRTY

CONGREGATIONS,

GATHERED ACCORDING TO THE

PRIMITIVE PATTERN.

Published (in love) by consent of two from
each Congregation, appointed for that purpose.
1. To inform those who have a desire to know what
Religious Duties they hold forth.
2. To undecieve those that are mis-informed thereof.
3. To the end that the said Congregations may in love,
and the spirit of Meekness, be informed by any
that conceive they walk amiss.

Rom. 12. 18. *If it be possible, as much as in you is,
have Peace with all men.*

London, Printed by *J. M. for Will. Larnar,*
at the Blackmore neer *Fleet-bridge,* 1651.

To all the Saints and Churches of God,
   who walk according to the commands
   of Jesus Christ, in *England, Wales,
   Army,* or else-where.

Dearly Beloved, and Fellow Citizens
of the household of God, Grace,
Mercy, and Peace be multiplyed
unto you from God, through Jesus
Christ; The Lord preserve your
minds and hearts by his holy Spirit, with all
those gifts of his Free Grace which he hath
bestowed upon you, to adorn the doctrine of
the Gospel in every thing whereunto ye are
called, to live to the glory and praise of his
Grace.

Loving Brethren, if we could have conveniently convayed this Copie unto your
hands before it went to the Press, doubtless
we might have gained your Christian Advice and Assistance herein, which might
have been very Beneficial to the Truth,
wherein you are with us alike concerned and
engaged; but by reason of the distance of
place, and also being unacquainted, hath
hindred our sending; but we hope our for-
wardness herein will not be any hinderance
to you for the future, to manifest your concurrence with us, so far as we own the
Truth; for the preserving our Union with
God, and our Joy and Peace with each
other, but the rather to give you occasion to
make use of the Ability and Power God
hath betrusted you with, for our Informati-
ons in what you judge is wanting, and for
our further Confirmation and Encouragement in those things you approve of with us,
have we published this ensuing Treatise;
That so we may agree with love in peace and
truth, by the Assistance of our blessed Lord

and Saviour Jesus Christ. So with our
Prayers, we subscribe our selves
> Your Servants in the Lord.
[Signatures of its sixty-one authors here.]

The Faith and Practise of
Thirty Congregations

Ezek. 43. 11.

*And if they be ashamed of all that they
have done, show them the form of the house,
and the fashion thereof, and the goings out
thereof, and the comings in thereof, and all
the forms thereof, and all the ordinances
thereof, and all the laws thereof; and write
it in their sight, that they may keep the whole
form thereof, and all the ordinances thereof,
and do them.*

Matth. 5. 16.
Let your light so shine before men, &c.

Hebr. 3. 6.
But Christ as a Son, over his own &c.

1. That that God whom we acknowledge, ought to be worshipped by
all, and above all that are called
Gods, and he is Infinite in power and
wisdom, universal, invisible, eternal. *Ps.* 96.
3. 4. *Ier.* 23. 24. *Col.* 1. 17. *Rom.* 1. 20.

2. That God created all creatures visible and invisible, by his own wisdome and
power, *Col.* 1. 16. *Ier.* 10. 12.

3. That God preserveth all creatures
which are in being. *Nehemiah.* 9. 6. *Rom.* 11. 36.

4. That the creation doth plainly declare the Power and Righteousness of
God; *Rom.* 1. 20. *Isa.* 40. 26.

5. That God commandeth men to take
a view of his Wise, Powerful, and Righteous workes of creation. *Isa.* 40. 26.

6. That God by his good creatures

called or calleth men to a serious consideration, or meditation, that they may further understand his Wisdom and Power. *Rom.* I. 20.

7. That God doth command men to speak or declare that which they have learned by the teaching of the creatures; *Psal.* 145. 5.

8. That the consideration of the Lord's handyworks in creatures, is a means to beget thoughts of God, and of our selves, sutable to his greatness, and our inferiority; *Psal.* 8. 3, 4.

9. That whatsoever good Meditations, or serious Considerations we have of the glorious works of Creation, ought to break forth with admiration unto thankfulness to God, *Psal.* 136. *from ver. 3. to ver. 9.*

10. That those who did refuse to worship or glorifie God answerably to the teaching of the Creation, the Lord gave them over, or forsook them so far, that they became so desperately wicked, that they did things contrary to nature, *Rom.* I. 26, 27.

11. God created or made *Adam* a living soul, and in his own Likeness in Soveraignty or Dominion; *Gen.* I. 26. 27.

12. That God gave unto *Adam* Lawes or commands, that he might know his Will; *Gen.* 2. 16. 17.

13. That God declared unto *Adam* what penalty or punishment he would cause to befall him, if he disobeyed his Will, *Gen.* 2. 17.

14. That *Adam* did sin or disobey the righteous commands of the Lord, *Gen.* 3. 6.

15. That God told *Adam* very plainly what death it should be that he would cause to come on him, and what sorrows should attend him in the meanwhile; *Gen.* 3. 17, 19.

M

16. That all mankind are liable to partake of the same death or punishment which the Lord in his righteous judgment caused to fall on *Adam* for his transgression; *Rom.* 5. 18.

17. That *Jesus Christ,* through (or by) the grace of God, suffered death for all mankind, or every man; *Heb.* 2. 9.

18. That *Christ Jesus,* the second *Adam,* will as certainly raise all mankind from that death which fell on them, through or by the first *Adam's* sin or offence, as surely as they partake of it; *Rom.* 5. 18.

19. That *Jesus Christ,* his Lordly or Kingly preheminence over all mankind, is vindicated or maintained in the Scriptures account, by vertue of his dying or suffering for them; *Rom.* 14. 9.

20. That God's Word, Son, or Spirit, are one, 1 *Ioh.* 5. 7. *Jude* 1. *Heb.* 10. 29. *Rom.* 15. 16.

God and his Word are one; *Ioh.* 1. 1. The Word quickneth, *Psal.* 119. 50. The Son quickeneth, *Eph.* 2. 1. And the spirit quickneth Ioh. 6. 63. So they are one. God giveth Gifts, and the Son doth the same, also the holy Ghost, So they are one. *Iam.* 1. 71. *Eph.* 4. 10, 11. *Acts* 2. 38. 1. *Thes.* 1. 5. *Ioh.* 6. 44. *Io.* 14. 6. *Eph.* 1. 18. 1 *Cor.* 12. 3. *Math.* 10. 40. *Gal.* 3. 2.

21. That the Lord of all mankind, *Jesus Christ,* hath the power of giving Lawes for the governing or ruling every man in the World in spiritual worship, *Isa.* 9. 6, 7. *Math.* 28. 18. 19, 20.

22. That this Prince of Peace, *Jesus Christ,* is the only or principal high Priest, which offered up sacrifice, or made reconciliation for the Sins of the people, *Heb.* 2. 17.

23. That the high Priest *Jesus Christ,*

is not onely King or Governour, but also
the Apostle or Prophet of the Truth professed, or the true profession of Saints
Heb. 3. 1.

24. That all the riches appertaining to
a spiritual and eternal life, were treasured up
in *Jesus Christ. Col.* 2. 3.

25. That there is not, neither ever was
any man endued with any abilities and
power to do the revealed will of God, but
it was given him from above. *Iam.* 1. 17.

26. That the gifts of God spring from
the pleasure of his will, or of his free grace;
even the Lord *Jesus Christ* sprung from
thence, from whom commeth all spiritual
mercies: *Rom.* 8. 32. *Heb.* 2. 9.

27. That *Iesus Christ* was faithfull in
all things whereunto he was appointed,
Heb. 3. 1, 2.

28. That *Iesus Christ* was not only the
Lawmaker, but the Law giver to every
man that liveth in the world, in that he
giveth every man therein some measure of
light. *Io.* 1. 9.

29. That God of his free love giveth
several gifts unto men, dividing severally as
it pleaseth him, by one and the same spirit;
1 *Cor.* 12. 11. *Eph.* 4. 7.

30. That the gifts of God given unto
men of his own free grace, though never so
richly they may be furnished both with abilities
and power, yet those gifts of grace do not
demonstrate, or declare them to be faithfull
servants; but it doth very plainly prove,
that they are called upon thereby to be
faithfull Servants; 1 *Cor.* 4. 1. 2.

31. That those gifts which God of his
free grace gives unto men to the enabling or
impowering them to obey or believe in his
name, are called the grace of God, as they

spring from the spirit of grace; *Acts.* 18.
17.

32. That when God of his own boun-
tifulness hath given gifts unto men to be
improved by them to the praise of his grace,
as to believe or obey, then those so endued
are Stewards of the grace of God, 1 *Pet.*
4. 10.

33. That God requireth or commandeth service of men, answerable to those gifts
of grace which he of his good pleasure
hath bestowed upon them, *Col.* 2. 6.
Ioh. 12. 37.

34. That it is the gracious pleasure of
God, that *Iesus Christ* his life, death, and
resurrection, should be made known unto
men, and by men, as arguments, or motives,
to allure or provoke them to live holy and
righteous in this present world; *Eph.* 5. 1. 2.
Rom. 6. 4, to *ver.* 14.

35. That God requireth that man
should worship him in Spirit and in truth, or
with all the heart, before they outwardly
make a profession of him: *Acts* 8. 36. 37.

36. That all actions performed by
man towards God, ought to flow from a
principle of Love; 1. *Cor.* 13. 1, 2, 3.

37. That God loves man first, and de-
clareth, or maketh known his love to men,
before any man can Act from a principle of
love in obedience to him, *Io.* 15. 16.

38. That whosoever obeyeth God
with those gifts of his free grace, (as a-
bilities and power to do his will) never so
faithfully, Evangelically, or Unfainedly,
giving him the glory of those performances;
yet thus believing or obeying doth not procure salvation as eternal life, neither are they
any cause at all to move God to bestow it;
Ezek. 16. from *ver.* 3. to *ver,* 10.
Eph. 2. 9.   *Rom.* 4. 2.   *Jo.* 15. 15.

39. That the ground or principal end
of mens believing or obeying God, ought
to be for the advancing of the glory of
God, or for the Praise of his free grace;
1. *Cor. 6.* 19, 20.

40. That those who serve or fear the
Lord, honouring or glorifying him with his
gifts bestowed on them, to the praise of his
free grace, do demonstratively of openly
manifest themselves to be his faithful servants, or children, 1. *Io. 3.* 10. Acts
10. 35.

41. That those which serve the Lord
with integrity of mind and spirit, improving their abilities and power given unto
them of God, to his glory and praise, are not
only called faithful Servants, or the children
of the living God, but they have the promises of God to be intrusted with more of
the manifestations of himself, which is called the misterie which hath bin hid from
many ages, and generations, which the disobedient shall not injoy. *Col. 1. 26. 27.*

42. That those which love the Lord
Jesus Christ, so as to walke in his appointed
ways with that strength of ability and
power which God of his own mercy hath
given unto them, they shall have peace of
conscience, being freed from anguish of spirit,
having their hearts comforted by the holy
Ghost; *Rom. 2.* 10.

43. That all those that continue sted-
fastly unto the end of their lives, pressing
forward to the mark (Jesus Christ) that is
set before them, shall not only have the
comfort and joy which is a part of their
portion in this life, but they shall also have
a Crown of eternal glory in the life to come;
Rev. 22. 14. 2 Tim. 4. 8.

44. That God of his free grace or love,
called or calleth sinners to repentance, and

afforded or affordeth them time or opportunity to repent or returne unto him; *Rom.* 4. 2.

45. That all those who refuse to improve the gifts of grace which God hath afforded them, so that they repent not, neither turne to him in obedience to his commands made manifest unto them, they do despise the goodness of God or his free grace, denying the Lord that bought them, and so are liable to destruction, 1 *Pet.* 2. 1, 2.

46. That whosoever shall preach, teach, or practise any doctrine in the worship of God, pretending it in the name of Jesus Christ, which is not to be heard or read of in the record of God, which was given by inspiration of the holy Ghost; such teachers are lyable to the curse of God, howsoever, countenanced by men, *Gal.* 1. 8, 9.

47. That the Baptisme which the Lord Jesus commanded his disciples to teach, ought to be known by every one, before they submit themselves, or obey it; *Acts.* 2. 38. 41.

48. That the way and manner of baptising, both before the death of Christ, and since his resurection and ascension, was to go into the water, and to be baptised; *Math.* 3. 6. *Math,* 1. 5. and 8. 9.

49. That when Baptisme is made known, or any other Action of obedience, then for men to refuse it, they are said to reject the counsel of God against themselves; *Luk.* 7. 30.

50. That those which received the word of God preached by the Ministrie of the Gospel, and were Baptized according to the Counsel of God, at the same time or day they were of the visible Church of God, *Acts.* 2. 41.

51. That the only foundation of the Church

of God, is the Doctrines of the Apostles or
Prophets, as they spring from Jesus Christ
the chiefe corner stone, whereon this or any-
other people are to be built together as the
house of God; *Eph.* 2. 20, 21.

52. That the chief or only ends of a people baptised according to the counsel of
God, when they meet together as the congregation or fellowship of Christ, are, or
ought to be, for to walk sutably; or to give
up themselves unto a holy conformity to all
the Laws or Ordinances of Jesus Christ,
answerable to the gifts and graces received,
improving them for the glory of God, and
the edification of each other in love, *Eph.*
4. 15, 16.

53. That Jesus Christ took Bread, and
the juice of the Vine, and brake, and gave
to his Disciples, to eat and drink with
thanksgiving; which practise is left upon
record as a memorial of his suffering, to
continue in the Church until he come a-
gain; 1 *Cor.* 11. 23, 24, 25, 26.

54. That the Church ought to call upon
God, seeking him by prayer in the name of
Jesus Christ, and to be thankful to him for
mercies received, sounding forth his praises
with understanding. *Eph.* 6. 16, 17, 18.

55. That if any one of the fellowship
neglect the watching over his own heart,
and so break out into an evill life and conversation, and all good meanes that God
hath appointed hath been used towards
such a one, and that person hath not performed, then ought not such a one to break
bread with obedient walkers, to shew forth
the death of Christ, seeing he doth deny
him in life and conversation; 1 *Cor.* 5. 12.

56. That the people of God ought to have
a tender respect towards them, as long as
there is any hope of being instrumental in the

use of that means which God hath appointed for the recovering them out of the snare of sin or wickedness. *2. Thes.* 3. 14, 15.

57. That there be contributions made for the relief of those that cannot help themselves with food and rayment, that are willing to the utmost to put forth their strength and skill in some lawful Way or Calling, especially those that are of the household of Faith; such as through sickness or weakness of body cannot labour. *Gal.* 6. 9. 10.

58. That it is the good pleasure of God, which hath given gifts of his grace to the Saints or Church of God, that some of the gifted men should be appointed or set apart to attend upon the preaching of the word, for the further edifying of the Churches, that they may be enabled to stand against all oppositions according as necessity requires, to the glory of God and their comfort. *Eph.* 4. 11, 21.

59. That it is the will of God that those Saints or members of the fellowship which are appointed so to spend their labors in teaching or exhorting them in the knowledge of God to their edification and consolation, ought to have maintenance of those that receive spiritual food by them. I *Cor.* 9. 11.

60. That the maintenance of the Ministers which labour in the Word of God, ought to be the free and Charitable Benevolence, or the chearful contribution of those that acknowledge themselves members of the same fellowship; 2 *Cor.* 9. 13.

61. That the servants of God, or the Ministers of the Gospel, ought to be content with necessary food and rayment, and to labour with their hands, that they may not be overchargeable, I *Cor.* 4. 12.

because they are to teach that doctrine to
every member. *Heb.* 13. 5.

62. That those servants of God which
labour in the word much, and well, ought
to be had in very good estimation; 1 *Tim.* 5. 17.

63. That the Church of Jesus Christ
ought not to think of any man above what
is meet, lest that they give that honour to
man, which properly and alone belongeth
to God; *Psal.* 115. 1. *2 Cor.* 12. 6.

64. That the Church hath directions of
God to set apart some men that are sute-
ably qualified, to oversee, or order the affairs concerning the poor distressed members of Christ, that they may not be neglected, and so perish for want of food and
rayment, and to take off that work from ly-
ing too heavy upon the care of those which
labour in the word and doctrine; *Acts.* 6. 3, 4.

65. That if the poor fearing God, cannot conveniently have a competent maintenance, for the supply of their necessities in
that society whereunto they must commonly resort, that then those men that have
the care laid upon them, send or give intelligence to the other Churches or saints of
God, who have ingaged themselves by
declaring their willingness towards the relief of such a distressed people, *Rom.* 15. 26.

66. That those men which the Church
of God are to make such uses of as the setting them to minister unto the saints in
things spritual or temporall, it is required
that the Church judge those men found in
the faith, that their lives and conversations
be unblameable, that those which are
without, cannot have any just occasion to
speak reproachfully of them, that they be
not covetous of filthy lucre, neither selfwill-
ed, but loving and patient towards all men,
apt to teach, and to do good works answer-

able to their abilities. *Titus* I. 7, 8. 9. *Acts*. 6. 3.

67. That some men amongst the brotherhood who are able to judge in causes of difference that may arise betwixt them in the Church, may be approved or appointed to put an end thereto without partiality, that there may be no unnecessary strivings in the Law to vex one another; I *Cor*. 6. 5, 6, 7.

68. That whosoever of the Society or Church of God which shall willfully or carelessly neglect any lawful way or calling, and to fall into hunger and nakedness, ought to be exhorted with love and meekness, to labour with their abilities in some honest way or calling for their relief which being done orderly, and he or they will not reform, so that sutable exhortations take no place, such an one shall be excluded or excommunicated, as one that hath denyed the faith; I. *Tim*. 5. 8.

69. That the offended ought to proceed according to rule, not delaying or prolonging time, but out of a tender care, that their hearts may not be hardned by a custome in sin, that thereby the reclaiming of them from sin may be done with less difficulty; *Mat*. 18. 15, 16, 17.

70. That if any controversie should so fall out, that the case cannot easily be determined by that society or church where it is first presented, that then use be made of some other society which they are in fellowship with, for their assistance therein; *Acts* 16. 1, 2.

71. That there be an orderly improving those gifts that God of his free grace hath bestowed on the Saints, that one may not hinder another, but as occasion serveth, one by one, speaking the things that they have learned of God, that the hearers may be

profited, and so put in a capacity to judge of
things concerning the glory of God, and
their own peace; 1 *Cor*. 14. 30, 31.

72. That if any one which hath been of
the fellowship of Christ, and hath so far
subjected himself to temptations that he de-
nyeth to live righteously, or in the fear and
love of God and makes shipwrack of Faith
and a good Conscience, for which he hath
been excommunicated according to Order,
that it be recorded, and made known to
other the Churches, for prevention of evils
in them; 1 *Tim*. 1. 19, 20.

73. That Fasting and Prayer ought to be
used, and laying on of hands, for the
Ordaining of servants or Officers to attend
about the service of God; *Acts* 13. 3.

74. That we ought to behave our selves
towards all men, no otherwise then we
would freely and cheerfully they in the like
case (if it should fall out) should do toward
us, and that we ought to seek a peaceable
life with all men, as far as possibly we can,
keeping faith and a good conscience; *Luke*
6. 31. *Rom*. 12. 18. 1 *Tim*. 1. 19.

75. That we ought to clear our selves,
not only from evil Thoughts harbouring in
our hearts, or the evils in life and conversation; but as far as we can, vindicate our
selves from all those scandalous aspersions
that daylie fall about our ears, setting our
good names on fire, to the dishonour of
God, whereof many are the Instruments by
their wilful contrivances, or by the mis-infor-
mations of others, which father upon us such
principles and practises as we abhor,
through ignorant mistakes cunningly suggested by some evil willers at least; 2 *Cor*. 2. 17.

Postscript.

THat we do own a Magistratical power
for the governing of this our English
Nation, to be determined in a just Parliamentary way; and that we ought to pray
for good Governors, and good Government; that we may live a peaceable and
godly life in all honesty; standing ready at
all times, as necessity may require, to vindicate such a Magistracy or Magistrates, not
only with arguments of sound reason, but
also with our Estates and Lives; that
Righteousness may reigne, and Vice may be
overthrown, without respect of persons.

FINIS.

C. *The True Gospel-Faith, 1654*

Early in his ministry, George Fox saw that he could not by himself effect the religious revolution he desired. In 1649 he had an
interview with the celebrated young preacher, Samuel Oates, then
itinerating as a representative of the parent General Baptist Church
in London, which was meeting in Bell Alley.[18] The idea of itinerating preachers seemed a good one to Fox, and soon he was sending
out an organized band of such preachers. In 1653 they numbered
at least thirty, and in 1654 their numbers grew to sixty or more.[19]
In the summer of the latter year, some of Fox's men moved to
"conquer London."[20] This was part of the larger Quaker strategy
of "occupying" the largest English cities. A number of preachers
started south at once: Howgill and Burrough went straight to London, arriving early in July; Hubberthorne and Whitehead stopped
for a short time at Oxford before going on to London; and Audland
and Ayrey went toward Bristol.[21] Once in London, the leaders
made their way to religious groups which were likely to show them
most sympathy, Baptist and Independent churches and Seeker meetings. It seems evident that they moved with caution and were well
received.

The London General Baptists do not seem at first to have sus-
pected danger to themselves in the Quaker movement; they had too

[18] Barclay, *Inner Life Religious Society of The Commonwealth*, 256.
[19] *Ibid.*, 265, and Emmott, *A Short History of Quakerism*, 137.
[20] Emmott, *op. cit.*, 137.
[21] Braithwaite, *The Beginnings of Quakerism*, 157-158.

much in common with it. But when Quakers began holding great rival public meetings of their own, to say nothing of private meetings in numerous houses,[22] the Baptists knew they must act quickly against them. The religious societies of London, on whose membership the Friends were making greatest inroads, cried out against them.[23] The element of surprise had operated in favor of the Quakers. Many religious groups looked frantically about for some defense against the almost irresistible enthusiasm of the new movement. Some General Baptist leaders held a meeting to consider what their churches might do. They decided to publish a thorough criticism of the Quaker positions and to issue a confession of their own faith. John Griffith, pastor (and founder in 1640) of the Dunning's Alley Church,[24] and apparently now the leader of this group, prepared an attack on the Quakers which he entitled, *A Voice from the word of the Lord to those grand Imposters called Quakers.* In it he levelled five accusations at his opponents, which may be summarized as follows:

1. ". . . thou art fleshly minded, for thou lookest upon the institutions of Christ with a fleshly carnal eye, witness Richard Hubberthorne in his Antipathy between flesh and Spirit, where he saith that the bread and wine, which Christ commanded . . . is carnal."

2. You are "spiritually proud . . . giving out yourselves to be great ones."

3. You "boast of your light within."

4. You "reject and despise" the Word.

5. "You have rejected the Law of the Lord."

The pamphlet, however, was not intended to be read by Quakers only, for the last section was "A word of caution" addressed to "All that are called to be Saints in this Nation," and "which may concern all people." Saints were strongly urged to "Labor to see an excellency" in three objects of loyalty which the Baptists held to be endangered: in Christ, in the Word of Christ, and in the Church and Ordinances of Christ.

Apparently time did not permit the working out of an original doctrinal statement. Someone remembered that Thomas Lover (deceased) had a few years previously prepared a Confession which

[22] Harvey, *The Rise of the Quakers,* 88.
[23] Penney (ed), *The Publishers of Truth,* 165.
[24] Whitley, *Minutes of the Gen. Assembly,* I, li-lii.

bore the title, "The True Gospel-Faith Witnessed by the Prophets and Apostles, And Collected into Thirty Articles, Presented to the world as the present Faith and Practice of the Church of Christ." This Confession may have been a private one, or it may originally have been adopted by one or more churches. Nothing is known of Thomas Lover or his church, though Lover must have been an early leader among General Baptists. His Confession was taken over as the official statement of faith of the represented congregations. It appears that no changes were made in it, and full credit for its authorship was given to Lover. Even Lover's original letter to the Reader was kept, and the first person singular in the first article as well. In Lover's letter the purpose of setting the Confession forth was shown to be partly apologetic and partly missionary, and the purpose of the group now concerned with the Confession was quite the same. The Confession as it stood seemed to have been made to order for just this occasion.

The Griffith group did take time to prepare a letter "To the Reader in behalf of the Author," and this was placed immediately after the author's letter. In their letter the leaders first gave thanks for the breaking forth of the Gospel light in England; at the same time, they said:

> there is a generation of men in the world that do hate the light, and endeavor to put it out, crying against the Scriptures of Truth, It's a dead Letter, and against the form of Doctrine therein contained, Rom. 6:17, as fleshly forms, and too low for them to walk in; insomuch that we say with David, It is time for the Lord to work, for they have made void the Law, Psalm 119.126.

The three leaders who, in addition to Griffith, signed this letter were John Foxwell, Thomas Parrett (or Perrott), and Francis Smith. It is to be supposed that all signed on behalf of their churches, but of the identity of the churches there is uncertainty. All four men were prominent in the largest circle of General Baptist affairs, the General Assembly. Smith was the well-known Croydon bookseller on whose co-operation much of the success of the General Baptist propaganda depended. As early as 1669, he was connected with the Glass-house Yard Church.[25] Probably not all

---

[25] Whitley, *Minutes*, I, 228 and *Baptists of London*, 114.

of the eleven General Baptist churches known to have existed in London before 1660 were represented in the Confession, but only such as were most fearful of the Quakers.

The form which the Confession of 1654 took is more like that of the Particular Baptist Confession of 1644 than the Midland Confession of 1651, but even the form shows complete independence, and the Confession possesses some novel aspects. The articles presenting the theological outlook of the authors are especially lacking in detail. There is no mention of deacons among the church officers listed.[26] There is no article on the Scriptures, though the leaders in 1654 did not overlook this omission. In their introductory letter they said:

> We therefore do desire that whosoever read it [the Confession] may weigh the Scriptures produced; and if it be according to the Scriptures, there is light in it; for its the Scriptures of the Prophets and Apostles that we square our faith and practice by, accounting that light within (not witnessed by the Scriptures without) which some so much talk of to be deep darkness . . . Let the Scripture therefore be the rule of thy faith and practice. . . .

The Confession always uses "dipped" for baptized. It also is the first Baptist Confession to prescribe the laying on of hands for all baptized believers. This practice appears to have been but lately brought to the attention of Baptists, and John Griffith was a leading exponent of it. It was not yet commonly used among General Baptists.

The Quakers took prompt notice of the stiffening opposition of the Baptists of whom Griffith was leader. In 1654 Edward Burrough answered Griffith's *A Voice from the Word of the Lord,* and in 1655 Richard Farnsworth published a critical answer to the Confession of 1654.[27] Perhaps the Confession steadied all London General Baptists, after making them aware of the serious danger in which they stood, for it does reflect a certain stability and maturity of thought which characterized the churches represented by it. It also gives the best picture of the reaction of Baptists to the first serious effort of the Quakers to win London.

---

[26] Article 22.
[27] Whitley, *A Baptist Bibliography*, pp. 56 and 60.

THE TRUE GOSPEL-FAITH DECLARED ACCORDING TO THE SCRIPTURES, 1654[28]

I

First, I believe there is but one God, I Cor 8.6 But to us there is but one God. See 2 Kings 19.15 Mark 12.42, who is eternal, invisible, the onely wise God etc. Rev. 15.3 Great and marvellous are thy works Lord God Almighty, just and true are thy ways. Psalm 145.9. The Lord is good to all, who is present in all places, knows all things, Pv. 15.3. The eye of the Lord is present in every place beholding the evil and the good, Acts 15.18. Known to the Lord are all his works from the beginning of the world. Iohn 6. For Iesus knew from the beginning who they were that believed not and who should betray him. See also Heb. 4.13. Who made Heaven, Earth, the Seas and all that is in them, Acts 17.14. God made the world and all things therein. See Rev. 14.7 Ionah 1.9 Iohn 1.3 Col. 1.15,16. And made man upright, Eccles. 7.29. This onely have I found that God made man upright and gave him power to rule over all creatures on the earth, Gen. 9.2. The fear and the dread of you shall be upon every beast of the earth; giving him a good law to keep Gen. 2.17. But of the tree of knowledg of good and evil thou shalt not eat; telling him he should die if he kept it not, Gen. 2.17. In the day that thou eatest thereof thou shalt surely die.

II.

Secondly, that man broke that law and brought death upon himself and all his posteritie, Rom. 5.12. Wherefore as by one man sin entered into the world, and death by sin, and so death passed on all men, for that all have sinned.

III.

Thirdly, that no man can redeem himself from this death, Psalm 47.7. None of them can by any means redeem his brother, or give to God a ransom for him, Ephes. 2.6. For by grace are you saved through faith, and that not of yourselves.

IV.

That God out of his love sent his son into the world to be born of a woman, to die for the sins of all men under the first Covenant,

[28] The Confession is very rare, copies of the original being found only at the Angus Library, Regent's Park College, Oxford, and at the British Museum. Apparently neither Underhill nor McGlothlin knew of its existence, and it has probably not been printed in modern times. A facsimile copy of the document found in the British Museum is given here.

Iohn 3.16. For God so loved the world, that he sent his only begotten son etc. Ga. 4.4 God sent forth his son made of a woman, made under the law to redeem them under the law, Heb. 2.9. That he by the grace of God should taste death for every man, Heb. 9.15. That by means of death for the redemption of the transgressors, that were under the first Testament.

v.

That he did do the will of his Father, in laying down his life for all sinners, Phil.2.8. And being found in the fashion as a man, he humbled himself, and became obedient unto death, even the death of the cross, I Tim.2.6, whò gave himself a ransom for all.

VI.

That he rose again from the dead the third day, and was seen bodily by his Disciples, Luke 24.6,7; Luke 29.39.

VII.

That he ascended bodily into Heaven, Acts 1.9; Eph.4.10.

VIII.

That he is now a Priest, a Prophet and a King, Heb.4.24; Acts 3.22; Rev.19.16.

IX.

That he hath given down the Holy Spirit to his Servants, that they might make known to all Nations the things that concern the Name of Iesus and the Kingdom of Heaven Acts 2.4; 2 Cor. 3.6; Acts 28.31.

X.

That all ought to believe the things declared by the Spirit Acts 17.30; Rom.16.26.

XI.

That they that believe the things so preached ought to be dipped in water, Acts 10.47. Can any man forbid water that these should not be baptized (which in English is Dipped) which have received the Holy Spirit as well as we? Acts 10.43; Acts 2.33; Acts 2.41; Acts 8.12.

XII.

That God gives his Spirit to believers dipped through the prayer of faith and laying on of hands, Acts 8.15; Acts 8.17; Acts 5.32; Ephes. 1.13,14.

N

XII.

That God gives his Spirit to believers dipped through the prayer of faith and laying on of hands, Acts 8.15; Acts 8.17; Acts 5.32; Ephes. 1.13,14.

XIII.

That every believer dipped is to be joyned with believers dipped, which is the Church of Christ, Acts 2.41; I Cor.12.13; I Pet. 2.5; Acts 2.42.

XIV.

That this company of believers dipped are subject to afflictions, 2 Tim.3.12; John 6.33.

XV.

That every one of them ought to be holy in life and conversation, 2 Cor.7.1; I Pet.1.15.

XVI.

That they ought to meet together to break bread, Acts 20.7; Lk.2.19.

XVII.

That they ought to be frequent in prayer, Rom.12.12; Ephes. 1.18; Luke 18.1:21,36.

XVIII.

That they ought to be obedient to the Magistrates in all things that are right, Rom.13.1; I Pet.2.13,14.

XIX.

That they ought to relieve the poor, that none want amongst them, except all want, they being diligent in their callings, Rom.12.13; Luke 3.11.

XX.

That it is the dutie of every one to tell his brother of his sin, seeing him to offend, Matt.18.15; Lev. 19.17.

XXI.

That they ought to cast out from among themselves all that walk disorderly, after admonition, they remaining obstinat, I Cor.5.11; I Cor.5.13; Titus 3.10.

XXII.

That they have power to chuse Messengers, Pastors, and Teachers from among themselves, Acts 1.21,22; Acts 1.26; Titus 1.5; Acts 6.3.

XXIII.

That they are to be chosen by fasting and prayer, with the laying on of hands, Acts. 13.3; Acts 6.6.

XXIV.

That the church is to assist them in the work they appoint them to do, with things needful, I Cor. 9.14; Rom.15.27; Gal. 6.6.

XXV.

That every member ought to exercise his gift for the benefit of others, Matth.25.27; I Pet.4.10.

XXVI.

That all ought to avoid the hearing of any Teachers so as to learn of them, except believers dipped, and making of marriages with any out of the Church lest they be drawn from the truth. 2 Jno.10 v..; I Iohn 4.6; I Cor.7.39; Deut.7.3,4; 2 Cor.6.14,15.

XXVII.

That Christ shall come personally to raise the just and unjust from the dead, Acts 1.11; Heb.9.29; I Cor.15.22.

XXVIII.

That he shall judg every one according to his work 2 Cor.5.10; Rom.2.6.

XXIX.

Whosoever believeth and is dipped, and abideth in the Commandments of God to the end, shall be saved, Mark 16.16; Matth. 24.13; Rev. 22.14.

XXX.

That whosoever believeth not and walketh not in the Commandments of God to the end, shall be forever cast out from the presence of God into everlasting punishment, which is the second death, Iohn 3.36; Matth.25.30; Matth.25.31; Rev. 21.8.

FINIS

D. *The Midland Association Confession, 1655*

In the Midlands in 1655, General Baptists far outnumbered their Calvinistic Brethren. The General Baptist Confession of 1651 had been signed by members of thirty congregations of the area, but when the Particular Baptists met in 1655 to constitute their Midland Association, there were but fourteen of their churches in the eight counties, and only seven of them were as yet willing to associate.

Two principal factors led to the formation of the Midland Association in 1655. One was the general trend among Baptists at that time toward associating. In promoting this trend the London churches took the lead, and they evidently were concerned with the beginnings of the organization in the Midlands. That Daniel King, who undoubtedly was leading the Midlands churches to associate, belonged to that circle is shown in a book of his published in London in 1650. In this book, *A Way to Sion,* which was an exposition of Baptist teaching, the Epistle Dedicatory was signed by four prominent London leaders. Probably at the suggestion of the London churches, he was by 1655 giving much of his time to building up associations of churches in various parts of the country.

The other factor promoting the organization of the Association was the great activity of the Quakers in the Midlands in 1654 and 1655. In 1654 George Fox returned to the Midlands, debated with some Baptists at Biddesley, Warwickshire,[29] and called a great "general meeting" which was attended by Quaker preachers from London, Bristol, and many other places.[30] Fox was present to direct his preachers for at least part of 1655, and to engage "several Baptists" in debate at Sileby, Leicestershire.[31] When King wrote *A Way to Sion,* he tried to refute the "Seekers" or "Waiters," but when the London leaders finally had the book published, a year later, their concern was to protest (in the Epistle Dedicatory) against the Quakers.

In the light of the Quaker activity, some Midland Particular Baptist churches listened readily to Daniel King's call to associate. Representatives of seven churches met at Warwick on May 3, 1655, in a preliminary session to consider certain Articles of Faith which might serve as the doctrinal basis for their intended Association. The churches were located in the Counties of Warwick, Gloucester, Oxford, and Derby. Correspondence had evidently made the messengers ready for their task, for they promptly considered the doctrines, agreement upon which would be a basis of union.

When they had examined and approved sixteen Articles, they appointed a second meeting to be held at Moreton-in-the-Marsh, on June 26, at which there would be the formal adoption of the Confession by the churches and the real beginning of their associational life. Before the June meeting each church carefully examined and solemnly adopted the Articles as its own creed. Full agreement was

---

[29] A. S. Langley, "Seventeenth Century Baptist Disputations," in *Transactions Baptist History Society,* VI (1918-19), 113-114.
[30] Harvey, *op. cit.,* p. 98.
[31] Langley, *supra.*

thus reported at Moreton, and signatures were affixed to the Articles and to a statement of purpose:

> We do therefore . . . mutually acknowledge each other to be true churches of Christ; and that it is our duty to hold communion with each other . . . and so to be helpful each to the other, as the Lord shall give opportunity and ability, endeavoring that we may all increase more and more, in faith and knowledge, in all purity and holiness, to the honor of our God. And it is our resolution, in the strength of Christ to endeavor to do so.[32]

Daniel King was a lay-preacher whose educational opportunities evidently had been limited. He had only laymen as his companions in preparing and signing the 1655 Confession. These were busy men who had little use for abstract language, so their Confession is brief and pointed. Its brevity fitted the purpose of its preparation. When the Circular Letter of the Association went out to the churches, reporting the proceedings of the meetings, the Confession appeared at its head as a kind of standard.[33] It also found its way into local church books.

The Confession must have been modeled on the London Confession of 1644, but its statements are original. In spite of its brevity, the theological portion is a careful and praiseworthy summary of Calvinistic Baptist doctrine of the middle of the seventeenth century. If Daniel King had at an earlier date been a General Baptist as Whitley[34] supposes, his reaction against Arminianism might explain the strength of the Calvinism of the Confession. The emphasis in Article 13 on the place of Christian works as outward evidences of conversion before baptism resembles the teaching of Menno Simons. Also, postponing of baptism shows the distance at which these Baptists stood from a sacramental understanding of the ordinance.

The primary purpose of the Confession was instructional rather than apologetic. Its usefulness was not soon lost. According to Stokes,[35] when the Particular Baptist General Assembly sought in 1689 to set forth an up-to-date doctrinal expression, the 1677 elaboration of the Midland Association Confession was adopted. This Assembly Confession became the best known of English Baptist

---

[32] Stokes, *op. cit.*, 26-28.
[33] Owen, *Records of an Old Association*, 72-73.
[34] *Minutes of General Assembly*, I, xxxviii.
[35] *Op. cit.*, 5-16.

Confessions. Thus, that which was wanting of breadth in the Midland Confession, was made up in the Confession of 1689.

SIXTEEN ARTICLES OF FAITH AND ORDER UNANIMOUSLY ASSENTED TO BY THE MESSENGERS MET AT WARWICK, THE 3RD DAY OF THE 3RD MONTH, 1655[36]

1st. We believe and profess, that there is only one true God, who is our God; who is eternal, almighty, unchangeable, infinite, and incomprehensible; who is a Spirit, having His being in Himself, and giveth being to all creatures; He doth what He will, in heaven and earth; working all things according to the counsel of His own will.

2nd. That this infinite Being is set forth to be the Father, the Word, and the Holy Spirit; and these three agree in one. I John v.7.

3rd. We profess and believe the Holy Scriptures, the Old and New Testament, to be the word and revealed mind of God, which are able to make men wise unto Salvation, through faith and love which is in Christ Jesus; and that they are given by inspiration of God, serving to furnish the man of God for every good work; and by them we are (in the strength of Christ) to try all things whatsoever are brought to us, under the pretence of truth. II Tim. iii.15-17; Isaiah viii.20.

4th. That though Adam was created righteous, yet he fell through the temptations of Satan; and his fall overthrew, not only himself, but his posterity, making them sinners by his disobedience; so that we are by nature children of wrath, and defiled from the womb, being shapen in iniquity and conceived in sin. Psalm li.5; Romans v.12-15.

5th. That God elected and chose, in His eternal counsel, some persons to life and salvation, before the foundation of the world, whom accordingly He doth and will effectually call, and whom He doth so call, He will certainly keep by His power, through faith to salvation. Acts xiii.48; Ephesians i.2-4; II Thessalonians ii.13; I Peter i.2, etc.

6th. That election was free in God, of His own pleasure, and not at all for, or with reference to, any forseen works of faith in the

---

[36] The Confession of 1655 probably was not published by its authors and subscribers. It was edited in 1905 from the Tewkesbury and Bourton Church books (Owen, *Records of an Old Association*, 72-73) by the Reverend W. Gwynne Owen. The Baptist Historical Society added this edition to its Supplement to McGlothlin's *Baptist Confessions of Faith* (pp. xviii-xx of the 1911 British Edition).

creature, as the motive thereunto. Ephesians i.4; Romans xi.5,6.

7th. That Jesus Christ was, in the fulness of time, manifested in the flesh; being born of a woman; being perfectly righteous, gave Himself for the elect, to redeem them to God by His blood. John x.15; Ephesians v.25-27; Rev. v.9.

8th. That all men until they be quickened by Christ are dead in trespasses—Ephesians ii.1; and therefore have no power of themselves to believe savingly—John xv.5. But faith is the free gift of God, and the mighty work of God in the soul, even like the rising of Christ from the dead—Ephesians i.19. Therefore consent not with those who hold that God hath given power to all men to believe to salvation.

9th. That Christ is the only true King, Priest, and Prophet of the Church. Acts iii.22-23; Hebrews iv.14, etc.; viii.1, etc.

10th. That every man is justified by Christ—Romans viii.33; I Cor. vi.11; apprehended by faith; and that no man is justified in the sight of God partly by Christ and partly by works. Romans iii.20,28,30; Gal. v.4.

11th. That Jesus of Nazareth, of whom the Scriptures of the Old Testament prophesied, is the true Messiah and Saviour of men; and that He died on the cross, was buried, rose again in the same body in which He suffered, and ascended to the right hand of the majesty on high, and appeareth in the presence of God, making intercession for us.

12th. That all who have faith wrought in their hearts by the power of God, according to His good pleasure, should be careful to maintain good works, and to abound in them, acting from principles of true faith and unfeigned love, looking to God's glory as their main end. Titus iii.8; Heb. xi.6; I Cor. vi.10 and 31.

13th. That all those who profess faith in Christ, and make the same appear by their fruits, are the proper subjects of Baptism. Matthew xxviii.18,19.

14th. That this baptizing is not by sprinkling, but dipping of the persons in the water, representing the death, burial, and resurrection of Christ. Romans vi.3,4; Colossians ii.12; Acts viii.38,39.

15th. That persons so baptized ought, by free consent, to walk together, as God shall give opportunity in distinct churches, or assemblies of Zion, continuing in the Apostles' doctrine and fellowship, breaking of bread and prayers, as fellow-men caring for one another, according to the will of God. All these ordinances of Christ are enjoined in His Church, being to be observed till His Second Coming, which we all ought diligently to wait for.

16th. That at the time appointed of the Lord, the dead bodies of all men, just and unjust shall rise again out of their graves, that all may receive according to what they have done in their bodies, be it good or evil.

E. *The Somerset (Particular Baptist) Confession, 1656*

The great Particular Baptist apostle to the West of England was Thomas Collier, a lay-preacher of extraordinary gifts and energy. There seems to have been scarcely a place in Wessex which he did not visit in his evangelistic tours. Of course, he founded churches, and to these he was writing "General Epistles" by 1649.[37] Collier himself may have been the chief link among the churches, but it is evident that there was a kind of brotherhood among them by 1651. On November 6-7, 1653, representatives of the churches met at Wells. The laying on of hands for all baptized believers was the foremost question discussed. Collier calls this one "the First" among several meetings of the Association between 1653 and 1657.[38]

The seventh meeting of the Association took place at Bridgewater on September 5-6, 1656, at which time a Confession of Faith was approved. It was evidently the work of Collier, but the fact that decisions in favor of some of the positions announced in the Confession were made at this meeting, might indicate that he had help in preparing the Confession. It is evident from the Epistle Dedicatory that the Quakers were chiefly responsible for the appearance of the Confession in 1656. The authors said that two facts caused them to set forth their beliefs. First, they denied the "general charge" that their churches were not Calvinistic and so were out of accord with the London Particular churches, and owned both the London brethren and their Confession. [39] Second, that they were:

> very sensible of the great distractions and divisions that are amongst professing people in this nation, the many ways and wiles of Satan to seduce and deceive souls, the great departing from the faith, and that under glorious notions of spiritualness and holiness. . . .

Collier had specific knowledge of the Quakers. Early in 1654 the Quaker pioneers, Audland and Ayrey, moved on Bristol, skirting Wales and preaching as they went. Once in Bristol, Audland ap-

[37] Whitley, *A Baptist Bibliography*, 40.
[38] Collier, *Several Resolutions and Answers to Queries*.
[39] Underhill, *Confessions of Faith*, 63.

pears to have gone straight to a Baptist meeting, where his preaching was well received. He and Ayrey soon moved on to preach in many places in Somersetshire and adjacent counties. Before leaving for London, however, they ran into Baptist opposition and in July were drawn into a debate with some Baptists at Broadmead, Bristol, on "the inner light."[40] By October, Audland had returned to Bristol with John Canne (formerly a Baptist) at his side.[41] They were given a tremendous reception, thousands attending their outdoor preaching. Many Baptists were attracted to the new movement, and Baptist churches faced a grim task in trying to maintain unity and peace in their fellowship. Braithwaite admits the Quaker movement became strong in Somerset largely through proselyting Baptists. More fuel was added to the Quaker fire with the coming of George Fox, toward the end of 1655, on a tour of the Southwest.

The Quaker fire was burning menacingly around the Baptists when their Western (or Somerset) Association met in September, 1656, at Bridgewater. The Confession which the churches at that meeting decided to publish may have been originally drawn up before 1656, possibly in 1653 when it, like the Midland Particular Association Confession, would have served as a basis of union, for the authors said that "when the Lord set us first upon this work, we did not think of bringing it to public view," but meant it to "try our unity in the faith."[42] In either case, Collier, who in 1654 was given the unique office of "General Superintendent and Messenger of all the Associated Churches," was its principal author.

The Confession bears the mark of careful preparation, and the impress of Collier can be seen at various points. While an effort is made to approximate the theological position of the London Confession, there is complete independence of expression, and there are some noteworthy omissions of material of the older document. Perhaps there was some ground for the saying that these Baptists did not quite have the same theological outlook as their London brethren. McGlothlin suggests that "some jealousy and fear" of the London churches prompted the setting forth of this Confession, but it seems improbable that this fear concerned the authority of the London churches as much as the theology of some London Baptists. The Calvinism of the Western Association was not of a rigid type.

[40] Langley, *loc. cit.*, in *Transacts. Baptist Historical Society.*
[41] Braithwaite, *op. cit.*, 165-167.
[42] Underhill, *op. cit.*, 63.

Collier, as a lay-evangelist, was troubled by some of the same practical difficulties which the General Baptists said they saw in the doctrine of a restricted or particular atonement, yet he liked the Calvinistic framework.

It is important to note that there were General Baptists within the area of the Western Association, and the Confession of 1656 probably represents an attempt to comprehend all Baptists of the district irrespective of their Calvinism or Arminianism.[43] Article 34 is one of the clearest statements on the missionary obligation of a church to be heard before the time of William Carey. This is the only Baptist Confession to include an article on the Jews and on the attitude that Christians should take toward them. The ubiquitous Quakers were partly responsible for the Article, having in 1656 debated with Collier the question of the Jews' admission to England.[44] The emphasis on obedience to "the ordinances of Christ" is due to the experience of Collier[45] and to the Quaker controversy. The angelology and eschatology of the Confession were called for by certain views of the Quakers.

This Confession is notable on two accounts: first, it represents the earliest important effort at bringing Particular and General Baptists into agreement and union; and, second, it clearly enunciates three distinctively Baptist principles,—the duty of a church to receive only those who give evidence of having been regenerated, the right of a church to call out and ordain its own ministers, and the obligation of the church to send representatives to preach the gospel to the world. These principles were brought to public attention by the Confession, and their practice defeated Quakerism among Baptists and fostered a united group of evangelistic churches, numbers of which continue to this day.

Original copies of this Confession are to be found in the British Museum; the Bodleian Library, Oxford; and the Manchester British College Library, Manchester. Facsimile copies of the Confession are in Underhill, *Confessions of Faith,* Crosby, *History of the English Baptists* (Vol. 1, Appendix III), and McGlothlin, *Baptist Confessions of Faith.* This copy is taken from McGlothlin.

---

[43] See the Association's view of the Atonement in 1655 in Collier, *Several Resolutions and Answers of Queries.*

[44] See *A brief answer to some of the objections made against the coming in of the Jews in this Commonwealth* (1656).

[45] In *The Right Constitution and True Subjects of the Visible Church* (Epistle Dedicatory), Collier says that he once was "against the practice of Ordinances," but that God had clea '
up his understanding.

A

CONFESSION

OF THE

FAITH

OF SEVERAL

CHURCHES OF CHRIST

In the County of Somerset, and of
some Churches in the Counties neer adjacent.

I Peter iii. 15.

Sanctifie the Lord God in your hearts, and be ready
alwaies to give an answer to every man that asketh
you a reason of the hope that is in you with meekness
and fear.

Mattew x. 32.

Whosoever therefore shall confess me before men, him
will I confess also before my Father, which is in
heaven.

Isaiah viii. 20.

To the Law and to the Testimony, if they speak not
according to this rule it is because there is no light in
them.

Acts xvii. 11.

These were more noble than those in Thessalonica, in
that they received the word with all readiness of minde,
and searched the Scriptures daily, whether those things
were so.

London, Printed by Henry Hills, and are to be
sold by Thomas Brewster, at the three Bibles
at the West end of Pauls, 1656.
August 10.

A CONFESSION of the FAITH of several congregations of Christ in the county of Somerset,. and some churches in the counties near adjacent. Printed at London, Anno 1656.

I.

WE believe that there is but one God (1 Cor. 8:6.), who is immortal, eternal, invisible, only wise (I Tim. 1:17.), holy (Lev. 11:44.), almighty (Gen. 17:1.), infinite (I Kings 8:27; Isa. 40:28; Ps. 147:5); a Spirit (John 4:24.), glorious in holiness (Ex. 15:11), just, merciful, gracious, long-suffering, abundant in mercy and truth (Ex. 34:6, 7.), faithful in all things (Deut. 7:9.).

II.

THAT this God, who is so in himself, did according to his own will in time, create all things, by, and for Jesus Christ (Heb. 1:2; Col. 1:16; John 2:3); who is the word of God (John 1:1) and upholds all things by the word of his power (Heb. 1:3.).

III.

THAT God made man after his own image (Gen. 1:27), in an estate of uprightness and human perfection (Eccles. 7:29.).

IV.

THAT God gave Adam a just law, requiring obedience under the penalty of death (Gen. 2:17), which law he brake, and brought himself and his posterity under the guilt and judgment denounced (Gen. 3:6; Rom. 5:12, 17, 18, 19.).

V.

MAN being in this undone estate, God did in the riches of his mercy hold forth Christ in a promise (Gen. 3:15.).

VI.

THAT in process of time God gave forth his laws by the hand of Moses (Exod. 20; John 1:17), to fallen man (Gal. 3:19), not for justification to eternal life (Gal.

3:17; Rom. 3:20.), but that all might appear guilty before the Lord by it (Rom. 3:19; 5:20).

VII.

THAT out of this condition none of the sons of Adam were able to deliver themselves (Rom. 8:3; Eph. 2:1, 5; Rom. 5:6.).

VIII.

THAT God continued and renewed the manifestation of his grace and mercy in Christ after the first promise made (Gen. 3), in other promises (Gen. 22:18 with Gen. 12:3; Gal. 3:16.); and in types, as the passover (Exod. 12:8 and ver. 13 with I Cor. 5:7.), and the brazen serpent (Numb. 21:9 compared with John 3:14); with the ministry and ministration of Moses and Aaron, the sacrifices, &c. being all figures of Christ (Heb. 7:8 and Chap. 9.); and in prophesies (as Isa. 9:6; 11:1, 2; 53:6 compared with I Pet. 2:24; I Cor. 15:3.).

IX.

THAT God in his son did freely, without respect to any work done, or to be done by them as a moving cause, elect and choose some to himself before the foundation of the world (Eph. 1:3, 4; 2 Tim. 1:9.), whom he in time hath, doth, and will call, justify, sanctify and glorify (Rom. 8:29, 30).

X.

THAT those that were thus elected and chosen in Christ were by nature (before conversion) children of wrath even as others (Eph. 2:3; Rom. 3:9.).

XI.

THAT those that are chosen of God, called and justified, shall never finally fall from him, but being born from above are kept by the power of God through faith unto salvation (John 6:39; 10:28; 11:26; I Pet. 1:5; Ps. 89:30, 31, 32, 33, 34; I John 3:9; John 14:19; Heb. 12:2; Jer. 31:3; John 10:29; Ps. 37:28; Jer. 32:40; Rom. 8:39; I Cor. 1:8, 9; Rom. 8:30; Ps. 48:14.).

XII.

THAT when the fulness of time was come, God sent forth his Son, made of a woman (Gal. 4:4, 5.) according to the promises and prophesies of the scriptures; who was conceived in the womb of Mary the virgin by the power of the Holy Spirit of God, (Luke 1:35; Matt. 1:20.), and by her born in Bethlehem (Matt. 2:11; Luke 2:6, 7.).

XIII.

WE believe that Jesus Christ is truly God (Isa. 9:6; Heb. 1:8; Rom. 9:5.) and truly man, of the seed of David (I Tim. 2:5; Acts 13:23; Rom. 1:3.).

XIV.

THAT after he came to be about thirty years of age, being baptized, he manifested himself to be the Son of God (Luke 3:21, 23 with John 2:7, 11.), the promised Messiah, by doing such works both in his life and in his death which were proper unto, and could be done by none but the Son of God, the true Messiah (John 1:49; 6:9, &c.).

XV.

THAT this man Christ Jesus suffered death under Pilate, at the request of the Jews (Luke 23:24.), bearing the sins of his people on his own body on the cross (I Pet. 2:24), according to the will of God (Isa. 53:6), being made sin for us, (2 Cor. 5:11) and so was also made a curse for us (Gal. 3:13, 14; I Pet. 3:18.), that we might be made the righteousness of God in him (2 Cor. 5:11.), and by his death upon the cross, he hath obtained eternal redemption and deliverance for his church. (Col 1:14; Eph. 1:7; Acts 20:28; Heb. 9:12; I Pet. 1:18, 19.).

XVI.

THAT this same Jesus having thus suffered death for our sins, was buried (Matt. 27:59, 60.), and was also raised by the power of God (Eph. 1:19.) the third day according to the scriptures (I Cor. 15:3, 4.), for our justification (Rom. 4:25.).

XVII.

THAT after he had been seen forty days upon the earth, manifesting himself to his disciples (Acts 1:3.), he ascended into the heavens (Acts 1:9, 10, 11; Heb. 4:14.), and is set on the right hand of the throne of God (Heb. 8:1; Heb. 1:3.), whom the heavens must receive until the time of the Restitution of all things. (Acts 3:21.).

XVIII.

THAT the Father having thus exalted him, and given him a name above every name (Phil. 2:9.), and hath made him who is mediator (I Tim. 2:5), priest (Heb. 10:21; 8:1), prophet (Acts 3:22.), and king to his people (Ps. 2:6; Rev. 15:3.). As he is our priest, so is he our peace and reconciliation (Eph. 2:14, 15; Rom. 5:9, 10.), and being enter'd into the holy place, even heaven itself, there to appear in the presence of God (Heb. 9:24.), making continual intercession for us (Heb. 7:24, 25.), he is become our advocate (I John 2:1.) by whom we have boldness and access unto the throne of grace with acceptance (Heb. 10:19; Eph. 3:12; Heb. 4:16.). As he is our prophet, so he hath given us the scriptures, the Old and New Testament, as a rule and direction unto us both for faith and practice (John 5:39; I Pet. 1:10, 11, 12; 2 Tim. 3:16; I Pet. 10:20, 21; Eph. 2:20; I Cor. 14:37; Tit. 1:2, 3.); and that he hath sent, doth and will (according to his promise) send his Holy Spirit the Comforter, by whom he leadeth us into all truth (John 14:26; 16:13.); and by his continual presence with us, and in us (John 14:16, 17.), teaching, opening and revealing the mysteries of the kingdom, and will of God unto us (I Cor. 2:10, 11, 12, 13; Rev. 2:29; 5:5.), giving gifts in his church for the work of the ministry, and edifying the body of Christ (Eph. 4:8, 12; I Cor. 12:4, 5, 6.), that through the powerful teachings of the Lord, by his Spirit in his church, they might grow up in him (Eph. 4:15.), be conformed to his will (Ezek. 36:27; I Pet. 1:2.), and sing praises unto his name (Heb. 2:12; I Cor. 14:15.). And as he is our prophet, and king, lord, and law-giver (Isa. 33:22; 55:4.), Prince of life (Acts 3:15.), Prince of peace (Isa. 9:6.), Master of his people (Matt. 23:8.), Head of his church (Col. 1:18.), the Almighty (Rev. 1:8.), so he hath given rules unto us, by the which he ruleth over us (Luke 6:46; John 10:16; I John 2:4; John 14:15; Matt. 28:20.), and ruleth over all things for his church (Eph. 1:22; Rev. 19:16.) and by the power of love ruleth by his Spirit in us (2 Cor. 5:14; I John 2:5.), making us (in a measure) both able and willing to honour him (Phil. 4:13; Heb. 13:21; Eph. 6:10; Phil. 2:13), and bow before him (Ps. 95:6; 110:3; Rev. 4:10, 11.), submitting ourselves to him alone in all his commands with joy (John 15:14; Rev. 14:4; 7:15; Ps. 119:2, 47; Rev. 15:3, 4.).

XIX.

THAT the Spirit is administred by or through the word of faith preached (Gal. 3:2.), which word was first declared by the Lord himself, and was confirm'd by them that heard him (Heb. 2:3.), which word is called the gospel of God's grace (Acts 20:24.), the word of reconciliation (2 Cor. 5:19.), the sword of the Spirit (Eph. 6:17.), the weapon of a Christian (2 Cor. 10:4.); a faithful (Rev. 22:6.), quick, powerful (Heb. 4:12.), plain (Prov. 8:9.), comfortable (Rom. 15:4.), pure (Ps. 12:6.), right, true (Ps. 33:4.), sound (Tit. 2:8.), and wholesome word (I Tim. 6:3.).

XX.

THAT this spirit of Christ, being administer'd by the word of faith, worketh in us faith in Christ (John 3:5; I Pet. 1:22; Acts 16:14; Gal. 5:22.) by virtue of which we come to receive our sonship (John 1:12; Gal. 3:26.), and is further administer'd unto us through faith in the promises of God (Eph. 1:13; Acts 2:38, 39; Acts 1:4.), waiting on him in those ways and means that he hath appointed in his word (John 14:15, 16, 17; Luke 11:9, 13.), this faith being the ground of things hoped for, and the evidence of things not seen (Heb. 11:1.).

XXI.

THAT justification is God's accounting and declaring that man justified from the guilt and condemnation of all his sin, who hath received Jesus Christ and doth believe in him (in truth and power) according to the record given of him by God in scripture (Rom. 4:5; I John 5:10, 11; Joh. 3:36.).

XXII.

THAT justification from the guilt and condemnation of sin is only obtained through faith in that man Jesus Christ, crucified at Jerusalem, and by God raised from the dead (Rom. 5:1, 9; Acts 13:38, 39; Rom. 4:25; 10:9.). And that those who bring in any other way of justification, do therein make void, and acquit themselves of having any interest in the gospel and grace of Christ (Gal. 2:21; 5:4.).

XXIII.

THAT this faith being wrought in truth and power, it doth not only interest us in our justification, sonship, and glory, but it produceth as effects and fruits, a conformity, in a measure, to the Lord Jesus, in his will, graces and virtues (Rom. 5:3, 4; I John 3:23, 24; 2 Pet. 1:5, 6, 7; Gal. 5:6; Acts 26:18; I Thess 1:3.).

XXIV.

THAT it is the duty of every man and woman, that have repented from dead works, and have faith towards God, to be baptized (Acts 2:38; 8:12, 37, 38.), that is, dipped or buried under the water (Rom. 6:3, 4; Col. 2:12.), in the name of our Lord Jesus (Acts 8:16.), or in the name of the Father, Son, and Holy Spirit (Matt. 28:19.), therein to signify and represent a washing away of sin (Acts 22:16.), and their death, burial, and resurrection with Christ (Rom. 6:5; Col. 2:12.), and being thus planted in the visible church or body of Christ (I Cor. 12:3.), who are a company of men and women separated out of the world by the preaching of the gospel (Acts 2:41; 2 Cor. 6:17.), do walk together in communion in all the commandments of Jesus (Acts 2:42.),

o

wherein God is glorified and their souls comforted (2
Thes. 1:11, 12; 2 Cor. 1:4.).

XXV.

THAT we believe some of those commandments
further to be as followeth.

    I.   CONSTANCY in prayer (Col. 2:23, 24.).

    2.   BREAKING of bread (I Cor. 11:23, 24.).

    3.   GIVING of thanks (Eph. 5:20.).

    4.   WATCHING over one another (Heb. 12:15.).

    5.   CARING one for another (I Cor. 12:25) by vis-
iting one another, especially in sickness and temptations
(Matt. 25:36.).

    6.   EXHORTING one another (Heb. 3:13.).

    7.   DISCOVERING to each other, and bearing one
another's burdens (Gal. 6:2.).

    8.   LOVING one another (Heb. 13:1.).

    9.   REPROVING when need is one another (Matt.
18:15.).

    10.   SUBMITTING one to another in the Lord (I
Pet. 5:5.).

    11.   ADMINISTERING one to another according
to the gift received, whether it be in spirituals, or tem-
porals (I Pet. 4:10.).

    12.   THE offender to seek reconciliation, as well as
the offended (Matt. 5:23, 24.).

    13.   LOVE our enemies and persecutors, and pray for
them (Matt. 5:44).

    14.   EVERY one to work if he be able, and none to
be idle (2 Thes. 3:10, 11, 12.

    15.   THE women in the church to learn in silence, and
in all subjection (I Tim. 2:11; I Cor. 14:37.).

    16.   PRIVATE admonition to a brother offending an-
other; and if not prevailing, to take one or two more; if
he hear not them, then to tell it to the church; and if he
hear not them, to be accounted as an heathen and publican (Matt. 18:15.).

    17.   PUBLICK rebuke to publick offenders (I Tim.
5:20.).

    18.   THE brethren in ministring forth their gifts,
ought to do it decently and in order, one by one, that all

may learn, and all may be comforted (I Cor. 14:31, 40.).

19. A SPECIAL care to assemble together, that their duty to God, and the church, may not be neglected (Heb. 10:24, 25.).

20. AND all things in the church, done in the name and power of the head, the Lord Christ Jesus (Col. 3: 17.).

21. THAT in admitting of members into the church of Christ, it is the duty of the church, and ministers whom it concerns, in faithfulness to God, that they be careful they receive none but such as do make forth evident demonstration of the new birth, and the work of faith with power (John 3:3; Matt. 3:8, 9; Acts 8:37; Ezek. 44:6, 7; Acts 2:38; 2 Cor. 9:14; Ps. 26:4, 5; 101:7.).

XXVI.

THAT those that truly repent, and believe, and are baptized in the name of the Lord Jesus, are in a fit capacity to exercise faith, in full assurance to receive a greater measure of the gifts and graces of the Holy Spirit (Acts 2:38, 39; Eph. 1:13.).

XXVIII. [Sic Original]

THAT it is the duty of the members of Christ in the order of the gospel, tho' in several congregations and assemblies (being one in the head) if occasion be, to communicate each to other, in things spiritual, and things temporal (Rom. 15:26; Acts 11:29; 15:22; 11:22.).

XXIX.

THAT the Lord Christ Jesus being the foundation and corner stone of the gospel church whereon his apostles built (Eph. 2:20; Heb. 2:3), He gave them power and abilities to propagate, to plant, to rule and order (Matt. 28:19, 20; Luke 10:16), for the benefit of that his body, by which ministry he did shew forth the exceeding riches of his grace, by his kindness towards it in the ages to come (Eph. 2:7), which is according to his promise (Matt. 28:20.).

XXX.

THAT this foundation and ministration aforesaid, is a sure guide, rule and direction, in the darkest time of the anti-christian apostacy, or spiritual Babylonish captivity, to direct, inform, and restore us in our just freedom and liberty, to the right worship and order belonging to the church of Jesus Christ (I Tim. 3:14, 15; 2 Tim. 3:15, 16, 17; John 17:20; Isa. 59:21; Rev. 2:24; Isa. 40:21; Rev. 2:5; I Cor. 14:37; Rev. 1:3; 2 Thes. 3:14; Rev. 2:11; I Pet. 1:25; I John 4:6; 2 Pet. 1:15, 16; Isa. 58:11, 12; 2 Pet. 3:2; Isa. 8:20.).

XXXI.

THAT the church of Jesus Christ with its ministry may from among themselves, make choice of such members, as are fitly gifted and qualified by Christ, and approve and ordain such by fasting, prayer, and laying on of hands (Acts 13:3; 14:23.), for the performance of the several duties, whereunto they are called (Acts 20:28; Rom. 12:6, 7, 8; 2 Tim. 4:2; Acts 6:3.).

XXXII.

THAT such a ministry labouring in the word and doctrine, have a power to receive a livelihood of their brethren, whose duty it is to provide a comfortable subsistance for them, if they be able, to whom for Christ's sake they are servants (I Cor. 9:4, 7; I Tim. 5:17, 18.). Yet it is commendable in cases of necessity, for them, for example sake, and that they may be able to support the weak, to labour and work with their hands (Acts 20:24, 25.).

XXXIII.

THAT the authority of Christ in an orderly ministry in his church, is to be submitted unto (Heb. 13:17; 2 Thes. 3:14.).

XXXIV.

THAT as it is an ordinance of Christ, so it is the duty of his church in his authority, to send forth such brethren as are fitly gifted and qualified through the Spirit of Christ to preach the gospel to the world (Acts 13:1, 2, 3; 11:22; 8:14.).

XXXV.

THAT it is the duty of us believing Gentiles, not to be ignorant of that blindness that yet lieth on Israel, that none of us may boast (Rom. 11:25.), but to have bowels of love and compassion to them, praying for them (Rom. 10:1.), expecting their calling, and so much the rather, because their conversion will be to us life from the dead (Rom. 11:15.).

XXXVI.

THAT it is the will of the Lord, and it is given to the saints not only to believe in him, but to suffer for his name (John 16:13; Phil. 1:26.) and so to pass through many tribulations into the kingdom of God (Acts 14:22; 2 Tim. 3:12; 2:12.).

XXXVII.

THAT the angels of the Lord are ministring spirits, sent forth for the good of those that shall be the heirs of salvation (Heb. 1:14; Ps. 91:11, 12; Acts 27:23; Luke 22:43.).

XXXVIII.

THAT the wicked angels (Ps. 78:49.) kept not their first estate in which they were created (Jude 6.), the prince of whom is called the devil (Matt. 8:28.), and the great dragon, and the old serpent, and satan (Rev. 12:9.), and the accuser of our brethren (Rev. 12:10.), and the prince of this world (John 14:30.), and a prince that ruleth in the air; a spirit working in the children of disobedience (Eph. 2:2.), and our adversary (I Pet. 5:8.), whose children the wicked are (Matt. 13:39; John 8:44.) To him we ought not to give place (Eph. 4:27.), whose power Christ hath overcome for us (Heb. 2:14.), and for him and his angels everlasting fire is prepared (Matt. 25:41.).

XXXIX.

THAT it is our assured expectation, grounded upon promises, that the Lord Jesus Christ shall the second time appear without sin unto salvation, unto his people, to raise and change the vile bodies of all his saints, to fashion them like unto his glorious body, and so to reign with him, and judge over all nations on the earth in power and glory (Phil. 3:20, 21; Heb. 9:28; Acts 3:19, 20, 21; Matt. 19:28; Rev. 2:26, 27; I Cor. 6:2; Ps. 72:8, 11; Dan. 7:27; Zech. 14:9; Ps. 2:8, 9; Jer. 23:5, 6; Ezek. 21:26, 27; Isa. 32:1; Rev. 11:15; Ps. 82:8; Rev. 5:9, 10; 20:6.).

XL.

THAT there is a day appointed, when the Lord shall raise the unjust as well as the righteous, and judge them all in righteousness (John 5:28, 29; Acts 24:15,), but every man in his own order (I Cor. 15:23; I Thes. 4: 16.), taking vengeance on them that know not God, and obey not the gospel of our Lord Jesus Christ, whose punishment will be everlasting destruction from the presence of the Lord (2 Thes. 1:7, 8, 9, 10; Jude 14, 15; Rev. 20:11, 12, 13, 14.).

XLI.

THAT there is a place into which the Lord will gather all his elect, to enjoy him for ever, usually in scripture called heaven (2 Cor. 5:1; John 14:2, 3.).

XLII.

THAT there is a place into which the Lord will cast the devil, his angels and wicked men, to be tormented for ever, from his presence and the glory of his power, usually in scripture called hell (Mark 9:43, 44, 45; Ps. 9:17; Matt. 25:41; 10:28; 23:33; Luke 10:15; 16: 23.).

XLIII.

THAT it is both the duty and privilege of the church of Christ (till his coming again) in their fellowship together in the ordinances of Christ, to enjoy, prize, and press after, fellowship through and in the Spirit with the Lord, and each with other (Acts 2:42; I Cor. 11:26; Eph. 2:21, 22; Eph. 4:3, 4, 5, 6; I Cor. 12:13; Eph. 3:9; Col. 2:2), which we believe to be attained through the exercise of faith in the death, resurrection, and life of Christ (2 Cor. 5:14, 15, 16; Col. 2:12; Phil. 3:9, 10, 11; I Pet. 2:5.).

XLIV.

THAT the ministry of civil justice (being for the praise of them that do well, and punishment of evil-doers) is an ordinance of God, and that it is the duty of the saints to be subject thereunto not only for fear, but for conscience sake (Rom. 13:1, 2, 3, 4, 5; I Pet. 2:13, 14.) and that for such, prayers and supplications are to be made by the saints (I Tim. 2:1, 2.).

XLV.

THAT nothing doth come to pass by fortune or chance, but all things are disposed by the hand of God, and all for good to his people (Gen. 45:5; 50:20; Rom. 8:28; Eph. 1:11; Job 14:5; Isa. 4:5, 7.).

XLVI.

AND that a church so believing, and so walking, though despised, and of low esteem, is no less in the account of her Lord and King, than though

BLACK, yet comely, Cant. 1:5.
FAIREST, without spot, Cant. 4:7.
PRECIOUS, Isa. 43:4.
BEAUTIFUL, Cant. 7:1.
HOLY, without blemish, Eph. 5:27.
PLEASANT, Cant. 1:15.
WHOSE soul loveth Christ, Cant. 1:7.
RUNNERS after Christ, Cant. 1:4.
HONOURABLE, Isa. 43:4.
THE desire of Christ, Cant. 7:10.
COMPLEAT in Christ, Col. 2:10.
LOVERS of the Father, John 16:27.

THE blessed of the Father, Matt. 25:34.

KEPT by the Lord, I Pet. 1:5; Isa. 27:3.

GRAVEN on the palms of his hands, Isa. 49:16.

TENDER to the Lord as the apple of his eye, Zech. 2:8.

TAUGHT of the Lord, Isa. 54:13.

ONE that hath obtained mercy, I Pet. 2:10.

ONE that hath a redemption, Eph. 1:7.

THE gates of hell shall not prevail against it, Matt. 16:18.

IN that church be glory unto God by Jesus Christ, throughout all ages, world without end. Amen. Eph. 2:21.

F. *An Antidote Against the Infection of the Times, 1656*

A document having the above name, published in Wales by a group of Particular Baptists in 1656, has been reckoned a Confession of Faith.[46] Its unique form has obscured its confessional character. The early growth of the Welsh Particular Baptist cause is largely to be accounted for by the zeal and administrative ability of John Myles, who is chiefly responsible for *An Antidote*. An Oxford graduate, Myles had begun to preach in Wales by 1644 or 1645, probably as an Independent.[47] Meeting some Particular Baptists who belonged to a detachment of the New Model Army, sent to Wales in 1648, he was converted to their views. In the spring of 1649 he journeyed to London, where he was baptized on profession of faith. The Glass-house Yard Church welcomed him with enthusiasm and recorded that his coming was an answer to prayer for home missionaries.

After a fortnight's stay in London, during which time he became acquainted with the practices of the leading Particular Baptist churches, he returned to Gower with the endorsement of the Glass-house Yard Church and threw himself into his work.[48] Five congregations were under his care by 1652, all practicing close communion. There were, however, other Baptists in Wales; and, to protect themselves against the easier discipline of the Arminian Baptists and the milder doctrinal views of certain Particular Baptists, Myles effected

---

[46] Isaac Backus, 17th Century American Baptist historian, reported that the churches of Myles and others published a confession of their faith, "wherein they adopted the words of David in Ps. 51.1" and which was publicly opposed by Geo. Fox (*History of N. England*, I, 460). This is that Confession.

[47] Gordon, A., in *Dictionary of National Biography*, XXXIX, 445.

[48] Richards, *The Puritan Movement in Wales, 1639-53*, 202.

an organization of his churches which gave the General Meetings so close a supervision over them as to approach presbyterianism.

Richards speaks of the "Close" Baptists' encasement in "a triple armour of aggressive Calvinism, strict communion, and the skill of a consummate dialectician,"[49] but even this armor did not prevent the rise of issues concerning state pay for ministers and the message of the Quakers. Myles made the mistake of accepting the office of lecturer at Llanelly under the Propagation Act, for which he was sharply criticized in 1655. The Quakers were playing havoc with many scattered bands of Baptists in South Wales, and they were circulating provocative and hurtful papers against the Baptists in Radnorshire, Llanafan, and Montgomeryshire.[50] Myles decided to prepare a direct refutation of Quakerism which would at the same time be a Confession of Faith for his churches. The approval of his brethren was sought at a meeting held at Brecknock on May 29-30, 1656. The Confession which was put forth was aimed at setting straight the disaffected brethren and at refuting the Quakers. It was "Published by the appointment of the Elders and messengers of the severall churches of Ilston, Abergavenny, Tredinog, Carmarthen, Hereford, Bradwardine, Cledoch, and Llangors. . . ."

The originality of the Confession must be traced to the genius of Myles, and both the symmetry of thought and the force of expression of the document do credit to the abilities of the author. The Confession is divided into three sections. The first, "Considerations presented to Sinners," is the doctrinal section; the second, "Admonitions to Saints," concerned the five "reigning corruptions" of the day; and the third, "Invitations to Backsliders," contained practical considerations for erring Christians.

The Confession served as a rallying point for the "Close" Baptists, while other Welsh Baptist groups were shattered by the Quaker movement. It drew from George Fox, in 1659, a harshly critical answer entitled *The Great Mystery of the Great Whore pinfolded and Antichrist's Kingdom Revealed.* . . . Copies of *An Antidote* being very scarce, the Welsh Baptist Historical Society published the work (edited by T. Shankland) in 1904 at Cardiff. The reply of Fox to *An Antidote* was included as an appendix. Original copies of the Confession are to be found only in the British Museum and

---

[49] *Religious Developments in Wales,* 1654-62, 262-264.
[50] Thomas, *History of the Baptist Association in Wales,* 17.

in the Angus Library, Regent's Park College, Oxford. The document is too lengthy to reproduce here, the Historical Society edition being 51 pages in length.

G. *Other Associational Confessions*

Interest in the pioneer seventeenth-century confessions should not be permitted to conceal the fact that new associational confessions occasionally appeared in the next century. A circle of Particular Baptist churches in the West Riding and in East Lancashire seem, by 1750, to have adopted a confession owned by the Rossendale Church about 1711. Another confession was adopted at the reorganization of the Yorkshire and Lancashire Association in 1787. Perhaps with some revision, this was later printed annually by the Lancashire and Cheshire Association, until near the end of the nineteenth century. Undoubtedly there were other associational confessions, though few of them were ever printed. They were widely circulated in manuscript and were incorporated in numerous church books.[51] Some are still in use.

---

[51] McGlothlin, *op. cit.*, Supplement to British Edition, 1911, xx-xxi.

4

English Baptist
General Confessions

THE FIRST GENERAL ASSEMBLY of the General Baptists of England appears to have been held in 1654. The stated purpose of the meeting was "to consider how and which way the affairs of the Gospell of Christ, so farre as it concerns them, might be best promoted. . . ."[1] Thirteen Messengers and twelve Elders signed a manifesto at that meeting disavowing sympathy with the Fifth Monarchy movement and declaring the willingness of General Baptists to assist in civil affairs and to support all measures of the new government which did not infringe on conscience. Politics continued to be a major interest of the Assembly. Many Baptists, while still supporting Cromwell, were by 1656 disappointed at the progress toward reform which he was making. With the death of Cromwell in 1659, it seemed to them that an advance beyond the Protectorate toward republican ideals might safely be ventured, and some of them actually petitioned for the establishment of a republic.[2] Richard Cromwell replaced his father and appeared to favor many of his precedents with regard to the liberties of the sectaries. His Parliament, however, showed little intention of following his policies. The resulting impasse seemed to present the sectaries an opportunity, so they turned to the Army.

How instrumental the Baptists were in effecting the change of government which came less than eight months after Oliver Cromwell's death is difficult to say; but they were very active in the effort. Richard Cromwell put himself into the hands of the Army in April, 1659, and dissolved his Parliament. He resigned on May 25, 1659, and the Army recalled the Rump Parliament. Conflict broke

---

[1] Whitley (ed), *Minutes of the General Assembly of General Baptists*, I, 2.
[2] Brown, *Baptists and Fifth Monarchy Men*, 173-174.

out anew and the Rump Parliament was expelled by the soldiers. A royalist reaction then set in quickly as the people, tired of confusion, saw that the restoration of the Stuarts was the one way of escaping military rule. Charles II was invited to return from exile in Holland to reclaim the throne of his fathers.

A. *The Standard Confession, 1660*

In the last six months before the Restoration, in spite of the general excitement, Baptists were remarkably quiet. Nonetheless, there was much talk in the nation of complicated political intrigues, and Baptists were commonly regarded as most dangerous plotters and sectaries. Many spoke of what the "Anabaptists" in the Army were about to do. The old stories of Münster were revived, and new editions of scurrilous writings against the Baptists were published. From declarations which Baptists put out in their own defense the offenses laid at their door may be learned. They included the following:

1. Opposition to magistracy.
2. Desiring to destroy the public ministry of the nation.
3. Countenancing the Quakers in their irregular practices.
4. Endeavoring "a toleration of all miscarriages in things ecclesiastical and civil, under pretense of Liberty of Conscience."
5. Desiring to "murder and destroy" those who differ from Baptists in matters of religion.

It was against this somber and confusing background that a General Assembly of General Baptists met in London in March, 1660. The Confession which they framed shows that the fearful slanders of their opponents were uppermost in their minds.[3] (see page 234). By the time the Assembly had approved its Confession of Faith, the Declaration of Charles II from Breda was less than a month away.

The forty men who signed the Confession of 1660 were a fairly representative group in that they represented the chief General Baptist districts. Of the thirty names tentatively identified, thirteen belonged to London, eight to Kent, and at least one each to Hertfordshire, Buckinghamshire, Lincolnshire, Sussex, Surrey, and Northampton. The representation of the great General Baptist fellowship in Lincolnshire and Leicestershire was disproportionately small.

---

[3] Whitley, *Minutes*, I, 20-21.

We may be reasonably sure that the Confession did not represent all of the General Baptists of England and Wales in 1660. From its concern with local (London) conditions, from the apparent absence of Leicestershire and Warwickshire names among the signatories, and from the fact that the Confession did not become the "Standard" Confession of General Baptists until 1663, it might be concluded that the Confession spoke in 1660 largely for people of London and vicinity, though not for all of them. There is significance in the indefiniteness of the legend which the Confession bears: "Set forth by many of us . . . called Anabaptists."

Among the signatories of this Confession a few were outstanding. Joseph Wright of Kent was a messenger who had received university training. William Jeffery, also of Kent, though a young man, was author of the remarkable doctrinal work, *The Whole Faith of Man,* which by 1660 was already "a standard work of reference and appeal" for General Baptists. It seems reasonable to suppose that Jeffery had very much responsibility in connection with the preparation of the Confession of 1660. Certainly McGlothlin was in error in supposing that Thomas Grantham composed the Confession. Grantham did not even sign the Confession in 1660 and he did not become prominent until some years later. Thomas Monck of Hertfordshire and Matthew Caffyn of Sussex and Kent may have made some contribution to the Confession.

The Standard Confession is more of a confession of faith and less of a statement of practice than *The Faith and Practice of Thirty Congregations.* In clarity and definiteness of statement it hardly matches the Particular Baptist Confession of 1644. The poor arrangement of subjects might indicate that the document was drawn up hurriedly. Theologically, the Confession is mildly Arminian. The Article on Christology is brief, vague, and in the words of Scripture; it was to be a bone of future contention. There is a more elaborate eschatology than in any other Baptist confession of the period, but the language of the three articles on the subject is strictly scriptural. The climax of the document is reached in the last two articles, Article 24 being one of the clearest statements of the seventeenth century in favor of absolute liberty of conscience. There is no mention of the place of messengers (though messengers signed the Confession) and no statement as to the meaning of the Lord's Supper.

The laying on of hands prescribed in Article 12 must have been something of an innovation for the Assembly, and there is doubt as to whether most General Baptist' churches already practiced it upon receiving new members. The practice was named in neither the 1611 nor the 1651 Confessions of General Baptists. The importance of the Ordinance was accentuated by the adoption in some quarters of the Six Principles of Hebrews 6:1-2 as a creedal standard and by the accession to Baptist ranks of several Anglican clergymen, who were used to the practice under the name of Confirmation. Those churches which adopted the practice were usually very strict in its observance, and there is evidence that the issue of laying on hands produced by 1660 a cleavage in the General Baptist fellowship which endangered the life of the young General Assembly. Neither John Griffith nor twenty-seven other London leaders who published a General Baptist declaration[4] early in 1660 signed the Confession of the Assembly.

It was in this declaration, indeed, that the Griffith group announced a new symbol or official basis, the "Doctrine of Christ or the Six Principles of Heb. vi:1-2." There had been for a number of years some interest among Baptists in this passage. As early as 1644 Christopher Blackwood, Particular Baptist leader and ex-clergyman, had spoken, in a work more concerned with other subjects, of "the six fundamental points" set forth in these verses.[5] His work was reprinted in 1653 under a new title,[6] and there was soon widespread discussion of the Six Points. By 1655 John Griffith was fully convinced concerning the authority of Hebrews 6:1-2, for in that year he published his book, *God's Oracle and Christ's doctrine, or the Six Principles of the Christian Religion.* This work became the textbook of the Six-Principle churches.

The dogmatic stand which the Griffith churches took on the Six Principles appears to have prevented their joining other General Baptists in approving an official confession of faith two months after the appearance of the Griffith work in January. Because the Assembly churches would not accept the Six Principles as the authoritative and only official platform, though they agreed to the

---

[4] *A Declaration of some of those people in and near London, called Anabaptists.* . . .
[5] *The Storming of Antichrist.* . . .
[6] *A Soul-searching Catechism.*

laying on of hands, the Griffith group withdrew.[7] In 1665 some kind of a reconciliation seems to have been effected; evidently it was a compromise, for the Assembly later had concurrent symbols: the Confession of 1660 and the Six Principles.[8] In 1690 there was another division, and the Six-Principle Baptists set up their own Assembly.[9] In America Six-Principle Baptists appeared early in the history of the colonies and have maintained a continuing separate existence.

The Confession of the Assembly was formally presented to King Charles II on July 26, 1660, along with an address.[10] The appearance of the Confession did little toward halting the persecution of Baptists, but they were spared temporarily by the official preoccupation with the more numerous and important Presbyterian dissenters. In 1663 the General Baptists thought it safe again to call a General Assembly. At that meeting the Confession was slightly revised and reaffirmed by a larger circle. From that date it was regarded as the "Standard" Confession of General Baptists. In 1678 Thomas Grantham edited the Confession, with "a few explanatory supplements, and the testimony of many ancient writers of Christianity," and the changes made by him were approved by the Assembly of 1691. A further revision was made about 1700 by Joseph Hooke of Hackenby, messenger in Lincolnshire, at the request of the General Assembly. The Assembly repeatedly approved the Confession, which also was known and used in America. It proved to be exceedingly important in the life of General Baptists, serving as a basis of union for over forty years and as a specific body of doctrine to which its people could hold in the dark years of persecution, 1664-1672, when little intercourse and organization were possible.

The only original copies are in Regent's Park College, Cambridge Library, and the British Museum. In 1739 Crosby conflated the original edition and that of 1691 in the second volume of *History of the English Baptists*. In 1854 Underhill conflated it in *Confessions of Faith*. Whitley, in *Minutes of the General Assembly*, offered a critical edition, and McGlothlin included the following original version in *Baptist Confessions of Faith*.

---

[7] The Griffith group also seems not to have been represented in an important Baptist joint defense declaration issued in 1661.

[8] Whitley, *Minutes of the General Assembly*, I, xix.

[9] Goadby, *Bye-paths in Baptist History*, 37.

[10] Crosby, *op. cit.*, II, 19 f; Taylor, *op. cit.*, I, 186 f.

A BRIEF

CONFESSION

OR

DECLARATION

OF

FAITH

Set forth by many of us, who are (falsely)
called Ana-Baptists, to inform all Men
(in these days of scandal and reproach) of our
inno | cent Belief and Practise; for which we
are not on | ly resolved to suffer Persecution,
to the loss of | our Goods, but also Life it self,
rather | than to decline the same.

Subscribed to by certain Elders, Deacons, and Brethren,
met at | *London,* in the first month (called *March,*
1660.) in the be | half of themselves, and many others
unto whom they belong, in | *London,* and in several
Counties of this Nation, who are of the | same Faith
with us.

*After the Way which men call Heresie, so Worship we
the God of our | Fathers; Believing all things which are
written in the Law, and | in the Prophets, Acts 24, 14.*

LONDON
Printed by *G. D.* for *F. Smith,* at the *Elephant* and
Castle, near | *Temple-Barr,* 1660.
[page 3]

A BRIEF
CONFESSION
OR
Declaration of Faith,

Set out by many of Us, who are (falsely) called
Ana-Baptists, to inform all men (in these days of
scandal | and reproach) of our innocent Belief, and
Practise: for which | we are not only resolved to suffer
persecution, to the loss of our | Goods, but also to life
it self, rather then to decline the same.

I. We Believe and are verily confident, that | there is but
one God the Father, of | whom are all things,
from everlasting | to everlasting, glorious, and
unword | able in all his attributes, I *Cor.* 8, 6.
Isa. 40. 28.

II. That God in the beginning made | Man
Upright, and put him into a state | and condition
of Glory, without the | least mixture of misery,
from which he | by *transgression* fell, and so
came into a miserable and mortal estate, | subject unto the
first death, *Gen.* I. 31. *Eccles.* 7. 29. *Gen.* 2. 17. 3.
17, 18, 19.

III. That there is one Lord Jesus Christ, by whom
are all things, | who is the only begotten Son of God, born
of the Virgin *Mary;* | yet as truly *Davids* Lord, and
Davids root, as *Davids* Son, and *Da* [page 4] *vids* Offspring, Luke 20. 44. *Revel.* 22. 16. whom God freely *sent*
| *into the World* (because of his great love unto the
World) who as | *freely gave himself a ransome for all,* I
Tim. 2. 5, 6. *tasting death* | *for every man, Heb.* 2. 9. *a*
propitiation for our sins; and not for ours | *only, but also*
for the sins of the whole World, I John 2. 2.

IV. That *God is not willing that any should perish, but*
that all | *should come to repentance,* 2 Pet. 3. 9. *and the*
knowledge of the truth, | *that they might be saved,* I Tim.
2. 4. For which end Christ hath | commanded, that the
Gospel (to wit, the glad tydings of remission | of sins)
should be preached to every creature, *Mark* 16. 15. So |
that no man shall eternally suffer in Hell (that is, the

P

second death) | for want of a Christ that dyed for them, but as the Scripture saith, | for *denying the Lord that bought them, 2 Pet. 2. 1.* or because they | *believe not in the name of the only begotten Son of God, John* 3. | 18. Unbelief therefore being the cause why the just and righteous | God, will condemn the children of men; it follows against all con | tradiction, that all men at one time or other, are put into such a | capacity, as that (through the grace of God) they may be eternally | saved, *John 1. 7. Acts 17. 30. Mark 6. 6. Heb. 3. 10, 18, 19. 1 John | 5. 10. John 3. 17.*

V. That such who first orderly comes into, and are brought up | in the School of Christs Church, and waiting there, comes to de|grees of Christianity, rightly qualified and considerably gifted by | Gods Spirit; ought to exercise their gifts not only in the Church, | but also (as occasion serves) to preach to the World (they being | approved of by the Church so to do) *Acts* 11. 22, 23, 24. *Acts* 11. | 19. 20. and that among such some are to be chosen by the Church, | and ordained by Fasting, Prayer, and Laying on of Hands, for the | work of the Ministry, *Acts* 13. 2, 3. *Acts* 1. 23. Such so ordained, | (and abiding faithful in their work) we own as Ministers of the Gos | pel; but all such who come not first to repent of their sins, believe | on the Lord Jesus, and so *Baptized* in his name for the remission of | Sins, but are only brought up in the Schools of humane learning, | to the attaining humane arts, and variety of languages, with ma | ny vain curiosities of speech, 1 *Cor.* 1. 19, 21. 2. 1, 4, 5. seeking | rather the gain of large revenues, then the gain of souls to God: | such (we say) we utterly deny, being such as have need rather to | be taught themselves, than fit to teach others, *Rom.* 2. 21. |

VI. That the way set forth by God for men to be justified in, is | by faith in Christ, *Rom.* 5. 1. | [page 5]

That is to say, when men shall assent to the truth of the Gospel, | believing with all their hearts, that there is remission of sins, and e | ternal life to be had in Christ.|

And that Christ therefore is most worthy their constant affecti | ons, and subjection to all his Commandements, and therefore re | solve with purpose of heart so to subject unto him in all things, and | no longer unto themselves, 2 *Cor.* 5. 15. |

And so, shall (with godly sorrow for the sins past) commit | themselves to his grace, confidently depending upon him for that | which they believe is to be had in him: such so believing are justifi | ed from all their sins, their faith shall be accounted unto them for | righteousness, *Rom.* 4. *22, 23, 24. Rom.* 3. *25, 26.* |

VII. That there is one holy Spirit, the pretious gift of God, free | ly given to such as *obey him, Ephes.* 4. 4. *Acts* 5. 32. that there | by they may be throughly sanctified, and made able (without which | they are altogether unable) to abide stedfast in the faith, and to | honour the Father, and his Son Christ, the Author and finisher of | their faith; 1 *Cor.* 6. 11. There are three that bear record in Hea | ven, the Father, the Word, the holy Spirit, and these three are one; | which Spirit of promise such have not yet received, (though they | speak much of him) that are so far out of *Love, Peace, Long-suffe* | *ring, Gentleness, Goodness, Meekness, and Temperance,* (*the* | *fruits of the Spirit, Gal.* 5. *22, 23.*) as that they breath out much | cruelty, and great envy against the Liberties, and peaceable living | of such, as are not of their judgment, though holy as to their conver | sations. |

VIII. That God hath even before *the foundation of the world* | *chosen,* (or elected) *to eternal life, such as believe,* and so are in | Christ, *John* 3. 16. *Ephes.* 1. 4, 2 *Thes.* 2. 13. yet confident we | are, that the purpose of God according to election, was not in the | least arising from fore-seen faith in, or works of righteousness done | by the creature, but only from the mercy, goodness, and com | passion dwelling in God, and so *it is of him that calleth, Rom.* 9. 11. | whose purity and unwordable holiness, cannot admit of any unclean | person (or thing) to be in his presence, therefore his decree of mer | cy reaches only the godly man, whom (saith *David*) God hath | *set apart for himself,* Psal. 4. 3. |

IX. That men not considered simply as men, but ungodly men, | *were of old ordained to condemnation,* considered as such, who turn [page 6] the grace of God

unto wantonness, and deny the only Lord God, | and our
Lord Jesus Christ, *Jude* 4. God indeed sends a strong
de | lusion to men, that they might be damned; but we
observe that they | are such (as saith the Apostle) that
*received not the love of the | truth, that they might be
saved,* 2 Thes. 2. 10, 11, 12. and so the | indignation and
wrath of God, is upon *every soul* of man that doth | *evil,*
(living and dying therein,) *for there is no respect of
persons | with God.* Rom. 2. 9, 10, 11. |

X. That all Children dying in Infancy, having not ac-
tually trans | gressed against the Law of God in their
own persons, are only sub | ject to the first death, which
comes upon them by the sin of the first | *Adam,* from
whence they shall be all raised by the second *Adam*; | and
not that any one of them (dying in that estate) shall suf-
fer for | *Adams* sin, eternal punishment in Hell, (which
is the second death) | *for of such belongs the Kingdome
of Heaven,* 1 Cor. 15. 22. Mat. 19. | 14. not daring
to conclude with that uncharitable opinion of others, |
who though they plead much for the bringing of children
into the | visible Church here on earth by *Baptism,* yet
nevertheless by their | Doctrine that Christ dyed but for
some, shut a great part of them out | of the Kingdome of
Heaven for ever. |

XI. That the right and only way, of gathering
Churches, (accor | ding to Christs appointment, *Mat.* 28.
19, 20.) is first to teach, or | preach the Gospel, *Mark* 16.
16. to the Sons and Daughters of | men; and then to
Baptise (that is in English to *Dip*) in the name of | the
Father, Son, and holy Spirit, or in the name of the Lord
Jesus | Christ; such only of them, as profess *repentance
towards God, and | faith towards our Lord Jesus Christ,*
Acts. 2. 38. Acts 8. 12. Acts | 18. 8. And as for all
such who preach not this Doctrine, but instead | thereof,
that Scriptureless thing of Sprinkling of Infants (*falsly
called\Baptisme*) whereby the pure *word of God is made
of no effect,* and the | new Testament-way of bringing
in Members, into the Church by re | generation, cast out;
when as the bond-woman & her son, that is to | say, the
old Testament-way of bringing in Children into the
Church | by generation, is cast out, as saith the Scrip-

ture, *Gal.* 4. 30, 22, 23, 24. | *Mat.* 3. 8, 9. all such we utterly deny, forasmuch as we are com | manded to *have no fellowship with the unfruitful works of darkness,* | *but rather to reprove them,* Ephes. 5. 11. |

XII. That it is the duty of all such who are believers *Baptized,* | to draw nigh unto God in submission to that principle of Christs [page 7] Doctrine, to wit, Prayer and Laying on of Hands, that they may | receive the promise of the holy Spirit, *Heb.* 6. 1. 2. *Acts* 8. 12, 15, | 17. *Acts* 19. 6. 2 *Tim.* 1. 6. whereby they may *mortifie the deeds of* | *the body,* Rom. 8. 13. and live in all things answerable to their pro | fessed intentions, and desires, even to the honour of him, *who hath* | *called them out of darkness into his marvellous light.* |

XIII. That it is the duty of such who are constituted as aforesaid, | to *continue stedfastly in Christs and the Apostles Doctrine, and assem* | *bling together, in fellow-ship, in breaking of Bread, and Prayer, Acts* | 2. 42. |

XIV. That although we thus declare the primitive way, and | order of constituting Churches, yet we verily believe, and also de | clare, that unless men so professing, and practising the forme and or|der of Christs Doctrine, shall also beautifie the same with a holy and | wise conversation, in all godliness and honesty; the profession of | the visible form will be rendered to them of no effect; *for without* | *holiness no man shall see the Lord,* Heb. 12. 14. Isa. 1. 11, 12, 15, | 16. |

XV. That the Elders or Pastors which God hath appointed to | oversee, and feed his Church (constituted as aforesaid) are such, | who first being of the number of Disciples, shall in time appear to *be* | *vigilent, sober, of good behavour, given to hospitality, apt to teach,* | &c. *not greedy of filthy lucre* (as too many National Ministers are) | *but patient; not a brawler, not covetuous,* &c. and as such chose, | and ordained to office (according to the order of Scripture, *Acts* 14. | 23.) who are to feed the flock with meat in due season, and in much | love to rule over them, with all care, seeking after such as go astray; | but as for all such who labour to feed themselves with the fat, more | than to feed the flock, *Ezek.* 34. 2, 3. seeking more after theirs, | than them, expresly

contrary to the practise of the Ministers of | old, who
said, *we seek not yours, but you,* 2 *Cor.* 12. 14. All such
we | utterly deny, and hereby bear our continued Testi-
mony against, | *Ezek.* 34.

XVI. That the Ministers of Christ, that have freely
received | from God, ought freely to Minister to others,
1 *Cor.* 9. 17. and | that such who have spiritual things,
freely Ministered unto them, | ought freely to communi-
cate necessary things to the Ministers, (up|on the account
of their charge) 1 *Cor.* 9. 11. *Gal.* 6. 6. And as for
[page 8] Tyths, or any forced Maintenance, we utterly
deny to be the Main | tenance of Gospel Ministers.

XVII. That the true Church of Christ, ought after the
first and | second admonition, to reject all Hereticks, *Tit.*
3. 10, 11. and in the | name of the Lord to withdraw from
all such, as profess the way of | the Lord, but walks dis-
orderly in their conversations, 2 *Thes.* 3. 6. | or any
wayes causes divisions or offences, contrary to the Doc-
trine | (of Christ) which they have learned, *Rom.* 16.
17. |

XVIII. That such who are true Believers, even
Branches in | Christ the Vine, (and that in his account,
whom he exhorts to a | bide in him, *John* 15. 1, 2, 3, 4, 5.)
or such who have charity out of | a pure heart, and of a
good conscience, and of Faith unfeigned, | 1 *Tim.* 1. 5.
may nevertheless for want of watchfulness, swerve and |
turn aside from the same, *vers.* 6, 7. and become as
withered Bran | ches, cast into the fire and burned, *John.*
15. 6. But such *who add un | to their Faith Vertue, and
unto Vertue Knowledge, and unto Know | ledge Temper-
ance,* &c. 2 Pet. 1. 5, 6, 7. such *shall never fall, vers.* | 8,
9, 10. 'tis impossible for all the false Christs, and false
Prophets, | that are, and are to come, to deceive such,
for they are *kept by the po | wer of God, through Faith
unto Salvation,* 1 Pet. 1. 5.

XIX. That the poor Saints belonging to the Church of
Christ, | are to be sufficiently provided for by the
Churches, that they neither | want food or rayment, and
this by a free and voluntary contributi | on, (and not of
necessity, or by the constraint or power of the Ma |
gistrate) 2 *Cor.* 9. 7. 1 *Cor.* 8. 11, 12, and this through

the free and | voluntary help of the Deacons, (called
Overseers of the poor) be | ing faithful men, chosen by
the Church, and ordained by Prayer | and Laying on of
Hands, to that Work, *Acts* 6. 1, 2. 3, 4, 5, 6. So | that
there is no need in the Church of Christ, of a Magesterial
compul | sion in this case, as there is among others, who
being constituted in | a fleshly and generational way, are
necessitated to make use of a | carnal sword, to compel
even a small, mean, and short Maintenance | for their
poor; when as many other Members of their Churches,
can | and do part with great and large Sums of Money, to
maintain their | vain fashions, Gold, Pearls, and costly
Array, which is expressly con | trary to the Word of God.
1 *Tim.* 2. 9, 10. 1 *Pet.* 3. 3. Alas, *what | will such do
when God riseth up, and when he visiteth, what will they
| answer him?* Job 31. 14. | [page 9]
XX. That there shall be (through Christ who was
dead, but is a | live again from the dead) a Resurrection
of all men from the graves | of the Earth, *Isa.* 26. 19.
both the just and the unjust, *Acts* 24. 15. | that is, the
fleshy bodies of men, sown into the graves of the earth, |
corruptable, dishonourable, weak, natural, (which so con-
sidered | cannot inherit the Kingdome of God) shall be
raised again, incor | ruptable, in glory, in power, spiritual,
and so considered, the | bodies of the Saints, (united
again to their spirits) which here suffer | for Christ, shall
inherit the *Kingdome, raigning* together with | Christ, 1
Cor. 15. 21, 22, 42, 43, 44, 49. |
XXI. That there shall be after the Resurrection from
the graves of | the Earth, *An eternal Judgement,* at
the appearing of Christ, and | his Kingdome, 2 *Tim.* 4. 1.
Heb. 9. 27. at which time of judgement | which is un-
alterable, and irrevocable, *every man shall receive ac |
cording to the things done in his body,* 2 Cor. 5. 10. |
XXII. That the same Lord Jesus who shewed himself
alive af | ter his passion, by many infallible proofs, *Acts*
1. 3. which was | taken up from the Disciples, and carried
up into Heaven, *Luke* | 24. 51. *Shall so come in like
manner as he was seen go into Heaven,* | Acts. 1. 9, 10,
11. *And when Christ who is our life shall appear, we |
shall also appear with him in glory, Col.* 3. 4. For then

shall he be | King of Kings, and Lord of Lords, *Rev.* 19. 16. for the Kingdome | is his, and he is the Governour among the Nations, *Psal.* 22. 28. | and King over all the earth, *Zech.* 14. 9. *and we shall raign (with | him) on the Earth*, Rev. 5. 10. the Kingdomes of this World, | (which men so mightily strive after here to enjoy) shall become the | Kingdomes of our Lord, and his Christ, *Rev.* 11. 15. for *all is yours,* | (O ye that overcome this world) *for ye are Christs, and Christ is* | *Gods,* 1 Cor. 3. 22, 23. *For unto the Saints shall be given the King* | *dome, and the greatness of the Kingdome, under* (mark that) *the* | *whole Heaven, Dan.* 7. 27. Though (alas) now many men be | scarce content that the Saints should have so much as being a | mong them; but when Christ shall appear, then shall be their day, | then shall be given unto them power over the Nations, to rule | them with a Rod of Iron, *Rev.* 2. 26, 27. then shall they receive a | Crown of life, which no man shall take from them, nor they by | any means turned, or overturned from it, for the oppressor shall | be broken in pieces, *Psal. 72.* 4. and their now vain, rejoycings | turned into mourning, and bitter Lamentations, as 'tis written, [page 10] *Job* 20. 5, 6, 7. *The triumphing of the wicked is short, and the joy* | *of the Hypocrite but for a moment; though his excellency mount up to* | *the Heavens, and his head reach unto the clouds, yet shall he perish* | *for ever, like his own dung; they which have seen him, shall say, where* | *is he?* |

XXIII. That the holy Scriptures is the rule whereby Saints both | in matters of Faith, and conversation are to be regulated, they being | able to make men wise unto salvation, through Faith in Christ | Jesus, profitable for Doctrine, for reproof, for instruction in | righteousness, that the man of God may be perfect, throughly | furnished unto all good works, 2 *Tim.* 3. 15, 16, 17. *John* 20. 31. | *Isa.* 8. 20. |

XXIV. That it is the will, and mind of God (in these Gospel | times) that all men should have the free liberty of their own **Consci** | **ences** in matters of Religion, or Worship, without the least op | pression, or persecution, as simply upon that account; and that | for any in Authority otherwise to act, we confidently believe is **ex** |

pressly contrary to the mind of Christ, who requires that
whatsoe | ver men would that others should do unto them,
they should even | so do unto others, *Mat. 7. 12.* and that
the Tares, and the Wheat | should grow together in the
field, (which is the world) until the | harvest (which is
the end of the world,) *Mat.* 13. 29, 30, 38, | 39. |

XXV. We believe that there ought to be civil Magis-
trates in all | Nations, *for the punishment of evil doers,*
and for the praise of them | that do well, 1 *Pet. 2.* 14. and
that all wicked lewdness, and fleshly | filthiness, contrary
to just and wholesome (Civil) Laws, ought | to be pun-
ished according to the nature of the offences; and this |
without respect of any Persons, Religion, or profession
whatsoe | ver; and that we and all men are obliged by
Gospel rules, to be | subject to the higher Powers, to obey
Magistrates, *Tit. 3.* 1. *and to | submit to every Ordinance*
of man, for the Lords sake, as saith *Peter 2.* | 13. But
in case the Civil Powers do, or shall at any time impose |
things about matters of Religion, which we through con-
science to | God cannot actually obey, then we with *Peter*
also do say, that we | ought (in such cases) to obey God
rather than men; *Acts* 5. 29. | and accordingly do hereby
declare our whole, and holy intent and | purpose, that
(through the help of grace) we will not yield, nor | (in
such cases) in the least actually obey them; yet humbly
pur [page 11] posing (in the Lords strength) patiently
to suffer whatsoever shall | be inflicted upon us, for our
conscionable forbearance. |

These things (O ye Sons and Daughters of Men) we
verily believe | to be the Lords will and mind, and there-
fore cannot but speak, | and if herein we differ from
many, yea from multitudes, from the | learned, the wise
and prudent of this World, we (with *Peter* and | *John*)
do herein make our solemne, and serious appeale, namely,
| *whether it be right in the sight of God, to hearken unto*
men, (of a con | trary perswasion) *more than unto God?*
Oh let the judicious, | judge righteous judgement! *Acts*
4. 19, 20.

And in the beleife, and practise of these things, (it
being the | good old Apostolical way) our souls have
found that rest, and soul | peace, which the world knows

not, and which they cannot take | from us; of whom then should we be afraid? *God is become our | strength, our light, our salvation; therefore,* we are resolved | (through grace) to seal the truth or these things in way of suffer | ing persecution, not only to the loss of our goods, free- domes, or | liberties, but with our lives also (if called thereunto.) |

Moreover we do utterly, and from our very hearts, in the | Lords fear, declare against all those wicked, and divillish reports, | and reproaches, falsly cast upon us, as though some of us (in & about | the City of *London*) had lately gotten **knives, booked knives,** & the | like, & great store of Arms besides what was given forth by order of | Parliament, intending to cut the throats of such as were contrary | minded to us in matters of Religion, and that many such **knives,** and | Armes, for the carrying on some secret design, hath been found in | some of our houses by search; we say, from truth of heart, in the | Lords fear, that we do utterly abhor, and abominate the thoughts | thereof, and much more the actions; and do hereby challenge both | City, and Coun- try (in our innocency herein) as being not able | to prove the things whereof they accuse us; and do for evermore | declare the Inventors of such reports, to be lyers, and wicked de | visers of mischeife, and corrupt designs: God that is above all will | justifie our innocency herein, who well knows our integrity, in what | we here declare, the Lord lay it not to their charge. |

In the time of building the decayed House of *God,* Samballet, & | Tobiah, (*wicked Counsellors*) *hired* Shemaiah *to make good* Nehemiah | *afraid;* and la- boured against him, that they might have *matter for* [page 12] *an evil report,* that they might reproach him, & hinder the building | of the house of God, Neh. 6. 12. *For I have heard (saith the Prophet)* | *the defaming of many; report, say they, and we will report it,* Jer. 20. | 10. |

Suscribed by certain Elders, Deacons, and Brathren met | àt *London,* in the first Month (called *March,* 1660.) in the | behalf of themselves, and many others unto whom they be | long, in *London,* and in several

Counties of this Nation, | who are of the same Faith
with Us.

Joseph Wright,	*John Hammersly,*
William Jeffery,	*William Russel,*
Thomas Monck,	*Joseph Keeich,*
John Hartnoll,	*Nicholas Newberry,*
Benjamine Morley,	*Samuel Lover,*
Francis Stanley,	*George Wright,*
George Hammon,	*John Parsons, Junior,*
William Smart,	*John Claton,*
John Reeve,	*Thomas Seele,*
Thomas Parrot,	*Michaiel Whiticar,*
John Wood,	*Giles Browne,*
Francis Smith,	*John Wells,*
Edward Jones,	*Stephen Torie,*
Humphrey Jones,	*Thomas Lathwel,*
Matthew Caffen,	*William Chadwell,*
Samuel Loveday,	*William Raph,*
John Parsons, Senior	*Henry Browne,*
Thomas Stacy,	*William Paine,*
Edward Stanley,	*Richard Bowin,*
Jonathan Gennings,	*Thomas Smith,*

THE END

B. *The Assembly or Second London Confession, 1677 and 1688*

By 1661 the Episcopalians had recaptured the machinery and
endowments of the Church of England, and they were bent upon
achieving uniformity in religion. A series of coercive acts which
form the Clarendon Code were put into effect to suppress dissent in
the years 1661 to 1665. These acts were aimed primarily at the
Presbyterians but they affected all dissenters alike. One of them,
the Conventicle Act of 1664, revived the Elizabethan Conventicle
Act but omitted the death penalty. Its enforcement depended upon
the temper of the local magistrates, but Baptist meetings were everywhere proscribed by it. King Charles actually favored the restoration of Catholicism, and in 1672 he issued a Declaration of Indulgence which suspended all penal laws of an ecclesiastical nature
against Protestant dissenters and Romanists. Teachers and meeting
places of Dissenters might now be licensed. There was only a brief
respite from persecution, however, as Parliament, perceiving that the
Declaration was aimed at restoring popery, forced the withdrawal
of the Indulgence in 1673. Parliament quickly passed the Test Act

(1673), which barred non-conformists from all military and civil offices. Persecution began anew as the Clarendon Code was again put into operation.

The renewal of persecution brought dissenting groups nearer to one another and especially brought Baptists and Congregationalists nearer to Presbyterians. Defiance of the Conventicle Act by the large Presbyterian party, which had been the dominant ecclesiastical group under the Commonwealth, made enforcement of that Act all but impossible. Observing the success of the Presbyterians, other Dissenters were emboldened. Moreover, it was important that Dissenters form a united front, which might be demonstrated by a show of doctrinal agreement among themselves. The very document which would be best proof of this agreement on essential matters was at hand, the Westminster Confession. This Confession had been prepared by the Westminster Assembly and published in 1646, had become the official Confession of Scotland, had been adopted by the English Parliament with slight alteration, and was still the authoritative creed of English Presbyterians. Also, the Congregationalists had adopted it as their Confession, after making some changes in conformity with their views of the Church, at the Savoy Conference in 1658.

The Particular Baptists of London and vicinity determined, therefore, to show their agreement with Presbyterians and Congregationalists by making the Westminster Confession the basis of a new confession of their own. A circular letter was sent to the Particular Baptist churches in England and Wales asking that representatives be sent to a general meeting in 1677. By the time this meeting was held, it appears that Elder William Collins of the Petty France Church in London had worked over the Westminster document, altering it as he saw fit. At the meeting the product of Collins' labors was approved and the Confession was issued in the name of the gathered representatives. Although published anonymously, it was said to have been "put forth by the Elders and Brethren of many Congregations of Christians (baptized upon Profession of their Faith) in London and the Country." Its purpose was clearly stated as showing:

> our hearty agreement with them (Presbyterians and Congregationalists) in that wholesome protestant doctrine, which, with so clear evidence of Scriptures they have asserted.

Essential agreement with the London Confession of 1644 was claimed in the introductory note, but scarcity of copies and general ignorance of that Confession, as well as the need for more full and distinct expression of views than that Confession offered, were given as reasons for preparing the new Confession.

As a matter of fact, there are numerous and marked differences between this Confession and that of 1644. To be sure, certain phrases were taken from the former confession, and there are evidences that other reminiscences from it were included, but, nevertheless, a number of significant and far-reaching changes were made. Among the innovations were the treatment of such subjects as the Scriptures, the Sabbath, and marriage. Moreover, the views of the church and of the ordinances were altered. Being based on one of the noblest of all Evangelical creeds, the Westminster Confession, this Confession is far more complete and better ordered than that of 1644. The Westminster order of chapters is followed, except that a new Chapter XX, "Of the Gospel, and of the extent of the Grace thereof," is added after XIX, and Chapters XXX and XXXI, "Of Church Censures" and "Of Synods and Councils," respectively, are omitted. The chapter on the doctrine of the Church is greatly expanded, having fifteen sections in all. It borrows material from the Savoy Confession.

The Calvinism of this Confession at points is more pronounced than that of the London Confession of 1644. This is true of the chapter on the doctrine of the Church. Chapter XXVII, Section 1, of the Westminster Confession is expanded in the Assembly Confession in an almost rhapsodic proclamation of faith in perseverance of the saints. However, Section 7 of Chapter III, on Reprobation, is omitted and the matter is dealt with in Chapter III,(3), in the words, "others being left to act in their sin, to their just condemnation." Also, the sections on the Covenants in Chapter VII (2,3,5,6) are omitted, as is the portion of Chapter XXIII which speaks of the duties of the civil magistrate to preserve peace in the Church, to suppress heresies and corruptions, and to call and order synods.

Evidences are not lacking of the independence of thought of the author or authors of the Assembly Confession. The Lord's Supper is not restricted to scripturally baptized people, as in the 1644 Confession. Peculiarly Baptist emphases appearing in the Assembly Confession concern the following subjects: the obligation to preach

the Gospel in all ages and nations (new Chapter XX)[11]; the singing of "Hymns and Spiritual Songs" (added to the Westminster's
injunction to sing Psalms, Chapter XXII); disuse of the term
"Sacrament" and of the Presbyterian definition of sacraments (Chapter XXVII); and provision for lay preaching (Chapter XXVI:11).
In addition, the characteristic Baptist emphasis on the Church is
made by enlarging Chapter XXVI into nine detailed chapters. As
the first Particular Baptist Confession to represent London and the
Counties, this Confession was historic, but its future usefulness
could scarcely have been imagined in 1677.

Following the ascension of William and Mary to the English
throne in 1689, the Act of Toleration was set forth on May 24.
Within two months thereafter, seven London Particular Baptist
pastors, William Kiffin, Hanserd Knollys, John Harris, George
Barrett, Benjamin Keach, Edward Man, and Richard Adams
unitedly sent a circular letter to Particular Baptist churches throughout England and Wales calling for a general meeting. Practical
objects of the meeting were to consider the low estate of the churches
and to deal with the problem of ministerial scarcity. In response to
this call, one hundred and seven churches sent messengers to a
meeting in London which began on September 3, and continued in
session until September 12. This first English Particular Baptist
General Assembly, in the course of its deliberations, approved the
Confession of 1677, a second edition of which had appeared in
1688.[12] The Assembly published the Confession, without the appendix of the original edition, but with the following prefixed addition "In the name and behalf of the whole Assembly":

"We the Ministers and Messengers of, and concerned for,
upwards of one hundred baptized congregations in England
and Wales (denying Arminianism) being met together in London, from the third of the seventh month to the eleventh of the
same, 1689, to consider of some things that might be for the
glory of God, and the good of these congregations; have
thought meet (for the satisfaction of all other Christians that
differ from us in the point of Baptism) to recommend to their

[11] Chapter XV, "Of Repentance unto Life," in the Westminster Confession defines the
doctrine in general terms; in the Assembly Confession the chapter begins with an illustra-
tion of the doctrine in the case of a person converted "at riper years" and ends with the
fine evangelical note: "which makes the constant preaching of repentance necessary."
[12] McGlothlin, op. cit., 217-218.

perusal the confession of our faith, which confession we own, as containing the doctrine of our faith and practice, and do desire that the members of our churches respectively do furnish themselves therewith."

Hanserd Knollys	Pastor	Broken Wharf	London
William Kiffin	Do.	Devonshire-Sq.	Do.
John Harris	Do.	Joiners' Hall	Do.
William Collins	Do.	Petty France	Do.
Hercules Collins	Do.	Wapping	Do.
Robert Steed	Do.	Broken Wharf	Do.
Leonard Harrison	Do.	Limehouse	Do.
George Barret	Do.	Mile End Green	Do.
Isaac Lamb	Do.	Pennington-St.	Do.
Richard Adams	Minister	Shad Thames	Southwark
Benjamin Keach	Pastor	Horse-lie-down	Do.
Andrew Gifford	Do.	Bristol, Fryars	Som. & Glouc.
Thomas Vaux	Do.	*Broadmead*	Do.
Thomas Winnel	Do.	Taunton	Do.
James Hitt	Preacher	Dalwood	Dorset
Richd. Tidmarsh	Minister	Oxford City	Oxon
William Facey	Pastor	Reading	Berks
Samuel Buttall	Minister	Plymouth	Devon
Christopher Price	Do.	Abergavenny	Monmouth
Daniel Finch	Do.	Kingsworth	Herts
John Ball		Tiverton	Devon
Edmond White	Pastor	Evershall	Bedford
William Prichard	Do.	Blaenau	Monmouth
Paul Fruin	Minister	Warwick	Warwick
Richard Ring	Pastor	Southampton	Hants
John Tomkins	Minister	Abingdon	Berks
Toby Willis	Pastor	Bridgewater	Somset
John Carter		Steventon	Bedford
James Web		Devizes	Wilts
Richard Sutton	Pastor	Tring	Herts
Robert Knight	Do.	Stukely	Bucks
Edward Price	Do.	Hereford City	Hereford
William Phips	Do.	Exon	Devon
William Hawkins	Do.	Dimmock	Gloucester
Samuel Ewer	Do.	Hempstead	Herts
Edward Man	Do.	Houndsditch	London
Charles Archer	Do.	Nook-Norton	Oxon

In the name and behalf of the whole Assembly."

Intended as an apologetic and educative instrument, the Confession became one of the most important of all Baptist confessions. New editions were prepared in 1693, 1699, 1719, 1720, 1791, 1809, among other years. Benjamin Keach of the Horsleydown Church, London, who had been associated with Collins in reissuing the Confession in 1688, worked over and condensed the Confession in 1697.

Then, with the concurrence of his son Elias Keach, pastor at Tallow Chandler's Hall, London, the document was set forth as the confession of faith of the two congregations. Benjamin Keach had also, in 1693, shared with Collins the task assigned by the General Assembly of preparing the *Baptist Catechism* (commonly called Keach's Catechism).[13] The Confession of the two Keaches was published, according to the letter "To the Reader," to relieve the general ignorance of Baptist doctrines and usages, to remedy the bulkiness, expensiveness, and scarcity of the Confession of 1677, to supply some omissions of that Confession, to distinguish themselves from some who bore the same name, and to arm members of the two churches against error. Articles on the imposition of hands and the singing of psalms in public worship were added, and some minor doctrinal changes were made.

An appendix on discipline entitled, "The Glory and Ornament of a True Gospel-constituted Church," written by Keach but drawn largely from Chauncey, was attached to the Keach document. Occupying sixteen octavo pages, it is a vigorous attack on infant baptism, designed to explicate and to defend the clause of Article XXIX which declares the subjects of baptism to be believers only. It also indicates the lack of agreement of the churches on close communion, saying that "others of us have a greater liberty and freedom in our spirits that way." Probably most of the churches practiced "strict communion" in 1689, but difference of practice was tolerated in the Assembly. Neither Rippon nor Crosby in their copies of the Confession included the Appendix, nor did Rippon put it in his "Narrative of the Proceedings of the General Assembly" which adopted the Confession.

The Keach Confession, which had only one edition in England, found its way to America, through Elias Keach's influence, and became the body of the Philadelphia Confession, the dominant early Calvinistic Baptist Confession in the New World.

A copy of the original edition of 1677, from McGlothlin, *Baptist Confessions of Faith*, 220-274, follows. Original copies may be found in the Angus Library, Regent's Park College, Oxford; Bristol Baptist College; University Library, Cambridge; the British Museum; and Sion College Library, London (Whitley, *Bibliography*, 108).

---

[13] Whitley, *A Baptist Bibliography*, I, 127.

CONFESSION

OF

FAITH

Put forth by the

ELDERS and BRETHREN

Of many

CONGREGATIONS

OF

Christians (baptized upon Profession of their Faith) in *London* and the Country.

With the Heart man believeth unto Righteousness, and with the Mouth Confession is made unto Salvation, Rom. 10. 10. *Search the Scriptures,* John 5. 39.

Printed in the Year, 1677.

Q

THE

CONTENTS.

[Page]

[Page]

TO THE
JUDICIOUS AND IMPARTIAL
READER.

Courteous Reader,—It is now many years since divers of
us (with other sober Christians then
living and walking in the way of
the Lord that we professe) did conceive
our selves to be under a necessity of Publishing a *Confession of our Faith*, for the
information, and satisfaction of those,
that did not thoroughly understand what
our principles were, or had entertained
prejudices against our Profession, by
reason of the strange representation of
them, by some men of note, who had
taken very wrong measures, and accord [page]
ingly led others into misapprehensions, of
us, and them: and this was first put forth
about the year, 1643, in the name of
seven Congregations then gathered in
London; since which time, diverse im-
pressions thereof have been dispersed
abroad, and our end proposed, in good
measure answered, inasmuch as many
(and some of those men eminent, both
for piety and learning) were thereby satisfied, that we were no way guilty of
those Heterodoxies and fundamental errors, which had too frequently been
charged upon us without ground, or occasion given on our part. And forasmuch as that *Confession* is not now commonly to be had; and also that many
others have since embraced the same
truth which is owned therein; it was
judged necessary by us to joyn together
in giving a testimony to the world; of
our firm adhering to those wholesome
Principles, by the publication of this
which is now in your hand.

And forasmuch as our method, and [page]
manner of expressing our sentiments in
this doth vary from the former (although the
substance of the matter is the same)
we shall freely impart to you the reason and
occasion thereof. One thing that greatly prevailed
with us to undertake this work, was (not only to
give a full account of ourselves to those Christians that differ from us about the subject

of baptism, but also) the profit that might
from thence arise unto those that have any
account of our labours, in their instruction
and establishment in the great truths of the
gospel; in the clear understanding and steady
belief of which our comfortable walking with
God, and fruitfulness before him in all our ways
is most nearly concerned. And therefore
we did conclude it necessary to express ourselves the more fully and distinctly, and also to fix
on such a method as might be most comprehensive of those things which we designed to explain our sense and belief of; and finding no
defect in this regard in that fixed on by the
Assembly, and after them by those of the Congregational way, we did readily conclude it
best to retain the same order in our present
Confession. And also when we observed [page]
that those last mentioned did, in their Confession
(for reasons which seemed of weight both to
themselves and others), choose not only to express their mind in words concurrent with
the former in sense, concerning all those articles wherein they were agreed, but also for
the most part without any variation of
the terms, we did in like manner conclude
it best to follow their example, in making
use of the very same words with them both, in
those articles (which are very many) wherein
our faith and doctrine is the same with theirs.
And this we did, the more abundantly to
manifest our consent with both, in all the
fundamental articles of the Christian religion, as also with many others whose
orthodox confessions have been published
to the World, on the behalf of the protestants
in diverse nations and cities; and also to
convince all that we have no itch to clog religion with new words, but to readily ac-
quiesce in that form of sound words which
hath been, in consent with the holy scriptures,
used by others before us; hereby declaring
before God, angels, and men, our hearty
agreement with them, in that wholesome [page]
protestant doctrine, which, with so clear
evidence of scriptures they have asserted.
Some things, indeed, are in some places
added, some terms omitted, and some
few changed; but these alterations are of
that nature, as that we need not doubt any
charge or suspicion of unsoundness in

the faith, from any of our brethren upon the account of them.

In those things wherein we differ from others,
we have expressed ourselves with all candour
and plainness, that none might entertain
Jealousy of aught secretly lodged in our breasts,
that we would not the world should be
acquainted with; yet we hope we have also
observed those rules of modesty and humility
as will render our freedom in this respect
inoffensive, even to those whose sentiments
are different from ours.

We have also taken care to affix texts of
scripture in the margin, for the confirmation of each article in our Confession; in
which work we have studiously endea-
vored to select such as are most clear
and pertinent for the proof of what is
asserted by us; and our earnest desire [page]
is, that all into whose hands this may
come would follow that (never
enough commended) example of the
noble Bereans, who searched the scriptures daily that they might find out
whether the things preached to them were
so or not.

There is one thing more which we
sincerely profess, and earnestly desire credence in, viz., that contention
is most remote from our design in
all that we have done in this matter;
and we hope the liberty of an inge-
nuous unfolding our principles and
opening our hearts unto our brethren,.
with the scripture-grounds on which
our faith and practice leans, will
by none of them be either denied to
us, or taken ill from us. Our
whole design is accomplished if we
may obtain that justice, as to be measured
in our principles and practice and the [page]
judgement of both by others, according
to what we have now published; which
the Lord (whose eyes are as a flame of
fire) knoweth to be the doctrine, which
with our hearts we most firmly believe,
and sincerely indeavour to conform our
lives to. And oh that other contentions
being laid asleep, the only care and contention of all upon whom the name of
our blessed Redeemer is called, might

for the future be, to walk humbly with
their God, and in the exercise of all
Love and Meekness towards each other,
to perfect holyness in the fear of the Lord,
each one endeavouring to have his conversation such as becometh the Gospel;
and also, suitable to his place and capacity, vigorously to promote in others the
practice of true Religion and undefiled in
the sight of God and our Father. And that
in this backsliding day, we might not
spend our breath in fruitless complaints of
the evils of others; but may every one
begin at home, to reform in the first place
our own hearts, and wayes; and then
to quicken all that we may have influence [page]
upon, to the same work; that if the will
of God were so, none might deceive
themselves, by resting in, and trusting
to, a form of Godliness, without the power of it, and inward experience of the
efficacy of those truths that are professed
by them.

And verily there is one spring and
cause of the decay of Religion in our
day, which we cannot but touch upon, and earnestly urge a redress of;
and that is the neglect of the worship of God
in Families, by those to whom the charge
and conduct of them is committed. May
not the grosse ignorance, and instability
of many; with the prophaneness of others,
be justly charged upon their Parents
and Masters, who have not trained them
up in the way wherein they ought to
walk when they were young; but have
neglected those frequent and solemn commands which the Lord hath laid upon
them so to catechise, and instruct them,
that their tender years might be seasoned
with the knowledge of the truth of God
as revealed in the Scriptures; and also by [page]
their own omission of Prayer, and other
duties of Religion in their families, together with the ill example of their loose
conversation, have inured them first to a
neglect, and then contempt of all Piety
and Religion? we know this will not excuse the blindness, or wickedness of any; but
certainly it will fall heavy upon those
that have been thus the occasion thereof;

they indeed dye in their sins; but will not their blood be required of those under whose care they were, who yet permitted them to go on without *warning*, yea led them into the paths of destruction? and will not the diligence of Christians with respect to the discharge of these duties, in ages past, rise up in judgment against, and condemn many of those who would be esteemed such now?

We shall conclude with our earnest prayer, that the God of all grace, will pour out those measures of his holy Spirit upon us, that the profession of truth may be accompanyed with the sound belief, and diligent practise of it by us; that his name may in all things be glorified, through Jesus Christ our Lord, *Amen.*

A

CONFESSION OF

FAITH.

Chap. I.

Of the Holy Scriptures.

1. THe Holy Scripture is the only sufficient, certain, and infallible[1] rule of all saving Knowledge, Faith, and Obedience; Although the[2] light of Nature, and the works of Creation and Providence do so far manifest the goodness, wisdom and power of God, as to leave men unexcusable; yet are they not sufficient to give that knowledge [page] of God and His will, which is necessary unto Salvation.[3] Therefore it pleased the Lord at sundry times, and in divers manners, to reveal himself, and to declare that His will unto his Church; and afterward for the better preserving, and propagating of the Truth, and for the more sure Establishment and Comfort of the

[1] 2 Tim. 3. 15, 16, 17. Isa. 8. 20. Luk. 16. 29, 31. Eph. 2. 20. [2] Rom. 1. 19, 20, 21 etc. ch. 2. 14, 15. Psal. 19. 1, 2, 3.

[3] Heb. 1. 1.

Church against the corruption of
the flesh, and the malice of Satan,
and of the World, to commit the same

⁴ Pro. 22.
19, 20, 21.
Rom. 15.
4. 2 Pet. 1.
19, 20.

wholly unto⁴ writing;
which maketh the Holy Scriptures
to be most necessary, those former
ways of Gods revealing his will
unto his people being now ceased.

2. Under the Name of Holy
Scripture, or the Word of God
written; are now contained all
the Books of the Old and New
Testament, which are these, [page]

Of the Old Testament.

Genesis, Exodus, Leviticus,
Numbers, Deauteronomy, Joshua,
Judges, Ruth, 1 Samuel, 2 Samuel, 1 Kings, 2 Kings, 1 Chronicles, 2 Chronicles, Ezra, Nehemiah, Esther, Job, Psalms, Pro-
verbs, Ecclesiastes, The Song of
Songs, Isaiah, Jeremiah, Lamen-
tations, Ezekiel, Daniel, Hosea,
Joel, Amos, Obadiah, Jonah, Micah, Nahum, Habakkuk, Zepha-
niah, Haggai, Zechariah, Mala-
chi.

Of the New Testament.

Matthew, Mark, Luke, John,
The Acts of the Apostles, Pauls
Epistle to the Romans, 1 Corin-
thians, 2 Corinthians, Galatians,
Ephesians, Philippians, Colossians, [page]
1 Thessalonians, 2 Thessalonians,
1 Timothy, 2 Timothy, to Titus,
to Philemon, the Epistle to the
Hebrews, the Epistle of James,
The first and second Epistles of
Peter, The first, second, and third
Epistles of John, the Epistle of
Jude, the Revelation. All which

⁵ 2 Tim. 3. 16.

are given by the⁵ inspiration
of God, to be the rule of Faith
and Life.

3. The Books commonly called

⁶ Luk. 24.
27, 44.
Rom. 3. 2.

Apochypha not being of⁶ Divine
inspiration, are no part of the Ca-
non (or rule) of the Scripture, and

therefore are of no authority to
the Church of God, nor to be any
otherwise approved or made use
of, then other humane writings.

4. The Authority of the Holy
Scripture for which it ought to be
believed dependeth not upon the
testimony of any man, or Church;
but wholly upon[7] God (who [page]
is truth it self) the Author thereof; therefore it is to be received,
because it is the Word of God.

5. We may be moved and induced by the testimony of the
Church of God, to an high and
reverent esteem of the Holy Scriptures; and the heavenliness of the
matter, the efficacy of the Doctrine, and the Majesty of the stile,
the consent of all the parts, the
scope of the whole (which is to
give all glory to God) the full discovery it makes of the only way
of mans salvation, and many o-
ther incomparable Excellencies,
and intire perfections thereof, are
arguments whereby it doth abundantly evidence it self to be the
Word of God; yet, notwithstanding; our[8] full perswasion, and
assurance of the infallible truth,
and divine authority thereof, is
from the inward work of the Holy
Spirit, bearing witness by and [page]
with the Word in our Hearts.

6. The whole Councel of God
concerning all things[9] necessary
for his own Glory, Mans Salvation,
Faith and Life, is either expresse-
ly set down or necessarily contained in the *Holy Scripture;* unto
which nothing at any time is to be
added, whether by new Revelation of the
Spirit, or traditions of
men.

Nevertheless we acknowledge
the[11] inward illumination of
the Spirit of God, to be necessary for the saving understanding of
such things as are revealed in the
Word, and that there are some

[7] 2 Pet. 1.
19, 20, 21,
2 Tim. 3.
16.
2 Thes. 2.
13. 1 Joh.
5. 19.

[8] Joh. 16.
13, 14.
1 Cor. 2.
10, 11, 12,
1 Joh. 2.
2, 20, 27.

[9] 2 Tim.
3. 15, 16.
17. Gal. 1.
8, 9.

[11] John 6.
45. 1 Cor.
2. 9, 10,
11, 12,

circumstances concerning the worship of God, and government of the Church common to humane actions and societies; which are to be[12] ordered by the light of nature, and Christian prudence according to the general rules of the Word, which are always to be observed. [page]

7. All things in Scripture are not alike[13] plain in themselves, nor alike clear unto all; yet those things which are necessary to be known, believed, and observed for Salvation, are so[14] clearly propounded, and opened in some place of Scripture or other, that not only the learned, but the unlearned, in a due use of ordinary means, may attain to a sufficient understanding of them.

8. The Old Testament in[15] *Hebrew,* (which was the Native language of the people of God of old) and the New Testament in *Greek,* (which at the time of the writing of it was most generally known to the Nations being immediately inspired by God, and by his singular care and Providence kept pure in all Ages, are therefore[16] authentical; so as in all controversies of Religion, the Church is finally to appeal unto them[17]. But be- [page] cause these original tongues are not known to all the people of God, who have a right unto, and interest in the scriptures, and are commanded in the fear of God to read[18] and search them, therefore they are to be translated into the vulgar language of every Nation, unto which they[19] come, that the Word of God dwelling[20] plentifully in all, they may worship him in an acceptable manner, and through patience and comfort of the Scriptures may have hope.

9. The infallible rule of interpretation of Scripture is the[21]

12 1 Cor.
11. 13, 14.
& ch. 14.
26 & 40.

13 2 Pet.
3. 16.

14 Ps. 19. 7.
and 119.

15 Rom.
3. 2.

16 Isa. 8. 20.

17 Act. 15. 15.

18 John 5.
39.

19 1 Cor.
14. 6, 9, 11,
12, 24, 28.
20 Col. 3. 16.

21 2 Pet. 1.
20, 21.
Act. 15.
15, 16.

Scripture it self: And therefore when there is a question about the true and full sense of any Scripture (which is not manifold but one) it must be searched by other places that speak more clearly. [page]

10. The supream judge by which all controversies of Religion are to be determined, and all Decrees of Councels, opinions of antient Writers, Doctrines of men, and private Spirits, are to be examined, and in whose sentence we are to rest, can be no other but the Holy Scripture delivered by the Spirit, into which [24] Scripture so delivered, our faith is finally resolved.

[21] Mat. 22. 29, 31. Eph. 2. 20. Acts 28. 23.

CHAP. II.

Of God and of the Holy Trinity.

1. THE Lord our God is but [1] one only living, and true God; whose [2] subsistence is in and of himself, [3] infinite in being, and perfection, whose Essence cannot be comprehended by [page] any but himself; [4] a most pure spirit, [5] invisible, without body, parts, or passions, who only hath immortality, dwelling in the light, which no man can approach unto, who is [6] immutable, [7] immense, [8] eternal, incomprehensible, [9] Almighty, every way infinite, [11] most holy, most wise, most free, most absolute, [12] working all things according to the councel of his own immutable, and most righteous will, [13] for his own glory, most loving, gracious, merciful, long-suffering, abundant in goodness and truth, forgiving iniquity, transgression and sin, [14] the rewarder of them that diligently seek him, and withal most just, [15] and terrible in his judgments, [16] hating all sin, and who will

[1] 1 Cor. 8. 4, 6. Deut. 6. 4.
[2] Jer. 10. 10. Isaiah 48. 12.
[3] Exod. 3. 14.
[4] Joh. 4. 24.
[5] 1 Tim. 1. 17. Deut. 4. 15, 16.
[6] Mal. 3. 6.
[7] 1 King. 8: 27. Jer. 23. 23.
[8] Psal. 90. 2.
[9] Gen. 17. 1.
[11] Isa. 6. 3.
[12] Psal. 16. 3. Isa. 46. 10.
[13] Pro. 16. 4. Rom. 11. 36.

[14] Exod. 34. 6, 7. Heb. 11. 6.
[15] Neh. 9. 32, 33.
[16] Ps. 5. 5, 6.

[17] Exod. 34. 7.
Nahum. 1. 2, 3.
[18] Joh. 5.
26.
[19] Ps. 148.
13.
[20] Ps. 119.
68.
[21] Job 22.
2, 3.

[24] Rom.
11. 34, 35,
36.

[25] Dan. 4.
25 & 5. 34, 35.

[20] Heb. 4.
13.

[1] Ezek. 11.
5. Act. 15.
18.

[2] Ps. 145.
17.

[3] Rev. 5.
12, 13, 14.

[4] 1 Joh.
5. 7. Mat.
28. 19.
2 Cor. 13.
14.

[5] Exod. 3.
14. Joh.
14. 11.
1 Cor. 8. 6.

[6] Joh. 1.
14, 18.

Joh. 15.
26.
Gal. 4. 6.

by no means clear the [17] guilty. [page]
2. God having all [18] life, [19]
glory, [20] goodness, blessedness,
in and of himself: is alone in,
and unto himself all-sufficient, not [21]
standing in need of any Crea-
ture which he hath made, nor de-
riving any glory from them, but
onely manifesting his own glory
in, by, unto, and upon them, he
is the alone fountain of all Being, [24]
of whom, through whom, and
to whom are all things, and he
hath most soveraign [25] dominion
over all creatures, to do by them,
for them, and upon them, whatsoever himself pleaseth; in his sight [26]
all things are open and manifest, his knowledge is [1] infinite,
infallible, and independant upon
the Creature, so as nothing is to
him contingent, or uncertain; he is
most holy in all his Councels, in [2]
all his Works, and in all his
Commands; to him is due [3] from
Angels and men, whatsoever
worship, service, or obedience as [page]
Creatures they owe unto the
Creator, and whatever he is further pleased to require of them.
3. In this divine and infinite
Being there are three subsistences, [4]
the Father the Word (or Son)
and Holy Spirit, of one substance,
power, and Eternity, each having
the whole Divine Essence, [5] yet
the Essence undivided, the Father
is of none neither begotten nor
proceeding, the Son is [6] Eternally begotten of the Father, the
holy Spirit [7] proceeding from
the Father and the Son, all infinite, without beginning, therefore
but one God, who is not to be divided in nature and Being; but
distinguished by several peculiar,
relative properties, and personal
relations; which doctrine of the
Trinity is the foundation of all
our Communion with God, and
comfortable dependence on him. [page]

CHAP. III.

Of Gods Decree.

1. GOD hath [1] *Decreed* in himself from all Eternity, by the most wise and holy Councel of his own will, freely and unchangeably, all things whatsoever comes to passe; yet so as thereby is God neither the author of sin,[2] nor hath fellowship with any therin, nor is violence offered to the will of the Creature, nor yet is the liberty, or contingency of second causes taken away, but rather [3] established, in which appears his wisdom in disposing all things, and power, and faithfulness [4] in accomplishing his *Decree*.

2. Although God knoweth whatsoever may, or can come to passe upon all [5] supposed condi- [page] tions; yet hath he not *Decreed* anything,[6] because he foresaw it as future, or as that which would come to pass upon such conditions.

3. By the *decree* of God, for the manifestation of his glory [7] some men and Angels are predestinated, or fore-ordained to Eternal Life, through Jesus Christ, to the [8] praise of his glorious grace; others being left to act in their sin to their [9] just condemnation, to the praise of his glorious justice.

4. These Angels and Men thus predestinated, and fore-ordained, are particularly, and unchangeably designed, and their [11] number so certain, and definite, that it cannot be either increased, or diminished.

5. Those of mankind that are predestinated to life, God, be- [page] fore the foundation of the world was laid, according to his eternal and immutable purpose, and the secret Councel and good pleasure of his will, hath chosen in Christ unto everlasting glory, out of his meer free grace and love; [13] without any other thing in the

[1] Is. 46. 10. Eph. 1. 11. Heb. 6. 17. Rom. 9. 15, 18.

[2] Jam. 1. 15, 17. 1 Joh. 1. 5.

[3] Act. 4. 27, 28, Joh. 19. 11.
[4] Numb. 23. 19. Eph. 1. 3, 4, 5.

[5] Act. 15. 18.

[6] Rom. 9. 11, 13, 16, 18.

[7] 1 Tim. 5. 21. Mat. 25. 41.
[8] Eph. 1. 5, 6.

[9] Rom. 9. 22, 23. Jud. 4.

[11] 2 Tim. 2. 19. Joh. 13. 18.
[12] Eph. 1. 4, 9, 11. Rom. 8. 30. 2 Tim. 1. 9. 1 Thes. 5. 9.

[13] Rom. 9. 13, 16. Eph. 1. 6, 12.

creature as a condition or cause moving him thereunto.

6. As God hath appointed the Elect unto glory, so he hath by the eternal and most free purpose of his will, fore-ordained [15] all the means thereunto, wherefore they who are elected, being faln in Adam,[16] are redeemed by Christ, are effectually [17] called unto faith in Christ, by his spirit working in due season, are justifyed, adopted, sanctified, and kept by his power through faith [18] unto salvation; neither are any other redeemed by Christ, or effectually called, justified, adopted, sanctifi- [page] ed, and saved, but the Elect [19] only.

7. The Doctrine of this high mystery of predestination, is to be handled with special prudence, and care; that men attending the will of God revealed in his word, and yielding obedience thereunto, may from the certainty of their effectual vocation, be assured of their [20] eternal election; so shall this doctrine afford matter [21] of praise, reverence, and admiration of God, and [24] of humility, diligence, and abundant [25] consolation, to all that sincerely obey the Gospel. [page]

CHAP. IV.

Of Creation.

1. IN the beginning it pleased *God* the Father,[1] Son, and Holy Spirit, for the manifestation of the glory of [2] his eternal power, wisdom, and goodness, to *Create* or *make* the world, and all things therein,[3] whether visible or invisible, in the space of six days, and all very good.

2. After God had made all other Creatures, he *Created* [4] man, male and female, with [5] reasonable and immortal souls, ren-

[15] 1 Pet. 1. 2.
2 Thes. 2.
[16] 13.
1 Thes. 5. 9, 10.
[17] Rom. 8. 30.
2 Thes. 2. 13.
[18] 1 Pet. 1. 5.

[19] Joh. 10. 26.
Joh. 17. 9.
Joh. 6. 64.

[20] 1 Thes. 1. 4, 5.
2 Pet. 1. 10..
[21] Eph. 1. 6. Rom. 11. 33.
[24] Rom. 11. 5, 6.
[25] Luk. 10. 20.

[1] John 1. 2, 3.
Heb. 1. 2.
Job 26. 13.
[2] Rom. 1. 20.
[3] Col. 1. 16.
Gen. 2. 1, 2.
[4] Gen. 1. 27.
[5] Gen. 2. 7.

dring them fit unto that life to
God, for which they were *Created;*
being[6] made after the image
of God, in knowledge, righteousness, and true holyness; having the [page]
Law of God[7] written in their
hearts, and power to fulfill it;
and yet under a possibility of
transgressing, being left to the liberty of their own will, which
was[8] subject to change.

3. Besides the Law written in
their hearts, they received[9] a
command not to eat of the tree of
knowledge of good and evil;
which whilst they kept, they were
happy in their Communion with
God, and had dominion[11] over
the Creatures. [page]

[6] Eccles.
7. 29.

[7] Rom. 2.
14, 15.

[8] Gen. 3.
6.
[9] Gen. 6.
17. & ch.
3. 8, 9, 10.

[11] Gen. 1.
26, 28.

CHAP. V.

Of Divine Providence.

1. GOD, the good *Creator* of all
things, in *his* infinite power,
and wisdom, doth[1] uphold, direct, dispose, and govern all Creatures, and things, from the greatest even to the[2] least, by *his*
most wise and holy providence, to
the end for the which they were
Created; according unto his infallible foreknowledge, and the free
and immutable Councel of *his*[3]
own will; to the praise of the
glory of *his* wisdom, power, justice, infinite goodness and mercy.

[1] Heb. 1.
3. Job 38.
11. Isa. 46.
10, 11. Ps.
135. 6.
[2] Mat. 10.
29, 30, 31.

[3] Eph. 1.
11.

2. Although in relation to the
foreknowledge and *Decree* of *God,*
the first cause, all things come to [page]
pass[4] immutably and infallibly;
so that there is not any thing, befalls any[5] by chance, or without
his Providence; yet by the same
Providence he ordereth them to
fall out, according to the nature
of second causes, either[6] necessarily, freely, or contingent-
ly.

Act. 2. 23.

[5] Prov. 16.
33.

[6] Gen. 8.
22.

3. God in *his* ordinary *Prov-*

7 Act. 27.
31, 44.
Isa. 55. 10,
11.
8 Hos. 1. 7.
9 Rom. 4.
19, 20, 21.
11 Dan. 3.
27.
12 Rom. 11.
32, 33, 34.
2 Sam. 24.
1. 1 Chro.
21. 1.

13 2 Kings
19. 28.
Ps. 76. 10.

14 Gen. 50.
20. Isa. 10.
6, 7, 12.

15 Ps. 50. 21.
1 Joh. 2.
16.

16 2 Chro.
32. 25, 26,
31.
2 Sam. 24.
1. 2 Cor.
12. 7, 8, 9.

17 Rom. 8.
28.

18 Rom. 1.
24, 26, 28,
ch. 11. 7, 8.
19 Deut.
29. 4.

idence [7] maketh use of means; yet is free [8] to work, without, [9] above, and [11] against them at *his* pleasure.

4. The Almighty power, unsearchable wisdom, and *infinite* goodness of *God*, so far manifest themselves in *his* Providence, that *his* determinate Councel [12] extendeth it self even to the first fall, and all other sinful actions both of Angels, and Men; (and that not by a bare permission) which also he most wisely and [page] powerfully [13] boundeth, and otherwise ordereth, and governeth, in a manifold dispensation to *his* most holy [14] ends: yet so, as the sinfulness of their acts proceedeth only from the Creatures, and not from *God;* who being most holy and righteous, neither is nor can be, the author or [15] approver of sin.

5. The most wise, righteous, and gracious *God*, doth oftentimes, leave for a season *his* own children to manifold temptations, and the corruptions of their own heart, to chastise them for their former sins, or to discover unto them the hidden strength of corruption, and deceitfulness of their hearts, [16] that they may be humbled; and to raise them to a more close, and constant dependence for their support, upon himself; and to make them more watchful against all future occasions of sin, and for [page] other just and holy ends.

So that whatsoever befalls any of his elect is by his appointment, for his glory, [17] and their good.

6. As for those wicked and ungodly men, whom God as a righteous judge, for former sin doth [18] blind and harden; from them he not only withholdeth his [19] Grace, whereby they might have been inlightened in their understanding, and wrought upon in

R

their hearts: But sometimes also withdraweth [20] the gifts which they had, and exposeth them to such [21] objects as their *corruptions* makes occasion of sin; and withal [24] gives them over to their own lusts, the temptations of the world, and the power of Satan, whereby it comes to pass, that they [25] harden themselves, even under those means which God useth for the softening of others. [page]

7. As the *Providence* of *God* doth in general reach to all *Creatures,* so after a most special manner it taketh care of his [26] Church, and disposeth of all things to the good thereof.

[20] Mat. 13. 12.
[21] Deut. 2. 30.
2 King. 8. 12, 13.
[24] Psal. 81. 11, 12.
2 Thes. 2. 10, 11, 12.
[25] Exod. 8. 15, 32.
Is. 6. 9, 10.
1 Pet. 2. 7, 8.

[26] 1 Tim. 4. 10.
Amos 9. 8, 9.
Isa. 43. 3, 4, 5.

CHAP. VI.
Of the fall of Man, of Sin, and of the Punishment thereof.

1. Although *God created Man* upright, and perfect, and gave him a righteous law, which had been unto life had he kept it,[1] and threatened death upon the breach thereof; yet he did not long abide in this honour;[2] Satan using the subtilty of the serpent to seduce *Eve,* then by her [page] seducing *Adam,* who without any compulsion, did wilfully transgress the Law of their *Creation,* and the command given unto them, in eating the forbidden fruit; which *God* was pleased according to *his* wise and holy *Councel* to permit, having purposed to order it, to *his* own glory.

2. Our first *Parents* by this *Sin,* fell from their [3] original righteousness and communion with *God,* and we in them, whereby death came upon all;[4] all becoming dead in *Sin,* and wholly defiled,[5] in all the faculties, and parts, of soul, and body.

3. They being the [6] root, and by *Gods* appointment, stand.

[1] Gen. 2. 16, 17.

[2] Gen. 3. 12, 13.
2 Cor. 11. 3.

[3] Rom. 3. 23.
[4] Rom. 5. 12 etc.
[5] Tit. 1. 15.
Gen. 6. 5.
Jer. 17. 9.
Rom. 3. 10-19.
[6] Rom. 5. 12-19.
1 Cor. 15. 21, 22, 45, 49.

ing in the room, and stead of all mankind; the guilt of the *Sin* was imputed, and *corrupted* nature conveyed, to all their posterity descending from them by ordina- [page] ry generation, being now [7] conceived in *Sin,* and by nature children [8] of wrath, the servants of *Sin,* the subjects [9] of *death* and all other miseries, spiritual, temporal and eternal, unless the *Lord Jesus* [11] set them free.

[7] Ps. 51. 5.
[8] Job 14. 4. Eph. 2. 3.
[9] Rom. 6. 20 & ch. 5. 12.
[11] Heb. 2. 14.

4. From this original *corruption,* whereby we are [12] utterly indisposed, disabled, and made oppo.ite to all good, and wholly inclined to all evil, do [13] proceed all actual transgressions.

[1] Thes. 1. 10.
[12] Rom. 8. 7. Col. 1. 21.
[13] Jam. 1. 14, 15. Mat. 15. 19.

5. This *corruption* of nature, during this Life, doth [14] remain in those that are regenerated: and although it be through *Christ* pardoned, and mortified, yet both it self, and the first motions thereof, are truely and properly [15] *Sin.* [page]

[14] Rom. 7. 18, 23. Eccles. 7. 20. 1 Joh. 1. 8.
[15] Rom. 7. 24, 25. Gal. 5. 17.

CHAP. VII.

Of Gods Covenant.

1. THE distance between *God* and the *Creature* is so great, that although reasonable *Creatures* do owe obedience unto him as their *Creator,* yet they could never have attained the reward of Life, but by some [1] voluntary condescension on *Gods part,* which he hath been pleased to express, by way of *Covenant.*

[1] Luk. 17. 10. Job 35. 7, 8.

2. Moreover *Man* having brought himself [2] under the *curse* of the Law by his fall, it pleased the *Lord* to make a *Covenant* of *Grace* wherein he freely offereth unto *Sinners,* [3] Life and Salvation by *Jesus Christ,* requiring of them Faith in him, that they may be saved; and [4] promising to [page] give unto all those that are ordained unto eternal Life, his Holy *Spi-*

[2] Gen. 2. 17. Gal. 3. 10, Rom. 3. 20, 21.
[3] Rom. 8. 3. Mark 16. 15, 16. Joh. 3. 16.
[4] Ezek. 36. 26, 27. Joh. 6. 44, 45. Ps. 110. 3.

rit, to make them willing, and
able to believe.

3. This *Covenant* is revealed in
the Gospel; first of all to *Adam*
in the promise of Salvation by the[5]
seed of the woman, and afterwards by farther steps, until the
full[6] discovery thereof was
compleated in the new Testament;
and it is founded in that * Eternal
Covenant transaction, that was between the *Father* and the *Son,*
about the Redemption of the
Elect; and it is alone by the
Grace of this *Covenant,* that all
of the posterity of fallen *Adam,*
that ever were[7] saved, did obtain life and a blessed immortality; *Man* being now utterly uncapable of acceptance with *God* upon those terms, on which *Adam*
stood in his state of innocency. [page]

[5] Gen. 3.
15.

[6] Heb. 1.
1.

* 2 Tim.
1. 9.
Tit. 1. 2.

[7] Heb. 11.
6, 13.
Rom. 4. 1,
2, etc.
Act. 4. 12.
Joh. 8. 56.

CHAP. VIII.
Of Christ the Media-
tor.

1. IT pleased *God* in his eternal
purpose, to chuse and ordain
the *Lord Jesus* his only begotten
Son, according to the *Covenant*
made between them both,[1]
to be the *Mediator* between
God and *Man;* the[2] Prophet,[3]
Priest and[4] King; Head
and Saviour of his Church, the
heir of all things, and judge of
the world: Unto whom he did
from all Eternity[5] give a people
to be his seed, and to be by him
in time redeemed, called, justified,
sanctified, and glorified.

2. The *Son* of *God,* the second
Person in the *Holy Trinity,* being [page]
very and eternal *God,* the brightness of the Fathers glory, of one
substance and equal with *him:*
who made the World, who up-
holdeth and governeth all things
he hath made: did when the fullness of time was come take upon
him[6] mans nature, with all

[1] Is. 42. 1.
1 Pet. 1.
19, 20.
[2] Act. 3.
22.
[3] Heb. 5.
5, 6.
[4] Ps. 2. 6.
Luk. 1. 33.
Eph. 1. 23.
Heb. 1. 2.
Act. 17. 31.
[5] Is. 53. 10.
Joh. 17. 6.
Rom. 8.
30.

[6] Joh. 1. 1,
14.
Gal. 4. 4.

the Essential properties, and common infirmities thereof,[7] yet without sin: being conceived by the *Holy Spirit* in the *Womb* of the *Virgin Mary,* the *Holy Spirit* coming down upon her, and the power of the most *High* overshadowing her,[8] and so was made of a *Woman,* of the Tribe of *Judah,* of the Seed of *Abraham,* and *David* according to the *Scriptures:* So that two whole, perfect, and distinct natures, were inseparably joined together in one *Person:* without *conversion, composition,* or *confusion:* which *Person* is very *God,* and very *Man;* yet one[9] *Christ,* the only *Mediator* between *God* and *Man.* [page]

3. The *Lord Jesus* in his human nature thus united to the divine, in the Person of the *Son,* was sanctified, anointed[11] with the *Holy Spirit,* above measure; having in him[12] all the treasures of wisdom and knowledge; in whom it pleased the *Father* that[13] all fullness should dwell: To the end that being[14] holy, harmless, undefiled, and full[15] of *Grace,* and *Truth,* he might be thoroughly furnished to execute the office of a *Mediator,* and[16] *Surety;* which office he took not upon himself, but was thereunto[17] called by his *Father;* who also put[18] all power and judgement in his hand, and gave him Commandement to execute the same.

4. This office the *Lord Jesus* did most[19] willingly undertake, which that he might discharge he was made under the Law,[20] and did perfectly fulfill it, and under- [page] went the[21] punishment due to us, which we should have born and suffered, being made[24] *Sin* and a *Curse* for us: enduring most grievous sorrows[25] in his *Soul;* and most painful sufferings in his body; was crucified, and died,

[7] Rom. 8. 3. Heb. 2. 14, 16, 17. ch. 4. 15.

[8] Luk. 1. 27, 31, 35.

[9] Rom. 9. 5. 1 Tim. 2. 5.

[11] Ps. 45. 7. Act. 10. 38. Joh. 3. 34.
[12] Col. 2. 3.

[13] Col. 1. 19.

[14] Heb. 7. 26.
[15] Joh. 1. 14.
[16] Heb. 7. 22.
[17] Heb. 5. 5.
[18] Joh. 5. 22, 27. Mat. 28. 18. Act. 2. 36.
[19] Ps. 40. 7, 8. Heb. 10. 5-11. Joh. 10. 18.
[20] Gal. 4. 4. Mat. 3. 15.
[21] Gal. 3. 13. Isa. 53. 6. 1 Pet. 3. 18.
[24] 2 Cor. 5. 21.
[25] Mat. 26. 37, 38. Luk. 22. 44. Mat. 27. 46.

and remained in the state of the
dead; yet saw no [26] *corruption*:
on the [1] third day he arose from
the dead, with the same [2] body in
which he suffered; with which he
also [3] ascended into heaven:
and there sitteth at the right hand
of *his Father*, [4] making intercession; and shall [5] return to judge
Men and *Angels*, at the end of the World.

5. The *Lord Jesus* by his perfect obedience and sacrifice of himself, which he through the Eternal *Spirit* once offered up unto
God, [6] hath fully satisfied the
Justice of *God*, procured reconciliation, and purchased an Everlast- [page]
ing inheritance in the Kingdom of
Heaven, [7] for all those whom
the *Father* hath given unto him.

6. Although the price of Redemption was not actually paid by
Christ, till after his *Incarnation*,[*]
yet the vertue, efficacy, and benefit
thereof were communicated to the
Elect in all ages successively, from
the beginning of the World, in
and by those Promises, Types, and
Sacrifices, wherein he was revealed, and signified to be the Seed of
the *Woman*, which should bruise
the Serpents head; [8] and the
Lamb slain from the foundation of
the World: [9] Being *the same
yesterday, and to-day, and for ever*.

7. Christ in the work of *Mediation* acteth according to both natures, by each nature doing that
which is proper to it self; yet by
reason of the Unity of the Person,
that which is proper to one na- [page]
ture, is sometimes in *Scripture* at-
tributed to the Person [11] denominated by the other nature.

8. To all those for whom Christ
hath obtained eternal redemption, he doth certainly, and effectually [12] apply, and communicate the same; making intercession for them, uniting them to himself by his spirit, [13] revealing

[26] Act. 13.
37.
[1] 1 Cor. 15. 3, 4
[2] Joh. 20.
25, 27.
[3] Mark 16.
19.
Act. 1. 9,
10, 11.
[4] Rom. 8.
34.
Heb. 9. 24.
[5] Act. 10.
42. Rom.
14. 9, 10.
Act. 1. 10.

[6] Heb. 9.
14. Ch. 10.
14. Rom.
3. 25, 26.

[7] Joh. 17.
2. Heb. 9.
15.

[*] 1 Cor. 4.
10.
Heb. 4. 2.
1 Pet. 1.
10, 11.

[8] Rev. 13.
8.

[9] Heb. 13.
8.

[11] Joh. 3.
13.
Act. 20.
28.
[12] Joh. 6.
37. ch. 10.
15, 16.
& ch. 17.
9.
[13] Joh. 17.
6. Eph. 1.
9. 1 Joh.
5. 20.

unto them, in and by the word, the mystery of salvation; perswading them to believe, and obey;[14] governing their hearts by his word and spirit, and[15] overcoming all their enemies by his Almighty power, and wisdom; in such manner, and wayes as are most consonant to his wonderful, and[16] unsearchable dispensation; and all of free, and absolute Grace, without any condition foreseen in them, to procure it. [page]

9. This office of Mediator between God and man, is proper[17] onely to Christ, who is the Prophet, Priest, and King of the Church of God; and may not be either in whole, or any part thereof transfer'ed from him to any other.

10. This number and order of Offices is necessary; for in respect of our[18] ignorance, we stand in need of his prophetical Office; and in respect of our alienation from God,[19] and imperfection of the best of our services, we need his Priestly office, to reconcile us, and present us acceptable unto God: and in respect of our averseness, and utter inability to return to God, and for our rescue, and security from our spiritual adversaries, we need his Kingly office,[20] to convince, subdue, draw, uphold, deliver, and preserve us to his Heavenly Kingdome.

CHAP. IX.

Of Free Will.

1. GOD hath indued the Will of Man, with that natural liberty, and power of acting upon choice; that it is[1] neither forced, nor by any necessity of nature determined to do good or evil.

2. Man in his state of innocency, had freedom, and power, to

Marginal references:

[14] Rom. 8. 9, 14.

[15] Ps. 110. 1. 1 Cor. 15. 25, 26.

[16] Joh. 3. 8. Eph. 1. 8.

[17] 1 Tim. 2. 5.

[18] Joh. 1. 18.

[19] Col. 1. 21. Gal. 5. 17.

[20] Joh. 16. 8. Ps. 110. 3. Luk. 1. 74, 75.

[1] Mat. 17. 12. Jam. 1. 14. Deut. 30. 19.

will, and to do that[2] which was
good, and well-pleasing to God;
but yet[3] was mutable, so that he
might fall from it.

3. Man by his fall into a state
of sin hath wholly lost[4] all ability of Will, to any spiritual good
accompanying salvation; so as a [page]
natural man, being altogether a-
verse from that good,[5] and dead
in *Sin*, is not able, by his own
strength, to[6] convert himself;
or to prepare himself thereunto.

4. When God converts a sinner, and translates him into the
state of Grace,[7] he freeth him
from his natural bondage under
sin, and by his grace alone, enables him[8] freely to will, and to
do that which is spiritually good;
yet so as that by reason of his[9]
remaining corruptions he doth not
perfectly nor only will that which
is good; but doth also will that
which is evil.

5. The Will of Man is made[11]
perfectly, and immutably free
to good alone, in the state of Glory only. [page]

CHAP. X.

Of Effectual Calling.

1. THose whom God hath predestinated unto Life, he is
pleased, in his appointed, and accepted time,[1] effectually to call
by his word, and Spirit, out of that
state of sin, and death, in which
they are by nature, to grace and
Salvation[2] by Jesus Christ; in-
lightning their minds, spiritually,
and savingly to[3] understand the
things of God; taking away their[4]
heart of stone, and giving unto them an heart of flesh; renewing their wills, and by his Almighty power determining them[5] to
that which is good, and effectually drawing them to Jesus Christ;
yet so as they come[6] most free- [page]

[2] Eccl. 7.
29.
[3] Gen. 3. 6.

[4] Rom. 5.
6. ch. 8. 7.

[5] Eph. 2.
1, 5.
[6] Tit. 3. 3,
4, 5. Joh.
6. 44.

[7] Col. 1.
13. Joh. 8.
36.

[8] Phil. 2.
13.

[9] Rom. 7.
15, 18, 19,
21, 23.

[11] Eph. 4.
13.

[1] Rom. 8.
30. Rom.
11. 7. Eph.
1. 10, 11.
2 Thes. 3.
13, 14.
[2] Eph. 2.
1-6.
[3] Act. 26.
18. Eph.
1. 17, 18.
[4] Ezek. 36.
26.

[5] Deut. 30.
6. Ezek.
36. 27,
Eph. 1. 19.
[6] Ps. 110.
3. Cant. 1.
4.

ly, being made willing by his Grace.

2. This Effectual Call is of God's free, and special grace a-lone [7] not from anything at all foreseen in man, nor from any po-wer, or agency in the Creature, coworking with his special Grace, [8] the Creature being wholly pas-sive therein, being dead in sins and trespasses, until being quickened & renewed by the holy Spirit, he is thereby enabled to answer this call, and to embrace the Grace of-fered and conveyed in it; and that by no less [9] power, then that which raised up Christ from the dead.

3. Elect Infants dying in infan-cy, are [11] regenerated and saved by Christ through the Spirit; who worketh when, and where, and [12] how he pleaseth: so also are [page] all other elect persons, who are uncapable of being outwardly called by the Ministry of the Word.

4. Others not elected, although they may be called by the Mini-stry of the word, [13] and may have some common operations of the Spirit, yet not being effectual-ly drawn by the Father, they nei-ther will nor can truly [14] come to Christ; and therefore cannot be saved: much less can men that receive not the Christian Religi-on [15] be saved; be they never so diligent to frame their lives ac-cording to the light of nature, and the Law of that Religion they do profess. [page]

Chap. XI.

Of Justification.

1. THose whom God Effectual-ly calleth, he also freely [1] justifieth, not by infusing Righteousness into them, but by [2] pardoning their sins, and by accounting, and accepting their

[7] 2 Tim. 1. 9. Eph. 2. 8.

[8] 1 Cor. 2. 14. Eph. 2. 5. Joh. 5. 25.

[9] Eph. 1. 19, 20.

[11] Joh. 3. 3, 5, 6.
[12] Joh. 3. 8.

[13] Mat. 22. 14. ch. 13. 20, 21. Heb. 6. 4, 5.
[14] Joh. 6. 44, 45, 65. 1 Joh. 2. 24, 25.

[15] Act. 4. 12. Joh. 4. 22. ch. 17. 3.

[1] Rom. 3, 24. ch. 8. 30.
[2] Rom. 4, 5, 6, 7, 8. Eph. 1. 7.

Persons as [3] Righteous; not for any thing wrought in them, or done by them, but for Christ's sake alone, not by imputing faith it self, the act of believing, or any other [4] evangelical obedience to them, as their Righteousness; but by imputing Christs active obedience unto the whole Law, and passive obedience in his death, for their whole and sole Righteousness, they [5] receiving, and resting on him, and his Righteousness, [page] by Faith; which faith they have not of themselves, it is the gift of *God.*

2. Faith thus receiving and resting on Christ, and his Righteousness, is the [6] alone instrument of Justification: yet it is not alone in the person justified, but is ever accompanied with all other saving Graces, and is no dead faith, [7] but worketh by love.

3. Christ by his obedience, and death, did fully discharge the debt of all those that are justified; and did by the sacrifice of himself, in the blood of his cross, undergoing in their stead, the penalty due unto them: make a proper, real, and full satisfaction [8] to *Gods* justice in their behalf: yet in asmuch as he was given by the Father for them, and his Obedience and Satisfaction accepted in their stead, and both [9] freely, not for any- [page] thing in them; their Justification is only of Free Grace, that both the exact justice and rich Grace of *God,* might be [11] glorified in the Justification of sinners.

4. God did from all eternity decree to [12] justifie all the Elect, and Christ did in the fulness of time die for their sins, and rise [13] again for their Justification; Nevertheless they are not justified personally, untill the *Holy Spirit,* doth in due time [14] actually apply *Christ* unto them.

[3] 1 Cor. 1. 30, 31. Rom. 5. 17, 18, 19.

[4] Phil. 3. 8, 9. Eph. 2. 8, 9, 10.

[5] Joh. 1. 12. Rom. 5. 17.

[6] Rom. 3. 28.

[7] Gal. 5. 6. Jam. 2. 17, 22, 26.

[8] Heb. 10. 14. 1 Pet. 1. 18, 19. Isa. 53. 5, 6.

[9] Rom. 8. 32. 2 Cor. 5. 21.

[11] Rom. 3. 26. Eph. 1. 6, 7. ch. 2. 7.

[12] Gal. 3. 8. 1 Pet. 1. 2. 1 Tim. 2. 6.

[13] Rom. 4. 25.

[14] Col. 1. 21, 22. Tit. 3. 4, 5, 6, 7.

[15] Mat. 6.
12.
1 John 1.
7, 9.
[16] Joh. 10.
28.
[17] Ps. 89.
31, 32, 33.

5. God doth continue to [15]
Forgive the sins of those that are
justified, and although they can
never fall from the state of [16]
justification; yet they may by their
sins fall under Gods [17] Fatherly
displeasure; and in that condition, they have not usually the
light of his Countenance restored
unto them, until they [18] hum- [page]
ble themselves, confess their sins,
beg pardon, and renew their faith,
and repentance.

[18] Psal. 32.
5. & 51.
Mat. 26.
75.

[19] Gal. 3. 9.
Rom. 4.
22, 23, 24.

6. The Justification of Believers under the Old Testament
was in all these respects,[19] one
and the same with the justification of Believers under the New Testament.

CHAP. XII.
Of Adoption.

[1] Eph. 1.
5. Gal. 4.
4, 5.
[2] Joh. 1. 12.
Rom. 8. 17.
[3] 2 Cor. 6.
18. Rev. 3.
12.
[4] Rom. 8. 15.
[5] Gal. 4. 6.
Eph. 2. 18.
[6] Ps. 103.
13.
[7] Prov. 14.
26.
[9] 1 Pet. 5.
7.
[11] Heb. 12.
6.
[12] Is. 54. 8,
9. Lam. 3.
31.
[13] Eph. 4.
30.
[14] Heb. 1.
14. ch. 6.
12.

ALL those that are justified, *God*
vouchsafed, in, and for the
sake of his only *Son Jesus Christ*, to
make partakers of the Grace [1]
of *Adoption;* by which they are taken into the number, and enjoy
the Liberties, and [2] Privileges
of Children of *God;* have his [3]
name put upon them,[4] receive [page]
the *Spirit of Adoption*,[5] have
access to the throne of Grace with
boldness, are enabled to cry *Abba
Father*, are [6] pitied,[7] pro-
tected,[9] provided for, and [11]
chastned by him, as by a *Father;*
yet never [12] cast off; but sealed [13]
to the day of Redemption,
and inherit the promises,[14] as
heirs, of everlasting Salvation.

CHAP. XIII.
Of Sanctification.

[1] Act. 20.
32.
Rom. 6. 5,
6.

1. THey who are united to
Christ, Effectually called,
and regenerated, having a new
heart, and a new *Spirit created* in
them, through the vertue of
Christ's death, and Resurrection;
are also [1] farther sanctified, real-

ly, and personally, through the same vertue,[2] by his word and [page] *Spirit* dwelling in them;[3] the dominion of the whole body of sin is destroyed,[4] and the several lusts thereof, are more and more weakened, and mortified; and they more and more quickened, and[5] strengthened in all saving graces, to the[6] practice of all true holyness, without which no man shall see the Lord.

2. This Sanctification is[7] throughout, in the whole man, yet imperfect[8] in this life; there abideth still some remnants of *corruption* in every part, whence a-riseth a[9] continual, and irre-concilable war; the Flesh lusting against the Spirit, and the Spirit against the Flesh.

3. In which war, although the remaining *corruption* for a time may much[11] prevail; yet through the continual supply of strength from the sanctifying *Spirit* of *Christ* [page] the[12] regenerate part doth over-come; and so the Saints grow in Grace, perfecting holiness in the fear of God,[13] pressing after an heavenly life, in Evangelical Obe-dience to all the commands which *Christ* as *Head* and *King*, in his *Word* hath prescribed to them.

CHAP. XIV.
Of Saving Faith.

1. THE Grace of *Faith*, where-by the Elect are enabled to believe to the saving of their souls, is the work of the *Spirit* of *Christ*[1] in their hearts; and is ordina-rily wrought by the Ministry of the[2] Word; by which also, and by the administration of *Bap-tisme*, and the *Lords Supper, Prayer* [page] and other *Means* appointed of God, it is increased,[3] and streng-thened.

2. By this *Faith* a Christian be-lieveth to be true,* whatsoever is

[2] Joh. 17. 17. Eph. 3. 16, 17, 18, 19. 1 Thes. 5. 21, 22, 23.
[3] Rom. 6. 14.
[4] Gal. 5. 24.
[5] Col. 1. 11.
[6] 2 Cor. 7. 1. Heb. 12. 14.
[7] 1 Thes. 5. 23.
[8] Rom. 7. 18, 23.
[9] Gal. 5. 17. 1 Pet. 2. 11.

[11] Rom. 7. 23.

[12] Rom. 6. 14.

[13] Eph. 4. 15, 16. 2 Cor. 3. 18. ch. 7. 1.

[1] 2 Cor. 4. 13. Eph. 2. 8.
[2] Rom. 10. 14, 17.
[3] Luk. 17. 5. 1 Pet. 2. 2. Act. 20. 32.
* Act. 24. 14.

⁴ Ps. 19.
7, 8, 9, 10.
Ps. 119. 72.

revealed in the *Word,* for the Authority of *God* himself; and also apprehendeth an excellency therein,[4] above all other *Writings;* and all things in the *world:* as it bears forth the glory of *God* in his *Attributes,* the excellency of *Christ* in his Nature and Offices; and the Power and Fullness of the *Holy Spirit* in his Workings, and Operations; and so is enabled

⁵ 2 Tim.
1. 12.

to[5] cast his Soul upon the truth thus believed; and also acteth differently, upon that which each particular, passage thereof containeth; yielding obedience to

⁶ Joh. 15.
14.
⁷ Is. 66. 2.
⁸ Heb. 11.
13.

the[6] commands, trembling at the [7] threatenings, and embracing the[8] promises of *God,* for this life, and that which is to come: [page] But the principal acts of Saving Faith, have immediate relation to *Christ,* accepting, receiving, and

⁹ Joh. 1.
12. Act. 16.
31. Gal. 2.
20. Act.
15. 11.

resting upon[9] him alone, for Justification, Sanctification, and Eternal Life, by vertue of the Covenant of Grace.

3. This *Faith* although it be different in degrees, and may be

¹¹ Heb. 5.
13, 14.
Matt. 6. 30.
Rom. 4. 19,
20.
¹² 2 Pet. 1.
1.
¹³ Eph. 6.
16.
1 Joh. 5.
4, 5.
¹⁴ Heb. 6.
11, 12.
Col. 2. 2.
¹⁵ Heb. 12.
2.

weak,[11] or strong; yet it is in the least degree of it, different in the kind, or nature of it (as is all other saving Grace) from the Faith,[12] and common grace of temporary believers; and therefore though it may be many times assailed, and weakened; yet it gets [13] the victory; growing up in many, to the attainment of a full [14] assurance through *Christ,* who is both the Author[15] and finisher of our *Faith.* [page]

CHAP. XV.
Of Repentence unto Life and Salvation.

¹ Tit. 3. 2,
3, 4, 5.

1. SUch of the Elect as are converted at riper years, having[1] sometimes lived in the state of nature, and therein served divers lusts and pleasures, *God* in their

Effectual Calling giveth them Re-
pentence unto Life.

2. Whereas there is none that
doth good, and sinneth[2] not;
and the best of men may, through
the power, and deceitfulness of
their corruption dwelling in
them, with the prevalency of
temptation, fall into great sins,
and provocations; God hath in
the Covenant of Grace, merciful- [page]
ly provided that Believers so sinning, and falling,[3] be renewed
through Repentance unto Salvation.

3. This saving Repentance is
an[4] evangelical Grace, whereby a person, being by the *Holy Spirit* made sensible of the manifold
evils of his sin, doth, by Faith in
Christ, humble himself for it, with
godly sorrow, detestation of it,
and self-abhorrency;[5] praying
for pardon, and strength of grace,
with a purpose and endeavour by
supplies of the *Spirit,* to[6] walk
before God unto all well pleasing
in all things.

4. As Repentance is to be continued through the whole course
of our lives, upon the account of
the body of death, and the motions thereof; so it is every mans
duty, to repent of his[7] particular known sins, particularly. [page]

5. Such is the provision which
God hath made through Christ in
the Covenant of Grace, for the
preservation of Believers unto
Salvation, that although there is
no sin so small, but it deserves[8]
damnation; yet there is no sin so
great, that it shall bring damnation on them that[9] repent;
which makes the constant preaching of Repentance necessary.

CHAP. XVI.
Of Good Works.

1. GOod Works are only such as
God hath[1] commanded

[2] Eccl. 7.
20.

[3] Luk. 22.
31, 32.

[4] Zech.
12. 10.
Act. 11.
18.

[5] Ezek.
36. 31.
2 Cor. 7.
11.
[6] Ps. 119.
6. Ps. 119.
128.

[7] Luk 19.
8. 1 Tim.
1. 13, 15.

[8] Rom. 6.
23.

[9] Is. 1. 16,
18.
Is. 55. 7.

[1] Mic. 6.
8. Heb. 13.
21.

in his Holy word; and not such as without the warrant thereof, are devised by men, out of blind zeal,[2] or upon any pretence of good intentions. [page]

2. These good works, done in obedience to Gods commandments, are the fruits, and evidences[3] of a true, and lively faith; and by them Believers manifest their[4] thankfullness, strengthen their[5] assurance, edifie their[6] brethren, adorn the profession of the Gospel, stop the mouths of the adversaries, and glorifie[7] God, whose workmanship they are, created in Christ Jesus[8] thereunto, that having their fruit unto holiness, they may have the end[9] eternal life.

3. Their ability to do good works, is not at all of themselves; but wholly from the *Spirit*[11] of Christ; and that they may be enabled thereunto, besides the graces they have already received, there is necessary an[12] actual influence of the same *Holy Spirit*, to work in them to will, and to do, of his good pleasure; yet are they not [page] hereupon to grow negligent, as if they were not bound to perform any duty, unless upon a special motion of the Spirit; but they ought to be diligent in[13] stirring up the Grace of God that is in them.

4. They who in their obedience attain to the greatest height which is possible in this life, are so far from being able to superrogate, and to do more than God requires, as that[14] they fall short of much which in duty they are bound to do.

5. We cannot by our best works merit pardon of Sin or Eternal Life at the hand of God, by reason of the great disproportion that is between them and the glory to come; and the infinite di-

[2] Mat. 15. 9. Isa. 29. 13.

[3] Jam. 2. 18, 22.
[4] Ps. 116. 12, 13.
[5] 1 Joh. 2. 3, 5. 2 Pet. 1. 5-11.
[6] Mat. 5. 16.
[7] 1 Tim. 6. 1. 1 Pet. 2. 15. Phil. 1. 11.
[8] Eph. 2. 10.
[9] Rom. 6. 22.

[11] Joh. 15. 4, 6.

[12] 2 Cor. 3. 5. Phil. 2. 13.

[13] Phil. 2. 12. Heb. 6. 11, 12. Isa. 64. 7.

[14] Job 9. 2, 3. Gal. 5. 17. Luk. 17. 10.

stance that is between us and God, whom by them we can neither profit, nor satisfie for the debt of our [15] former sins; but when we [page] have done all we can, we have done but our duty, and are unprofitable servants; and because as they are good they proceed from his [16] Spirit, and as they are wrought by us they are defiled [17] and mixed with so much weakness and imperfection that they cannot endure the severity of Gods judgment.

6. Yet notwithstanding the persons of Believers being accepted through Christ their good works also are accepted in [18] him; not as though they were in this life wholly unblameable and unreprovable in Gods sight; but that he looking upon them in his Son is pleased to accept and reward that which is [19] sincere although accomplished with many weaknesses and imperfections.

7. Works done by unregenerate men, although for the matter [page] of them they may be things which God commands, and of good use, both to themselves and [20] others; yet because they proceed not from a heart purified by [21] faith, nor are done in a right manner according to the [22] word, nor to a right end the [24] glory of God; they are therefore sinful and cannot please God; nor make a man meet to receive grace from [25] God; and yet their neglect of them is more sinful and [26] displeasing to God. [page]

[15] Rom. 3. 20. Eph. 2. 8, 9. Rom. 4. 6.

[16] Gal. 5. 22, 23.

[17] Isa. 64. 6. Ps. 143. 2.

[18] Eph. 1. 6. 1 Pet. 2. 5.

[19] Mat. 25. 21, 23. Heb. 6. 10.

[20] 2 King. 10. 30. 1 King. 21. 27, 29. [21] Gen. 4. 5. Heb. 11. 4, 6. [22] 1 Cor. 13. 1. [24] Mat. 6. 2, 5. [25] Amos 5. 21, 22. Rom. 9. 16. Tit. 3. 5. [26] Job 21. 14, 15. Mat. 25. 41, 42, 43.

CHAP. XVII.
Of Perseverence of the Saints.

1. THose whom God hath accepted in the beloved, effectually called and Sanctified by his *Spirit,* and given the precious faith of his Elect unto, can neither

¹ Joh. 10.
28, 29.
Phil. 1. 6.
2 Tim. 2.
19. 1 Joh.
2. 19.

totally nor finally fall from the
state of grace;[1] but shall certainly persevere therein to the
end and be eternally saved, seeing the gifts and callings of God
are without Repentance, (whence
he still begets and nourisheth in
them Faith, Repentance, Love,
Joy, Hope, and all the graces of the
Spirit unto immortality) and
though many storms and floods
arise and beat against them, yet
they shall never be able to take
them off that foundation and rock [page]
which by faith they are fastned
upon: notwithstanding through
unbelief and the temptations of
Satan the sensible sight of the light
and love of God, may for a time

² Psal. 89.
31, 32.
1 Cor. 11.
32.
³ Mal. 3. 6.

be clouded, and obscured from [2]
them, yet he is still the same,[3]
and they shall be sure to be
kept by the power of God unto
Salvation, where they shall enjoy
their purchased possession, they
being engraven upon the palms of
his hands, and their names having
been written in the book of life
from all Eternity.

2. This perseverance of the
Saints depends not upon their own
free will; but upon the immuta-

⁴ Rom. 8.
30. ch. 9.
11, 16.
⁵ Rom. 5.
9, 10.
John 14.
19.
⁶ Heb. 6.
17, 18.
⁷ 1 Joh. 3.
9.
⁸ Jer. 32.
40.

bility of the decree of[4] Election, flowing from the free and unchangeable love of God the Father; upon the efficacy of the merit and intercession of Jesus Christ[5]
and Union with him, the[6]
oath of God, the abiding of his [page]
Spirit & the[7] seed of God within them, and the nature of the[8]
Covenant of Grace from all which
ariseth also the certainty and infallibility thereof.

3. And though they may,
through the temptation of Satan
and of the world, the prevalency
of corruption remaining in them,

⁹ Mat. 26.
70, 72, 74.

and the neglect of the means of their
preservation fall into grievous[9]
sins, and for a time continue there-

S

in; whereby they incur [11] Gods displeasure, and grieve his holy Spirit, come to have their graces and [12] comforts impaired have their hearts hardened, and their Consciences wounded, [13] hurt, and scandalize others, and bring temporal judgements [14] upon themselves: yet they shall renew their [15] repentance and be preserved through faith in Christ Jesus to the end. [page]

[11] Is. 64. 5.
9.
Eph. 4. 30.

[12] Psal. 51. 10, 12.

[13] Psa. 32. 3, 4.

[14] 2 Sam. 12. 14.

[15] Luk. 22. 32 & 5. 61, 62.

CHAP. XVIII.
Of the Assurance of Grace and Salvation.

1. ALthough temporary Believers, and other unregenerate men, may vainly deceive themselves with false hopes, and carnal presumptions, of being in the favour of God, and in a state of salvation, [1] which hope of theirs shall perish; yet such as truly believe in the Lord Jesus, and love him in sincerity, endeavouring to walk in all good Conscience before him, may in this life be certainly assured [2] that they are in the state of Grace; and may rejoice in the hope of the glory of God which [page] hope shall never make them [3] ashamed.

[1] Job 8. 13, 14. Mat. 7. 22, 23.

[2] 1 Joh. 2. 3. ch. 3. 14, 18, 19, 21, 24. ch. 5. 13.
[3] Rom. 5. 2, 5.

2. This certainty is not a bare conjectural and probable perswasion, grounded upon [4] a fallible hope; but an infallible assurance of faith, founded on the Blood and Righteousness of Christ [5] revealed in the Gospel; and also upon the inward [6] evidence of those graces of the Spirit unto which promises are made, and on the testimony of the [7] Spirit of adoption, witnessing with our Spirits that we are the children of God; and as a fruit thereof keeping the heart both [8] humble and holy.

[4] Heb. 6. 11, 19.

[5] Heb. 6. 17, 18.

[6] 2 Pet. 1. 4, 5, 10, 11.

[7] Rom. 8. 15, 16.

[8] 1 Joh. 3. 1, 2, 3.

3. This infallible assurance doth

not so belong to the essence of faith, but that a true Believer, may wait long and conflict with many difficulties before he be [9] partaker of it; yet being enabled by the Spirit to know the things [page] which are freely given him of God, he may without extraordinary revelation in the right use of means [11] attain thereunto: and therefore it is the duty of every one, to give all diligence to make their Calling and Election sure, that thereby his heart may be enlarged in peace and joy in the holy Spirit, in love and thankfulness to God, and in strength and chearfulness in the duties of obedience, the proper [12] fruits of this Assurance; so far is it [13] from inclining men to looseness.

4. True Believers may have the assurance of their Salvation divers ways shaken, diminished, and intermitted; as [14] by negligence in preserving of it, by [15] falling into some special Sin, which woundeth the Conscience, and grieveth the Spirit, by some sudden or [16] vehement temptation, by Gods withdrawing the [17] light of his coun- [page] tenance and suffering even such as fear him to walk in darkness and to have no light; yet are they never destitute of the [18] seed of God, and Life [19] of Faith, that Love of Christ, and the brethren, that sincerity of Heart, and Conscience of duty, out of which by the operation of the Spirit, this Assurance may in due time be [20] revived: and by the which in the mean time they are [21] preserved from utter despair.

CHAP. XIX.
Of the Law of God.

1. GOd gave to *Adam* a Law of universal obedience,[1] written in his Heart, and a particular precept of not eating the

[9] Isa. 50. 10. Ps. 88. & Ps. 77. 1-12.

[11] 1 Joh. 4. 13. Heb. 6. 11, 12.

[12] Rom. 5. 1, 2, 5. ch. 14. 17. Ps. 119. 32.
[13] Rom. 6. 1, 2. Tit. 2. 11, 12, 14.
[14] Cant. 5. 2, 3, 6.
[15] Ps. 51. 8, 12, 14.
[16] Psa. 116. 11. Ps. 77. 7, 8. Ps. 31. 22.
[17] Ps. 30. 7.

[18] 1 Joh. 3. 9.
[19] Luk. 22. 32.

[20] Ps. 42. 5, 11.
[21] Lam. 3. 26. 27-31.

[1] Gen. 1. Eccl. 7. 29.

Fruit of the tree of knowledge of [page]
good and evil; by which he
bound him, and all his posterity to
personal entire exact and perpetual [2] obedience; promised life
upon the filfilling, and [3] threatened death upon the breach of it,
and indued him with power and
ability to keep it.

2. The same Law that was first
written in the heart of man,[4]
continued to be a perfect rule of
Righteousness after the fall; & was
delivered by God upon Mount *Sinai,* in [5] Ten Commandments and
written in two Tables; the four
first containing our duty towards
God, and the other six our duty
to man.

3. Besides this law commonly
called moral, God was pleased to
give to the people *Israel* Ceremonial Laws, containing several
typical ordinances, partly of worship,[6] prefiguring Christ, his [page]
graces, actions, sufferings, and benefits; and partly holding forth
divers instructions [7] of moral
duties, all which Ceremonial Laws
being appointed only to the time
of reformation, are by Jesus Christ
the true *Messiah* and only Law-
giver, who was furnished with power from the Father, for that end,[8]
abrogate and taken away.

4. To them also he gave sundry
judicial Laws, which expired together with the state of that people, not obliging and now by vertue of that institution; their general [9] equity onely, being of
moral use.

5. The moral Law doth for e-
ver bind all,[11] as well justified
persons as others, to the obedience thereof, and that not only in
regard of the matter contained in
it, but also in respect of the [12]
authority of God the Creator, [page]
who gave it: Neither doth *Christ*
in the Gospel any way dissolve,[13]

[2] Rom. 10.
5.
[3] Gal. 3.
10, 12.

[4] Rom. 2.
14, 15.

[5] Deut. 10.
4.

[6] Heb. 10.
1. Col. 2.
17.

[7] 1 Cor. 5.
7.

[8] Col. 2.
14, 16, 17.
Eph. 2.
14, 16.

[9] 1 Cor. 9.
8, 9, 10.

[11] Rom. 13.
8, 9, 10.
Jam. 2. 8,
10, 11, 12.
[12] Jam. 2.
10, 11.
[13] Mat. 5.
17, 18, 19,
Rom. 3.
31.

but much strengthen this obligation.

6. Although true *Believers* be not under the Law, as a Covenant of *Works*,[14] to be thereby Justified or condemned; yet it is of great use to them as well as to others: in that, as a Rule of *Life*, informing them of the Will of *God*, and their Duty, it directs and binds them, to walk accordingly [15] discovering also the sinfull pollutions of their Natures, Hearts and Lives; so as Examining themselves thereby, they may come to further Conviction of, Humiliation for, and Hatred against Sin; together with a clearer sight of the need they have of *Christ* and the perfection of his Obedience: It is likewise of use to the Regenerate to restrain their Corruptions, in that it forbids Sin; and the Threatnings of it serve to shew what even their Sins deserve; and what afflictions in this Life they may expect for them, although free'd from the Curse and unallayed Rigor thereof. The Promises of it likewise shew them Gods approbation of Obedience, and what blessings they may expect upon the performance thereof, though not as due to them by the Law as a Covenant of Works; so as mans doing Good and refraining from Evil, because the Law incourageth to the one and deterreth from the other, is no Evidence of his being [16] under the Law and not under Grace.

7. Neither are the forementioned uses of the Law [17] contrary to the Grace of the Gospel; but do sweetly comply with it; the *Spirit* of *Christ* subduing [18] and inabling the Will of man, to do that freely and chearfully, which the will of God revealed in the Law, requireth to be done.

---

[14] Rom. 6. 14.
Gal. 2. 16.
Rom. 8. 1.
cha. 10. 4.

[15] Rom. 3. 20.
chap. 7. 7, etc.

[16] Rom. 6. 12, 13, 14. 1 Pet. 3. 8 -13.

[17] Gal. 3. 21.

[18] Eze. 36. 27.

CHAP. 20.

Of the Gospel, and of the extent of the Grace thereof.

1. THE Covenant of Works being broken by Sin, and made unprofitable unto Life; God was pleased to give forth the promise of *Christ*,[1] the Seed of the Woman, as the means of calling the Elect, and begetting in them Faith and Repentance; in this Promise, the[2] Gospel, as to the substance of it, was revealed, and therein Effectual, for the Conversion and Salvation of Sinners. [page]

2. This Promise of *Christ*, and Salvation by him, is revealed only by[3] the Word of God; neither do the Works of Creation, or Providence, with the light of Nature,[4] make discovery of *Christ*, or of *Grace* by him; so much as in a general, or obscure way; much less that men destitute of the Revelation of him by the Promise, or Gospel;[5] should be enabled thereby, to attain saving Faith, or Repentance.

3. The Revelation of the Gospel unto Sinners, made in divers times, and by sundry parts; with the addition of Promises, and Precepts for the Obedience required therein, as to the Nations, and Persons, to whom it is granted, is meerly of the[6] Soveraign Will and good Pleasure of God; not being annexed by vertue of any Promise, to the due improvement of mens natural abilities, by vertue of Common light received with- [page] out it; which none ever did[7] make, or can so do: And therefore in all Ages the preaching of the Gospel hath been granted unto persons and Nations, as to the extent, or streightning of it, in great variety, according to the Councell of the Will of God.

4. Although the Gospel be the

[1] Gen. 3. 15.

[2] Rev. 13. 8.

[3] Rom. 1. 17.

[4] Ro. 10. 14, 15, 17.

[5] Pro. 29. 18. Isa. 25. 7, with ch. 60. 2, 3.

[6] Ps. 147. 20. Act. 16. 7.

[7] Rom. 1. 18 etc.

only outward means, of revealing *Christ,* and saving Grace; and is, as such, abundantly sufficient thereunto; yet that men who are dead in Trespasses, may be born again, Quickened or Regenerated; there is morover necessary, an effectual, insuperable[8] work of the Holy *Spirit,* upon the whole Soul, for the producing in them a new spiritual Life; without which no other means will effect[9] their Conversion unto God. [page]

**Ps. 110.
3.
1 Cor. 2.
14.
Eph. 1. 19,
20.**
**Joh. 6.
44.
2 Cor. 4.
4, 6.**

CHAP. XXI.
*Of Christian Liberty
and Liberty of
Conscience.*

1. THE Liberty which *Christ* hath purchased for Believers under the Gospel, consists in their freedom from the guilt of Sin, the condemning wrath of God, the Rigour and[1] Curse of the Law; and in their being delivered from this present evil[2] World, bondage to[3] Satan, and Dominion[4] of Sin; from the[5] Evil of Afflictions; the Fear, and Sting[6] of Death, the Victory of the Grave, and[7] Everlasting Damnation; as also in their[8] free access to God; and their yielding Obedience unto him not out of a slavish fear,[9] but a Child-like [page] love, and willing mind.

**1 Gal. 3.
13.**
2 Gal. 1. 4.
**3 Act. 26.
18.**
**4 Rom. 8.
3.**
**5 Rom. 8.
28.**
**6 1 Cor.
15. 54, 55,
56, 57.**
**7 2 Thes.
1. 10.**
**8 Rom. 8.
15.**
**9 Luk. 1.
74, 75.
1 Joh. 4.
18.**
**11 Gal. 3.
9, 14.**

All which were common also to Believers under the Law[11] for the substance of them; but under the new Testament, the Liberty of Christians is further enlarged in their freedom from the yoke of the Ceremonial Law, to which the *Jewish* Church was subjected; and in greater boldness of access to the Throne of Grace; and in fuller Communications of the[12] Free *Spirit* of God, then Believers under the Law did ordinarily partake of.

2. God alone is[13] Lord of the

**12 Joh. 7.
38, 39.
Heb. 10.
19, 20, 21.**

**13 Jam. 4.
12.
Rom. 14.
4.**

Conscience, and hath left it free
from the Doctrines and Commandments of men [14] which are in
any thing contrary to his Word, or
not contained in it. So that to
Believe such Doctrines, or obey
such Commands out of Consci-
ence,[15] is to betray true liberty [page]
of Conscience; and the requiring of
an [16] implicit Faith, and absolute
and blind Obedience, is to destroy
Liberty of Conscience, and Reason also.

3. They who upon pretence of
Christian Liberty do practice any
sin, or cherish any sinfull lust; as
they do thereby pervert the main
design of the Grace of the Gospel [17]
to their own Destruction; so
they wholly destroy [18] the end
of *Christian* Liberty, which is,
that being delivered out of the
hands of all our Enemies we might
serve the Lord without fear in
Holiness, and Righteousness before him, all the days of our Life. [page]

[14] Act. 4. 19.
& 5. 29.
1 Cor. 7.
23.
Mat. 15. 9.

[15] Col. 2. 20,
22, 23.

[16] 1 Cor. 3.
5.
2 Cor. 1.
24.

[17] Rom. 6.
1, 2.

[18] Gal. 5.
13.
2 Pet. 2.
18-21.

CHAP. XXII.
Of Religious Wor-
ship, and the Sabbath
Day.

1. THE light of Nature shews
that there is a God, who
hath Lordship, and Soveraigntye
over all; is just, good, and doth
good unto all; and is therefore
to be feared, loved, praised, called upon, trusted in, and served,
with all the Heart, and all the
Soul,[1] and with all the Might.
But the acceptable way of Worshipping the the true God, is [2] instituted by himself; and so limited by his own revealed will, that
he may not be worshipped according to the imaginations, and [page]
devices of Men, or the suggestions
of Satan, under any visible representations, or [3] any other way,
not prescribed in the Holy Scriptures.

2. *Religious Worship* is to be gi-

[1] Jer. 10.
7. Mar.
12. 33.
[2] Deut. 12.
32.

[3] Exo. 20.
4, 5, 6.

4 Mat. 4.
9, 10.
Joh. 6. 23.
Mat. 28.
19.
5 Rom. 1.
25.
Col. 2. 18.
Revel. 19.
10.
6 Joh. 14.
6.
7 1 Tim. 2. 5.
8 Psal. 95.
1-7.
Psal. 65. 2.
9 Joh. 14.
13, 14.
11 Rom. 8.
26.
12 1 Joh. 5.
14.
13 1 Cor.
14. 16, 17.
14 1 Tim.
2. 1, 2.
2 Sam. 7.
29.
15 2 Sam.
12. 21, 22,
23.
16 1 Joh. 5.
16.
17 1 Tim.
4. 13.
18 2 Tim.
4. 2.
Luk. 8. 18.

19 Col. 3.
16.
Eph. 5. 19.
20 Mat. 28.
19, 20.
21 1 Cor. 11.
26.

24 Esth. 4.
16.
Joel. 2. 12.
25 Exo. 15.
1 etc. Ps.
107.

26 Joh. 4.
21. Mal. 1.
11. 1 Tim.
2. 8.

ven to *God* the *Father, Son* and *Holy Spirit,* and to him [4] alone; not to *Angels, Saints,* or any other [5] *Creatures;* and since the fall, not without a [6] *Mediator,* nor in the *Mediation* of any other but [7] *Christ* alone.

3. Prayer with thanksgiving, being one special part of natural worship, is by *God* required of [8] all men. But that it may be accepted, it is to be made in the [9] Name of the Son, by the help [11] of the Spirit, according to [12] his Will; with understanding, reverence, humility, fervency, faith, love, and perseverance; [page] and when with others, in a [13] known tongue.

4. Prayer is to be made for things lawful, and for all sorts of men living, [14] or that shall live hereafter; but not [15] for the dead, nor for those of whom it may be known that they have sinned [16] the sin unto death.

5. The [17] reading of the Scriptures, Preaching, and [18] hearing the word of God, teaching and admonishing one another in Psalms, Hymns and Spiritual songs, singing with grace in our Hearts to [19] the Lord; as also the Administration [20] of Baptism, and [21] the Lords Supper are all parts of Religious worship of *God,* to be performed in obedience to him, with understanding, faith, reverence, and godly fear; moreover solemn humiliation, [24] with [page] fastings; and thanksgiving upon [25] special occasions, ought to be used in an holy and religious manner.

6. Neither *Prayer,* nor any other part of Religious worship, is now under the Gospel tied unto, or made more acceptable by, any place in which it is [26] performed, or towards which it is directed; but God is to be worshipped every where in *Spirit,* and in truth;

as in[1] private families[2] daily,
and[3] in secret each one by himself, so more solemnly in the public Assemblies, which are not
carelessely, nor willfully, to be[4]
neglected, or forsaken, when
God by his word, or providence
calleth thereunto.

7. As it is of the Law of nature,
that in general a proportion of
time by Gods appointment, be set
apart for the Worship of God; so [page]
by his Word, in a positive moral,
and perpetual commande-
ment, binding all men, in all Ages, he
hath particularly appointed one
day in seven for a[5] Sabbath to be
kept holy unto him, which from
the beginning of the World to
the Resurrection of Christ, was
the last day of the week; and
from the resurrection of Christ,
was changed into the first day of
the week[6] which is called the
Lords day; and is to be continued to the end of the World, as
the *Christian sabbath;* the obser-
vation of the last day of the week
being abolished.

8. The *Sabbath* is then kept
holy unto the Lord, when men after a due preparing of their hearts,
and ordering their common affairs
aforehand, do not only observe an
holy[7] rest all the day, from their
own works, words, and thoughts,
about their worldly employment, [page]
and recreations, but also are tak-
en up the whole time in the publick and private exercises of his
worship, and in the duties[8] of
necessity and mercy.

CHAP XXIII.
Of Lawful Oaths and Vows.

1. A lawful Oath is a part of religious worship,[1] wherein
the person swearing in Truth,
Righteousness, and Judgment,
solemnly calleth God to witness
what he sweareth;[2] and to

[1] Act. 10.
2.
[2] Mat. 6.
11. Ps. 55.
17.
[3] Mat. 6. 6.
[4] Heb. 10.
25.
Act. 2. 42.

[5] Exo. 20.
8.

[6] 1 Cor.
16. 1, 2.
Act. 20. 7.
Rev. 1. 10.

[7] Isa. 58.
13.
Neh. 13.
15-23.

[8] Mat. 12.
1-13.

[1] Exo. 20.
7. Deut. 10.
20. Jer. 4.
2.

[2] 2 Cro. 6.
22, 23.

judge him according to the Truth or falseness thereof.

2. The Name of God only is [page] that by which men ought to swear; and therein it is to be used, with all Holy Fear and reverence, therefore to swear vainly or rashly by that glorious, and dreadful name; or to *swear* at all by any other thing, is sinful and to be[3] abhorred; yet as in matter of weight and moment for confirmation of truth,[4] and ending all strife, an Oath is warranted by the word of God; so a *lawful Oath* being imposed,[5] by lawful Authority, in such matters, ought to be taken.

3. Whosoever taketh an *Oath* warranted by the word of God, ought duely to consider the weightiness of so solemn an act; and therein to avouch nothing, but what he knoweth to be the truth; for that by rash, false, and vain *Oaths* the[6] Lord is provoked, and for them this Land mournes. [page]

4. An *Oath* is to be taken in the plain, and[7] common sense of the words; without equivocation, or mental reservation.

5. A Vow, which is not to be made to any *Creature,* but to God alone,[8] is to be made and performed with all Religious care, and faithfulness; but Popish *Monastical Vows,*[9] of perpetual single life, professed[11] poverty, and regular obedience, are so far from being decrees of higher perfection, that they are superstitious,[12] and sinful snares, in which no *Christian* may intangle himself.

CHAP. XXIV.

Of the Civil Magistrate.

1. God the supream Lord, and King of all the World,

---

[3] Mat. 5. 34, 37. Jam. 5. 12.
[4] Heb. 6. 16. 2 Cor. 1. 23.

[5] Neh. 13. 25.

[6] Levit. 19. 12. Jer. 23. 10.

[7] Ps. 24. 4.

[8] Psal. 76. 11. Gen. 28. 20, 21, 22.
[9] 1 Cor. 7. 2, 9.
[11] Eph. 4. 28.

[12] Mat. 19. 11.

hath ordained *Civil*[1] *Magistrates* to be under him, over the people, for his own glory, and the publick good; and to this end hath armed them with the power of the Sword, for defence and encouragement of them that do good, and for the punishment of evil doers.

[1] Rom. 13. 1, 2, 3, 4.

2. It is lawful for Christians to Accept, and Execute the Office of a *Magistrate,* when called thereunto; in the management whereof, as they ought especially to maintain[2] Justice, and Peace, [page] according to the wholesome Laws of each Kingdome, and Commonwealth: so for that end they may lawfully now under the New Testament[3] wage war upon just and necessary occasions.

[2] 2 Sam. 23. 3. Ps. 82. 3, 4.

[3] Luk. 3. 14.

3. *Civil Magistrates* being set up by God, for the ends aforesaid; subjection in all lawful things commanded by them, ought to be yielded by us, in the Lord; not only for wrath[4] but for Conscience sake; and we ought to make supplications and prayers for Kings, and all that are in Authority,[5] that under them we may live a quiet and peaceable life, in all godliness and honesty.

[4] Rom. 13. 5, 6, 7. 1 Pet. 2. 17.

[5] 1 Tim. 2. 1, 2.

CHAP. XXV.

Of Marriage.

1. MArriage is to be between one *Man and one Woman;*[1] neither is it lawful for any man to have more then one *Wife,* nor for any *Woman* to have more then one *Husband* at the same time.

[1] Gen. 2. 24. Mal. 2. 15. Mat. 19. 5, 6.

2. Marriage was ordained for the mutual help[2] of *Husband* and *Wife,*[3] for the increase of Man-kind, with a legitimate issue, and for[4] preventing of uncleanness.

[2] Gen. 2. 18.
[3] Gen. 1. 28.

[4] 1 Cor. 7. 2, 9.

3. It is lawful for[5] all sorts of people to *Marry,* who are able with judgment to give their con-

[5] Heb. 13. 4. 1 Tim. 4. 3.

sent; yet it is the duty of *Christi-ans* [6] to *marry* in the Lord,
and therefore such as profess the [page] true Religion, should not *Marry* with infidels,[7] or Idolators; neither should such as are godly be unequally yoked, by *marrying* with such as are wicked, in their life, or maintain damnable He-resie.

4. *Marriage* ought not to be within the degrees of consanquini-ty,[8] or Affinity forbidden in the word; nor can such incestu-ous *Marriage* ever be made law-ful, by any law of *Man* or consent of parties,[9] so as those persons may live together as *Man* and *Wife*. [page]

CHAP. XXVI.

Of the Church.

1. The Catholick or universal Church, which (with re-spect to internal work of the Spirit, and truth of grace) may be called invisible, consists of the whole[1] number of the Elect, that have been, are, or shall be ga-thered into one, under Christ the head thereof; and is the spouse, the body, the fulness of him that fil-leth all in all.

2. All persons throughout the world, professing the faith of the Gospel, and obedience unto God by Christ, according unto it; not destroying their own profession by any Errors everting the foundati- [page] on, or unholyness of conversation,[2] are and may be called visible Saints;[3] and of such ought all particular Congregations to be constituted.

3. The purest Churches under heaven are subject[4] to mixture, and error; and som have so de-generated as to become[5] no Churches of Christ, but Synago-gues of Satan; nevertheless Christ

[6] 1 Cor. 7. 39.

[7] Neh. 13. 25, 26, 27.

[8] Levit. 18.

[9] Mat. 6. 18. 1 Cor. 5. 1.

[1] Heb. 12. 23. Col. 1. 18. Eph. 1. 10, 22, 23, & ch. 5. 23, 27, 32.

[2] 1 Cor. 1. 2. Act. 11. 26.
[3] Rom. 1. 7. Eph. 1. 20, 21, 22.

[4] 1 Cor. 15. Rev. 2 & ch. 3.
[5] Rev. 18. 2. 2 Thes. 2, 11, 12.

always hath had, and ever shall
have a [6] Kingdome, in this world,
to the end thereof, of such as believe in him, and make profession
of his Name.

4. The Lord Jesus Christ is the
Head of the Church, in whom by
the appointment of the Father,[7]
all power for the calling, institution, order, or Government of the
Church, is invested in a supream &
soveraigne manner, neither can the
Pope of *Rome* in any sense be head [page]
thereof, but is [8] that Antichrist,
that Man of sin, and Son of perdition, that exalteth himself in
the Church against Christ, and all
that is called God; whom the
Lord shall destroy with the brightness of his coming.

5. In the execution of this power wherewith he is so intrusted,
the Lord Jesus calleth out of the
World unto himself, through the
Ministry of his word, by his Spirit,[9]
those that are given unto him
by his Father; that they may
walk before him in all the [11]
ways of obedience, which he pre-
scribeth to them in his Word.
Those thus called he commandeth
to walk together in particular societies, or [12] Churches, for their
mutual edification; and the due
performance of that publick worship, which he requireth of them
in the World. [page]

6. The Members of these
Churches are [13] Saints by calling, visibly manifesting and evi-
dencing (in and by their profession and walking) their obedience
unto that call of Christ; and do
willingly consent to walk together
according to the appointment of
Christ, giving up themselves, to the
Lord & one to another by the will
of God,[14] in professed subjection
to the Ordinances of the Gospel.

7. To each of these Churches

[6] Mat. 16.
18. Ps. 72.
17 & Ps.
102. 28.
Rev. 12.
17.

[7] Col. 1.
18. Mat.
28. 18, 19,
20.
Eph. 4.
11, 12.

[8] 2 Thes.
2. 3-9.

[9] Joh. 10.
16. chap.
12. 32.

[11] Mat. 28.
20.

[12] Mat. 18.
15-20.

[13] Rom. 1.
9. 1 Cor.
1. 2.

[14] Act. 2.
41, 42.
ch. 5. 13.
14. 2 Cor.
9. 13.

thus gathered, according to his mind, declared in his word, he hath given all that [15] power and authority, which is any way needfull, for their carrying on that order in worship, and discipline, which he hath instituted for them to observe; with commands, and rules for the due and right exerting, and executing of that power.

[15] Mat. 18. 17, 18. 1 Cor. 5. 4, 5, with 5. 13.

8. A particular Church gathered, and compleatly Organized, according to the mind of Christ, consists of Officers, and Members; And the Officers appointed by *Christ* to be chosen and set apart by the Church (so called and gathered) for the peculiar Administration of Ordinances, and Execution of Power, or Duty, which he intrusts them with, or calls them to, to be continued to the end of the World, are [16] Bishops or Elders and Deacons.

[16] Act. 20. 17, with v. 28. Phil. 1. 1.

9. The way appointed by *Christ* for the Calling of any person, fitted, and gifted by the Holy *Spirit,* unto the Office of Bishop, or Elder, in a Church, is, that he be chosen thereunto by the common [17] suffrage of the Church it self; and Solemnly set apart by Fasting and Prayer, with imposition of hands of the [18] Eldership of the Church, if there be any before [page] Constituted therein; And of a Deacon [19] that he be chosen by the like suffrage, and set apart by Prayer, and the like Imposition of hands.

[17] Act. 14. 23. See the original. [18] 1 Tim. 4. 14.

[19] Act. 6. 3, 5, 6.

10. The work of Pastors being constantly to attend the Service of *Christ,* in his Churches, in the Ministry of the Word, and Prayer,[20] with watching for their Souls, as they that must give an account to him; it is incumbent on the Churches to whom they Minister, not only to give them all due respect,[21] but also to communicate to them of all

[20] Act. 6. 4. Heb. 13. 17.

[21] 1 Tim. 5. 17, 18. Gal. 6.

their good things according to   6, 7.
their ability, so as they may have
a comfortable supply, without   [24] 2 Tim.
being themselves [24] entangled in   2. 4.
Secular Affairs; and may also be
capable of exercising [25] Hospita-   [25] 1 Tim.
lity towards others; and this is re-   3. 2.
quired by the [26] Law of Nature,   [26] 1 Cor.
and by the Express order of our [page]   9.
Lord Jesus, who hath ordained   6-14.
that they that preach the Gospel,
should live of the Gospel.

11. Although it be incumbent
on the Bishops or Pastors of the
Churches to be instant in Preaching the Word, by way of Office;
yet the work of Preaching the
Word, is not so peculiarly confin-   [1] Act. 11.
ed to them; but that others also [1]   19, 20, 21.
gifted, and fitted by the Ho-   1 Pet. 4.
ly *Spirit* for it, and approved, and   10, 11.
called by the *Church,* may and
ought to perform it.

12. As all Believers are bound
to joyn themselves to particular
Churches, when and where they
have opportunity so to do; So all
that are admitted unto the privi-
ledges of a *Church,* are also [2]   [2] 1 Thes.
under the Censures and Govern-   5. 14.
ment thereof, according to the   2 Thes. 3.
Rule of *Christ.* [page]   6, 14, 15.

13. No Church-members upon
any offence taken by them, having performed their Duty required
of them towards the person they
are offended at, ought to disturb
any *Church* order, or absent themselves from the Assemblies of the
Church, or Administration of any
Ordinances, upon the account of
such offence at any of their fellow-
members; but to wait upon *Christ,*[3]   [3] Mat. 18.
in the further proceeding of the   15, 16, 17.
Church.   Eph. 4. 2,
                                                3.
14. As each *Church,* and all the
Members of it, are bound to [4]   [4] Eph. 6.
pray continually, for the good   18. Ps.
and prosperity of all the *Churches* of   122. 6.
Christ, in all places; and upon
all occasions to further it (every

one within the bounds of their places, and callings, in the Exercise of their Gifts and Graces) so the *Churches* (when planted by the providence of God so as they may injoy opportunity and advantage for it) ought to hold [page] [5] communion amongst themselves for their peace, increase of love, and mutual edification.

[5] Rom. 16. 1, 2. 3 Joh. 8, 9, 10.

15. In cases of difficulties or differences, either in point of Doctrine, or Administration; wherein either the Churches in general are concerned, or any one Church in their peace, union, and edification; or any member, or members, of any Church are injured, in or by any proceedings in censures not agreeable to truth, and order: it is according to the mind of Christ, that many Churches holding communion together, do by their messengers meet to consider, [6] and give their advice in, or about that matter in difference, to be reported to all the Churches concerned; howbeit these messengers assembled, are not entrusted with any Church-power properly so called; or with any jurisdiction over the Churches themselves, to exercise any censures either over any [page] Churches, or Persons: or [7] to impose their determination on the Churches, or Officers.

[6] Act. 15. 2, 4, 6. & 22, 23, 25.

[7] 2 Cor. 1. 24. 1 Joh. 4. 1.

CHAP. XXVII.
On the Communion of Saints.

1. All *Saints* that are united to Jesus Christ their *Head*, by his Spirit, and Faith; although they are not made thereby one person with him, have [1] fellowship in his Graces, sufferings, death, resurrection, and glory; and being united to one another in love, they [2] have communion in each others gifts, and graces; and obliged to the perfor-

[1] 1 Joh. 1. 3. Joh. 1. 16. Phil. 3. 10. Rom. 6. 5, 6.
[2] Eph. 4. 15, 16. 1 Cor. 12. 7. 1 Cor. 3. 21, 22, 23.

T

mance of such duties, publick and
private, in an orderly way,[3] as
do conduce to their mutual good,
both in the inward and outward
man. [page]

2. *Saints* by profession are
bound to maintain an holy fellowship and communion in the
worship of God, and in performing such other spiritual services,[4]
as tend to their mutual edification; as also in relieving each
other in [5] outward things according to their several abilities,
and necessities; which communion, according to the rule of the
Gospel, though especially to be exercised by them, in the relations
wherein they stand, whether in [6]
families, or [7] Churches;
yet as God offereth opportunity
is to be extended to all the houshold of faith, even all those who
in every place call upon the name
of the Lord Jesus; nevertheless
their communion one with another as *Saints,* doth not take away
or [8] infringe the title or propriety, which each man hath in his
goods and possessions. [page]

[3] 1 Thes.
5. 11, 14.
Rom. 1.
12. 1 Joh.
2. 17, 18.
Gal. 6. 10.

[4] Heb. 10.
24, 25
with ch.
3. 12, 13.

[5] Act. 12.
29, 30.

[6] Eph. 6.
4.
[7] 1 Cor.
12. 14
-27.

[8] Act. 5. 4
Eph. 4. 28

CHAP. XXVIII.
Of Baptism and the
Lords Supper.

1. BAptism and the Lords Supper
are ordinances of positive, and
soveraign institution; appointed by the Lord Jesus the only Law-giver, to be continued in
his Church [1] to the end of the
world.

2. These holy appointments are
to be administered by those only,
who are qualified and thereunto
called according [2] to the commission of Christ. [page]

[1] Mat. 28.
19, 20.
1 Cor.
11. 26.

[2] Mat. 28.
19. 1 Cor.
4. 1.

CHAP. XXIX.
Of Baptism.

1. BAptism is an Ordinance of
the New Testament, ordain-

ed by Jesus Christ, to be unto the party Baptized, a sign of his fellowship with him, in his death,[2] and resurrection; of his being engrafted into him; of[4] remission of sins; and of his[5] giving up unto God through Jesus Christ, to live and walk in newness of Life.

2. Those who do actually profess[6] repentance towards *God*, faith in, and obedience, to our Lord Jesus, are the only proper subjects of this ordinance. [page]

3. The outward element to be used in this ordinance[7] is water, wherein the party is to be baptized, in the name of the Father, and of the Son, and of the Holy Spirit.

4. Immersion, or dipping of the person[8] in water, is necessary to the due administration of this ordinance.

CHAP. XXX.

Of the Lords Supper.

1. THE Supper of the Lord Jesus, was instituted by him, the same night wherein he was betrayed, to be observed in his Churches unto the end of the [page] world, for the perpetual remembrance, and shewing forth the sacrifice in his death[1] confirmation of the faith of believers in all the benefits thereof, their spiritual nourishment, and growth in him, their further ingagement in, and to, all duties which they owe unto him;[2] and to be a bond and pledge of their communion with him, and with each other.

2. In this ordinance Christ is not offered up to his Father, nor any real sacrifice made at all, for remission of sin of the quick or dead; but only a memorial of that[3] one offering up of himself, by

[2] Rom. 6. 3, 4, 5. Col. 2. 12. Gal. 3. 27.
[4] Mar. 1. 4. Act. 26. 16.
[5] Rom. 6. 2, 4.

[6] Mar. 16. 16. Act. 8. 36, 37.

[7] Mat. 28. 19, 20, with Act. 8. 38.

[8] Mat. 3. 16. Joh. 3. 23.

[1] 1 Cor. 11. 23, 24, 25, 26.

[2] 1 Cor. 10. 16, 17, 21.

[3] Heb 9. 25, 26, 28.

himself, upon the crosse, once for all; and a spiritual oblation of all [4] possible praise unto God for the same; so that the Popish sacrifice of the Mass (as they call it) is most abominable, injurious to Christs own only sacrifice, the [page] alone propitiation for all the sins of the Elect.

3. The Lord Jesus hath in this Ordinance, appointed his Ministers to Pray, and bless the Elements of Bread and Wine, and thereby to set them apart from a common to an holy use, and to take and break the Bread; to take the Cup,[5] and (they communicating also themselves) to give both to the Communicants.

4. The denyal of the Cup to the people, worshiping the Elements, the lifting them up, or carrying them about for adoration, and reserving them for any pretended religious use,[6] are all contrary to the nature of this Ordinance, and to the institution of Christ.

5. The outward Elements in this Ordinance, duely set apart to [page] the uses ordained by Christ, have such relation to him crucified, as that truely, although in terms used figuratively, they are sometimes called by the name of the things they represent, to wit [7] body and Blood of Christ; albeit in substance, and nature, they still remain truly, and only [8] Bread, and Wine, as they were before.

6. That doctrine which maintains a change of the substance of Bread and Wine, into the substance of Christs body and blood (commonly called Transubstantiation) by consecration of a Priest, or by any other way, is repugnant not to Scripture [9] alone, but even to common sense and reason; overthroweth the [11] nature of the ordinance, and hath been and is the

[4] 1 Cor. 11. 24. Mat. 26. 26, 27.

[5] 1 Cor. 11. 23, 24, 25, 26, etc.

[6] Mat. 26. 26, 27, 28. Mat. 15. 9. Exod. 20. 4, 5.

[7] 1 Cor. 11. 27.

[8] 1 Cor. 11. 26 & 5. 28.

[9] Act. 3. 21. Luk. 24. 6 & 5. 39.
[11] 1 Cor. 11. 24, 25.

cause of manifold superstitions, yea, of gross Idolatries. [page]

7. Worthy receivers, outwardly partaking of the visible Elements in this Ordinance, do then also inwardly by faith, really and indeed, yet not carnally, and corporally, but spiritually receive, and feed upon Christ crucified [12] & all the benefits of his death: the Body and Blood of *Christ,* being then not corporally, or carnally, but spiritually present to the faith of Believers, in that Ordinance, as the Elements themselves are to their outward senses.

[12] 1 Cor. 10. 16. ch. 11. 23-26.

8. All ignorant and ungodly persons, as they are unfit to enjoy communion [13] with *Christ;* so are they unworthy of the Lords Table; and cannot without great sin against him, while they remain such, partake of these holy mysteries,[14] or be admitted thereunto: yea whosoever shall receive unworthily are guilty of the Body and Blood of the Lord, eating and drinking judgment to themselves. [page]

[13] 2 Cor. 6. 14, 15.

[14] 1 Cor. 11. 29. Mat. 7. 6.

CHAP. XXXI.

Of the State of Man after Death and of the Resurrection of the Dead.

1. THE Bodies of Men after Death return to dust,[1] and see corruption; but their Souls (which neither die nor sleep) having an immortal subsistence, immediately [2] return to God who gave them; the Souls of the Righteous being then made perfect in holiness, are received into paradise where they are with *Christ,* and behold the face of *God,* in light [3] and glory; waiting for the full Redemption of their Bodies; and the souls of the wicked, are cast into hell; where they [page] remain in torment and utter dark-

[1] Gen. 3. 19. Act. 13. 36.

[2] Eccl. 12. 7.

[3] Luk. 23. 43. 2 Cor. 5. 1, 6, 8. Phil. 1. 23. Heb. 12. 23.

ness, reserved to [4] the judgement of the great day; besides
these two places for Souls separated from their bodies, the Scripture acknowledgeth none.

2. At the last day such of the
Saints as are found alive shall not
sleep but be [5] changed; and all
the dead shall be raised up with
the self same bodies, and [6] none
other; although with different [7]
qualities, which shall be united again to their Souls for ever.

3. The bodies of the unjust
shall by the power of *Christ,* be
raised to dishonour; the bodies of
the just by his spirit unto honour, [8]
and be made conformable to
his own glorious Body. [page]

[4] Jud. 6.
7. 1 Pet.
3. 19.
Luk. 16.
23, 24.

[5] 1 Cor.
15. 51, 52.
1 Thes. 4.
17.
[6] Job 19.
26, 27.
[7] 1 Cor.
15. 42, 43.

[8] Act. 24.
15. Joh. 5.
28, 29.
Phil. 3. 21.

CHAP. XXXII.

Of the Last Judge-
ment.

1. GOD hath appointed a Day
wherein he will judge the
world in Righteousness, by [1] Jesus Christ; to whom all power
and judgement is given of the Father; in which Day not only the [2]
Apostate Angels shall be judged; but likewise all persons that
have lived upon the Earth, shall
appear before the Tribunal of
Christ; [3] to give an account of
their thoughts, Words, and
Deeds, and to receive according
to what they have done in the
body, whether good or evil. [page]

2. The end of Gods appointing this Day, is for the manifestation of the glory of his Mercy, in
the Eternal Salvation of the Elect; [4]
and of his Justice in the Eternal damnation of the Reprobate,
who are wicked and disobedient; for then shall the Righteous
go into Everlasting Life, and receive that fulness of Joy, and Glory, with everlasting reward, in
the presence [5] of the Lord:

[1] Act. 17.
31.
Joh. 5. 22,
27.
[2] 1 Cor. 6.
3. Jud. 6.

[3] 2 Cor.
5. 10.
Eccles. 12.
14. Mat.
12. 36.
Rom. 14.
10, 12.
Mat. 25.
32 etc.

[4] Rom. 9.
22, 23.

[5] Mat. 25.
21, 34.
2 Tim.
4. 8.

6 Mat. 25.
46.   Mar. 9.
48.
2 Thes. 1.
7, 8, 9, 10.

7 2 Cor.
5. 10, 11.

8 2 Thes.
1. 5, 6, 7.

9 Mar. 13.
35, 36, 37.
Luk. 13.
35, 36.
11 Rev. 22.
20.

but the wicked who know not
God, and obey not the Gospel of
Jesus Christ, shall be cast into E-
ternal torments, and 6 punished
with everlasting destruction, from
the presence of the Lord, and
from the glory of his power.
3. As Christ would have us to
be certainly perswaded that there
shall be a Day of judgement, both 7
to deter all men from sin, and
for the greater 8 consolation of
the godly, in their adversity; so [page]
will he have that day unknown to
Men, that they may shake off all
carnal security, and be always
watchful, because they know not
at what hour, the 9 Lord will
come; and may ever be prepared
to say,11 *Come Lord Jesus, Come quickly,*
Amen.

C. The "Orthodox Creed," 1678

The example of the Particular Baptists in publishing a new confession was closely followed by the General Baptists when, in 1678,
they drew up their so-called "Orthodox Creed" to "unite and confirm all true protestants in the fundamental articles of the Christian
religion. . . ." Additional inspiration for the Creed lay in the desire
to refute the Hoffmanite Christology which Matthew Caffyn, a
General Baptist messenger, was preaching in Kent and Sussex, and
in the fear of a return of popery to England.

The Creed was not published in the name of the General Assembly
but of a group of the more earnestly orthodox General Baptist
churches of the Midlands, in the counties of Buckinghamshire, Hertfordshire, Bedfordshire, and Oxford. On Jan. 30, 1678, fifty-four
Messengers, Elders, and Brethren met "in the name of many baptized Christians or congregations in the several counties." The Creed
is supposed to have been particularly the work of Thomas Monck,
a farmer and a Messenger in Buckinghamshire, who in 1673 had
published *A cure for the cankering error of the new Eutychians.*

The preoccupation of the Creed with Christology is indicated by
the remark in the preface, "We are sure that the denying of baptism
is a less evil than to deny the Divinity or Humanity of Christ."

The first eight articles are devoted entirely to the Trinity, those on the Incarnation and the Union of the Two Natures in Christ being especially full. Sections with similar fullness to that on the Trinity contain articles on ecclesiology and cultic problems. The Westminster Confession served as the model, but it was followed less closely than was the case with the Confession of 1677. In the Creed large freedom was exercised in changing the order of articles and their contents.

Theologically, in keeping with its unionistic purpose, the Confession approaches Calvinism more closely than any other General Baptist confession. This disposition is particularly evident in the articles on "Predestination and Election" (IX), "The Covenants" (XVI), "Original Sin" (XV), "Perseverance" (XXXVI), and "The Invisible Church" (XXIX). Perhaps, indeed, the Creed is principally noteworthy as an early attempt at compromise between the two great systems of theology, thus anticipating the work of Andrew Fuller and others of the latter eighteenth century. It also presents clear evidence of the tendency among General Baptists in the late years of the seventeenth century to elevate the ministry and to centralize authority. It is the only confession of the century to elevate the association as an institution above local churches. Article XXXIV commits the "executive part" of church discipline to ministers and Article XXXIX gives to general assemblies "lawful power to hear and determine, as also to excommunicate." There were General Baptists, however, who strongly resisted this view of the power of general councils. Article XXXI shows that messengers (or bishops) were ordained by "bishops of the same function," and that they ordained pastors and governed congregations. The Creed is alone among Baptist confessions in including and setting forth the Apostles', the Nicene, and the Athanasian Creeds.

As a means of rallying the orthodox General Baptists of the Midlands against the drift toward Hoffmanism, the Creed seems to have served a useful purpose, but the Confession does not appear to have enjoyed large influence beyond the Midlands. Original copies of the Creed are in the Angus Library, Oxford, and in the Baptist College, Rawdon, Leeds, England. Reprints have been made by Crosby (III, Appx. I), Underhill (121 ff), McGlothlin (124 ff), and the Baptist Historical Society (in 1911). Crosby's text is reproduced here as it appears in McGlothlin.

AN

ORTHODOX CREED,

OR

A PROTESTANT CONFESSION OF FAITH,

BEING AN

ESSAY TO UNITE AND CONFIRM ALL TRUE
PROTESTANTS

IN THE FUNDAMENTAL ARTICLES OF THE
CHRISTIAN RELIGION, | AGAINST THE
ERRORS AND HERESIES OF ROME.

LONDON, Printed in the year, 1679.

An orthodox CREED.

I. ARTICLE.

Of the Essence of God.

We verily believe, that there is but one, only living and true God; whose subsistence is in and of himself, whose essence cannot be comprehended by any but himself; a most pure, spiritual, or invisible substance; who hath an absolute, independent, unchangeable, and infinite being; without matter or form, body, parts, or passions.

For I am the Lord, I change not; God is a spirit. Now unto the king eternal, immortal, invisible, the only wise God, be honour and glory, for ever and ever, Amen. Ye heard a Voice, but saw no similitude.

Deut. 6 : 4; 5 : 26.
Ps. 42 : 2.
Jer. 10 : 10.
Exod. 3 : 14.
Ps. 147 : 5.
Hab. 1 : 13.
Deut. 4 : 15, 16.
Col. 1 : 15.
Acts 17 : 28.
Luke 24 : 39.
Mal. 3 : 6.
John 4 : 24.
I Tim. 1 : 17.
Deut. 14 : 12.

II. ARTICLE.

Of the divine Attributes in God.

Every particle of being in heaven and earth, leads us to the infinite being of beings, namely God, who is simplicity, viz. one mere and perfect act, without all composition, and an immense sea of perfections; who is the only eternal being, everlasting without time, whose immense presence, is always every where present, having immutability without any alteration in being, or will; in a word, God is infinite, of universal, unlimited, and incomprehensible perfection, most holy, wise, just, and good; whose wisdom is his justice, whose justice is his holiness, and whose wisdom, justice, and holiness, is himself. Most merciful, gracious, faithful, and true, a full fountain of love, and who is that perfect, sovereign, divine will, the Alpha of supreme being.

Is it true, indeed, that God will dwell on the earth? Behold, the heaven, and heaven of heavens, cannot contain thee: how much less this house which I have built. Great is the Lord, and worthy to be praised, and his greatness is incomprehensible.

John 5 : 26.
I John 1 : 5.
Matt. 5 : 48.
Exod. 6 : 3.
Isaiah 40 : 28.
Ps. 90 : 2 : 39 : 9.
Heb. 6 : 17.
James 1 : 17.
Mal. 3 : 6.
Num. 23 : 19.
Lev. 20 : 26.
Rom. 16 : 27.
Ps. 119 : 68.
Deut. 32 : 4.
Exod. 34 : 6.
Isaiah 41 : 4.
Job 33 : 13.
I Kings 8 : 27.
Ps. 145 : 3.

III. ARTICLE.

Of the holy Trinity.

In this divine, and infinite being, or unity of the Godhead, there are three persons, or subsistences, the father, the word, or son, and the holy spirit, of one substance, power, eternity, and will, each having the whole divine essence, yet the essence undivided. The father is of none, neither begotten nor proceeding; the son is eternally begotten of the father; the holy ghost is of the father, and the son, proceeding. All infinite, without beginning, therefore but one God, who is indivisible, and not to be divided in nature, or being, but distinguished by several properties and personal relations; and we worship and adore a Trinity in Unity, and a Unity in Trinity, three persons, and but one God; which doctrine of the Trinity, is the foundation of all our communion with God, and comfortable dependance on him.

And there are three that bare record in heaven, the father, the word, and the holy spirit, and these three are one. Baptizing them in the name of the father, son, and holy Ghost, &c.

I John 5 : 7.
John 15 : 26.
2 Cor. 13 : 13.
Gen. 1 : 26.
Matt. 3 : 16, 17.
John 5 : 17.
Gal. 1 : 3.
Matt. 16 : 16; 12 : 32.
Heb. 1 : 3.
Gen. 1 : 2, 26.
Rev. 1 : 8.
John 1 : 5.
1 Cor. 12 : 6, 11.
John 14 : 11.
I John 5 : 7, 26.
Gal. 4 : 6.
I Pet. 1 : 11.
2 Cor. 13 : 14.
I John 5 : 7.
Matt. 28 : 19.

IV. ARTICLE.

Of the divine Nature, or Godhead of Christ.

We confess and believe, that the Son of God, or the eternal word, is very and true God, having his personal subsistance of the father alone, and yet for ever of himself as God; and of the father as the son, the eternal son of an eternal father; not later in beginning. There was never any time when he was not, not less in dignity, not other in substance, begotten without diminution of his father that begat, of one nature and substance with the father; begotten of the father, while the father communicated wholly to the son, which he retained wholly in himself, because both were infinite, without inequality of nature, without division of essence, neither made, nor created, nor adopted, but begotten before all time; not

John 5 : 20; 1 : 1, 2, 3.
Heb. 1 : 3.
I Cor. 15 : 16, 17.
Col. 1 : 2, 9.
Mic. 5 : 2.
Gnolam, or Eternity.
Matt. 2 : 6.
Prov. 8 : 22, 23, 35.
Phil. 2 : 6.

John 16 : 27, 28.
1 : 18.
Isaiah 40 : 11, 12, 22.
Rev. 1 : 8, 11.

a metaphorical, or subordinate God; not a God by office, but a God by nature, co-equal, coessential, and coeternal, with the father and the holy ghost.

Phil. 2 : 6.
John 10 : 30.
Isaiah 9 : 6.
John 17 : 5; 8 : 58.

Jesus said unto them, Verily, verily, I say unto you, before Abraham was, I am. Jesus Christ the same yesterday, and to day, and for ever. David therefore calleth him Lord, how is he then his son?

Heb. 13 : 8.
Luke 20 : 44.

V. ARTICLE.

Of the second Person of the holy Trinity, taking our flesh.

We believe that the only begotten son of God, the second person in the sacred Trinity, took to himself a true, real, and fleshly body, and reasonable soul, being conceived in the fulness of time, by the holy ghost, and born of the virgin Mary, and became very and true man like unto us in all things, even in our infirmities, sin only excepted, as appeareth by his conception, birth, life, and death. He was of a woman, and by the power of the holy ghost, in a supernatural and miraculous manner, was formed of the only seed, or substance of the virgin Mary, in which respect he hath the name of the son of man, and is the true son of David the fruit of the virgin's womb, to that end he might die for Adam.
Gen. 26: 17. Heb. 2. 16.

I John 5 : 7.
Isaiah 7 : 14.
John 1 : 14.
Luke 1 : 31, 32.
Heb. 2 : 16, 17.
John 19 : 34, 36.
Matt. 26 : 38.
Luke 2 : 6, 7; 1 : 35.

Matt.1 :18,20; 23:25.
Gal. 4 : 4.

Heb. 4 :15; 2 :13, 14.
Luke 2 : 52.
Gal. 4 : 4.
Rom. 1 : 3, 4.
Luke 3 : 23, 24.
Heb. 7 : 14.

VI. ARTICLE.

Of the union of the two natures in Christ.

We believe the person of the son of God, being a person from all eternity existing, did assume the most pure nature of man, wanting all personal existing of its own, into the unity of his person, or Godhead, and made it his own; the properties of each nature being preserved, and this inseparable and indissolvable union of both natures, and was made by the holy ghost, sanctifying our nature in the virgin's womb, without change of either nature, or mixture of both, and of two

Heb. 2 : 14, 16.
Acts 20 : 28.

Matt. 1 : 20.
Luke 1 : 35.
Rom. 1 : 3, 4.

natures is one Christ, God-man, or Imma-
nuel, God with us. Which mystery ex-
ceeds the conception of men, and is the
wonder of angels, one only mediator,
Jesus Christ, the son of God.

Matt. 1 : 23.
I Tim. 3 : 16; 2 : 5.

VII. ARTICLE.

Of the communication of Properties.

We believe that the two natures in
Christ, continue still distinct in substance,
properties, and actions, and remain one
and the same Christ: For the properties
of the Godhead, cannot agree to the
properties of the manhood, nor the properties of the manhood, to the properties
of the Godhead; for as the Godhead or
divine nature cannot thirst, or be hungry, no more can the manhood
be in all, or many places at once. Therefore, we believe, the Godhead was neither turned nor transfused into the manhood, nor the
manhood into the Godhead, but both, the
divine nature keepeth entire all his essential
properties to its self, so that the humanity is neither omnipotent, omniscient,
nor omnipresent: And the human also
keepeth his properties, tho' often that
which is proper to the one nature, is
spoken of the person denominated from
the other, which must be understood by
the figure synecdoche, viz. a part being
taken for the whole, by reason of the
union of both natures into one person.
Hereby perceive we the love of God, because he laid down his life for us.

John 10 : 30; 5 : 26,
27, &c.
I John 4 : 9.
Matt. 9 : 6.
John 7 : 42.

Acts 20 : 28.
I Cor. 2 : 8.
John 3 : 13.
Mark 2 : 10.

I John 3 : 16.

VIII. ARTICLE.

Of the holy Spirit.

We believe that there is one holy spirit, the third person subsisting in the sacred trinity, one with the father and son,
who is very and true God, of one substance
or nature with the father and son, coequal,
coeternal, and coessential with the father
and son, to whom with the father and son,
three persons, and but one eternal and
almighty God, be by all the hosts of
saints and angels, ascribed eternal glory,
and Hallelujahs. Amen.

John 5 : 7.
Matt. 28 : 19.
Gen. 1 : 26.
Acts 5 : 4.
2 Cor. 13 : 13.
I Cor. 12 : 6, 11.
Isaiah 6 : 8, 9.
Acts 28 : 25, 26.

Isaiah 6 : 3.

IX. ARTICLE.

Of Predestination and Election.

The decrees of God are founded on
infinite wisdom, and situate in eternity,
and are crowned with infallibility, as to
the event. Now predestination unto life,
is the everlasting purpose of God, whereby before the foundation of the world
was laid, he hath constantly decreed in
his counsel secret to us, to deliver
from curse and damnation, those whom
he hath chosen in Christ, and bring them
to everlasting salvation, as vessels made
to honour, thro' Jesus Christ, whom he
elected before the foundation of the
world, and is called God's elect, in
whom his soul delighteth, being the
lamb foreordain'd, and so predestinated
unto the superlative glory of the hypostatical union. And this not for any foreseen holiness in his human nature, sith all
that did flow out of the hypostatical
union, being elected of mere grace, as
are all the members of his mystical body.
And God the father gave this his elected
and beloved son, for a covenant to the
people, and said, that his covenant shall
stand fast with him; and his seed shall endure for ever. And albeit God the father
be the efficient cause of all good things
he intended to us, yet Christ is the meriting cause of all those good things God
intended to us in election, viz. repentance, faith and sincere obedience to all
God's commandments. And so God the
father, that he might bring about the
eternal salvation of his elect, chose the
man Christ, with respect to his human
nature, out of the fallen lump of mankind,
which in the fulness of time, he made of
a woman, made under the law, to redeem
those that were under it, that we might
receive the adoption of sons. And tho'
Christ came from Adam, as Eve did, yet
not by Adam, as Cain did, viz. by natural propagation. Therefore without any
stain of sin, and this second Adam, being
by God's eternal decree, excepted out of
the first covenant, as being neither God

Isaiah 46 : 10.
Acts 15 : 18; 17 : 26.

Eph. 1 : 11.
Matt. 25 : 34.
I Tim. 1 : 9.
John 6 : 37; 10 : 28, 29.
Eph. 1 : 4.
Rom. 11 : 33; 8 : 30;
        9 : 29.
I Thess. 1 : 4.
Tit. 1 : 1.
I Pet. 1 : 19, 20.
Isaiah 42.: 1.
Matt 12 : 17, 18.

I Pet. 2 : 6.
Luke 23 : 35.
I Pet. 1 : 19.
John 1 : 14.
Heb. 2 : 16.
Col. 2 : 9.
I Tim. 1 : 9.
Ps. 89 : 23, &c.
John 3 : 16.
I John 4 : 9, 10, 19.
Rom. 3 : 24, 25.
        8 : 3.
I Cor. 8 : 30.
Eph. 2 : 8, 9, 10.

Heb. 7:14; 10 : 5, 6, &c.
Gal. 4 : 3.
Eph. 1 : 5.
Gen. 2 : 21, &c.
        4 : 1.
        5 : 3.
Matt. 1 : 18, 19.
Luke 1 : 35.
2 Tim. 2 : 5.
Heb. 9 : 15.
Eph. 2 : 13, &c.

Isaiah 49 : 6, &c.
2 Thess. 2 : 13.
Eph. 1 : 17, &c.
I Cor. 2 : 13.

the father, who was justly offended, nor yet sinful Adam, who had offended him in breaking of it. Therefore Christ, the second Adam, was a fit mediator between God and man, to reconcile both in himself, by the shedding and sprinkling of his blood, according to God's eternal purpose in electing of Christ, and of all that do, or shall believe in him, which eternal election or covenant transaction between the father and son, is very consistent with his revealed will in the gospel; for we ought not to oppose the grace of God in electing of us, nor yet the grace of the son in dying for all men, and so for us, nor yet the grace of the holy ghost in propounding the gospel, and persuading us to believe it. For until we do believe, the effects of God's displeasure are not taken from us; for the wrath of God abideth on all them that do not believe in Christ; for the actual declaration in the court of conscience, is by faith as an instrument, not for faith as a meriting cause: for Christ is the meriting cause of eternal life to all that believe, but not of God's will to give eternal life to them, nor yet of God's decree to save us, albeit we are chosen in Christ before the foundation of the world. Now faith is necessary as the way of our salvation, as an instrumental cause: but the active and passive obedience of Christ, is necessary as a meriting cause of our salvation; therefore God's eternal decree doth not oppose his revealed will in the gospel, it being but one, not two diverse or contrary wills. For his decree as king, decreeth the event, or what shall be done infallibly; but his command as a lawgiver, sheweth not what shall be done, but what is the duty of man to do, and leave undone. Therefore God hath, we believe, decreed, that faith as the means, and salvation as the end, shall be joined together, that where one is, the other must be also, for it is written, he that believeth shall be saved; also, believe in the Lord Jesus Christ, and thou shalt be saved. Now here is a great mystery indeed, for God so administereth his absolute decree that he leaveth us

I Thess. 1 : 5.
John 3 : 18, 36.
Rom. 3 : 30.
Gal. 3 : 8, 11.
Phil. 3 : 9.
Rom. 5 : 1, 2.

I John 4 : 9, 10, 19.
Heb. 11 : 6.
John 1 : 11, 12.
Acts 13 : 39; 20 : 28.
Eph. 1 : 14.

Rom. 5 : 9, &c.
John 6 : 40.
I Tim. 2 : 3, 4.
Job 23 : 13.
Ps. 115 : 3.
Job 42 : 2.
Isaiah 33 : 22.
John 3 : 36.
Mark 16 : 16.
Acts 16 : 31.
Isaiah 14 : 24.
Ps. 115 : 3; 32 : 11, 12.

89 : 30, 31, &c.

much place for an efficacious conditional dispensation, as if the decree itself were conditional.

X. ARTICLE.

Of Preterition or Reprobation.

We do believe, that known unto God are all his works from eternity; therefore he foresaw Adam's fall, but did not decree it, yet foreseeing it in his eternal counsel and wisdom, did elect and chuse Jesus Christ, and all that do or shall believe in him, out of that fallen lump of mankind. And hath manifested his love and grace by Jesus Christ, his elect or beloved son, thro' the gospel means, to all; and hath given us his word and oath, to assure us that he desires not the death of the wicked, but rather that they repent, or return to him and live, and if any do perish, their destruction is of themselves: and hath decreed to punish all those wicked, or ungodly, disobedient, and unbelieving or impenitent sinners, that have, or shall despise his grace, love, and woings, or strivings of the holy ghost, or longsuffering, whether by a total and continued rejection of grace, or by an universal and final apostacy; and such persons, so living and dying, shall be punished with everlasting destruction in hell fire, with the fallen angels, or devils, and shall be fixed in an irrecoverable state of damnation, irrevocable under the wrath of God, they being the proper objects of it; and shall remain under his inexpressible wrath and justice, in inconceivable torment, soul and body, to all eternity.

Acts 15 : 18.

Ezek. 18 : 23, 32.
33 : 11.
Hos. 13 : 9.
Jam. 1 : 13, 14.
2 Thess. 1 : 9,
10; 2 : 12

Heb. 10 : 26, &c.

Isa. 30 : 33;
66 : 24.
Mark 9 : 45, 46.

Jude 4.

Matt. 25 : 41, 46.

Rev 20. : 13, 14.

XI. ARTICLE.

Of Creation.

In the beginning it pleased god the father, son, and holy ghost, according to his eternal, and immutable decree, for the manifestation of the glory of his eternal power, wisdom, and goodness, to create, or make out of nothing, the world, and all things

Gen. 1 : 1.
Rom. 11 : 36.
Rev. 4 : 11.
Heb. 11 : 3.
Col. 1 : 16.
Gen. 5 : 1, 2; 2 : 7.

ETERNAL CONCIOUS PUNISHMENT (HELL) IS A ROMAN CATHOLIC AND SO ORTHODOX WAY TO JUSTIFY PERCATDEY

THERE IS NO REPROBATION

therein, whether visible or invisible, and
created man male and female, with a
fleshly body, and a reasonable, and invisible, or spiritual, angelical, and immortal soul, made after the image of God,
in knowledge, righteousness, and true
holiness, having the law written in his
heart, and power or liberty of will to fulfil
it, yet mutable, or under a possibility
of transgressing, being left to the liberty
of their own will, which was subject to
change; and also gave them command
not to eat of the tree of knowledge of
good and evil, and while they kept this
command, they enjoyed most happy communion with God, and had dominion
over the creatures. And all this wonderful work of creation, both in heaven and
in earth, was finished in the space of six
days, and all very good, and altho' reason
cannot conceive nor comprehend it, yet
God's word hath plainly revealed it, and
faith believes it.

Matt.10:28; 22:31,32.
Rev. 6 : 9.
Luk 23 : 46.
Acts 7 : 59.
Gen. 1 : 27; 9 : 6.
Eph. 4 : 24.
Rom. 2 : 14, 15.
Eccles. 7 : 29.

Gen. 3 : 6; 2 : 16, 17.

Gen. 1 : 1, 2, 31.

XII. ARTICLE.

Of Divine Providence.

The Almighty God, that created all
things, and gave them their being, by
his infinite power and wisdom, doth sustain and uphold, and move, direct, dispose, and govern all creatures and things,
from the greatest to the least, according
to the counsel of his own good will and
pleasure, for his own glory, and his creatures good.

Heb. 1 : 3.
Job 28 : 11.
    26 : 7, &c.
Ps. 135 : 5, 6.

Matt. 10 : 19, &c.
Ps. 65 : 8, &c.
Eph. 1 : 11.

XIII. ARTICLE.

Of the first Covenant.

The first covenant was made between
God and man, before man had sinned in
eating of the forbidden fruit, in which
covenant God required of man perfect
obedience to all the commands thereof,
and in case he did so obey he promised
to be his God. And on the other part,
man promised to perform entire and perfect obedience to all God's holy commands in that covenant, by that strength
wherewith God endowed him in his first

Hos. 6 : 7; 8 : 1.

Deut. 26 : 17, 18, 19.

creation; by the improvement of which
he might have attained unto eternal life
without faith, in the blood of the mediator of the new covenant of grace; but
he sinning against this covenant, which
consisted in two roots, viz. To love God a-
bove all things; and his neighbour as himself; it being the substance of that law
which was afterwards written in two
tables of stone, and delivered unto Moses
upon mount Sinai, and fell under the just
sentence of eternal death, which was the
punishment that God had appointed for
the breach of it. And under this righteous
judgment of God, Adam and his natural
posterity, had for ever remained, as
the fallen Angels do, had not God of his
infinite grace and love, provided his son,
to take unto himself our nature, and so became a fit mediator between God the father, who was offended, and man, who
had offended him in breaking his holy
law and covenant.

Matt. 22 : 37, 40.
Rom. 2 : 14, 15.

Gen. 3 : 12, 13.

Deut. 29 : 19, 20, 21.
Eph. 2 : 3.
Rom. 1 : 20, 32.

Rom. 5 : 12, 18.

Eph. 2 : 13, 14.

XIV. ARTICLE.

Of the fall of man, of his sin, and of the punishment thereof.

The first man Adam, in eating voluntarily of the forbidden fruit, incurred the
curse of God upon himself, and all his
posterity, that came of him by natural
propagation, viz. corporal and spiritual
death, in body and soul eternally; but
this covenant was not only made with
him, but with his seed also, which should
descend from his loins by natural generation; he standing as a publick person
in the stead of all mankind. And, as St.
Paul saith, by him came sin, and death by
sin, &c. and so deprived himself, and all
his posterity, of that original righteousness, which God created him in.

Rom. 5 : 12, 14.

Gen. 3 : 10, 12.
Eph. 2 : 1, 3.
Rom. 5 : 15, 16, 17.

Heb. 7 : 9, 10.
Ps. 51 : 5.
Gen. 6 : 5.
Rom. 7 : 7.
James 1 : 14.

XV. ARTICLE.

Of original, or birth, sin.

Original sin, is the fault and corruption
of the nature of every man, that naturally

Rom. 7 : 21.
Gen. 6 : 5.

descendeth from Adam by natural generation, by means of which, man has not
only lost that original righteousness, that
God created him in, but is naturally inclined to all manner of evil, being conceived in sin, and brought forth in iniquity; and, as St. Paul saith, the flesh
lusteth against the spirit. And therefore
every man justly deserveth God's wrath,
and damnation. And this concupisence,
or indwelling lust, remaineth even in the
regenerate, that they cannot love nor
obey God perfectly in this life, according
to the tenour of the first covenant.

CALVINISTS OF THE FIRST COVENANT.

Tit. 1 : 15.
Rom. 3 : 23.
Gen. 5 : 3.
Jer. 17 : 9.
Ps. 51 : 4, 5.
Job 14 : 4.
Gal. 5 : 16, 17.
I Cor. 15 : 22.
Rom. 6 : 23.
Gen. 2 : 17.
John 5 : 24.
Isa. 64 : 6.
Gal. 3 : 10.
Rom. 7 : 17, 21, 22.
2 : 14, 15.
Gal. 3 : 21, 22.
Matt. 12 : 33.

XVI. ARTICLE.

Of the new covenant of grace.

The first covenant being broken by
mans disobedience, and by his sin, he was
excluded from the favour of God, and
eternal life, in which deplorable condition
of his, God being pleased, out of his free
grace and love to fallen man, in order to
his recovery out of this sinful and deplorable estate, hath freely offered him a
second, or a new covenant of grace,
which new covenant of grace is Jesus
Christ, in remission of sins, thro' faith in
his blood, which God hath promised to
give to all them that do obey and submit
to the conditions of this covenant, which
covenant of grace, and eternal salvation
annexed to it, is freely and fully offered
unto all men, upon the terms of the gospel, viz. repentance and faith. And the
benefits of this covenant, by God's free
grace, thro' the redemption that is in
Jesus Christ, whom God has set forth to
be a propitiation thro' faith in his blood,
to declare his righteousness for the remission of sins that are past thro' the for-
bearance of God, that he might be just,
and the justifier of him that believeth in
Jesus. Therefore, we conclude, that a
man is justified by faith, without the deeds
of the law; for by faith we receive that
righteousness that the law, or the first
covenant, required of the first Adam;
which righteousness Christ hath fulfilled

Deut. 27 : 26.
Col. 1 : 13.
2 Cor. 4 : 4.
John 3 : 16.
Jer. 31 : 31, 32.

Rom. 3 : 23, 24.
Gal. 3 : 21, 22.
Rom. 3 : 31.
Heb. 8 : 7.
Gen. 3 : 15.
Luk. 24 : 47.
Eph. 1 : 7.
Ps. 20 : 3.
Acts 10 : 43; 3 : 19;
26 : 18; 2 : 37, 38.
Mark 1 : 15.
Gal. 3 : 11, 17.
Jer. 32 : 40.
Isa. 42 : 6.
Rom. 3 : 23, &c.

Acts 10 : 43.
Isa. 93 : 11.
Rom. 5 : 9; 3 : 20.
Gal. 3 : 8; 2 : 16.
Rom. 5 : 10, 19;
10 : 4.
Matt. 3.
2 Cor. 5 : 21.
I Cor. 1 : 30.

in our nature which he took of the virgin Mary, by his active obedience, and is, by God's free donation, made over to us by imputation; for he hath made him to us wisdom, righteousness and sanctification. For as by one man's disobedience, many were made sinners, so by the obedience of one, that is Christ, shall many be made righteous. For Christ hath not only fulfilled the sanction of the law, viz. To love God with all his heart, and his neighbour as himself, but hath also voluntarily suffered the curse of the law, being made a curse for us, that we might receive the blessing of Abraham, and the promise of the spirit thro' faith in his blood. And now, albeit the essential righteousness of Christ, as he is God equal with his father, be not imputed unto us, nor yet his personal righteousness, as he was or is man, only, yet we believe his mediatorial righteousness, as God man, is imputed, reckoned, or made over to us, upon the terms of this new covenant of grace; and so being justified by his grace, we are thereby made heirs according to the hope of eternal life: for, as St. Paul saith, If righteousness come by the law, then Christ is dead in vain.

Gal. 3 : 13.
I Pet. 2 : 24.
Isa. 53 : 6, 7, 8.
Phil. 2 : 7, 8.
Gal. 3 : 13, 14.
Heb. 7 : 26.
Matt. 3 : 15.
Rom. 5 : 18.
Gal. 4 : 6, 7.
Rom. 4 : 3, 4, 23.
　3 : 25, 28.
Tit. 3 : 7; 1 : 2.

XVII. ARTICLE.

Of Christ and his mediatorial Office.

It pleased God, in his eternal purpose, to chuse and ordain the Lord Jesus Christ, his only begotten son, according to the covenant made between them both, to be the alone mediator between God and man, viz. God the father, who was by Adam's sin justly offended, and Adam, our common parent, the person offending. Now in order to reconcile God to man, and man to God, who were at a distance, Christ Jesus, the second person in the trinity, being very God, of the same substance with his father, did, when the fulness of time was come, take unto him man's nature, with all the essential properties, and common infirmities, sin

Zech. 6 : 12, 13.
Gal. 3 : 17.
Ps. 89 : 28; 109 : 10.

Gal. 3 : 19, 20.
Heb. 10 : 15; 12 : 24.

I Tim. 2 : 5.
Job 9 : 33.
any days-man betwixt | us, &c.
Gal. 3 : 16.
Gen. 3 : 15.
I Chron. 17 : 11.

only excepted, being made of a woman,
of the seed of Abraham and David; and
altho' he came from Adam, and had truly the nature of man, yet not by Adam;
and the person of Christ took our nature
into union with the divine nature, but he
did not take the person of Adam which
sinned, therefore we believe he was neither
the covenantee, nor yet the coventanter,
and so, by consequence, neither the cre-
ditor nor the debtor. And being concerned by this office or appointment of the
father to make peace, it plainly appears,
that he is the only fit mediator between
God and man, who is very God, and very
man; yet one Christ, who was sanctified,
and anointed with the holy spirit above
measure, and was superlatively and ad-
mirably fitted for, and called unto this
office by his father, who put all judgment into his hand, and power to execute the same, and he willingly under-
took the same; and being made under
the law, did perfectly fulfil or keep it,
and underwent the punishment due to us,
which we should have suffered; our sin,
and the punishment of it, being reckoned
or imputed to him, he being made a curse
for us, and underwent and trod the wine-
press of his father's wrath for us, in do-
lorous pangs and agony of soul, and painful sufferings in his body, was crucified,
dead, and buried, or remained in the state
of the dead, yet saw no corruption,
and on the third day he arose from the
dead, with the same body in which he
suffered, with which he also ascended,
and there sitteth at the right hand of his
father, making intercession for his saints,
and shall return to judge men and angels
at the end of the world. And the same
Lord Jesus, by his perfect obedience to
the whole law, and sacrifice of himself,
which he, thro' the eternal spirit offered
up unto the father, hath fully satisfied the
justice of God and reconciled him
to us; and hath purchased an everlasting inheritance in the kingdom of
heaven, for all those that the father hath
given unto him, and now, by a continued act of intercession in heaven, doth

Luke 1 : 35.
Heb. 7 : 26.
Rom. 9 : 5.
Heb. 5 : 5; 7 : 21, &c.
Eph. 2 : 14.
Ps. 42 : 1, 6.
I Pet. 1 : 19, 20.
Heb. 9 : 15; 1 : 9.
Ps. 45 : 7.
Isaiah 61 : 1.
Col. 2 : 3.
Heb. 5 : 5.
John 5 : 22, 27.
Rom. 10 : 4.
2 Cor. 5 : 21.
Gal. 3 : 13.
Luke 22 : 44, 45.

Isaiah 53 : 10, 11, 12
I Pet. 2 : 24.
Matt. 27 : 46.
26 : 37, 38.
Acts 13 : 28, &c.

Luke 24 : 7.
John 20 : 25, 27.
Acts 1 : 9, 10, 11.

Mark 16 : 19.
Rom. 8 : 34.
Matt. 25 ; 31, &c.
Heb. 9 : 14, 15.

Eph. 2 : 14, &c.
John 17 : 2.
I Pet. 1 : 2, &c.

apply the benefits he hath purchased
unto the elect. And in this office of
mediator, he hath the dignity of three
offices, viz. Priest, Prophet, and King:
all which offices are necessary for the benefit
of his church, and without which
we can never be saved. For, in
respect of our ignorance, we stand
in need of his prophetical office, and
in respect of our alienation from God,
and imperfect services, and God's wrath
and justice, we stand in need of his
priestly office, to reconcile God to us,
and us to God; and in respect of our
bondage to sin and Satan, and averseness to return to God, we need his
kingly office to subdue our enemies, and
deliver us captives out of the kingdom
and power of sin, and preserve us to
his heavenly kingdom. And thus, in
our nature, he living the life of the
law, and suffering the penalty due to
us, continually presents us at the
throne of grace; so is a most wonderful and compleat mediator for his
elect.

Heb. 7 : 17.
Acts 3 : 22.
Ps. 45 : 5, &c.
Acts 4 : 11, 12.

2 Tim. 4 : 18.
Col. 1 : 13, 14.
Heb. 4 : 14, &c.

XVIII. ARTICLE.

Of Christ dying for all mankind.

God the father, out of his royal bounty,
and fountain of love, when all mankind
was fallen by sin, in breaking of the first
covenant of works made with them in
Adam, did chuse Jesus Christ, and sent
him into the world to die for Adam, or
fallen man. And God's love is manifest to all mankind, in that he is not
willing, as himself hath sworn, and abundantly declared in his word, that mankind
should perish eternally, but would have all
to be saved, and come to the knowledge of
the truth. And Christ died for all men,
and there is a sufficiency in his death and
merits for the sins of the whole world,
and hath appointed the gospel to be
preached unto all, and hath sent forth
his spirit to accompany the word in
order to beget repentance and faith:
so that if any do perish, it's not for

Rom. 5 : 8.
Matt. 20 : 28.
Rom. 8 : 3.
Heb. 9 : 15.
Ezek. 18 : 23.
Heb. 2 : 9.
I John 2 : 2.
I Tim. 2 : 3, &c.
Heb. 10 : 12, &c.
Mark 16 : 16.
Tit. 2 : 11, 12.
I Thess. 1 : 5, 6, 7.

John 5 : 39, 40.
Matt. 23 : 37, 38.
24 : 12.
Acts 13 : 46, 48.

want of the means of grace manifested
by Christ to them, but for the non-
improvement of the grace of God, offered freely to them through Christ in
the gospel.

XIX. ARTICLE.

Of the agreement between the Old and New Testament.

The Gospel, or new Covenant, was
held forth, or preached to the fathers,
from Adam to Christ's coming in the flesh,
though it was revealed by sundry degrees,   Gal. 3 : 8.
and in diverse manners, in types and sha-   Gen. 12 : 3.
dows, darkly; yet it was the same gos-   Heb. 4 : 2, 3; 1 : 1, 2.
pel, the same Christ, the same faith for kind,   10 : 1.
and the very same covenant, that they
were justified and saved by, before Christ
took flesh of the virgin, that we have
now, and is to continue to the end of
the world. For as the church of the   Heb. 9, 10, and
Jews, in their gospel types, had a priest,   11 chapt.
and an altar, and a lamb, and a fire, and
without all these no sacrifice could, or
was accepted of God, then, nor now,
without faith in the anti-type, Christ,
whose human nature is the true lamb,
the union of natures, the high priest, the
divine nature, the altar, and the holy
ghost, the heavenly fire. And again: Heb. 9 : 14.
The blood shed upon the brazen altar,
may be applied to our justification, and
the sprinkling of it upon the incense altar,
may be applied to the work of sanctification by Christ's spirit, sprinkling his
blood upon us. And the blood that was   Eph. 5 : 2.
carried within the vail, into the most   I Pet. 1 : 2.
holy place, is applied to our glorifica-
tion in heaven. And as they had in
their church the ark, a figure of Christ's
presence, so have we the promise of   Heb. 9 : 7, &c.
his presence to the end of the world.
And as they had the tables of the old
covenant or law, in the ark, so have
we the law fulfilled by Christ; and meet-   Matt. 18 : 20.
ing God in Christ, it's handed forth by   28 : 19, 20.
Christ now to us, as the only rule of our   Rom. 3 : 31; 8 : 3, 4
sanctification and obedience through his   10 : 4.
grace. And as they had the manna   I John 2 : 6, 7, 8.
to nourish them in the wilderness to

Canaan; so have we the sacraments, to
nourish us in the church, and in our
wilderness-condition, till we come to
heaven. And as they had the rod that
corrected them; so have we the church
censures now to correct us, when we offend his law; and their burnt offerings
may be applied to Christ, killing of o-
riginal sin in us, and their sin offering
may be applied to Christ, killing, or
taking away our actual sins, and their
peace offering may be applied to our
reconciliation with God in Christ by his
spirit, and so all the rest of those gos-
pel-antitypes may be applied. And thus
the Old and New Testaments, like the
faces of the Cherubins, look one toward
another, and hold forth the self-same
gospel, salvation to them and us.

James 4 : 12.
John 16 : 14, 15.

I Cor. 4 : 19, &c.

XX. ARTICLE.

Of Free-Will in Man.

God hath endued the will of man with
that natural liberty and power of acting
upon choice, that it's neither forced, nor
by any necessity of nature determined, to
do good or evil: but man, in the state
of innocency, had such power and liberty of will to chuse and perform that
which was acceptable and well pleasing
to God, according to the requirement
of the first covenant; but he falling from
his state of innocency, wholly lost all
ability, or liberty of will, to any spiritual
good, for his eternal salvation, his will
being now in bondage under sin and Satan, and therefore not able of his own
strength to convert himself nor prepare
himself thereunto, without God's grace
taketh away the enmity out of his will,
and by his special grace, freeth him from
his natural bondage under sin, enabling
him to will freely and sincerely, that
which is spiritually good, according to
the tenure of the new covenant of grace
in Christ, tho' not perfectly, according to
the tenure of the first covenant, which
perfection of will is only attainable in the

Matt. 17 : 12.

Eccles. 7 : 29.
Rom. 5 : 6; 8 : 7, 8
John 8 : 44.

Eph. 2 : 8, &c.
Phil. 2 : 13.
Rom. 7 : 14, &c.
　8 : 23.
Eph. 4 : 13.

state of glory, after the redemption, or resurrection of our fleshly bodies.

XXI. ARTICLE.

Of Vocation and effectual Calling.

Vocation, or calling, general, or common, is, when God by the means of his word and spirit, freely of his own gràce and goodness, doth ministerially acquaint mankind with his gracious good purpose of salvation, by Jesus Christ; inviting and wooing them to come to him, and to accept of Christ revealing unto them the gospel covenant, and those that with cordial hearts do improve this common grace, he in time worketh unfeigned faith, and sincere repentance in them; and by his grace they come to accept of Christ, as their only Lord and Saviour, with their whole heart; and God becomes their father in Christ, and they being then effectually called, are by faith united to Jesus Christ by grace unto salvation.

Matt. 11 : 28.
Acts 20 : 21.
Rom. 16 : 25, 26.
Tit. 2 : 11.
Acts 5 : 31; 11 : 18.
Rom. 8 : 28, 30.
11 : 5, 7.

Eph. 1 : 11, &c.
Rom. 5 : 1.
Eph. 2 : 8.
Rom. 4 : 16.

XXII. ARTICLE.

Of evangelical Repentance.

Unfeigned repentance, is an inward and true sorrow of heart for sin, with sincere confession of the same to God, especially that we have offended so gracious a God, and so loving a father, together with a settled purpose of heart, and a careful endeavor to leave all our sins, and to live a more holy and sanctified life, according to all God's commands. Or it is a turning, or change of the whole man to God, with endeavour, thro' his grace, to mortify the indwelling lust, or corruptions, and obtain a great reformation both in the outward and inward man, according to the will of God, and this repentance, for the nature of it, must be continued throughout the whole course of our lives, and is wrought in us by the spirit of God; by the ministry of the law and gospel, in order to our obedience to

Tit. 2 : 3, 4, 5.
Acts 2 : 37, 38.
2 Cor. 7 : 10, 11.
Acts 17 : 30.
Ps. 51 : 4.
Luke 15 : 17, &c.

Ezek. 18 : 30.
Eph. 2 : 10.
Rom. 8 : 13.
Eph. 4 : 20, &c.

John 8 : 31, &c.

Rom. 8 : 13.

Christ, or being baptized in his name, but this repentance unto life, is not wrought without faith in the soul; for by faith we receive that grace, that perfects, or carrieth on the work of repentance in the soul, from first to last.

I Thess. 1 : 5, 6.
Acts 3 : 19, 26.
2 : 38.
Heb. 11 : 6.
Gal. 3 : 26, &c.

XXIII. ARTICLE.

Of justifying, and saving Faith.

Faith is an act of the understanding, giving a firm assent to the things contained in the holy scriptures. But justifying faith is a grace, or habit, wrought in the soul, by the holy ghost, through preaching the word of God, whereby we are enabled to believe, not only that the Messias is offered to us, but also to take and receive him, as a Lord and Saviour, and wholly and only to rest upon Christ, for grace and eternal salvation.

Rom. 10 : 14, 17.
Matt. 13 : 20, 21.

Acts 24 : 14.
Ps.19:7,&c.; 119:72.
2 Pet. 1 : 1.
I John 5 : 4, 5.
2 Cor. 4 : 13.
Eph. 2 : 8.
Acts 31 : 31 ; 15 : 11.
2 Pet. 1 : 5, 11.
Phil. 3 : 8, 9.
Acts 8 : 37.

XXIV. ARTICLE.

Of Justification by Christ.

Justification is a declarative, or judicial sentence of God the father, whereby he of his infinite love, and most free grace, for the alone and mediatorial righteousness of his own son, performed in our nature and stead, which righteousness of God man, the father imputing to us, and by effectual faith, received and embraced by us, doth free us by judicial sentence from sin and death, and accept us righteous in Christ our surety, unto eternal life; the active and passive obedience of Christ being the accomplishment of all that righteousness and sufferings the law, or justice of God required, and this being perfectly performed by our mediator, in the very nature of us men, and accepted by the father in our stead, according to that eternal covenant-transaction, between the father and the son. And hereby we have deliverance from the guilt and punishment of all our sins, and are accounted righteous

Acts 13 : 38, 39.
Rom. 8 : 34, 35.
3 : 23, &c.
4 : 22, &c.
I Cor. 1 : 30, 31.

2 Thess. 1 : 3, 4.
Acts 15 : 9.
Gal. 5 : 6.
Rom. 8 : 1; 4:6, 7, 8.
Gal. 3 : 13, 14.
John 5 : 24.
Rom. 3 : 22, 30;
5 : 19.
2 Cor. 1 : 30.
Eph. 1 : 7.
Rom. 5 : 9; 10 : 4.
Gal. 3 : 13.
Heb. 2 : 9, &c.
2 Cor. 5 : 21.
Isaiah 53 : 10, &c.

before God, at the throne of grace,
by the alone righteousness of Christ the
mediator, imputed, or reckoned unto us
through faith; for we believe there are
six necessary causes of man's justification,
or salvation; viz. First, The efficient
cause of our justification, is God's free
grace. Secondly, The meritorious cause   Rom. 3 : 24.
is the blood of Christ. Thirdly, The ma-   Rom. 5 : 9.
terial cause is Christ's active obedience.   5 : 19; 4 : 6.
Fourthly, The imputation of Christ, his   5 : 1.
obedience for us, is the formal cause.   Eph. 1 : 11, 12
Fifthly, The instrumental cause is faith.
Sixthly, God's glory, and man's salvation,
is the final cause. Now we principally apply the first and last to God the
father; the second and third to Christ the
mediator; the fourth and fifth to the blessed
comforter, the holy ghost; hence it   Matt. 28 : 19.
is we are baptized in the name of the   2 Cor. 13 : 14.
father, of the son, and holy ghost, and   1 John 5 : 7.
so we worship a trinity in unity, and unity
in trinity.

XXV. ARTICLE.

Of Reconciliation, and Sonship by Christ.

Two privileges flow out of our justification by faith in Christ, viz. our reconciliation, and adoption, or sonship. Reconciliation is a gracious privilege, whereby we that were enemies are made friends; or
we that were enemies, rebels, and
aliens, are received into favour, or brought
near to God through faith in Christ Jesus.
And adoption is that power and privilege   Rom. 5 : 8, &c.
to be the sons of God, through faith in   Eph. 2 : 12, &c.
Christ our surety, who being the eternal   1 : 5.
son of God, became by incarnation our   Gal. 4 : 4, 5, 6.
brother, that by him God might bring   Rom. 8 : 16, 17.
many sons unto glory, according to his
eternal decree of preserving the human   Heb. 2 : 10, &c.
nature of Christ, that it never fell in   4 : 15.
Adam. And so we are, by faith accord-   Matt. 1 : 18.
ing to God's free grace, and Christ's pur-   Heb. 7 : 26.
chase, or redemption, and the holy spi-   Rom. 8 : 16, 17.
rit's application of it to us, made heirs
and joint heirs with Christ, our elder brother,
of the same kingdom, and stupendous
and unutterable glory, for ever and ever.

XXVI. ARTICLE.

Of Sanctification, and good Works.

Those that are united unto Christ by effectual faith, are regenerated, and have a new heart and spirit created in them, through the virtue of Christ his death, resurrection, and intercession, and by the efficacy of the holy spirit, received by faith, and are sanctified by the word and spirit of truth, dwelling in them, by destroying and pulling down the strong holds, or dominion of sin and lust, and more and more quickened and strengthened in all saving graces, in the practice of holiness, without which no man shall see the lord. And this sanctification is throughout the whole man, tho' imperfect in this life, there abiding still in the best saints, some remnants of corruption, which occasions a continual war in the soul, the flesh lusting against the spirit, and the spirit against the flesh; yet through the continual supply of strength from Christ, which flows from him to believers by means of the covenant of grace or hypostatical union with our nature, the regenerate part doth overcome, pressing after a heavenly life, in evangelical obedience to all the commands that Christ, their king, and law-giver, hath commanded them in his word, or holy scriptures, which are the only rule, and square of our sanctification and obedience in all good works, and piety. And sith our only assistance to good works, such as God hath commanded, is of God, who worketh in us both to will and to do, we have no cause to boast, nor ground to conclude, we merit any thing thereby, we receiving all of free and undeserved grace, and when we have done the most, yet we are unprofitable servants, and do abundantly fall short; and the best duties that we can now perform, will not abide the judgment of God. Neither do any good works whatsoever, that are done by unregenerate men, or without faith in, and love to Christ, please God, or are accepted of him. Yet good works are of great ad-

Ezek. 36 : 26.
Eph. 4 : 24.
2 Cor. 5 : 17.
I John 3 : 9.
Tit. 3 : 5.
1 Cor. 4 : 15.
2 Cor. 3 : 18.
I Tim. 2 : 20.
Ps. 110 : 3.
2 Cor. 10 : 4, 5; 5 : 17.
John 17 : 17; 16:14,15.
Heb. 12 : 14.
Rom. 7 : 20.
Gal. 5 : 16, 17.
I John 3 ; 8 ; 2 : 20.

Rom. 6 : 14.
Eph. 4 : 15.
2 Cor. 3 : 18; 7 : 1.
Ps. 112 : 1; 119 : 48.

John 15 : 4, 6.
Isaiah 43 : 13; 26:12.
Phil. 2 : 13.
2 Cor. 3 : 5.
Job 9 : 2, 3, 20.
25 : 4.
Gal. 2 : 16.
James 2 : 9, 10; 3 : 2.
Heb. 11 : 6.
Isa. 64 : 6.
Prov. 8 : 17.
I Cor. 16 : 22.
James 1 : 18, &c.

vantage, being done in faith, and love, and wrought by the holy spirit, and are to be done by us, to shew our thankfulness to God, for the grace of the new covenant by Christ, and to fit us more and more for glory. And in this sense the ten commandments, as handed forth by Christ the mediator, are a rule of life to a believer, and shew us our duty to God and man, as also our need of the grace of God, and merit of Christ.

Gal. 5 : 22, 23.
John 4 : 14; 5 : 25.

Gal. 5 : 6.
I Cor. 6 : 9, &c.
Heb. 12 : 28, 29.

I Cor. 13 : 2, 3.
Ps. 50 : 14.

XXVII. ARTICLE.

Of Baptism, and the Lord's-supper.

Those two sacraments, viz. Baptism, and the Lord's-supper, are ordinances of positive, sovereign, and holy institution, appointed by the Lord Jesus Christ, the only lawgiver, to be continued in his church, to the end of the world; and to be administred by those only who are rightly qualified, and thereunto called, according to the command of Christ.

Matt. 28 : 19, 20.
I Cor. 11 : 26; 4 : 1

XXVIII. ARTICLE.

Of the right subject and administration of holy Baptism.

Baptism is an ordinance of the new testament, ordained by Jesus Christ, to be unto the party baptized, or dipped, a sign of our entrance into the covenant of grace, and ingrafting into Christ, and into the body of Christ, which is his church; and of remission of sin in the blood of Christ, and of our fellowship with Christ, in his death and resurrection, and of our living, or rising to newness of life. And orderly none ought to be admitted into the visible church of Christ, without being first baptized; and those which do really profess repentance towards God, and faith in, and obedience to our Lord Jesus Christ, are the only proper subjects of this ordinance, according to our Lord's holy institution, and primitive practice; and ought by the minister, or administrator, to be done in a solemn manner, in the

Rom. 6 : 3, 4, 5.
I Cor. 12 : 13.
Gal. 3 : 27.
Mark 16 : 16.
Matt. 3 : 11.
Acts 2 : 38.
Rom. 6 : 1, &c.
Matt. 28 : 19.

Acts 8 : 37.
Matt. 3 : 6.
Heb. 6 : 1, 2.
Acts 2 : 37, 38;
   8 : 35, 36, &c.

name of the father, son, and holy ghost, Matt. 28 : 19.
by immersion or dipping of the person in John 1 : 2, 8, 31.
the element of water; this being necessary 3 : 22, 23.
to the due administration of this holy
sacrament, as holy scripture sheweth and Mark 1 : 9, 10.
the first and best antiquity witnesseth for
some centuries of years. But the popish doctrine
which they teach and believe, that
those infants that die without baptism,
or have it not actually, or in desire,
are not, nor cannot be saved, we do not
believe. Nor yet their practice of admitting persons only upon an implicit
faith of the church, nor their superstitious
and popish ceremonies of salt, and spittle,
and breathing on the face of the party
baptized, together with their chrisoms
and hallowed lights. Neither do we
believe, that infants dying in infancy,
without baptism, go to purgatory or lim-
bus infantum, as they erroneously teach.
Nor do we believe, that the Pope of
Rome, or any other persons whomsoever,
have power to alter, or change, this ordinance of Christ, as they have done by
this superstitious, and such like idolatrous
inventions and practices of the Romish
church. All which superstitions of theirs,
are contrary to Christ's institution, or the
apostles practice of holy baptism.

XXIX. ARTICLE.

Of the invisible catholick Church of Christ.

There is one holy catholick church, Heb. 12 : 22, 23.
consisting of, or made up of the whole Rev. 14 : 1, &c.
number of the elect, that have been, are, Col. 1 : 18.
or shall be gathered, in one body under Eph. 1 : 10, 22;
Christ, the only head thereof; which 5 : 23, 26, 27.
church is gathered by special grace, and
the powerful and internal work of the John 10 : 16.
spirit; and are effectually united unto Gal. 3 : 28.
Christ their head, and can never fall Ps. 72 : 17; 102 : 28.
away. Rev. 13 : 8.

XXX. ARTICLE.

Of the catholick Church as visible.

Nevertheless, we believe the visible
church of Christ on earth, is made up of

several distinct congregations, which make up that one catholick church, or mystical body of Christ. And the marks by which she is known to be the true spouse of Christ, are these, viz. Where the word of God is rightly preached, and the sacraments truly administred, according to Christ's institution, and the practice of the primitive church; having discipline and government duly executed, by ministers or pastors of God's appointing, and the church's election, that is a true constituted church; to which church, and not elsewhere, all persons that seek for eternal life, should gladly join themselves. And altho' there may be many errors in such a visible church, or congregations, they being not infallible, yet those errors being not fundamental, and the church in the major, or governing part, being not guilty, she is not thereby unchurched; nevertheless she ought to detect those errors, and to reform, according to God's holy word, and from such visible church, or congregations, no man ought, by any pretence whatever, schismatically to separate.

Gal. 3 : 26, &c.
Acts 2 : 41, &c.

Eph. 2 : 19, &c.

I Cor. 11 : 23, &c.
Gal. 3 : 1.
Eph. 3 : 21.
Acts 18 : 8.
I Cor. 12 : 13.
I John 2 : 19.
Rev. 2 : 2, 14, &c.
Tit. 3 : 10, 11.
Jude 17 : 18, 19.
Jam. 3 : 13, &c.
I Tim. 4 : 1.
2 Tim. 1 : 13, &c.

Acts 20 : 29, &c.
I Cor. 12 : 25.

XXXI. ARTICLE.
Of Officers in the Church of Christ.

The visible church of Christ, being completely gathered and organized, according to the mind of Christ, consists of officers and members; and the officers, appointed by Christ, to be chosen by his church, for the peculiar administration of ordinances, and execution of the power and duty Christ hath enjoined them to the end of the world, are these three, viz. *Bishops, or Messengers; and Elders, or Pastors; and Deacons, or Overseers of the poor; and the way appointed by Christ, for the calling of any person fitted and gifted by the holy ghost, unto the office of bishop, or messenger, in the churches, is, viz, That he be chosen thereunto by the common suffrage of the church, and solemnly set apart by fasting and prayer,

Acts 1 : 20, &c.
13 : 2, 3; 14 : 23.
20 : 17, 18.
6 : 3, 4, 5, 6.
1 : 23, 24, &c.
14 : 23.

*Or overseer, or shepherd.

with imposition of hands, by the bishops
of the same function, ordinarily, and
those bishops so ordained, have the government of those churches, that had
suffrage in their election, and no other
ordinarily; as also to preach the word,
or gospel, to the world, or unbelievers.
And the particular pastor, or elder, in
like manner is to be chosen by the common suffrage of the particular congrega-
tion, and ordained by the bishop or mes- I Tim. 1 : 3.
senger God hath placed in the church he Tit. 1 : 5.
hath charge of; and the elder, so ordain- Rev. 2 : 1, 2, &c.
ed, is to watch over that particular Matt. 28 : 19.
church; and he may not ministerially act
in any other church before he be sent, Mark 16 : 16.
neither ought his power, or office, any Acts 1 : 22.
way to infringe the liberty, or due power, 2 Tim. 4 : 2.
or office of his bishop *, God being a Acts 14 : 23.
God of order, having ordained things Rom. 10 : 15.
most harmoniously, tending every way to Acts 13 : 2, 3, 4.
unity. The deacons are in like manner I Cor. 16 : 16.
to be chosen by election and ordination, I Tim. 1 : 3.
and are in their particular congregations, Acts 20 : 28.
to receive the charity and free benevo- I Cor. 11 : 34.
lence of the people; and the bisops and Tit. 1 : 5.
elders so chosen, and ordained, to the Heb. 13 : 17.
I Cor. 14 : 33.
work of God, ought to be enabled and Acts 6 : 1, 2, &c.
capacitated thereunto, by a sufficient and I Tim. 3 : 8, &c.
honourable maintenance of the people 1 Cor. 3 : 9.
that chose them, answerable to the dignity I Tim. 3 : 5; 4 : 6, 16.
of their places, and charge committed to 2 Tim. 4 : 5.
them, without which they cannot dis- Tit. 1 : 7.
charge their duty, as they ought to do, 1 Cor. 9 : 1, &c.
in studying to divide the word of God Phil. 4 : 15, &c.
aright, as St. Paul adviseth Timothy, and I Tim. 5 : 17, 18.
also to give themselves wholly to it; and
this maintenance is to be given out of the Gal. 6 : 6, 10.
labours, profits, and estates of the people, Deut. 25 : 4.
by equality, and proportionable to their 2 Cor. 11 : 7, 8.
ability, in liberality, God having reserved I Tim. 3 : 5, &c.
a portion for all his labourers, out of all 11 : 13, &c
the members worldly goods and possessions. 2 Tim. 1, 2, &c.
3 : 14, &c.
Col. 4 : 11, 17: 2 Cor. 8 : 12, &c.; 2 Cor. 9 : 5, 6, &c. 4 : 1, 2, 5.

XXXII. ARTICLE.

Of Prayer, with laying on of Hands.

Prayer, with imposition of hands by Acts 8 : 12, &c.
the bishop, or elder, on baptized be- 19 : 6, 7.

lievers, as such, for the reception of the holy promised spirit of Christ, we believe is a principle of Christ's doctrine, and ought to be practised and submitted to by every baptized believer in order to receive the promised spirit of the father and son.

2 Tim. 1 : 6, 7.
Heb. 6 : 2.
John 13 : 16, &c.
16 : 7.
Eph. 1 : 13, 14.
2 Tim. 1 : 6.
Acts 2 : 38, 39.

XXXIII. ARTICLE.

Of the End, and right Administration of the Lord's-supper.

The supper of the Lord Jesus, was instituted by him the same night wherein he was betrayed; to be observed in his church, to the end of the world, for the perpetual remembrance, and showing forth the sacrifice of himself in his death; and for the confirmation of the faithful believers in all the benefits of his death and resurrection, and spiritual nourishment and growth in him; sealing unto them their continuance in the covenant of grace, and to be a band and pledge of communion with him, and an obligation of obedience to Christ, both passively and actively, as also of our communion and union each with other, in the participation of this holy sacrament. And the outward elements of bread and wine, after they are set apart by the hand of the minister, from common use, and blessed, or consecrated, by the word of God and prayer, the bread being broken, and wine poured forth, signify to the faithful, the body and blood of Christ, or holdeth forth Christ, and him crucified; and the minister distributing the bread and wine to the communicants, who are to take, or receive, both the bread and wine at the hands of the minister, applying it by faith, with thanksgiving to God the father, for so great a benefit, and no unbaptized, unbelieving, or open profane, or wicked heretical persons, ought to be admitted to this ordinance to profane it.

Luk. 22 : 17, &c.
Matt. 26 : 26, &c.
I Cor. 11 : 23, &c.

Matt. 28 : 20.

Gal. 3 : 1.

I Cor. 10 : 16, 17.

Gal. 3 : 1.

I Cor. 11 : 27, &c.

Matt. 26 : 30.
I Cor. 5 : 7, 8, 15.

Acts 2 : 41, &c.

Neither is that popish doctrine of transubstantiation to be admitted of, nor adoration of the unbloody sacrifice of the mass, as they call it, together with their denying of the cup to the laity,

See the popish catechism, p. 286, &c.

v

and many more idolatrous and superstitious practices, decreed in the popish councils of Lateran and Trent. In opposition
to which, and such like idolatry of Rome,
many of our worthy and famous antients,
and renowned protestants, lost their lives
by fire and faggot in England, whose
spirits we hope are now in heaven, as
worthy martyrs and witnesses of Christ,
in bearing a faithful testimony to this
holy ordinance of their Lord and master.
Neither may we admit of consubstantiation, it being not consonant to God's word.
Nor are little infants, that cannot examine
themselves, nor give account of their
faith, nor understand what is signified by
the outward signs of bread and wine, to
be admitted to this sacrament. Though
St. Austin taught so from John 6:63.
and many of the Greek churches so believe
and practise to this day. And this holy
ordinance ought to be often celebrated
among the faithful, with examination of
themselves, viz. of their faith, and love,
and knowledge of these holy and divine
mysteries, lest they eat and drink their
own damnation, for prophaning of God's
holy ordinance, as many, we fear, have
done, and yet do at this day; whose hard
and blind hearts the Lord in mercy open,
if it be his blessed will.

Ib. p. 197, &c.

See Mr. Fox's Book of Martyrs.

I Cor. 11 : 18, &c.

XXXIV. ARTICLE.

Of the Discipline and Government of the Church of Christ.

We believe that the great king, and
lawgiver, Christ, the universal and only
head of his church, hath given to his
visible church, a subordinate power, or
authority, for the well-being, ordering,
and governing of it, for his own glory,
and the church's profit, and good, the
executive part of which derivative
power of discipline and government, is
committed to his ministers, proportionable
to their dignities and places in the
church in a most harmonious way, for
the beauty, order, government, and e-
stablishment of the same, and consisteth

Isaiah 9 : 6.
Matt. 28 : 18.
18 : 17, 11.
Rev. 2 : 3.
I Cor. 5 : 4.
Heb. 13 : 7, 17.

in the exercise and execution of the censors, or rod of correction, he hath appointed therein, for the purgation, or pruning of the same, in order to prevent scandals and offences, both publick and private. And in case of personal and private trespasses between party and party, that the member so offended, tell his offence to his brother, between them alone; and if he shall not hear him, to take one or two more; if he will not hear him then, to tell it unto the church: And the ministers of Christ ought to rebuke them sharply, that sin before them in the church; and in case there be any wicked, publick, and scandalous sinners, or obstinate hereticks, that then the church ought speedily to convene such her members, and labour to convict them of their sin and heresy, schism, and prophaneness, whatsoever it be; and after such regular suspension, and due admonition, if such sinners repent not; that then for the honour of God, and preserving the credit of religion, and in order to save the sinner's soul, and good of the church, in obedience to God's law, to proceed and excommunicate the sinner, by a judicial sentence in the name of Christ and his church, tendring an admonition of repentance to him, with gravity, love, and authority, and all this without hypocrisy, or partiality, praying for the sinner, that his soul may be saved in the day of the Lord; and under this second degree, of withdrawing, or excommunication, to account him as a heathen, or publican, that he may be ashamed. But upon the third and highest act of excommunication, it being a most dreadful thunderclap of God's judgment, it is most difficult for any church now to proceed in, it being difficult to know when any man hath sinned the unpardonable sin, and so to incur a total cutting off from the church.

2 Thess. 3 : 6.
I Thess. 5 : 12, &c.
2 Cor. 2 : 5, 6, 7.

Lev. 19 : 17, 18.

Matt. 18 : 15, &c.
I Tim. 5 : 20.
2 Tim. 2 : 14.
Tit. 1 : 12, 13, 14.

Lev. 13 : 1, &c.
Numb. 12 : 14, 15.

2 Thess. 3 : 6.

I Cor. 5 : 4, &c.
Tit. 3 : 10.
Rev. 2 : 14, 20, &c.

Matt. 18 : 17.
I Cor. 16 : 22.

XXXV. ARTICLE.

Of Communion of Saints, and giving to the Poor.

All christians that have been baptized into one faith, and united in one true

Eph. 4 : 5.
Col. 3 : 15.

visible way of worshipping the true God, by Christ Jesus our Lord, should keep the unity of the spirit, in the bond of peace, seeing there is but one mystical body of Christ, and should have fellowship and communion in each other's sufferings, or afflictions, for if one member suffer, all are pained with it. Hence it is also they partake of each other's gifts in great variety, which make the harmony of dependency on each other, seeing a need of every member, for the publick use, and common profit of the whole, both in the private as well as more publick, and solemn worship of God's house; as also an interest in each other's goods and possessions, so far as comports with necessity and charity, according to the charter privileges, or law of their king; and tho' no equality, or property, be pleaded for; yet the works of charity and mercy, must be minded as a duty to lend to the Lord, and pity and relieve the Lord's poor, weekly laying out for them, as God hath prospered us, according to our ability in freedom, liberality, and charity, according to our brethrens necessity, whether sick, or in prison, to visit and relieve them, and not only within the church, but to all as we have opportunity, and ability to be doing good.

Acts 2 : 46.
Eph. 4 : 3, 4, &c.
I Cor. 12 : 12, 13.
Acts 4 : 32.
I Cor. 12 : 26; 12 : 4, 5, &c.

2 Cor. 8 : 9, 11, &c.
Ps. 37 : 26.
Prov. 11 : 25.
19 : 17.
22 : 22.
Deut. 15 : 10.
Eph. 4 : 28.
I Cor. 16 : 1, 2; 3 : 14, 15.
Deut. 15 : 7, &c.
Matt. 25 : 35, &c.

XXXVI. ARTICLE.

Of Perseverance.

Those that are effectually called, according to God's eternal purpose, being justified by faith do receive such a measure of the holy unction, from the holy spirit, by which they shall certainly persevere unto eternal life.

Jer. 31 : 33, 34. Rom. 8 : 30.

Rom. 8 : 28.
Gal. 3 : 14.
John 1 : 12, 13.
John 17 : 12, 21.
10 : 28, 29.
Rom. 1 : 17.

XXXVII. ARTICLE.

Of the sacred Scripture.

The authority of the holy scripture dependeth not upon the authority of any

2 Pet. 1 : 19, &c.
2 Tim. 3 : 15, &c.

man, but only upon the authority of God, who hath delivered and revealed his mind therein unto us, and containeth all things necessary for salvation; so that whatsoever is not read therein, nor may be proved thereby, is not to be required of any man, that it should be believed as an article of the christian faith, or be thought requisite to salvation. Neither ought we, since we have the scriptures delivered to us now, to depend upon, hearken to, or regard the pretended immediate inspirations, dreams, or prophetical predictions, by or from any person whatsoever, lest we be deluded by them. Nor yet do we believe, that the works of creation, nor the law written in the heart, viz. natural religion, as some call it, or the light within man, as such, is sufficient to inform man of Christ the mediator, or of the way to salvation, or eternal life by him; but the holy scriptures are necessary to instruct all men into the way of salvation, and eternal life. And we do believe, that all people ought to have them in their mother tongue, and diligently, and constantly to read them in their particular places and families, for their edification, and comfort; and endeavour to frame their lives, according to the direction of God's word, both in faith and practice, the holy scriptures being of no private interpretation, but ought to be interpreted according to the analogy of faith, and is the best interpreter of itself, and is sole judge in controversy. And no decrees of popes, or councils, or writings of any person whatsoever, are of equal authority with the sacred scriptures. And by the holy scriptures we understand, the canonical books of the old and new testament, as they are now translated into our English mother-tongue, of which there hath never been any doubt of their verity, and authority, in the protestant churches of Christ to this day.

John 20 : 30, 31.
  21 : 25.
Matt. 22 : 29.
John 5 : 39, 46, 47.
  10 : 35.
  17 : 12.
Prov. 30 : 5, 6.

Joshua 1 : 7.
Rev. 22 : 18.
Deut. 12 : 32.
Isaiah 8 : 20.
2 Pet. 1 : 19.
2 John 7 : 8, 9, 10.
Matt. 24 : 23, &c.
2 Thess. 2 : 7, &c.

I Cor. 1 : 20, &c.
  2 : 6, 7, &c.

Rom.15:4,5; 16:25,26.
  1 : 16, &c.
Gal. 5 : 22.
Rom. 11 : 31, 32.

  10 : 13, &c.
I Cor. 14 : 4, 9, &c.
Col. 3 : 16.
2 Pet. 1 : 20, 21.
Acts 15 : 15, 16.

Matt. 22 : 29, 30,

Acts 17 : 10, &c.
  18 : 28.

" Then follows the names of the books of the Old and New Testament, as acknowledged in all Protestant confessions, after which follow these words "[Crosby's note]:

All which are given by the inspiration
of God, to be the Rule of faith and
life.

XXXVIII. ARTICLE.

Of the three Creeds.

The three creeds, viz. Nicene creed,
Athanasius's creed, and the Apostles creed,
as they are commonly called, ought
throughly to be received, and believed.
For we believe, they may be proved, by
most undoubted authority of holy scripture, and àre necessary to be understood
of all christians; and to be instructed in
the knowledge of them, by the ministers
of Christ, according to the analogy of
faith, recorded in sacred scriptures, upon
which these creeds are grounded, and ca-
techistically opened, and expounded in all
christian families, for the edification of
young and old, which might be a means
to prevent heresy in doctrine, and practice, these creeds containing all things in
a brief manner, that are necessary to be
known, fundamentally, in order to our
salvation; to which end they may be considered, and better understood of all men,
we have here printed them under their
several titles as followeth, viz.

The Apostles Creed.

I believe in God the father almighty, &c.

The Nicene Creed.

We believe in one God, the father al-
might, &c.

Athanasius his Creed.

Whosoever will be saved, before all
things, &c.

" I have omitted inserting the creeds at length, they being to be found in every common prayer-book, and only
observe, that upon the article in the Apostles' Creed, he

descended into hell, they thus comment, Not that he, to wit, Christ, went into the place of the damned, but that he went absolutely into the state of the dead. See Doctor Usher in his body of Divinity, p. 174, and Mr. Perkins on the creed " [Crosby's note].

XXXIX. ARTICLE.

Of general Councils, or Assemblies.

General councils, or assemblies, consisting of Bishops, Elders, and Brethren, of the several churches of Christ, and being legally convened, and met together out of all the churches, and the churches appearing there by their representatives, make but one church, and have lawful right, and suffrage in this general meeting, or assembly, to act in the name of Christ; it being of divine authority, and is the best means under heaven to preserve unity, to prevent heresy, and superintendency among, or in any congregation whatsoever within its own limits, or jurisdiction. And to such a meeting, or assembly, appeals ought to be made, in case any injustice be done, or heresy, and schism countenanced, in any particular congregation of Christ, and the decisive voice in such general assemblies is the major part, and such general assemblies have lawful power to hear, and determine, as also to excommunicate.

Acts 15 : 1, &c.

Acts 15 : 11, &c.
Matt. 18 : 20.

Acts 15 : 30, 31.

Matt. 18 : 18, 19.
I Cor. 5 : 4, 5, 6.

XL. ARTICLE.

Of religious Worship, and the Sabbath-day.

The light of nature sheweth there is a God, who hath a sovereignty over all, but the holy scripture hath fully revealed it; as also that all men should worship him according to God's own institution and appointment. And hath limited us, by his own revealed will, that he may not be worshipped according to the imaginations and devices of men, or the suggestions of Satan, under any visible representations whatsoever, or any other way not pre-

Rom. 1 : 19, 20; 2 : 15.

I Chron. 16 : 29.
Ps. 95 : 6, 7, 8.

scribed in the holy scriptures; and all religious worship is to be given to the
father, son, and holy ghost, and to God
alone, not to angels, saints, or any other
creature, and since the fall, not without a
mediator, nor in the mediation of any
other but Christ alone; nor is this worshipping of God now under the gospel,
tied to any place, or made more acceptable by one place than another. Yet the
assembly of the church, ought not to be
neglected by any. And in order to his
being worshipped, and served, God hath
instituted one day in seven, for his sabbath
to be kept holy unto him, which from
the resurrection of Christ, is the first day
of the week, which is called the Lord's-
day, and is to be observed and continued
to the end of the world, as a christian
sabbath, the last day of the week being
abolished. And this christian sabbath is
to be kept after a due and reverent manner, in preparing of our hearts, and ordering of affairs so beforehand, that we
may rest that day from worldly and carnal
employments, and frequent the solemn
assemblies of the church, and in all publick and private duties of religion, as
hearing, meditating, and conferring, and
reading in, or of the holy scriptures, together with prayer, publick and private,
and in the duties of necessity, charity,
and mercy, and not in any vain or worldly discourse, or idle recreations whatsoever.

Luke 21 : 36. Acts 16 : 13, 16. Isa. 56 : 2, 6.

97 : 7.
99 : 5.
Deut. 8 : 6.
Ps. 103 : 7; 14 : 6.

Mark 7 : 7.
Ps. 99 : 8, 9.
  106 : 29, 39.
John 4 : 24.
Rev. 9 : 20.
Exod. 34 : 14.
I Cor. 8 : 4.
Matt. 28 : 19.
Deut. 5 : 26, &c.
John 14 : 6.
Gal. 3 : 9.
Heb. 9 : 15.
I Tim. 2 : 5.
Matt. 18 : 20.
John 4 : 21.
Mal. 1 : 11.
I Tim. 2 : 8.
Heb. 10 : 25.
Acts 2 : 42.
Exod. 20 : 8.
I Cor. 16 : 1, 2.
Acts 20 : 7.
Rev. 1 : 10.
Isaiah 58 : 13.
Neh. 13 : 15, &c.
Heb. 10 : 25.
Rev. 1 : 3.
James 1 : 23, 25.
Rom. 10 : 14.
Ps. 119 : 15.
Zech. 7 : 2.

XLI. ARTICLE.

Of publick and private Prayer.

Prayer is an holy, religious, and sacred
ordinance of God, and the duty of all
men to perform, by the law of God;
and to God alone, and no other, whether
saint or angel, and in the name of Christ
the mediator, and in his name alone, and
no other, whether saint or angel, or any
other creature. And that for all men
living, except they have sinned the un-

Matt. 6 : 7.
Jude 20.
Heb. 12 : 28.
Isaiah 55 : 6.
Jer. 29 : 12; 10 : 6, 25.

Ps. 32 : 6.
Matt. 26 : 41.
Isaiah 30 : 2.
Hos. 4 : 12.

pardonable sin, both high and low; especially for ministers and magistrates. And not for dead saints, nor infernal spirits. And prayer is to be made in a tongue understood by the people: And we ought to pray for all things necessary according to the will of God in Christ Jesus, in a solemn and reverent manner, every way suitable and agreeable to the platform, or manner of prayer, which Christ taught his disciples, and us, in his holy gospel, which is the only perfect rule of all prayers; and by the assistance of the holy spirit of God, without which we cannot pray aright. And this religious worship all men are bound, and required to serve God in, both public and private, at least two times a day, in all christian families, by prayers, and supplications, intercessions, and giving of thanks to God the father, in the name and mediation of Christ Jesus our Lord.

James 1 : 5.
John 14 : 13, 14.
15 : 16.
16 : 23.
I Tim. 2 : 1, 2, 3.
James 5 : 16.
I Thess. 5 : 17, 25.

2 Thess. 3 : 1, 2.
Matt. 9 : 38.
I Cor. 14 : 14, &c.

Matt. 6 : 6, &c.
Rom. 8 : 26, 27.
I Thess. 5 : 18.
Isa. 17 : 65.
Jer. 18 : 14, 15.

Hos. 5 : 4.
Ps. 69 : 6.
Dan. 6 : 10.
Ps. 5 : 2, 3.

Ps. 55 : 15, 16, 17. Zach. 8 : 21. Phil. 1 : 4, 6.
I Tim. 4 : 5. Isaiah 1 : 15. Rev. 5 : 8.

XLII. ARTICLE.

Of publick Humiliation, by Fasting and Prayer.

Publick humiliation, by fasting and prayer, is an ordinance of God, appointed for his church and people. And it being an extraordinary duty, especially as it hath respect to the church generally, or the nation as such, and therefore we must have due regard to the grounds, ends, and manner, of its being performed; confessing of, and reforming from sin, both in publick as well as private fasts. Abstaining from our pleasures, as also our common food, in a sensible and real afflicting of our souls before the Lord; or to seek to God by prayer and fasting for some spiritual, or temporal good, that God hath promised us, or that we stand in need of having due regard to God's word and glory, in this solemn or divine ordinance.

Joel 1 : 14, 15.
2 : 12, 13, &c.
2 Chron. 20 : 3.

Lev. 23 : 27, &c.
Ezra 8 : 21; 9 : 4.
10 : 1.
Neh. 9 : 1, 2, 3.

Isaiah 58 : 3, 4, &c.

Jonah 3 : 4, 6, &c.

Zech. 7 : 5.
Matt. 6 : 16, &c.
2 Sam. 12 : 21, 22.

Esther 4 : 16.

XLIII. ARTICLE.

Of Family, or relative Duties therein.

Parents, and masters, are a sort of subordinate governors, and rulers, in their
respective jurisdictions and families; in
their respective relative places, according
to their capacities, and opportunities;
and are engaged from God's word, to
take charge of their families, and
rule and govern them according to the
word of God, both husbands, parents,
masters, and all others concerned in any
such relation; and by their godly and religious example, instruct their families;
they being found carefully keeping of the
sabbath-day, in the holy and religious
services of hearing the word preached,
with publick and private prayer. As also
requiring and instructing their families
and relations, to follow their godly and
religious example, in the private and publick exercises of religion; and calling
them to an account, how they spend the
sabbath, and other times, and mercies
they enjoy; especially the reading of the
scriptures, and hearing the word preached, with publick prayer with them, and
for them, in order to a blessing for them,
and their families. The neglect of which
duty, or power of godliness, and religion
in families, is one main cause of that
wicked atheism, and impiety in the world
and families; and of the carnal luke-
warmness, and ignorance in churches, to
gether with contempt of government;
because many professors make so little account, or conscience of performing any
duty at home in their own families.

Gen. 18 : 19.
I Sam. 2 : 23, &c.
Prov. 30 : 11, &c.
I Tim. 5 : 8.
Matt. 7 : 9, 10.
Col. 4 : 1.
Eph. 4 : 25, &c.
    5 : 4.

Josh. 24 : 15.
Eph. 5 : 19, &c.
    6 : 1, 2, &c.
Prov. 1 : 1.
Acts 10 : 30, 33
I Tim. 3 : 4.
I Kings 2 : 1, 2, 3.
Gen. 49 : 28, 29.

Job 1 : 5.
I Chron. 29 : 19.
Prov. 22 : 6, 15.
2 Kings 2 : 24.

Prov. 29 : 15, 21.
2 Tim 3 : 15.

XLIV. ARTICLE.

Of Children dying in Infancy.

We do believe, that all little children,
dying in their infancy, viz. before they
are capable to chuse either good or evil,
whether born of believing parents, or unbelieving parents, shall be saved by the
grace of God, and merit of Christ their
redeemer, and work of the holy ghost,

Isaiah 7 : 16; 8 : 4.

2 Sam. 12 : 19, &c.
Ezek. 18 : 4, &c.

I Kings 14 : 13.
Matt. 18 : 2, 3, 4.

and so being made members of the invisible church, shall enjoy life everlasting; for our Lord Jesus saith, of such belongs the kingdom of heaven. Ergo, we conclude, that that opinion is false, which saith, that those little infants dying before baptism, are damned.

Jer. 31 : 29, 30.
Deut. 1 : 39.
Matt. 19 : 13, 14.
Mark 10 : 13, &c.

XLV. ARTICLE.

Of the civil Magistrate.

The supreme lord and king of all the world, hath ordained civil magistrates to be under him, over the people for his own glory, and the publick good. And the office of a magistrate, may be accepted of, and executed by christians, when lawfully called thereunto; and God hath given the power of the sword, into the hands of all lawful magistrates, for the defence and encouragement of them that do well, and for the punishment of evil doers, and for the maintenance of justice, and peace, according to the wholesome laws of each kingdom, and commonwealth, and they may wage war upon just and necessary occasions. And subjection in the Lord ought to be yielded to the magistrates in all lawful things commanded by them, for conscience sake, with prayers for them, for a blessing upon them, paying all lawful and reasonable custom, and tribute to them, for the assisting of them, against foreign, domestical, and potent enemies.

Rom. 13 : 1, &c.
Prov. 8 : 15.
I Pet. 2 : 14.
Prov. 20 : 26.
2 Sam. 23 : 3.
Ps. 82 : 3, 4; 72 : 4, 7.
Eccles. 3 : 8.
Prov. 20 : 18.
Luke 3 : 15.
Acts 10 : 22.
I Chron. 5 : 22.
Prov. 24 : 6.
Tit. 3 : 1.
2 Pet. 2 : 13, 17.
Eccles. 10 : 20.
Prov. 21 : 22.
Rom. 13 : 5.
I Tim. 2 : 1, 2.
Matt. 22 : 17, 21.
   17 : 25, 27.
2 Sam. 21 : 16, 17.
   23 : 15, 16.

XLVI. ARTICLE.

Of Liberty of Conscience.

The Lord Jesus Christ, who is king of kings, and lord of all by purchase, and is judge of quick and dead, is only Lord of Conscience; having a peculiar right so to be. He having died for that end, to take away the guilt, and to destroy the filth of sin, that keeps the consciences of all men in thraldom, and bondage, till they are set free by his special grace. And therefore he would not have the consciences of men in bondage to, or im-

I Tim. 6 : 15.
Acts 10 : 36; 4:17,&c.
James 4 : 12.
Rom. 14 : 4.
Acts 5 : 29.
I Cor. 7 : 23.
Matt. 15 : 9; 24 : 9.
Col. 2 : 20, &c.
I Cor. 11 : 23.
I Pet. 5 : 2, 3.
Matt. 15 : 14

posed upon, by any usurpation, tyranny, or command whatsoever, contrary to his revealed will in his word, which is the only rule he hath left, for the consciences of all men to be ruled, and regulated, and guided by, through the assistance of his spirit. And therefore the obedience to any command, or decree, that is not revealed in, or consonant to his word, in the holy oracles of scripture, is a betraying of the true liberty of conscience. And the requiring of an implicit faith, and an absolute blind obedience, destroys liberty of conscience, and reason also, it being repugnant to both, and that no pretended good end whatsoever, by any man, can make that action, obedience, or practice, lawful and good, that is not grounded in, or upon the authority of holy scripture, or right reason agreeable thereunto.

Deut. 12 : 32.
Micah 6 : 6, 7, 8.
Acts 17 : 25, &c.
Deut. 4 : 17, 19.

I Cor. 10 : 18.
I Sam. 15 : 3, &c.
Rom. 14 : 10, 12.

Gal. 1 : 14.
Phil. 3 : 6.
John 4 : 22.
2 Sam. 3 : 6, &c.

XLVII. ARTICLE.

Of Marriage.

Marriage is to be between one Man, and one Woman; neither is it lawful for any Man, to have more than one wife, nor for any woman to have more than one husband, at the same time. And it is lawful for all sorts of people to marry, who are able of judgment to give their consent. But marriage must not be within the degree of consanguinity, or affinity, forbidden in the word, nor can any such incestuous marriages ever be made lawful by any law of man, or consent of parties, to live together as man and wife. And it is the duty of christians to marry in the Lord, and therefore those that profess the true religion, ought not to marry with infidels, or idolaters, nor prophane wicked persons in their life, nor yet with any that maintain damnable heresies.

Matt. 19 : 5, 6.
Gen. 2 : 24.
Mal. 2 : 15.
I Cor. 7 : 36.
Heb. 13 : 4.
I Tim. 4 : 3.
Exod. 22 : 16, 17.
Gen. 29 : 23.
Lev. 18 : 6, &c.
2 Sam. 13 : 14.
Gen. 38 : 16.
Deut. 22 : 28.

Eph. 5 : 3.
I Cor. 7: 2; 5: 1, 4, 13.
Gen. 6 : 2.
I Cor. 7 : 39.
Numb. 25 : 1, 2;
2 Cor. 6 : 14, &c.

XLVIII. ARTICLE.

Of the Lawfulness of an Oath.

A lawful oath, is a part of religious worship, wherein the person swearing in

Exod. 20 : 7.
Deut. 6 : 13; 10 : 20.

truth, righteousness, and judgment, solemnly calleth God to witness what he sweareth, and to judge him according to the truth or falseness thereof. And we are to swear by no other name, but by the name of God only, when we are called before a lawful magistrate, upon a lawful matter, warranted by God's holy word; and an oath is to be taken in the plain and common sense of the words, without equivocation, or mental reservation, in a solemn and reverent using of God's holy name; and such an oath, we believe all christians, when lawfully called thereunto by the magistrate, may take. But the foolish monastical vows of papists, and all idle and vain swearing, is an abominable, and wicked prophaning of the holy name of God.

Jer. 4 : 2.
Ps. 15 : 4.
Zech. 5 : 4.
2 Chron. 6 : 22, 23.
Isa. 65 : 16.
Jer. 12 : 16.
Matt. 5 : 34.
Neh. 13 : 25.
2 Kings 11 : 4, 17.
Ps. 24 : 4.
Heb. 6 : 16.
Jer. 23 : 10.
Lev. 19 : 12.
Eph. 4 : 28.
Amos 8 : 14.
James 5 : 12.
1 Sam. 14 : 29.
2 Kings 6 : 31.
Isaiah 48 : 1.
Zeph. 1 : 5.

XLIX. ARTICLE.

TOTAL ERROR

Of the State of man after Death, and of the Resurrection of the Dead.

The bodies of men after death, return to dust, and see corruption; but their souls, or spirits, which neither die nor sleep, having an immortal subsistence, immediately return to God who gave them; the souls of the righteous being then made perfect in holiness, are received into paradise where they are with Christ, and behold the face of God in light and glory, waiting for the full redemption of their bodies, and the souls of the wicked are cast into hell, where they remain in torment and utter darkness, reserved to the judgment of the great day. And besides these two places, for souls separated from their bodies, the holy scripture mentions none. And at the last day, such of the saints as shall be found alive, shall not sleep, but be changed, and all the dead shall be raised up with the self same bodies and none other, although with different qualities, which shall be united to their souls for ever and ever, but the bodies of the unjust, shall by the power of Christ, as a severe and just judge, be raised to dishonour; and the bodies

Gen. 3 : 19.
Acts 13 : 36.
Eccles. 12 : 7.
Acts 7 : 59.
Luke 23 : 43.
2 Cor. 5 : 1, 6, 8.
Phil. 1 : 23.
Heb. 12 : 23.
Jude 6.
I Pet. 3 : 19.
Luke 16 : 23, 24.
I Cor. 15 : 51, 52.
I Thess. 4 : 17.
Job 19 : 26, 27.
I Cor. 15 : 42, &c,
John 5 : 28, 29.
Dan. 12 : 2.
I Cor. 15 : 21, &c.

Rev. 20 : 5, 6.
Acts 24 : 15.
Phil. 3 : 21.
Rev. 19 : 1, &c.
14 : 37.

of the just and righteous, by his spirit,
as he is head of the catholick church,
unto honour, and be made conformable
with his glorious body, and shall enjoy
everlasting life; in singing perpetual
praises, and hallelujahs to God for ever
and ever. Amen.

L. ARTICLE. TOTAL ERROR

Of the last Judgment.

And lastly, we believe, God hath appointed a day, wherein he will judge the
world in righteousness, by Jesus Christ,
to whom all power, and judgment is
given of the father; in which day, not
only the apostate angels shall be judged,
but likewise all persons that have lived
upon the earth, shall appear before the
tribunal of Christ, to give an account of
their thoughts, words, and deeds, and
shall receive a just sentence, according to
what they have done in their bodies,
whether good, or evil, when God, according to his purpose, will manifest the
glory of his mercy, in the salvation of
his elect, and of his justice in the eternal
damnation of the wicked and disobedient;
for then shall the righteous go into everlasting life, and receive the fullness of joy
and glory, but the wicked, who know
not God, nor obey the gospel offered
them in Christ, shall be cast into eternal
torments, and punished with everlasting
destruction, from the presence of the
Lord, and from the glory of his power.
Amen.

Acts 17 : 31.
John 5 : 22, 27.
Rom. 2 : 16.
2 Tim. 4 : 1.
I Cor. 6 : 3.
Jude 6.
Matt. 12 : 36.
2 Cor. 5 : 10.
Eccles. 12 : 14.
Rom. 14 : 10, 12.
Matt. 25 : 32.
Luke 21 : 28.
I Thess. 4 : 17.
Ps. 16 : 11.
Luke 12 : 32.
Matt. 25 : 46.
Ps. 58 : 10.
2 Tim. 4 : 8.
Luke 16 : 28.
Rev. 14 : 11.
John 8 : 24.
2 Thess. 1 : 8, &c.
Rev. 20 : 10, 11, &c.
22 : 11, 15.

D. *A Short Confession or A Brief Narrative of Faith, 1691*

In the West Country during the last quarter of the seventeenth
century there was a remarkable current away from Calvinism
among some Particular Baptist churches founded by Thomas Collier,
the "Apostle to the West." Explanation for this drift may be found
in Collier's change of views and his desire to comprehend General
as well as Particular Baptists in his circle. London Particular
churches sent deputations to the West to persuade Collier of his

error and to halt the tide of his influence. A few churches were reclaimed, some joined the Particular Baptist General Assembly in 1689. Others followed Collier in remaining aloof from it. These seem to have prepared the Somerset Confession of 1691 in response to the Assembly Confession of two years earlier, against which Collier dissented at a number of points.[14]

The Somerset Confession could not have been prepared by a General Baptist group, as McGlothlin says,[15] in spite of the General Baptist tone of some of its articles. General Baptists were few in the Somerset area in 1691, and they do not seem to have had an associational life until after 1693.[16] What is more important, the Confession clearly shows its author's Calvinistic patterns of thought, and in its longest chapter (XXIII) it speaks with deliberate criticism of a learned ministry. The Particular Baptist General Assembly had recently given much attention to the problem of raising up a trained ministry, and this article apparently gives the answer of the extra-Assembly Particular churches of the West to this emphasis. Two reasons were stated for publishing the Confession: to provide a basis of agreement for churches in the area and to clear the authors of suspicion in the eyes of Baptists that they were "a people degenerated from almost all other baptized congregations."[17]

The Confession is notable for its clarity and force of expression. It is concerned primarily with doctrine, though there is an elaborate and informative article on the Church.[18] The order and form of the articles are entirely independent; neither the Westminster nor the 1656 Somerset Confession is followed. The Confession probably did not find use beyond the West of England. Its significance lies in the departure shown in it by one Particular Baptist group from the heightening Calvinism of the late seventeenth century, and in its attempt to speak for both Particular and General Baptists.

This Confession of twenty-seven articles is too lengthy to give here in full, but the doctrinal articles of particular interest are listed. Crosby's text is followed.[19]

---

[14] Collier, *A Confession of Faith*, 42-62, indicates his disagreement with seven articles, all Calvinistic.
[15] *Op. cit.*, 161.
[16] *Minutes of the General Assembly*, I, 38-39
[17] Crosby, *History English Baptists*, III, 259 ff.
[18] Article XXIII.
[19] Vol. IV, No. 1, 1-42. Original copies are in the Angus and Bodleian Libraries, Oxford, and the Manchester College Library, Manchester.

A SHORT CONFESSION OR A BRIEF NARRATIVE OF FAITH

CHAPTER VI.

OF THE EXTENT OF THE DEATH OF CHRIST

Concerning the extent of the death of our dear redeemer, we believe, that suitable to the great end of God the father in sending him into the world, to give himself a ransom for all mankind; for the world, the whole world; and that thereby the world hath its present being; and that thereby there is a way of reconciliation, acceptation, and salvation opened for all men: From whence we conclude, that if any man come short of obtaining reconciliation, acceptation, and salvation, it is not for want of grace in the father, nor a sacrifice in the son.

CHAPTER VIII.

OF THE POWER AND WILL OF MAN

Concerning the power and will of man, we believe,

1. That the power and will of man are proper attributes and faculties of the soul; and if so, that it's God's workmanship, and properly of and from God: so then man hath neither will nor power, but what he receives from the Lord, tho' he improves it to contrary ends, and not for that end which was and is given him.

2. Notwithstanding all the power and abilities that men have, are of and from the Lord, yet we are strongly inclined to believe, that the will and power of man is greatly debilitated by the fall, but not wholly lost; man in all his parts, is weaken'd by the fall, but no part wholly lost.

3. We believe that there remaineth still in man, a power to will his own good.

4. Yet we believe, that man knoweth not what is good any otherwise but as he is taught of the Lord.

5. Man being taught of God what is good, and how and when to will this good, being thus shewed of the Lord, he hath now a capacity, in the use of the means that God hath appointed, to bring his will to an inclinable frame, truly to be seeking after his eternal well-being: so, in short, we sum up all thus: That man hath neither power nor will, nor a matter what to will for his own good, nor how, nor when, in respect of a seasonable time, but what he hath from God, for all power belongeth to God; yet we believe, that man ought to employ

his will, yea, all the powers and faculties of his soul, in and about spiritual things, which if men were faithful in, God would have the glory and they the advantage.

CHAPTER XVII.

OF PERSEVERANCE

Concerning perseverance we believe, That it is absolutely necessary, in order to the obtaining of the end (namely salvation with eternal glory) for believers to cleave to the Lord, and to keep close to him in the way of duty. 1. To watch and pray. 2. To keep close to the publick worship and service of God. 3. To be mortifying the corrupt deeds of the body. 4. To be continuing in the exercise of faith. 5. To be growing and encreasing in all the graces of the new covenant. In which way of keeping close to the Lord, watching and praying, worshipping and serving God, mortifying the corrupt deeds of the body, growing and encreasing in all the graces of the new covenant; to wit, faith, love, humility, patience, &c. they shall be supplied with sufficiency of grace here, to preserve them safely to the kingdom of glory hereafter.

2. Yet we believe, that it's possible for true believers, through their remissness or negligence in point of duty towards God, through the temptations of Satan, and corruptions of their own deceitful hearts, finally to apostatize from the truth they once made profession of, and in so doing render their latter end to be worse than their beginning.

CHAPTER XVIII.

OF GOD'S DECREES

Concerning God's decrees we believe, that the word of God is his decreed will; and that there is no secret will or decree in God, contrary to his revealed word and will; and that his decree is, that whosoever believeth and obeyeth him, persevering therein to the end, shall be saved; and he that believeth not shall be damned.

2. We believe, that whatsoever God hath absolutely decreed, shall certainly and inevitably come to pass. But then,

3. We believe, that many things that do come to pass are not decreed of God, For it seems to us not only unscriptural, but also altogether irrational, to imagine, that the righteous and holy God should decree any sin, or unholiness, either in angels or men, tho' God doth permit them to come to pass, yet there is no decree of his, that do necessitate the being of them. It might suit the nature of

W

the Devil or of wicked men, to decree wickedness; but far be it from the righteous God so to do; shall not the judge of all the earth do right?

CHAPTER XX.

OF ELECTION

Concerning election we believe, not as some who express themselves after this manner, in these words, by the decree of God, for the manifestation of his glory, some men and angels are predestined or fore-ordained to eternal life, thro' Jesus Christ; and that these angels and men, thus predestined and fore-ordained, are particularly, and unchangeably designed, and their number so certain, and definite that it cannot be either increased or diminished.

2. And affirmatively we believe, that the infinitely wise and holy God, suitable to his name and nature, did elect or choose unto himself from eternity, and (merely of his own good pleasure) out of the whole body and bulk of mankind, an entire species, or sort of men, namely those that in time do believe, and sincerely obey him, patiently continuing in the way of well doing unto the end.

3. We believe this election to be in Jesus Christ, of God's eternal purpose and grace, before the foundation of the world.

4. We do believe that God's electing grace doth extend itself to the whole number of the godly in all nations, throughout all ages, under the various dispensations, under which they live.

CHAPTER XXI.

OF REPROBATION

Concerning reprobation we believe, that God hath not decreed from eternity, the reprobation of any person of mankind, considered as such, who may not very possibly be saved, notwithstanding any decree in God; much less do we hold a decree of reprobation, from eternity, of the greatest part of mankind, excluding a possibility of their being saved; for we believe that God doth not hate or reprobate any man, as his creature, before he considers him as an actual sinner.

2. We believe, that whensoever God doth reject or reprobate any person of mankind, it is for their own wilful and actual transgressions, as the just deserving cause thereof, and not from his own will, any otherwise considered.

3. That the intent (at least the primary or antecedent intent) of God in his decree of reprobation, is the salvation and not the damna-

tion of men. The Lord declares that he had rejected or reprobated them, yet exhorts them to duty, with promises on their performance; and if ever the Lord does finally reprobate any person or persons, it is for their final rejecting him, in his many calls, and gracious invitations.

4. From whence we conclude, that those that own personal election, and personal reprobation before time, so as to deny the love of God to the world, do not own the faith of the gospel.

5. We believe, that God hath not decreed the reprobation of any infant, dying before the commission of actual sin.

E. *The Unity of the Churches, 1704*

Early in the history of General Baptists, individual leaders raised questions concerning the doctrines of the Trinity and the divinity of Christ. Their biblicism led some to reject the term Trinity as noncanonical, and the Hoffmanite view that Christ received nothing of his manhood from Mary seems to have lingered in some General Baptist minds. The ambiguity of the Confession of 1660 has been regarded as evidence of some uncertainty on the subject of the Trinity. The speculations of Matthew Caffyn, pastor at Horsham in Sussex, who had studied at Oxford and who became an outstanding messenger in Sussex and Kent, first raised Christological questions to the status of general issues in the denomination. Beginning with a denial of the humanity of Christ and concluding, years later, with a denial of his divinity, Caffynism was the source of local ruptures among General Baptists by 1677.

The issue reached the General Assembly by 1686, but that body, jealous of its unity, refused to discipline Caffyn.[20] For the next ten years, the Assembly referred disputants, when it did not silence them, to the Confession of 1660 or took refuge in the Six Principles. In 1693, the body, seeking to assert its orthodoxy, pronounced as heretical the opinions ascribed to Caffyn, but it refused to proceed against Caffyn himself. This refusal brought a protest from a minority of the members, and when the Assembly met again in 1696, the minority withdrew, after lengthy contention, from the Assembly. Seven seceding churches proceeded to organize the General Association on the basis of a clear statement of the doctrine of the Trinity.

Reconciliation between Assembly and Association, whose numbers

---

[20] Whitley, *Minutes General Assembly*, II, xiii-xiv.

were steadily increasing, was sought unsuccessfully until 1704. The Assembly's overtures for peace and unity were presented in that year in a book, *A Vindication of the ancient General Assembly,* and the Association responded favorably. A joint committee was appointed which drew up a basis of reunion entitled "The Unity of the Churches." Individual subscription to this document by all members of the General Assembly was required forthwith. Of the seven articles the two concerning doctrine are as follows:[21]

> First, respecting Almighty God.—We do believe, and are very confident, that there is one, and but one living and true God, who is from everlasting to everlasting, and changeth not; without body, parts, or imperfections; essentially present in all places; of infinite power, wisdom, and goodness; the Maker of all things in heaven and earth, visible and invisible: and, that in this divine and infinite Being, or Unity of the Godhead, there are Three Persons, the Father, Word, and Holy Ghost, of one substance, power, and eternity. Secondly, respecting the Lord Jesus Christ—We do believe, that there is but one Lord Jesus Christ, the second Person in the Trinity, and the only begotten Son of God; and that he did, in the fulness of time, take to himself our nature, in the womb of the blessed Virgin Mary, of whom, in respect of the flesh, he was made; and so is true God, and true Man, our Immanuel.

The reconciliation was of short duration. Friends of Caffyn retired in 1708, and constituting themselves as the Kent Association they adopted the Six Principles and the Confession of 1660 as doctrinal bases. Moreover, the drift to Socinianism continued in the General Assembly. With the passing of the older leadership, represented especially in Thomas Grantham, laxity of principle became increasingly evident. The union of rival Assemblies in 1731 did little to check the decline of the group, which fell victim to the general religious stagnation of the nation in the first half of the eighteenth century.

F. *Articles of Religion of the New Connexion, 1770*

Revival came to the General Baptists from beyond their own ranks in the second half of the eighteenth century as a consequence of the Evangelical Awakening. A new beginning resulted from

---

²¹ Taylor, *op. cit.,* I. 47

activity in two centers in the East Midlands. Starting with the preaching of David Taylor, a servant in the household of the Countess of Huntingdon, groups of Christians formed on Methodist lines were gathered in Leicestershire. By 1755, numbers of the members of these groups had independently concluded in favor of believers' baptism and had instituted the ordinance anew among themselves. There were five distinct societies of this circle by 1760, maintaining close relations with one another but living in isolation from other Christians. Meanwhile, Daniel Taylor, a young miner of Yorkshire, was converted under Wesleyan preaching. Disagreeing with Wesley's views on discipline, he became in 1762 minister of a little group of Methodist seceders at Wadsworth, near Hebden Bridge, Yorkshire. His study of the Scriptures soon led him to reject infant baptism, and in 1763 he was baptized at the hands of a General Baptist pastor at Gamston, Nottinghamshire.

Taylor carried some of his people with him in his change of views, and he represented them at the Assembly of the Lincolnshire General Baptists that year. Members of this Assembly assisted him in forming the Wadsworth society into a General Baptist church. On attending the General Assembly in London, however, Taylor was distressed at the doctrinal laxity and the backwardness of outlook of that body. He found more congenial fellowship among the Leicestershire evangelical groups, and he sought to draw them into the General Baptist fellowship of Lincolnshire. The evangelicals shrank from associating with a group which tolerated unorthodox views, and so Taylor conceived the idea of uniting the societies of Leicestershire with such General Baptist churches as remained orthodox. The consent of the Leicestershire leaders to this scheme was secured in a preliminary meeting, and the New Connexion of General Baptists was formed in London on June 6, 1770. Member churches in addition to those of Leicestershire were located in Lincolnshire, London, Kent, and Essex. The announced design of the New Connexion was "to revive experimental religion or primitive Christianity in faith and practice."

To indicate their doctrinal position and to guard against the prevalent Socinianism, the members drew up and signed Six Articles. These Articles did not pretend to be a thorough summary of the Christian faith, but rather to indicate the distinguishing tenets of the New Connexion. They were composed by Daniel

Taylor, who continued to lead the denomination to the end of his life. Some of the old General Baptist churches which retained their evangelical emphasis joined the movement from time to time, and new churches were planted in the Midlands, Yorkshire, and elsewhere. New ministers entering the Connexion in the first five years of its life had to subscribe to the Articles. After 1775, however, the new ministers had only to relate a convincing experience of grace before the Association. Still, the Articles did not fall into disuse; no new document superseded them among New Connexion Baptists.

From 1786 to 1803 the group again had an affiliate relationship to the General Assembly, being known simply as the Leicestershire Association, but it participated only in token fashion and finally withdrew in protest against the admission into the Assembly of a Unitarian-Universalist minister. Even this interval, however, did not send the Articles into oblivion. In 1813 the Connexion in describing the design of the body in maintaining an institution for ministerial education said that the purpose was "to promote and cherish the sentiments contained in the articles, drawn up and signed in the year 1770, at the formation of the New Connexion."[22] In 1815 the Association reaffirmed its faith in the principles of the Articles and ordered:

> that all churches which may hereafter be admitted into it, satisfy it that they maintain the same, and if any church in the connection depart from these principles either in doctrine or practice, and by proper steps cannot be reclaimed, it shall be excluded from the connection.[23]

Daniel Taylor gave further circulation to the Articles when he incorporated their views in a catechism for children and young people and when, in more elaborate form, he prepared a confession of faith based upon the Articles for his London church (1785).[24]

The Articles as given by Taylor, *History of English General Baptists*, II, 139-142, are as follows:

ARTICLES OF RELIGION

ARTICLE 1. *On the Fall of Man.* We believe, that man was made upright in the image of God, free from all disorder natural and

---

[22] Taylor, *op. cit.*, II, 456.
[23] *Ibid.*, 459.
[24] *Ibid.*, 470-477. The original is in "Original Proceedings of the yearly meetings of the NEW CONNEXION from 1770 to 1796," Angus Library, Regent's Park College, Oxford.

moral; capable of obeying perfectly the will and command of God his
Maker; yet capable also of sinning: which he unhappily did, and
thereby laid himself under the divine curse; which, we think, could
include nothing less than the mortality of the body and the eternal
punishment of the soul. His nature also became depraved; his mind
was defiled; and the powers of his soul weakened—that both he
was, and his posterity are, captives of Satan till set at liberty by
Christ.

ARTICLE 2. *On the Nature and Perpetual Obligation of the Moral
Law.* We believe, that the moral law not only extends to the outward actions of the life, but to all the powers and faculties of the
mind, to every desire, temper and thought; that it demands the
entire devotion of all the powers and faculties of both body and soul
to God: or, in our Lord's words, to love the Lord with all our
heart, mind, soul and strength:—that this law is of perpetual duration and obligation, to all men, at all times, and in all places or parts
of the world. And, we suppose that this law was obligatory to Adam
in his perfect state—was more clearly revealed in the ten commandments—and more fully explained in many other parts of the bible.

ARTICLE 3. *On the Person and Work of Christ.* We believe, that
our Lord Jesus Christ is God and man, united in one person: or
possessed of divine perfection united to human nature, in a way which
we pretend not to explain, but think ourselves bound by the word of
God firmly to believe:—that he suffered to make a full atonement
for all the sins of all men—and that hereby he has wrought out for
us a compleat salvation; which is received by, and as a free gift
communicated to, all that believe in him; without the consideration
of any works done by us, in order to entitle us to his salvation.—
Though we firmly believe, that no faith is the means of justification,
but that which produces good works.

ARTICLE 4. *On Salvation by Faith.* We believe, that as this salvation is held forth to all to whom the gospel revelation comes without
exception, we ought in the course of our ministry, to propose or
offer this salvation to all those who attend our ministry: and, having
opened to them their ruined wretched state by nature and practice,
to invite all without exception, to look to Christ by faith, without any
regard to any thing in, or done by, themselves; that they may, in
this way alone, that is, by faith be possessed of this salvation.

ARTICLE 5. *On Regeneration by the Holy Spirit.* We believe, that,
as the scriptures assure us, we are justified, made the children of

God, purified and sanctified by faith:—that when a person comes to believe in Jesus (and not before) he is regenerated or renewed in his soul, by the spirit of God, through the instrumentality of the word, now believed and embraced; which renewal of his soul naturally produces holiness in heart and life:—that this holiness is the means of preparing us for the enjoyments and employments of the heavenly world; and of preserving in our souls a comfortable sense of our interest in the Lord, and of our title to glory; as well as to set a good example before men, and to recommend our blessed Redeemer's cause to the world.

ARTICLE 6. *On Baptism.* We believe, that it is the indispensible duty of all who repent and believe the gospel, to be baptized, by immersion in water, in order to be initiated into a church state; and that no person ought to be received into the church without submission to that ordinance.

G. *Statements of the Baptist Union of Great Britain and Ireland*

After 1704 English Particular Baptists published no confessions of note in the eighteenth century. Local church confessions were occasionally used, as in the church of Dr. John Gill in London in 1764. Particular Baptists suffered with others through the period of general religious decline, and particularly from antinomian tendencies. A new temper toward antinomianism appeared, however, in the second half of the century in the influence of Andrew Fuller of Kettering. As the leading theologian of his era, Fuller sought to unite the doctrinal strength of Calvinism with the evangelical fervor of the old General Baptists. He did this through his theory of redemption, according to which he separated the doctrine of a general atonement from the doctrine of a particular redemption. Keeping the Calvinistic framework, he added to it the old General Baptist emphasis on a General Atonement.

Thus Baptists were prepared to offer the gospel to every creature and to pioneer in the foreign missions enterprise. The practical rather than the theoretical side of Christianity came to have first consideration in men's minds. The era of confession-making passed as theological formulae and controversies faded. Little remained to keep Calvinistic and Arminian Baptists apart, and they gradually were drawn together. Common tasks called for united effort. The Baptist Union, formed as early as 1813 as a Particular Baptist national body, was to be the inclusive organization. In 1887 the Council and Assembly of the Union voted for amalgamation of the two bodies and referred the matter to local associations, who generally replied favorably. In 1891 the New Connexion Association accepted the invitation of the Union to membership. No confession of faith was asked for or given by either group. A brief doctrinal statement had been drawn up by the Council and adopted by the Union in 1888. Some members, including Charles H. Spurgeon of the Metropolitan Tabernacle, London, who withdrew from the Union in 1888, were dissatisfied with the statement. The proceedings of the Union carried the statement in 1888, but it was not published again. It ran as follows:[25]

> Whilst expressly disavowing and disallowing any powers to control belief, or to restrict enquiry, yet, in view of the uneasiness produced in the churches by recent discussions, and to show our agreement with one another, and with our fellow-Christians on the great truths of the Gospel, the Council deem it right to say that:
>
> A. Baptized into the name of the Father, and the Son, and the Holy Ghost, we have avowed repentance towards God and faith in the Lord Jesus Christ—the very elements of a new life; as in the Supper we avow our union with one another, while partaking of the symbol of the body of our Lord, broken for us, and of the blood shed for the remission of sins. The Union, therefore, is an association of Churches and Ministers professing not only to believe the facts and doctrines of the Gospel, but to have undergone the spiritual change expressed or implied in them. This change is the fundamental principle of our church life.
>
> B. The following facts and doctrines are commonly believed by the churches of the Union:—
>
> (1), The Divine Inspiration and Authority of the Holy Scripture as the supreme and sufficient rule of our faith and practice; and the right and duty of individual judgment in the interpretation of it.
>
> (2), The fallen and sinful state of man.
>
> (3), The Deity, the Incarnation, the Resurrection of the Lord Jesus Christ, and His Sacrificial and Mediatorial work.

---

[25] McGlothlin, *op. cit.*, 291-292.

(4), Justification by faith—a faith that works by love and produces holiness.

(5), The work of the Holy Spirit in the conversion of sinners and in the sanctification of all who believe.

(6), The Resurrection; the Judgment at the last day, according to the words of our Lord in Matt. 25.46.

Later the Baptist Union published annually a brief *Declaration of Principle,* reading as follows:[26]

The basis of this Union is:—

1. That the Lord Jesus Christ, our God and Saviour, is the sole and absolute authority in all matters pertaining to faith and practice, as revealed in the Holy Scriptures, and that each church has liberty to interpret and administer His Laws.

2. That Christian Baptism is the immersion in water into the Name of the Father, the Son, and the Holy Ghost, of those who have professed repentance towards God and faith in our Lord Jesus Christ who "died for our sins according to the Scriptures; was buried, and rose again the third day."

3. That it is the duty of every disciple to bear personal witness to the Gospel of Jesus Christ, and to take part in the evangelisation of the world.

---

[26] McGlothlin, *op. cit.,* Supplement to British Edition, 1911, p. xxi.

5

American Baptist
Confessions

THE FIRST CALVINISTIC BAPTISTS in America did not own a confession of faith; there was no Calvinistic confession among Baptists when their first churches were formed in New England. As churches gradually increased in that area, the non-confessional tradition was followed. In the Middle Colonies, however, where relations with English Calvinistic Baptists were more intimate, the use of confessions became common in the eighteenth century. The fact that the early New England churches at first often comprehended Arminian as well as Calvinistic Baptists may have prevented the setting forth of particular theological views in confessional form there. In Virginia and North Carolina the earliest Baptists held Arminian views, and they seem generally to have acknowledged the Standard General Baptist Confession of 1660.[1]

In this area, if not throughout the country, these Baptists at first promised to be the dominant type in American life. Their movement was shattered, however, by the twofold offensive of Regular and Separate Baptists after the middle of the eighteenth century. Calvinistic Regular Baptist influence began to be felt in North Carolina following the preaching there of Robert Williams of Welsh Neck, S. C., around 1750. Other preachers of the Charleston Association followed Williams to the area, and General Baptist ministers quickly defected to the Calvinistic position. Williams appealed to the Philadelphia Association to take an interest in North Carolina Baptists, and that body sent several of its outstanding evangelists to North Carolina. The result was the reconstitution of most of the General Baptist churches on a Calvinistic basis. This process was carried

---

[1] Burkitt and Read, *History of the Kehukee Association.* 28.

to completion after 1755 in the revival enthusiasm of the Separate Baptist movement, springing from the Great Awakening in New England. Few General Baptist churches remained in the Virginia-North Carolina region by 1790; nor did General Baptists flourish in other parts of the country before the last years of the eighteenth century.

A. *The Philadelphia Confession, 1742*

Toward the end of the seventeenth century, Baptists were becoming active in the Middle Atlantic Colonies. In 1688, the Pennepack Baptist Church was organized in an area which today is within the city of Philadelphia, Pa. Elias Keach, son of the London minister, Benjamin Keach, became the pastor of this church. He was a strenuous worker who preached to congregations in such places as Philadelphia, Trenton, Piscataway, Cohansey, and Chester. He did much to encourage the idea of connectionalism among the assemblages with which he worked in America. At first, groups of Baptists in various locations were members of the Pennepack Baptist Church, but as it was discovered that the distances between the groups was great, and as the numbers of members in each location increased, separate churches were established. Within the churches, questions and differences of opinion arose in matters of doctrine and practice. Because of this, joint meetings of several churches were held for several years, culminating, in 1707, in the formation of the Philadelphia Baptist Association. This Association became the pattern for numerous other Calvinistic Baptist associations.

Elias Keach returned to England in 1692, and assumed the pastorate of the Tallow Chandler's Hall Church in London. There, in 1697, he concurred with his father to publish a set of articles of faith in the name of his church. These articles were almost exactly the Assembly Confession of 1689 with the addition of articles on hymn-singing and the laying on of hands upon baptized believers. Concerning both of the additions, Benjamin Keach had been an innovator among Particular Baptists. He began to use vernacular hymns in his Horsleydown Church by 1691, and he urged the laying on of hands as a "sacred Ordinance" in a book written in the 1670's and reissued in 1697.[2]

---

[2] *Laying on of Hands upon Baptized Believers* was written in answer to a book by Danvers. Keach taught toleration of differences in churches on the subject, though he urged the practice.

This so-called Keach's Confession is the first generally-used Baptist confession of which we hear in America.[3] When the church at Middletown, N. J., experienced doctrinal difficulty in 1712, a council of neighboring Baptists called in to help settle the dispute recommended that the members "should subscribe to Elias Keach's Confession of Faith, at least the Covenant annexed to it." The subscribing majority became the reconstituted church. Records of the Welsh Tract Church, in New Jersey, show that the Assembly Confession in 1716 was translated into Welsh by Abel Morgan, a Philadelphia minister. To the Confession he added "An article relative to Laying on of hands; Singing Psalms; and Church Covenants." This Confession then was signed by members at the quarterly meeting (May 4, 1716), though it may never have been published. The Welsh had earlier refused to enter into friendly relationship with the pioneer Pennepack Church because Pennepack did not acknowledge the Laying on of Hands.

The earliest known reference by an association to a confession occurred in 1724, when the Philadelphia Association, in reply to a query concerning the Sabbath, referred to "the Confession of Faith, set forth by the elders and brethren met in London, 1689, and owned by us." Whether the Confession had been formally adopted is not indicated, but that it was the accepted standard of doctrine is evident. Formal adoption certainly is shown by September 25, 1742, for on that date the Association in session at Philadelphia ordered a printing of a new edition. The churches paid for the printing job, which was done by Benjamin Franklin in 1743.

The new edition had two additional articles, indications of the influence of Keach's Confession and of the Welsh Baptists. They are in fact reprints of Articles 27 and 28 of Keach's Confession. One, numbered XXIII, concerned the singing of Psalms, hymns, and spiritual songs as of "divine institution," and the other, numbered XXXI, considered the imposition of hands upon baptized believers as "an ordinance of Christ." This brought the number of articles in the Philadelphia Confession to 34, and caused the renumbering of the articles from XXIII to XXXIV. A facsimile of the title page and a copy of the two added articles follow.

---

[3] A local confession was prepared for the Lower Dublin (Pa.) Church in 1700. It was used for instructional purposes. Even earlier, in 1697, a community of Keithian Baptists (former Quakers) in the same area had published a confession based upon the Apostles' Creed.

A
CONFESSION
OF
FAITH,

Put forth by the
Elders and *Brethren*
Of many
CONGREGATIONS
OF
CHRISTIANS

(Baptized upon Profession of their Faith)
In *London* and the *Country*.

Adopted by the Baptist ASSOCIATION
met at Philadelphia, Sept. 25. 1742.

The SIXTH EDITION.

To which are added,
Two Articles *viz.* Of Imposition of Hands,
and Singing of Psalms in Publick Worship.

ALSO
A Short Treatise of Church Discipline.

*With the Heart Man believeth unto Righteousness, and with the
Mouth Confession is made unto Salvation,* Rom. 10. 20.
Search the Scriptures, John 5. 39.

PHILADELPHIA: Printed by B. FRANKLIN.
M,DCC,XLIII.

CHAPTER XXIII.

OF SINGING PSALMS, &C.

We believe that 'acts 16 25 eph 5 19 col 3 16' singing the praises of God, is a holy Ordinance of Christ, and not a part of natural religion, or a moral duty only; but that it is brought under divine institution, it being injoined on the churches of Christ to sing psalms, hymns, and spiritual songs; and that the whole church in their public assemblies, as well as private christians, ought to 'heb 2 12 jam 5 13' sing God's praises according to the best light they have received. Moreover, it was practiced in the great representative church, by 'matt 26 30 mat 14 26' our Lord Jesus Christ with his disciples, after he had instituted and celebrated the sacred ordinance of his Holy Supper, as a commemorative token of redeeming love.

CHAPTER XXXI.

OF LAYING ON OF HANDS

We believe that (Heb 5 12 and 6 1 2 Acts 8 17 18 and 19 6) laying on of hands (with prayer) upon baptized believers, as such, is an ordinance of Christ, and ought to be submitted unto by all such persons that are admitted to partake of the Lord's Supper; and that the end of this ordinance is not for the extraordinary gifts of the Spirit, but for (Eph 1 13 14) a farther reception of the Holy Spirit of promise, or for the addition of the graces of the Spirit, and the influences thereof; to confirm, strengthen, and comfort them in Christ Jesus; it being ratified and established by the (Acts 8 and 19 6) extraordinary gifts of the Spirit in the primitive times, to abide in the Church, as meeting together on the first Day of the week was, Acts 2 1 that being the day of worship, or Christian Sabbath, under the gospel; and as preaching the word was, Acts 10 44 and as Baptism was, Mat 3 16 and prayer was, Acts 4 31 and singing Psalms, &c was Acts 16 25 26 so this of laying on of hands was, Acts 8 & ch 19 for as the whole gospel was confirmed by (Heb 2 3 4) signs and wonders, and divers miracles and gifts of the Holy Ghost in general, so was every ordinance in like manner confirmed in particular.

The Philadelphia Association omitted the Appendix of the original edition of the 1677 Confession, but it authorized Jenkin Jones and

Benjamin Griffith to "prepare a short treatise of discipline, to be annexed to the Confession of faith."[4] This Discipline was actually prepared by Griffith, who used in its preparation a tract of Elias Keach, a manuscript of Abel Morgan, writings of Owen and Goodwin, and previous actions of the Association on matters of discipline. It was adopted by the Association in 1743 and added as an appendix to the Confession. In an edition of the Confession published in 1831, this Discipline occupies the last thirty-three pages of a 108-page volume.

The Philadelphia Association published many editions of the Confession, and it was adopted by many churches and associations. Among associations, the Ketockton of Virginia led the way in 1766.[5] The Warren Association of Rhode Island adopted it in 1767. The Charleston Association of South Carolina, founded in 1751, also adopted the Confession in 1767; here the Confession exerted extraordinary influence especially in the churches of the coastal section where Arminian sentiments had earlier been dominant. The article on Laying on of Hands, however, was omitted in all editions of the Charleston Confession. The second edition (1813) included with the Confession a *Summary of Church Discipline* and *The Baptist Catechism*. A later edition (that of 1831) retained the summary of discipline and added an appendix dealing with questions of Baptist polity and practice, supposedly prepared originally by Oliver Hart and other pioneers of the Association.[6] A fourth edition appeared in 1850 and is an indication of the continued use of the Confession in the South. Indeed in this region it influenced Baptist thought generally and has been perhaps the most influential of all confessions. Local church covenants still reflect its outlook and summarize its doctrines.

On the early American frontier the Confession was not always received with enthusiasm, though two early Associations there, the Elkhorn of Kentucky and the Holston of Tennessee, adopted it in 1785 and 1788, respectively. The Separate Baptist movement, com-

---

[4] Minutes, Philadelphia Association, 1742.

[5] In 1774 David Thomas, pastor in the Ketockton Association and graduate of Rhode Island College, published a revision of the Confession in seventeen articles, in his work, *The Virginian Baptist or a View and Defense of the Christian Religion as it is Professed by the Baptists of Virginia*. Fristoe in his *History of the Ketocton Association* (1808) condensed the Confession's "leading doctrines" in eleven paragraphs. This condensation, reaffirmed in 1927, forms the present Articles of Faith of the Ketocton (Primitive) Association (Vid. *The Primitive Baptist*, Feb. 16, 1956, 59-60).

[6] McGlothlin, *op. cit.*, 298, and Cathcart, *Baptist Encyclopedia*, I, 266.

ing out of the Great Awakening in New England and reaching Virginia and the Carolinas in the period 1755 to 1760, at first rejected all confessions of faith. In 1783, however, the Separate General Association of Virginia agreed to adopt the Philadelphia Confession, with the proviso that the acceptance did

> not mean that every person is to be bound to the strict observance of everything therein contained, nor do we mean to make it, in any respect, superior or equal to the scriptures in matters of faith and practice: although we think it the best composition of the kind now extant. . . .[7]

With a similar understanding the Confession became the basis of union of Separate and Regular Baptists of Virginia in 1787. A revision of the Philadelphia Confession, proposed by the Ketockton Association, was undertaken by several associations in Virginia in the years 1800-1802. It was never approved by a majority of the associations represented in the General Meeting of Correspondence of Virginia, but the Ketockton and the Culpeper Associations published the revision in 1806, as *The Baptist Declaration of Faith. Revised and Adapted by Several District Associations of the United Baptists in Virginia.* Thirteen of the thirty-four chapters (or articles) of the Philadelphia Confession were unchanged, fourteen were abbreviated, four were rewritten, and three were omitted. One on regeneration was added. Among the omissions was the chapter on the laying on of hands, a practice which had fallen into disuse in Virginia by 1780.

The Philadelphia Confession passed into the background of Baptist affairs in the nineteenth century, but it still was often referred to in America as "the Baptist Confession."

B. *Articles of Faith of the Kehukee Association, 1777*

The Kehukee was one of the early Regular[8] Baptist associations. It was formed in 1769 of churches which missionaries of the Philadelphia and Charleston Associations had helped build. Some of these churches had originally been General Baptist churches but had been converted to Calvinistic views by the work of itinerant preachers like Gano, Vanhorn, and Miller. When the revivalistic

---

[7] Semple, *History of the Rise and Progress of Baptists of Virginia*, 68.

[8] The rise of the Separate Baptists in North Carolina and Virginia after 1755 gave currency to the term "Regular" as applied to those Baptists who looked to Philadelphia as their center and acknowledged the Philadelphia Confession of Faith.

X

Separate Baptists had arisen in the same region, the Kehukee Association sought to establish communion with them. The first effort in this direction was rebuffed by the Separates on the grounds that the Kehukee churches were not strict enough in receiving members, countenanced extravagance of dress, and retained some members who acknowledged that they had been baptized in a state of unbelief.

The North Carolina General Baptist churches, in point of fact, had required no profession of conversion prior to baptism, and when they became Regular churches they failed to eliminate some members who had never made such a profession. As a result of the Separate Baptists' criticisms, a reformation movement was attempted in the Kehukee Association by a majority of its leaders in 1774. The majority agreed not to have fellowship with any people who confessed that they had been baptized before being converted. A minority group of the churches opposed the reformation, and a division of the Association occurred in 1775. Several Separate churches quickly joined the reforming group.[9]

The Kehukee Association was concerned about winning back the dissident churches and securing union with the Separates. Difficulties with both groups were in view in 1777 when the Association drew up a brief Confession of Faith. The Confession, which probably was the first Baptist associational confession of faith to be written in America, was designed to meet the objections of the Separates to the Philadelphia Confession and, at the same time, to declare against Arminianism and lax disciplinary standards. It served as the principal instrument for restoring harmony to the Calvinistic Baptist churches of the area of the Kehukee Association. A reconciliation was effected at Sappony Meeting-house, Sussex County, Virginia, in August, 1777.[10] Separate Baptist churches were formally incorporated into the Association in 1788.[11]

In the anti-missions controversy of the period 1818-1840, the Kehukee Association was badly rent. In 1827 the Association agreed "that we discard all Missionary Societies, Bible Societies and Theological Seminaries, and the practices heretofore resorted to for their support, in begging money from the public. . . ." Missionary churches seceded in numbers by 1830 leaving the Primitive minority

---

[9] Hassell, *History of the Church of God . . . including . . . The History of the Kehukee Primitive Baptist Association,* 698.
[10] *Ibid.*
[11] *Ibid.,* 707.

and the associational name. The Kehukee Association did not alter its Articles of Faith in the controversy, an indication that sources of the anti-missions movement were more practical than theological.

The Kehukee Primitive Baptist Association has retained its Articles to the present, publishing them annually in connection with the minutes of the associational meetings.

ARTICLES OF FAITH
KEHUKEE PRIMITIVE BAPTIST ASSOCIATION[12]

1. We believe in the being of God as almighty, eternal, unchangeable, of infinite wisdom, power, justice, holiness, goodness, mercy, and truth; and that this God has revealed Himself in His word under the characteristics of Father, Son and Holy Ghost.

2. We believe that Almighty God has made known His mind and will to the children of men in His word which word we believe to be of divine authority, and contains all things necessary to be made known for the salvation of men and women. The same is comprehended or contained in the Books of the Old and New Testaments as are commonly received.

3. We believe that God, before the foundation of the world, for a purpose of His own glory, did elect a certain number of men and angels to eternal life and that His election is particular, eternal and unconditional on the creature's part.

4. We believe that, when God made man first, he was perfect, holy and upright, able to keep the law, but liable to fall, and that he stood as a federal head, or representative, of all his natural offspring and that they were partakers of the benefits of his obedience or exposed to the misery which sprang from his disobedience.

5. We believe that Adam fell from his state of moral rectitude, and that he involved himself and all his natural offspring in a state of death; and, for that original transgression, we are both guilty and filthy in the sight of our holy God.

6. We believe that it is utterly out of the power of men, as fallen creatures, to keep the law of God perfectly, repent of their sins truly, or believe in Jesus Christ, except they be drawn by the Holy Ghost.

7. We believe that in God's appointed time and way (by means

---

[12] *Minutes of Kehukee Baptist Association,* 1955.

which He has ordained) the elect shall be called, justified, pardoned and sanctified, and that it is impossible they can utterly refuse the call, but shall be made willing by divine grace to receive the offers of mercy.

8. We believe that justification in the sight of God is only by the imputed righteousness of Jesus Christ, received and applied by faith alone.

9. We believe, in like manner, that God's elect shall not only be called, and justified, but that they shall be converted, born again, and changed by the effectual workings of God's holy Spirit.

10. We believe that such as are converted, justified and called by His grace, shall persevere in holiness, and never fall finally away.

11. We believe it to be a duty incumbent on all God's people to walk religiously in good works; not in the old covenant way of seeking life and favor of the Lord by it, but only as a duty from a principle of love.

12. We believe baptism and the Lord's Supper are gospel ordinances both belonging to the converted or true believers; and that persons who are sprinkled or dipped while in unbelief are not regularly baptized according to God's word, and that such ought to be baptized after they are savingly converted into the faith of Christ.

13. We believe that every church is independent in matters of discipline; and that Associations, Councils and Conferences of several ministers, or churches, are not to impose on the churches the keeping, holding or maintaining of any principle or practice contrary to Church's judgment.

14. We believe in the resurrection of the dead, both of the just and unjust, and a general judgment.

15. We believe the punishment of the wicked is everlasting and the joys of the righteous are eternal.

16. We believe that no minister has no [sic] right to administration of the ordinances, only as are regularly called and come under the imposition of hands by the presbytery.

17. Lastly, we believe that, for the mutual comfort, union and satisfaction of the several churches of the aforesaid faith and order, we ought to meet in an Association way, wherein each church ought to represent their case by their delegates and attend as often as is necessary to advise the several churches in conference and that the

decision of matters in such Associations are not to be imposed, or in any wise binding, on the churches, without their consent, but only to sit as an advisory council.

C. *Principles of Faith of the Sandy Creek Association, 1816*

In the Great Awakening in New England in the fifth decade of the eighteenth century numerous divisions occurred in the established (Congregational) churches. Revivalistic members often left their churches on the basis of their insistence upon experimental religion and organized separate churches; thus they were popularly known as "Separates." Many of them came to require personal faith prior to baptism in their churches, and so they were reckoned "Separate Baptists." In New England they quickly merged with the older Baptist movement in that area.

The Separate Baptist movement went south from New England in 1754 especially in the persons of Shubael Stearns and Daniel Marshall. These pioneers ministered for a while in northern Virginia in the midst of some Baptists who were connected with the Philadelphia Association, before moving on to settle at Sandy Creek, Guilford (now Randolph) County, N. C. The church which the Separates established at Sandy Creek had phenomenal growth and became the center of an evangelistic movement which spread throughout the South. In seventeen years the mother church planted forty-two Separate Baptist churches and sent out one hundred twenty-five ministers.[13] The Sandy Creek Association, organized by Stearns in 1758, was ever characterized by its missionary zeal.

The early Separate Baptists were prejudiced against confessions of faith and this opposition to confessions hindered their uniting with the Regular Baptists in North Carolina, Virginia, and elsewhere. At their 1816 meeting at Brush Creek Church, Randolph County, N. C., however, they consented to ten principles of faith. Perhaps the influence of Luther Rice was determinative in this decision. Rice was present as "a representative of the Board of Foreign Missions," and he and six leaders of the Association were appointed to prepare a Constitution and Rules of Decorum, as well as Articles of Faith for the Association. The following Articles, adopted on October 28, 1816, reflect the outlook of the most influential Baptist association in the South during the eighteenth century.

<hr />

[13]Newman, *A History of the Baptist Churches of the U. S.,* 294.

PRINCIPLES OF FAITH OF THE SANDY CREEK ASSOCIATION[14]

Art. I. We believe that there is only one true and living God; the Father, Son, and Holy Ghost, equal in essence, power and glory; yet there are not three Gods but one God.

II. That the Scriptures of the Old and New Testaments are the word of God, and only rule of faith and practice.

III. That Adam fell from his original state of purity, and that his sin is imputed to his posterity; that human nature is corrupt, and that man, of his own free will and ability, is impotent to regain the state in which he was primarily placed.

IV. We believe in election from eternity, effectual calling by the Holy Spirit of God, and justification in his sight only by the imputation of Christ's righteousness. And we believe that they who are thus elected, effectually called, and justified, will persevere through grace to the end, that none of them be lost.

V. We believe that there will be a resurrection from the dead, and a general or universal judgment, and that the happiness of the righteous and punishment of the wicked will be eternal.

VI. That the visible Church of Christ is a congregation of faithful persons, who have obtained fellowship with each other, and have given themselves up to the Lord and one another; having agreed to keep up a godly discipline, according to the rules of the Gospel.

VII. That Jesus Christ is the great head of the church, and that the government thereof is with the body.

VIII. That baptism and the Lord's Supper are ordinances of the Lord, and to be continued by his church until his second coming.

IX. That true believers are the only fit subjects of baptism, and that immersion is the only mode.

X. That the church has no right to admit any but regular baptized church members to communion at the Lord's table.

D. *Terms of Union Between the Elkhorn and South Kentucky, or Separate, Associations, 1801*

Early efforts of uniting Regular and Separate Baptists in Kentucky failed. During the great Frontier Revival, however, the Elkhorn (Regular) Association appointed a committee in 1801 to visit the South Kentucky (Separate) Association for the purpose of arranging with that body to hold a convention for uniting the

---

[14] Copied from Purefoy, *History of the Sandy Creek Association*, 104-105.

two groups. The convention was planned, and it was held at Howard's Creek (Old Providence) Meeting-house, in Clark County, on the second Saturday in October, 1801. The Separates, being unwilling to accept the Philadelphia Confession, desired a brief set of terms of union. Such an instrument was drawn up, approved by the convention, and, shortly afterward, approved by the churches. Only the two oldest frontier associations were immediately concerned with the transaction, but the articles were published under the style of *The Terms of General Union*. Very soon then, there took place a general union of Kentucky Baptist churches.[15] The unifying instrument reads as follows:[16]

TERMS OF UNION BETWEEN THE ELKHORN AND SOUTH KENTUCKY, OR SEPARATE, ASSOCIATIONS.

We, the committees of Elkhorn and South Kentucky Associations, do agree to unite on the following plan:

1st. That the Scriptures of the Old and New Testament are the infallible word of God, and the only rule of faith and practice.

2d. That there is one only true God, and in the Godhead or divine essence, there are Father, Son and Holy Ghost.

3d. That by nature we are fallen and depraved creatures.

4th. That salvation, regeneration, sanctification and justification are by the life, death, resurrection and ascension of Jesus Christ.

5th. That the saints will finally persevere through grace to glory.

6th. That believers' baptism by immersion is necessary to receiving the Lord's Supper.

7th. That the salvation of the righteous and punishment of the wicked will be eternal.

8th. That it is our duty to be tender and affectionate to each other, and study the happiness of the children of God in general; to be engaged singly to promote the honor of God.

9th. And that the preaching Christ tasted death for every man, shall be no bar to communion.

10th. And that each may keep up their associational and church government as to them may seem best.

11th. That a free correspondence and communion be kept up between the churches thus united.

Unanimously agreed to by the joint committee.

---

[15] Spencer, *A History of Kentucky Baptists*, 544-545.
[16] Taken from Spencer, *ibid.*, 546.

E. *The New Hampshire Confession, 1833*

On June 24, 1830, the Baptist Convention of New Hampshire appointed a committee to prepare and present at the next annual sessions "such a Declaration of Faith and Practice, together with a Covenant, as may be thought agreeable and consistent with the views of all our churches in this State." The resolution calling for this action indicates that the feeling of the body was that the known Baptist declarations of faith were not "in precisely the same language as it is desirable they should be." In point of fact, the theological views of Calvinistic Baptists in the New Hampshire area had been considerably modified after 1780 by the rise of the Free Will Baptists (later called Free Baptists) following the leadership of Benjamin Randall. The Free Will Baptist message was welcomed with enthusiasm by the great middle class in New England and its warm evangelism produced a revolt against the rigid theological system of some Calvinistic Baptists. The New Hampshire Convention thus sought to restate its Calvinism in very moderate tones.

N. W. Williams, William Taylor, and I. Person were named as the committee to draw up and present the new Confession, but their work being unfinished the next year, the assignment was committed to I. Person alone. As instructed by the Convention, Person submitted the draft of a Confession to the Board of the Convention on June 26, 1832. The draft was then referred to a committee of Baron Stow, John Newton Brown, Jonathan Going, and the author for revamping. The committee recommended to the Convention the adoption of the articles, but the Convention referred the articles "to the disposal of the Board" and never took up the matter again. The Board, however, discussed the articles and referred them for further revision to Brown and Stow. After more discussion, alterations were made upon the report of this committee, and Brown was appointed to prepare a final copy. This copy was presented to the Board on January 15, 1833, and approved after slight alterations. The Confession was published by the Board of the Convention and was recommended to the churches for adoption.[17]

The Confession might never have been known outside of New Hampshire except for the work of J. Newton Brown who, twenty

---

[17] McGlothlin, *op. cit.*, 300. Details taken from *Minutes New Hampshire Baptist Historical Society*, 1891.

years later, in 1853, was editorial secretary of the American Baptist Publication Society. On his own authority, in that year, Brown revised the Confession and published it in *The Baptist Church Manual*. In revising it, he added two articles to the original sixteen, one on "Repentance and Faith" and one on "Sanctification." In various church manuals this Confession became the most widely disseminated creedal declaration of American Baptists. In 1867, J. M. Pendleton, pastor at Upland, Pa., incorporated it in his *Church Manual*, and as a leader in the "Landmark Baptist" movement he secured its adoption as the doctrinal statement of churches and associations of the Landmark type. Its silence on the doctrine of the universal Church made the confession particularly adaptable to the emphasis of this group on the local, visible congregation. Hiscox placed it in his *Standard Manual* and his *New Directory*, enlarging it each time.

The Confession has been reasserted or adapted by several groups in the twentieth century. Landmarkists of the Southwest organized in 1902 a General Association of Baptist Churches (now the American Baptist Association) which adopted the Confession, along with a supplementary Doctrinal Statement. In 1933 a group of about fifty churches of the North, protesting against theological liberalism and denominational policies, withdrew to organize the General Association of Regular Baptist Churches. This Association adopted the New Hampshire Confession, with a premillennial interpretation of its last article. In 1925 the Southern Baptist Convention worked over the Confession, adding ten new sections, and published it as an expression of the faith generally held by Southern Baptists.

The following copy of the New Hampshire Confession was taken by McGlothlin, pages 301-307, from William Crowell's *Church Members Hand-Book*. It is thought to be substantially like the original edition, copies of which have disappeared completely. Additions made by J. Newton Brown in 1853 are enclosed in brackets; other changes are indicated in footnotes.

Declaration of Faith.

i. Of the Scriptures.

We believe [that] the Holy Bible was written by men divinely inspired, and is a perfect treasure of heavenly instruction; that it has God for its author, salvation for its end, and truth, without any mixture of error, for its matter; that it reveals the principles by which God will judge us; and therefore is, and shall remain to the end of the world, the true centre of Christian union, and the supreme standard by which all human conduct, creeds, and opinions should be tried.

ii. *Of the True God.*

[We believe] That there is one, and only one, living and true [1] God, [an infinite, intelligent Spirit,] whose name is JEHOVAH, the Maker and Supreme Ruler of heaven and earth; inexpressibly glorious in holiness; [and] worthy of all possible honor, confidence, and love; revealed under the personal and relative distinctions of [2] the Father, the Son, and the Holy Spirit; [3] equal in every divine perfection, and executing distinct but harmonious offices in the great work of redemption.

iii. *Of the Fall of Man.*

[We believe] That man was created in a state of [4] holiness, under the law of his Maker; but by voluntary transgression fell from that holy and happy state; in consequence of which all mankind are now sinners, not by constraint but choice, being by nature utterly void of that holiness required by the law of God, wholly given to the gratification of the world, of Satan, and of their own sinful passions, [5] therefore under just condemnation to eternal ruin, without defense or excuse.

iv. *Of the Way of Salvation.*

[We believe] That the salvation of sinners is wholly of grace; through the Mediatorial Offices of the Son of God, who [by the appointment of the Father, freely] took upon him our nature, yet without sin; honored the [divine] law by his personal obedience, and made atone-

---

[1] "true and living" in ed. 1853.
[2] "revealed . . . of the Father," is as follows in ed. 1853, "that in the unity of the Godhead there are three persons, the Father," etc.
[3] "Ghost" in ed. 1853.
[4] "a state of," omitted in ed. 1853.
[5] "wholly given . . . sinful passions" is changed to "positively inclined to evil" in ed. 1853.

ment for our sins by his death[6]; being[7]risen from the dead he is now enthroned in heaven; and uniting in his wonderful person the tenderest sympathies with divine perfections, [he] is every way qualified to be a suitable, a compassionate, and an all-sufficient Saviour.

v. Of Justification

[We believe] That the great Gospel blessing which Christ of his fulness bestows on such[a] as believe in Him, is Justification; that Justification consists in[b] the pardon of sin and the promise of eternal life, on principles of righteousness; that it is bestowed not in consideration of any works of righteousness which we have done, but solely through His own redemption and righteousness,[8] [by virtue of which faith his perfect righteousness is freely imputed to us of God;] that it brings us into a state of most blessed peace and favor with God, and secures every other blessing needful for time and eternity.

vi. Of the Freeness of Salvation.

[We believe] That the blessings of salvation are made free to all by the Gospel; that it is the immediate duty of all to accept them by a cordial, [penitent,] and obedient faith; and that nothing prevents the salvation of the greatest sinner on earth except[9] his own [inherent depravity and] voluntary refusal to submit to the Lord Jesus Christ,[10] which refusal will subject him to[11] an aggravated condemnation.

vii. Of grace in Regeneration.

[We believe] That in order to be saved, we[12] must be regenerated or born again; that regeneration consists

[6] Ed. 1853 reads, "and by his death made a full atonement for our sins" for "and made . . . death."
[7] "that having risen" in ed. 1853.
[a] For "of his . . . such" ed. 1853 has "secures to such."
[b] For "consists in" ed. 1853 has "includes."
[8] For "His own redemption and righteousness" ed. 1853 has "faith in the Redeemer's blood."
[9] "But" in ed. 1853.
[10] For "refusal to . . . Jesus Christ" ed. 1853 has "rejection of the gospel."
[11] "which refusal . . . to" changed to "which rejection involves him in."
[12] "Sinners" in ed. 1853.

in giving a holy disposition to the mind; and [13] is effected
in a manner above our comprehension or calculation,[14]
by the power of the Holy Spirit, [in connection with
divine truth,] so as to secure our voluntary obedience to
the Gospel; and that its proper evidence is [15] found in
the holy fruit which we bring forth to the glory of God.

viii. *Of Repentance and Faith.*

[This article added in 1853.]

We believe that Repentance and Faith are sacred duties, and also inseparable graces, wrought in our souls
by the regenerating Spirit of God; whereby being deeply
convinced of our guilt, danger, and helplessness, and of
the way of salvation by Christ, we turn to God with
unfeigned contrition, confession, and supplication for
mercy; at the same time heartily receiving the Lord Jesus Christ as our Prophet, Priest, and King, and relying
on him alone as the only and all-sufficient Saviour.

ix. *Of God's Purpose of Grace.*

[We believe] That Election is the gracious [16] purpose
of God, according to which he [graciously] regenerates,
sanctifies, and saves sinners; that being perfectly consistent with the free agency of man, it comprehends all
the means in connection with the end; that it is a most
glorious display of God's sovereign goodness, being infinitely [free,] wise, holy, and unchangeable; that it utterly excludes boasting, and promotes humility, [love,]
prayer, praise, trust in God, and active imitation of his
free mercy; that it encourages the use of means in the
highest degree; that it is [17] ascertained by its effects in
all who [truly] believe the gospel; [that it] is the foundation of Christian assurance; and that to ascertain it with
regard to ourselves, demands and deserves our [18] utmost
diligence.

[13] For "and" ed. 1853 has "that it."
[14] "Or calculation" omitted in ed. 1853.
[15] "Is found . . . God" appears in ed. 1853 as follows: "appears in the
holy fruits of repentance, and faith, and newness of life."
[16] "eternal" in ed. 1853.
[17] "may be" in ed. 1853.
[18] "The" in ed. 1853.

x. *Of Sanctification.*
[Added in 1853.]

We believe that Sanctification is the process by which, according to the will of God, we are made partakers of his holiness; that it is a progressive work; that it is begun in regeneration; and that it is carried on in the hearts of believers by the presence and power of the Holy Spirit, the Sealer and Comforter, in the continual use of the appointed means—especially the Word of God, self-examination, self-denial, watchfulness and prayer.

xi. *Of the Perseverance of Saints.*

[We believe] That such only are real believers as endure unto the end; that their persevering attachment to Christ is the grand mark which distinguishes them from mere [19] professors; that a special Providence watches over their welfare; and [that] they are kept by the power of God through faith unto salvation.

xii. [Of the] *Harmony of the Law and the Gospel.*

[We believe] That the Law of God is the eternal and unchangeable rule of his moral government; that it is holy, just, and good; and that the inability which the Scriptures ascribe to fallen men to fulfill its precepts, arises entirely from their love of sin; to deliver them from which, and to restore them through a Mediator to unfeigned obedience to the holy law, is one great end of the Gospel, and of the means of grace connected with the establishment of the visible Church.

xiii. *Of a Gospel Church.*

[We believe] That a visible Church of Christ is a congregation of baptized believers, associated by covenant in the faith and fellowship of the Gospel; observing the ordinances of Christ; governed by his laws; and exercising the gifts, rights, and privileges invested in them by his word; that its only proper [20] officers are Bishops or

[19] " Superficial " in ed. 1853.
[20] " Scriptural " in ed. 1853.

Pastors, and Deacons, whose qualifications, claims, and duties are defined in the Epistles to Timothy and Titus.

xiv. *Of Baptism and the Lord's Supper.*

[We believe] That Christian Baptism is the immersion of a believer in water,[21] in the name of the Father [and] Son, and Spirit,[22] to show forth in a solemn and beautiful emblem, our faith in a [23] crucified, buried, and risen Saviour, with its purifying power[24]; that it is prerequisite to the privileges of a church relation; and to the Lord's Supper, in which the members of the church, by the [sacred] use of bread and wine, are to commemorate together the dying love of Christ; preceded always by solemn self-examination.

xv. *Of the Christian Sabbath.*

[We believe] That the first day of the week is the Lord's-Day, or Christian Sabbath; and is to be kept sacred to religious purposes, by abstaining from all secular labor and [sinful] recreations; by the devout observance of all the means of grace, both private and public; and by preparation for that rest which remaineth for the people of God.

xvi. *Of Civil Government.*

[We believe] That civil government is of divine appointment, for the interests and good order of human society; and that magistrates are to be prayed for, conscientiously honored, and obeyed, except [only] in things opposed to the will of our Lord Jesus Christ, who is the only Lord of the conscience, and the Prince of the kings of the earth.

xvii. *Of the Righteous and the Wicked.*

[We believe] That there is a radical and essential difference between the righteous and the wicked; that such

---

[21] " Immersion . . . in " reads "immersion in water of a believer, into."
[22] " Holy Ghost " in ed. 1853.
[23] " The" in ed. 1853.
[24] For " with its purifying power " is substituted the following: " with its effect in our death to sin and resurrection to a new life " in ed. 1853.

only as through faith are justified in the name of the
Lord Jesus, and sanctified by the Spirit of our God, are
truly righteous in his esteem; while all such as continue
in impenitence and unbelief are in his sight wicked, and
under the curse; and this distinction holds among men
both in and after death.

xviii. *Of the World to Come.*

[We believe] That the end of this [25] world is ap-
proaching: that at the last day, Christ will descend from
heaven, and raise the dead from the grave to final retribution; that a solemn separation will then take place;
that the wicked will be adjudged to endless punishment,
and the righteous to endless joy; and that this judgment
will fix forever the final state of men in heaven or hell,
on principles of righteousness.

F. *A Treatise on the Faith of the Free Will Baptists, 1834 and 1948*

General or Arminian Baptists appeared early in the story of Baptist life in New England, but having to move counter to the main
theological currents of the day, they did not flourish for a century
and a half. Their theology had its rebirth with the movement of
Benjamin Randall, which began about 1780.

Randall, a native of New Castle, N. H., was converted in 1770,
following, it is said, receipt of the news of George Whitefield's death.
He first joined a Congregational church in New Castle, but becoming
dissatisfied he withdrew from it. Study of the New Testament
convinced him of the doctrine of believers' baptism, and in October,
1776, he was baptized into the fellowship of the Baptist church at
Berwick, Me. Beginning to preach shortly afterward, he had
remarkable success as an evangelist. By 1779, however, sternly
Calvinistic Baptists of New Hampshire and Maine were becoming
very critical of his theological views. Therefore he removed his
membership to an Arminian Baptist church at Strafford, N. H., and
he was ordained in April, 1779, by two Arminian churches. His
founding of a Free Will church at Durham, N. H., in June, 1779,
was but the beginning of a highly successful ministry of gathering
churches and of binding them together in Quarterly and Yearly
Meetings. At his death in 1808, there were one hundred and thirty

---

[25] "The" in ed. 1853.

churches in his fellowship, principally in Maine, New Hampshire, and Vermont.[18]

For a time the new denomination had no confession of faith and was opposed to the use of confessions, but in the third decade of the nineteenth century this attitude began to change. The General Conference, organized in 1827, made up of delegates from Yearly Meetings, agreed in 1832 that a treatise on Free Will Baptist doctrine and practice was needed. Two years were spent in preparing the treatise, and it was adopted in April, 1834. It was published the same year with an introduction which told of the rise of the body, of its attitude toward the Bible, and its reason for publishing the Confession, and with an appendix on discipline and usages. Several editions appeared in this form, until 1848, when the treatise was revised and enlarged.

In view of the gradual changes in doctrine and practice, the General Conferences of 1865 and 1868 raised the question of a revision of both the "Confession" and the "Usages." A revision was attempted and completed by January 1, 1869, and the *Free Will Baptist Faith* was published (as a ninth edition) in that year.[19]

Early in the twentieth century it was evident that the Calvinistic theology of many Baptists, especially in the North, had been considerably modified. Free Will Baptists realized that the larger body of Baptists in the North had come to approximate their theological position, and in 1911 they merged with the Northern Convention.

In the South, the group known as The Original Free Will Baptists maintained a separate existence, and in the first half of the twentieth century exhibited considerable vitality. A General Conference of these churches, spread over six Southern states, existed by the close of the nineteenth century.[20] In 1916 representatives of churches in Kansas, Missouri, Oklahoma, Texas, and North Carolina met near Pattonsburg, Mo., and formed a general organization called the Cooperative General Association of Free Will Baptists. Approximately 300,000 Free Will Baptists were said to have been represented in this Association.[21] When the churches of North Carolina and Tennessee insisted on foot-washing as an ordinance, contrary to the practice of the mid-western churches, they withdrew and

---

[18] Torbet, *A History of the Baptists*, 274-276.
[19] McGlothlin, *op. cit.*, 309.
[20] Dodd, *The Free Will Baptist Story*, 110.
[21] *Ibid.*, 111.

revived the Eastern General Conference in 1921. Finally, however, on November 5, 1935, the Cooperative General Association and the Eastern General Conference merged to form the National Association of Free Will Baptists.[22] At the organizational meeting, at Nashville, Tenn., in 1935, a committee of this body formulated a Treatise to be used in Free Will churches. It was based upon several Treatises, especially that of Benjamin Randall of 1834, and Disciplines already in use among the churches. In 1947 the National Association named a committee to revise the Treatise, and the revision was adopted at the annual session in. July, 1948, at Pocahontas, Ark. It reads as follows:

TREATISE[23]
REVISION OF THE TREATISE AND THE FAITH AND PRACTICES OF THE FREE WILL BAPTISTS

CHAPTER I.

THE HOLY SCRIPTURES

These are the Old and the New Testaments; they were written by holy men, inspired by the Holy Spirit, and are God's revealed word to man. They are a sufficient and infallible rule and guide to Salvation and all Christian worship and service.

CHAPTER II.

BEING AND ATTRIBUTES OF GOD

The Scriptures teach that there is only one true and living God, who is Spirit, self-existent, eternal, immutable, omnipresent, omniscient, omnipotent, independent, good, wise, holy, just, and merciful; the Creator, Preserver, and Governor of the universe; the Redeemer, Saviour, Sanctifier, and Judge of men; and the only proper object of worship.

The mode of His existence, however, is a subject far above the understanding of men—finite beings cannot comprehend Him, for there is none like Him. He is the fountain of all perfection and happiness. He is glorified by the whole creation, and is worthy to be loved and served by all intelligence.

---

[22] *Ibid.*, 116 and 121.
[23] Copied from *A Treatise of the Faith and Practices of the Original Free Will Baptists.* 1953, 4-38. Scripture references omitted.

Y

CHAPTER III.

DIVINE GOVERNMENT AND PROVIDENCE

1. God exercises a providential care and superintendence over all His creatures, and governs the world in wisdom and mercy, according to the testimony of His Word.

2. God has endowed man with power of free choice, and governs him by moral laws and motives; and this power of free choice is the exact measure of man's responsibility.

3. All events are present with God from everlasting to everlasting; but His knowledge of them does not in any sense cause them, nor does He decree all events which He knows will occur.

CHAPTER IV.

CREATION, PRIMITIVE STATE OF MAN, AND HIS FALL

Section I

Creation

1. Of the World. God created the world, and all things that it contains, for His own pleasure and glory and the enjoyment of His creatures.

2. Of the Angels. The angels were created by God to glorify Him and obey His commandments. Those who have kept their first estate He employs in ministering blessings to the heirs of salvation and in executing judgments upon the world.

3. Of Man. God created man, consisting of a material body and a thinking rational soul. He was made in the image of God, to glorify his Maker.

Section II

Primitive Man and His Fall

Our first parents, in their original state, were upright. They naturally preferred and desired to obey their Creator, and had no preference or desire to transgress His will until they were influenced and inclined by the tempter to disobey God's commands. Previous to this, the only tendency of their nature was to do righteousness. In consequence of the first transgression, the state under which the posterity of Adam came into the world is so different from that of Adam that they have not that righteousness and purity which Adam had before the fall; they are not willing to obey God, but are inclined to evil. Hence none, by virtue of any natural goodness and mere work of their own, can become the children of God; but they are all dependent for salvation upon the redemption effected through the blood of Christ, and upon being created anew unto obedience through the operation of the Spirit; both of which are freely provided for every descendent of Adam.

CHAPTER V.

OF CHRIST

Section I

Jesus Christ, the Son of God, possesses all divine perfections. As He and the Father are one, He in His divine nature, filled all the offices and performed the works of God to His creatures that have been the subjects of revelations to us. As man, He performed all the duties toward God that we are required to perform, repentance of sin excepted.

His divinity is proved by His titles, His attributes, and His works.

1. His Titles. The Bible ascribes to Christ the titles of Saviour, Jehovah, Lord of hosts, the first and last, God, true God, great God, God over all, almighty God, and the everlasting Father.

2. The attributes of God are ascribed to the Holy Spirit. omniscient, omnipotent, holy, and is to be worshipped.

3. His Works. By Christ the world was created. He preserves and governs it; He has provided redemption for all men and He will be their final Judge.

Section II

The Incarnation of Christ

The Word, which in the beginning was with God and which was God, by whom all things were made, condescended to a state of humiliation in being united with human nature and become like us, pollution and sin excepted. In this state, as a subject of the law, He was liable to the infirmities of our nature; was tempted as we are, but lived our example, perfect obedience to the divine requirements. As Christ was made of the seed of David, according to the flesh, He is "the Son of man," and as the divine existence is the fountain from which He proceeded, and was the only agency by which He was begotten. He is "the Son of God," being the only begotten of the Father, and the only incarnation of the Divine Being.

CHAPTER VI.

THE ATONEMENT AND MEDIATION OF CHRIST

1. The Atonement. As sin cannot be pardoned without a sacrifice, and the blood of beasts could never wash away sin, Christ gave Himself a sacrifice for the sins of the world, and thus was made salvation possible for all men. He died for us, suffering in our stead, to make known the righteousness of God, that He might be just in justifying sinners who believe in His Son. Through the redemption effected by Christ, salvation is actually enjoyed in this world, and will be enjoyed in the next by all who do not in this life refuse obedience to the known requirements of God. The atonement for sin was necessary. For present and future obedience can no more blot out our past sins than past obedience can remove the guilt of present and future sins. If God pardoned the sins of men without satisfaction for the violation of His law, it would follow that transgression might go on with impunity; government would be abrogated, and the obligation of obedience to God would be, in effect, removed.

2. Mediation of Christ. Our Lord not only died for our sins, but He arose for our justification, and ascended up to heaven, where, as the only Mediator between God and man, He makes intercession for us until He comes again.

3. We believe that all children dying in infancy, having not actually transgressed against the law of God, in their own persons are only subject to the first death, which was brought on by the fall of the first Adam, and not that any one of them dying in that state shall suffer punishment in Hell by the guilt of Adam's sin for of such is the Kingdom of God.

CHAPTER VII.

THE HOLY SPIRIT

1. The Scriptures ascribe to the Holy Spirit the acts and attributes of an intelligent being. He guides, knows, moves, gives information, commands, forbids, sends forth, reproves, and can be sinned against.

2. The attributes of God are ascribed to the Holy Spirit.

3. The works of God are ascribed to the Holy Spirit; creation, inspiration, giving of life, and sanctification.

4. The apostles assert that the Holy Spirit is Lord and God.

From the foregoing the conclusion is that the Holy Spirit is in reality God, and one with the Father in all divine perfections. It has also been shown that Jesus Christ is God—one with the Father. Then these three: the Father, Son, and Holy Spirit, are one God.

The truth of this doctrine is also proved from the fact that the Father, the Son, and the Holy Ghost are united in the authority by which believers are baptized; and in the benedictions pronounced by the apostles, which are acts of the highest religious worship.

CHAPTER VIII.

THE GOSPEL CALL

The call of the Gospel is co-extensive with the atonement to all men, both by the word and strivings of the Spirit, so that salvation is rendered equally possible to all; and if any fail of eternal life, the fault is wholly his own.

CHAPTER IX.

REPENTANCE

The repentance which the Gospel requires includes a deep conviction, a penitential sorrow, an open confession, a decided hatred, and an entire forsaking of all sin. This repentance God has enjoined on all men; and without it in this life the sinner must perish eternally.

CHAPTER X.

FAITH

Saving faith is an assent of the mind to the fundamental truths of revelation, an acceptance of the Gospel, through the influence of the Holy Spirit, and a firm confidence and trust in Christ. The fruit of faith is obedience to the Gospel. The power to believe is the gift of God, but believing is an act of the creature, which is required as a condition of pardon, and without which the sinner cannot obtain salvation. All men are required to believe in Christ, and those who yield obedience to this requirement become the children of God by faith.

CHAPTER XI.

REGENERATION

As man is a fallen and sinful being, he must be regenerated in order to obtain salvation. This change is an instantaneous renewal of the heart by the Holy Spirit, whereby the penitent sinner receives new life, becomes a child of God, and is disposed to serve Him. This is called in Scripture being born again—born of the Spirit, being quickened, passing from death unto life, and a partaking of the divine nature.

CHAPTER XII.

JUSTIFICATION AND SANCTIFICATION

1. Justification. Personal justification implies that the person justified has been guilty before God; and, in consideration of the atonement of Christ, accepted by faith, the sinner is pardoned and absolved from the guilt of sin and restored to the divine favor. Christ's atonement is the foundation of the sinner's redemption, yet, without repentance and faith, it can never give him justification and peace with God.

2. Sanctification is the continuing of God's grace by which the Christian may constantly grow in grace and in the knowledge of our Lord Jesus Christ.

CHAPTER XIII.

PERSEVERANCE OF THE SAINTS

There are strong grounds to hope that the truly regenerate will persevere unto the end, and be saved, through the power of divine grace which is pledged for their support; but their future obedience and final salvation are neither determined nor certain, since through infirmity and manifold temptations they are in danger of falling; and they ought, therefore, to watch and pray lest they make shipwreck of their faith and be lost.

CHAPTER XIV.

THE SABBATH

This is one day in seven, which from the creation of the world God has set apart for sacred rest and holy service. Under the former dispensation, the seventh day of the week as commemorative of the work of creation, was set apart for the sabbath. Under the Gospel, the first day of the week, in commemoration of the resurrection of Christ, and by authority of Christ and the apostles, is observed as the Christian Sabbath. On this day all men are required to refrain from secular labor and devote themselves to the worship and service of God.

Chapter XV.

The Church

A Christian Church is an organized body of believers in Christ, who statedly assemble to worship God, and who sustain the ordinances of the Gospel according to the Scriptures. Believers in Christ are admitted to this church on giving evidence of faith in Christ, obtaining consent of the body, being baptized, and receiving the right hand of fellowship.

The Church of God, or members of the body of Christ, is the whole body of Christians throughout the whole world, and none but the regenerate are its members.

Chapter XVI.

Tithing

Both the Old and New Scriptures teach Tithing as God's financial plan for the support of His work.

Chapter XVII.

The Gospel Ministry

1. Qualification of Ministers. They must possess good, natural and acquired abilities, deep and ardent piety, be especially called of God to the work, and ordained by prayer and the laying on of hands.

2. Duties of Ministers. These are to preach the Word, administer the ordinances of the Gospel, visit their people, and otherwise perform the work of faithful ministers.

Chapter XVIII.

Ordinances of the Gospel

1. Christian Baptism. This is the immersion of believers in water, in the name of the Father, the Son, and the Holy Spirit, in which are represented the burial and resurrection of Christ, the death of Christians to the world, the washing of their souls from the pollution of sin, their rising to newness of life, their engagement to serve God, and their resurrection at the last day.

2. The Lord's Supper. This is a commemoration of the death of Christ for our sins, in the use of bread which He made the emblem of His broken body, and the cup, the emblem of His shed blood, and by

it the believer expresses his love for Christ, his faith and hope in Him, and pledges to Him perpetual fidelity.

It is the privilege and duty of all who have spiritual union with Christ to commemorate His death, and no man has a right to forbid these tokens to the least of His disciples.

3. Washing the Saint's Feet—This is a sacred ordinance, which teaches humility, and reminds the believer of the necessity of a daily cleansing from all sin. It was instituted by the Lord Jesus Christ, and called an "example" on the night of His betrayal, and in connection with the institution of the Lord's Supper. It is the duty and happy prerogative of every believer to observe this sacred ordinance.

Chapter XIX.

Death

Death. As a result of sin, all mankind is subject to the death of the body. The soul does not die with the body, but immediately after death enters into a conscious state of happiness or misery, according to the character here possessed.

Chapter XX.

Second Coming of Christ

The Lord Jesus who ascended on high and sits at the right hand of God, will come again to close the Gospel dispensation, glorify His saints, and judge the world.

Chapter XXI.

The Resurrection

The Scriptures teach the resurrection of the bodies of all men, each in its own order; they that have done good will come forth to the resurrection of life, and they that have done evil to the resurrection of damnation.

Chapter XXII.

The Judgment and Retribution

1. The Judgment. There will be a judgment, when time and man's probation will close forever. Then all men will be judged according to their works.

2. Retribution. Immediately after the judgment, the righteous will enter into eternal life, and the wicked will go into a state of endless punishment.

G. *Doctrinal Statements of the American Baptist Association (1905)
and the North American Baptist Association (1950)*

The Landmark Controversy of the last half of the nineteenth
century concerned a type of "high-churchism" which was preached
in the Southern Baptist Convention particularly by J. R. Graves of
Tennessee. Graves sought support for the "Old Landmarks," which
he identified as including a view of the church as only local and
visible, the necessity of a properly authorized administrator for
validation of the Ordinances, and belief in a direct succession of
Baptist churches (except for the name) from the time of Christ.
According to his teaching, all baptism other than that administered by
authorized Baptist preachers should be rejected, there should be no
"pulpit affiliation" with other denominations or preachers, and the
Lord's Supper should be an exclusively local church observance.
Graves was in favor of missions, but he was severely critical of the
boards of the Convention as a method of carrying on missionary
work.

Graves' ideas were long in taking organizational shape, though
they were spread widely in the South and Southwest. A Landmark
movement crystallized in Texas and Arkansas in the last decade of
the nineteenth century and the first years of the twentieth. Personal
antagonisms and opposition to the use of "executive boards" in
Texas, beginning in 1894, resulted in the withdrawal of a group
called the East Texas Baptist Convention from the Texas Convention in 1899. In the same year the name of the group was changed
to the Missionary Baptist Association of Texas. A similar group in
Arkansas, opposed to boards, conventions, and corresponding sec-
retaries, organized at Little Rock in 1902, calling itself the General
Association of Baptist Churches.[24]

A general organization, the United States General Association
of Landmark Baptists, drawing together Landmark groups in
Texas and Arkansas, began at Texarkana, Ark., in March, 1905,
though formal organization was deferred until November of that
year. At the earlier meeting, a committee of which Ben M. Bogard
was chairman was appointed to draw up a statement of principles,
but the committee's statement proved unsatisfactory. Representation

---

[24] Moore, D. O., *The Landmark Baptists and Their Attack upon the Southern Baptist
Convention Historically Analyzed* (unpublished doctoral thesis at the Southern Baptist Theological Seminary) gives a good account of these beginnings, Chapter III.

was much more general at the later meeting in Texarkana, in November, when messengers from one hundred and seven churches of twelve States and Territories attended, and contributions were received from churches in twenty States and Territories.[25] Committees rather than boards were set up for co-operative work. In November a new Statement of Principles was drawn up and agreed upon. The new denomination soon took the shorter name, the American Baptist Association, by which it is known today. Its early growth was rapid and by 1950 its churches were to be found in thirty-four States and had a combined membership of over 200,000.[26]

According to the Baptist Way-Book (B. M. Bogard, editor, 1946), published by the Sunday School Committee, the denomination holds to the following Doctrinal Statement:

DOCTRINAL STATEMENT OF THE AMERICAN BAPTIST ASSOCIATION[27]

We, your committee on the statement of our doctrinal belief, would respectfully submit the following and recommend:

That this body reaffirm its acceptance of the New Hampshire confession of faith; so long held by our American Baptist people, and that it be printed in full in the minutes of this session.

And that we would further recommend that in explanation of said Articles of Faith and in view of the attacks being made by the advocates of modern science, falsely so-called, on certain fundamentals of the revealed truth, do most positively emphasize our adherence to the following:

1. We believe in the infallible verbal inspiration of the whole Bible. II Tim. 3:16.

2. The Triune God. Matt. 28:19.

3. The Genesis Account of Creation.

4. The virgin birth of Jesus Christ. Matt. 1:21.

5. The deity of Jesus Christ.

6. His crucifixion and suffering as vicarious and substitutionary.

7. The bodily resurrection and ascension of Christ and the bodily resurrection of His saints. 1st Cor. 15th chapter.

---

[25] *Minutes of the Baptist General Association,* Texarkana, Tex., Nov. 24-26, 1905, 1-6
[26] Moore, *op. cit.,* 75-76.
[27] Appearing first in the year book of 1944.

8. The second coming of Christ, personal and bodily, as the crowning event of the Gentile age. Acts 1:11.

9. The Bible doctrine of eternal punishment of the finally impenitent. Matt. 25:46.

10. We also hold in common what real Baptists have ever held, That the great commission was given to the churches only. That in kingdom activities, the church is the unit, and the only unit that the churches have, and equal authority and responsibility should be met by them according to their several abilities.

11. That all co-operative bodies, such as Associations, Conventions and their Boards or Committees, etc., are, and properly should be, the servants of the churches.

12. We believe that the great commission teaches that there has been a succession of missionary Baptist churches from the days of Christ down to this day.

An important secession of member churches from the ranks of the American Baptist Association occurred in 1950, with the organization of the North American Baptist Association. The new body was formed in protest against what was called "one-church dictatorship" of the American Association.[28] Its formative meeting was held with the Temple Baptist Church, Little Rock, Ark., on May 25-26, 1950. Six hundred and eighty-five churches from twenty-one States were represented at the Association's 1955 sessions.[29] Missionaries working in seven foreign lands reported at the same meeting.[30]

The Doctrinal Statement of the North American Baptist Association adds a number of articles to that of the American Baptist Association and reads as follows:

DOCTRINAL STATEMENT OF THE NORTH AMERICAN BAPTIST ASSOCIATION[31]

The churches of this Association heartily subscribe to and agree to defend and promulgate the historic Missionary Baptist Faith and Practice, the interpretation of which is tersely stated as follows:

---

[28] Particularly against the dominant influence of the Antioch Church, Little Rock, Ark.
[29] *Yearbook of North American Baptist Association*, 1955, 81-117.
[30] *Ibid.*, 33-36
[31] *Ibid.*

1. The Trinity of God.

2. The infallibility and plenary verbal inspiration of the Scriptures.

3. The Biblical account of creation.

4. The personality of Satan.

5. Hereditary and total depravity of man in his natural state involving his fall in Adam.

6. The virgin birth and deity of Jesus Christ.

7. Christ's blood atonement for fallen man.

8. His bodily resurrection and ascension back to His Father.

9. The person and work of the Holy Spirit.

10. Justification before God by faith without any admixture of works.

11. Separation of God's children from the world.

12. Water baptism (immersion) to be administered to believers only and by Divine authority as given to Missionary Baptist churches.

13. The Lord's Supper as a church ordinance is to be ministered to baptized believers only and in Scriptural church capacity.

14. Eternal security of the believer.

15. Establishment of a visible church of Christ Himself during His personal ministry on earth.

16. World wide missions according to the Great Commission which Christ gave His church. (Matthew 28:19,20).

17. Perpetuity of Missionary Baptist churches from Christ's day on earth until His second coming.

18. That all Scriptural churches should ever be held as equal units as to their rights and privileges in their associated capacities.

19. That all Scriptural associational assemblies and their committees are servants of the churches.

20. That we brand as unscriptural open communion, alien baptism, pulpit affiliation with heretical ministers, unionism, modernism, modern conventionism, one-church dictatorship, and all kindred evils arising from these practices.

21. We believe that baptism to be valid must be administered by the authority of a true Scriptural Missionary Baptist Church, and we believe that a so-called Baptist church which knowingly receives alien immersion is not a Scriptural Baptist church, and its ordinances are not valid.

22. The personal, bodily and imminent return of Christ to earth.

23. The bodily resurrection of the dead.

24. The reality of heaven, involving Divine assurance of eternal happiness for the redeemed of God.

25. The reality of hell, involving everlasting punishment of the incorrigible wicked.

H. *Confession of Faith of the Fundamental Fellowship, 1921*

The Fundamentalist-Modernist controversy produced several confessions of faith in the third decade of the twentieth century. The first of these appeared in the Northern Convention in 1921. Tension between the two points of view heightened appreciably following the First World War. The reaction of Fundamentalists to the Convention's decision, in 1919, to establish a new weekly publication for promotion of optimistic post-war plans was the calling of a pre-convention Conference on the Fundamentals of the Baptist Faith at Buffalo, N. Y., "to stop our drift toward division and estrangement by stopping the drift toward rationalism and materialism."[32] The result of this meeting of June, 1920, was the formation of the Fundamental Fellowship of the Northern Baptist Convention, later called the National Federation of Fundamentalists of the Northern Baptists.[33] This organization struck out at evolutionary theories and at liberal teaching in Baptist schools, and sought to safeguard orthodoxy in the denomination by committing the Convention to a new confession of faith.

To the pre-convention Conference of 1921, at Des Moines, Iowa, an elderly minister, Frank M. Goodchild, presented a brief confession for adoption by the group. While some hesitated to vote for any confession, the statement was finally adopted almost unanimously. For the next three years, leaders of the Fellowship sought approval of such a declaration by the entire Convention, but that body opposed the use of creeds for attaining doctrinal uniformity. Even the 1922 resolution of W. B. Riley of Minneapolis, that the New Hampshire Confession be recommended to the churches, was defeated.[34] After 1925 the Fundamentalist Fellowship declined, though the controversy continued.

---

[32] Furniss, *The Fundamentalist Controversy, 1918-1931*, 104, quoting *Watchman-Examiner*, 8 (1929) 754.

[33] Furniss, *supra*, 104.

[34] The prevailing substitute motion affirmed that "the New Testament is the all-sufficient ground of our faith and practice, and we need no other statement." *Annual* of the Northern Baptist Convention, 1922, 133-134.

The Goodchild Confession was not forgotten, though it was passed over in favor of the New Hampshire Confession when in 1933 a number of Fundamentalist churches withdrew from the Convention to form the General Association of Regular Baptist Churches. The main body of the old Fundamentalist Fellowship, protesting against an "inclusive" policy of the Foreign Mission Society, continued in the Northern Convention, but organized the Conservative Baptist Foreign Mission Society in December, 1943. The Goodchild Confession was adopted by the Society under Article III of its Constitution and By-Laws, and Article IX of the Constitution, concerning amendments, indicates that Article III may not be altered or amended. In place of the Goodchild preamble to the Confession, the following statement was substituted by the Conservative Society:

> "Only those persons who, without reservation, fully and freely subscribe to the following doctrinal statement are eligible to vote, and only those who without reservation will subscribe to [sic] by signing the following doctrinal statement annually are eligible to serve as officers, regular employees, or missionary representatives of the society."[35]

At a pre-convention meeting in May, 1947, at Atlantic City, N. J., the Conservative Baptist Fellowship became the Conservative Baptist Association of America. Its constitution, drawn after the 1947 meeting, follows that of the Conservative Foreign Mission Society in requiring members to subscribe to its doctrinal platform. The Society's Doctrinal Statement is today practically the original Goodchild Confession in eight articles, the last article having become two articles.[36]

The Goodchild Confession, as published in *The Chronicle* (April, 1944),[37] is as follows:

A CONFESSION OF FAITH

The adoption of a creed to which allegiance is demanded would be contrary to our historic Baptist principles and repugnant to our deepest spiritual instincts. On the other hand, the adoption of a confession of faith, as a standard about which our Baptist people may rally, is consistent with the practice of our fathers from the

[35] *The Chronicle*, VII-VIII (April, 1944), 58.
[36] Bushwyler, Vincent, *The Story of the Conservative Baptist Foreign Mission Society* (Jan., 1949, pamphlet).
[37] VII-VIII, 57-58, reprinted from *The Baptist*, Chicago, July 2, 1921.

earliest days of our denominational history. Living in a day of doubt, unbelief, and irreligion, we feel that the time has come for Baptists publicly to reaffirm their faith in the great fundamentals. As Baptists and members of churches connected with the Northern Baptist Convention, we desire to restate the foundation doctrines of our faith in the following brief and simple confession which is but a re-affirmation of the substance of the historic Philadelphia and New Hampshire Confessions of faith:

1. We believe that the Bible is God's word, that it was written by men divinely inspired, and that it has supreme authority in all matters of faith and conduct.

2. We believe in God the Father, perfect in holiness, infinite in wisdom, measureless in power. We rejoice that he concerns Himself mercifully in the affairs of men, that He hears and answers prayer, and that He saves from sin and death all who come to Him through Jesus Christ.

3. We believe in Jesus Christ, God's only begotten Son, miraculous in His birth, sinless in His life, making atonement for the sins of the world by His death. We believe in His bodily resurrection, His ascension into heaven, His perpetual intercession for His people, and His personal visible return to the world according to His promise.

4. We believe in the Holy Spirit who came forth from God to convince the world of sin, of righteousness and of judgment, and to regenerate, sanctify and comfort those who believe in Jesus Christ.

5. We believe that men by nature and by choice are sinners but that "God so loved the world, that he gave his only begotten son, that whosoever believeth in him should not perish, but have everlasting life"; we believe therefore, that those who accept Christ as Saviour and Lord will rejoice forever in God's presence and those who refuse to accept Christ as Saviour and Lord will be forever separated from God.

6. We believe in the church—a living spiritual body of which Christ is the head and of which all regenerated people are members. We believe that a visible church is a company of believers in Jesus Christ, baptized on a credible confession of faith, and associated for worship, work, and fellowship. We believe that to these visible churches were committed, for perpetual observance, the ordinances of baptism and the Lord's Supper, and that God has laid upon these churches the task of persuading a lost world to accept Jesus Christ as Saviour, and to enthrone Him as the Lord and Master. We be-

lieve that all human betterment and social improvement are the inevitable by-products of such a gospel.

7. We believe that every human being has direct relations with God, and is responsible to God alone in all matters of faith; that each church is independent and autonomous and must be free from interference by any ecclesiastical or political authority; that therefore Church and State must be kept separate as having different functions, each fulfilling its duties free from the dictation or patronage of the other.

I. *Articles of Faith of the Baptist Bible Union of America, 1923*

Another Fundamentalist organization among Northern Baptists was the Baptist Bible Union, which had its beginning in a "Call and Manifesto" issued in 1921 by one hundred and thirty conservatives to reject Baptist agencies disloyal to traditional beliefs, to support only doctrinally sound schools and missionaries, and to circulate safe literature. The supposed ineffectiveness of the Federation of Fundamentalists in opposing modernism was the primary factor in forming the Union. The two groups differed in that while the Federation sought to avoid schism in the Convention, the Union was determined to stamp out heresy at whatever cost. When the Convention in 1925 refused to recall certain of its missionaries, the Union withdrew support from Convention missionary agencies and set up its own foreign and domestic missions departments. The Convention repeatedly rejected the Union's demands, and so the latter proceeded with plans to set up missions and publication societies and took over Des Moines University. At the height of its activity in 1928, the Union drew delegates from eighteen American states and five Canadian provinces to the annual meeting that year in Toronto. However, the waning of the Fundamentalist controversy after 1928 and unwise leadership policies of the Union led to rapid decline and to the sudden death of the body.[38]

The outstanding leader of the Union was T. T. Shields, head of the board of Des Moines University, and it appears that he was chiefly responsible for the Confession of Faith of the group. The Confession, remarkably concise and definite, was printed with Scripture passages quoted in full with each article and with a church covenant. The Confession, published in pamphlet form, is as follows:

---

[38] Furniss, *op. cit.*, 106-109.

ARTICLES OF FAITH
PUT FORTH BY THE BAPTIST BIBLE UNION
OF AMERICA

I. OF THE SCRIPTURES

We believe that the Holy Bible was (a) written by men supernaturally inspired; (b) that it has truth without any admixture of error for its matter; and (c) therefore is, and shall remain to the end of the age, the only complete and final revelation of the will of God to man; the true center of Christian union and the supreme standard by which all human conduct, creeds and opinions should be tried.

(Explanatory)

1. By "THE HOLY BIBLE" we mean that collection of sixty-six books, from Genesis to Revelation, which, as originally written, does not contain and convey the word of God, but IS the very Word of God.

2. By "INSPIRATION" we mean that the books of the Bible were written by holy men of old, as they were moved by the Holy Spirit, in such a definite way that their writings were supernaturally inspired and free from error, as no other writings have ever been or ever will be inspired.

II. OF THE TRUE GOD

We believe that there is (a) one, and only one, living and true God, an infinite, intelligent Spirit, the maker and supreme ruler of heaven and earth; (b) inexpressibly glorious in holiness, and worthy of all possible honor, confidence and love; (c) that in the unity of the Godhead there are three persons, the Father, the Son, and the Holy Ghost, equal in every divine perfection, and executing distinct but harmonious offices in the great work of redemption.

III. OF THE HOLY SPIRIT

That the Holy Spirit is a divine person; (a) equal with God the Father and (b) God the Son and (c) of the same nature; (d) that He was active in the creation; (e) that in His relation to the unbelieving world He restrains the Evil one until God's purpose is fulfilled; (f) that He convicts of sin, of judgment and of righteousness; (g) that He bears witness to the Truth of the Gospel in preaching and testimony; (h) that He is the agent in the New Birth; (i) that He seals, baptizes, endues, guides, teaches, witnesses, sanctifies, and helps the believer.

z

IV. OF THE DEVIL, OR SATAN

We believe that Satan was once (a) holy, and enjoyed heavenly honors; but through pride and ambition to be as the Almighty; fell and (b) drew after him a host of angels; that he is now (c) the malignant prince of the power of the air, and the unholy god of this world. (d) We hold him to be man's great tempter, (e) the enemy of God and His Christ; (f) the accuser of the saints, (g) the author of all false religions, the chief power back of the present apostasy; (h) the Lord of the anti-Christ, and (i) the author of all the powers of darkness—destined however (j) to final defeat at the hands of God's Son, and (k) to the judgment of an eternal justice in hell, a place prepared for him and his angels.

V. OF THE CREATION

We believe in the Genesis account of creation, and (a) that it is to be accepted literally, and not allegorically or figuratively; (b) that man was created directly in God's own image and after his own likeness; (c) that man's creation was not a matter of evolution or evolutionary change of species, or development through interminable periods of time from lower to higher forms; (d) that all animal and vegetable life was made directly, and God's established law was they should bring forth only "after their kind."

VI. OF THE FALL OF MAN

We believe (a) that man was created in innocence under the law of his Maker, but (b) by voluntary transgression fell from his sinless and happy state, (c) in consequence of which, all mankind are now sinners, not by constraint, but of choice; and (d) therefore under just condemnation without defense or excuse.

VII. OF THE VIRGIN BIRTH

We believe (a) that Jesus Christ was begotten of the Holy Ghost in a miraculous manner; (b) born of Mary, a virgin, as no other man was ever born or can ever be born of woman, and (c) that He is both the Son of God, and God, the Son.

VIII. OF THE ATONEMENT FOR SIN

We believe (a) that the salvation of sinners is wholly of grace; (b) through the mediatorial offices of the Son of God, who by the appointment of the Father, freely took upon him our nature, yet without sin, honored the divine law by His personal obedience, and by His death made a full and vicarious atonement for our sins; (c) that His atonement consisted not in setting us an example by His death as a martyr, but was the voluntary substitution of Himself in the sinner's place, the just dying for the unjust, Christ, the Lord, bearing our sins in His own body on the tree; (d) that, having risen from the dead, He is now enthroned in heaven, and uniting in His wonderful person the tenderest sympathies with divine perfection, He is every way qualified to be a suitable, a compassionate and an all-sufficient Saviour.

IX. OF GRACE IN THE NEW CREATION

We believe (a) that in order to be saved, sinners must be born again; (b) that the new birth is a new creation in Christ Jesus; (c) that it is instantaneous and not a process; (d) that in the new birth the one dead in trespasses and in sins is made a partaker of the divine nature and receives eternal life, the free gift of God; (e) That the new creation is brought about in a manner above our comprehension, not by culture, not by character, nor by the will of man, but wholly and solely by the power of the Holy Spirit in connection with divine truth, so as to secure our voluntary obedience to the gospel; (f) that its proper evidence appears in the holy fruits of repentance and faith and newness of life.

X. OF THE FREENESS OF SALVATION

We believe (a) in God's electing grace; (b) that the blessings of salvation are made free to all by the gospel; (c) that it is the immediate duty of all to accept them by a cordial, penitent and obedient faith; and (d) that nothing prevents the salvation of the greatest sinner on earth but his own inherent depravity and voluntary rejection of the gospel; (e) which rejection involves him in an aggravated condemnation.

XI. OF JUSTIFICATION

We believe that the great gospel blessing which Christ secures to such as believe in Him is Justification; (a) that Justification includes the pardon of sin, and the gift of eternal life on principles of righteousness; (b) that it is bestowed not in consideration of any works of righteousness which we have done; but solely through faith in the Redeemer's blood, His righteousness is imputed unto us.

XII. OF REPENTANCE AND FAITH

We believe that Repentance and Faith are (a) solemn obligations, and (b) also inseparable graces, (c) wrought in our souls by the quickening Spirit of God; (d) thereby, being deeply convicted of our guilt, danger and helplessness. and of the way of salvation by Christ, we turn to God with unfeigned contrition, confession, and supplication for mercy; (e) at the same time heartily receiving the Lord Jesus Christ and openly confessing Him as our only and all-sufficient Saviour.

XIII. OF THE CHURCH

We believe that a church of Christ is a congregation of baptized believers (a) associated by a covenant of faith and fellowship of the gospel; (b) observing the ordinances of Christ; (c) governed by His laws; and (d) exercising the gifts, rights and privileges invested in them by His word; (e) that its officers of ordination are pastors, elders and deacons, whose qualifications, claims and duties are clearly defined in the Scriptures; (f) we believe the true mission of the church is found in the great commission: First, to make individual disciples; Second, to build up the church; Third, to teach and instruct, as He has commanded. We do not believe in the reversal of this order; (g) we hold that the local church has the absolute right of self government, free from the interference of any hierarchy of individuals or organizations; and that the one and only superintendent is Christ, through the Holy Spirit; (h) that it is scriptural for true churches to cooperate with each other in contending for the faith and for the furtherance of the gospel; that every church is the sole and only judge of the measure and method of its cooperation; (i) on all matters of membership, of polity, of government, of discipline, of benevolence, the will of the local church is final.

XIV. OF BAPTISM AND THE LORD'S SUPPER

We believe that Christian baptism is (a) the immersion in water of a believer; (b) into the name of the Father, the Son, and the Holy Ghost; (c) to show forth in a solemn and beautiful emblem our faith in the crucified, buried and risen Saviour, with its effect in our death to sin and resurrection to a new life; (d) that it is prerequisite to the privileges of a church relation and to the Lord's Supper; (e) in which the members of the church, by the sacred use of bread and wine are to commemorate together the dying love of Christ; (f) preceded always by solemn self-examination.

XV. OF THE PERSEVERANCE OF THE SAINTS

We believe (a) that such only are real believers as endure unto the end; (b) that their persevering attachment to Christ is the grand mark which distinguishes them from superficial professors; (c) that a special providence watches over their welfare; and (d) that they are kept by the power of God through faith unto eternal salvation.

XVI. OF THE RIGHTEOUS AND THE WICKED

We believe that (a) there is a radical and essential difference between the righteous and the wicked; (b) that such only as through faith are justified in the name of the Lord Jesus, and sanctified by the Spirit of our God, are truly righteous in His esteem; (c) while all such as continue in impenitence and unbelief are in His sight wicked, and under the curse; (d) that this distinction holds among men both in and after death, in the everlasting felicity of the saved and the everlasting conscious suffering of the lost.

XVII. OF CIVIL GOVERNMENT

We believe that civil government is (a) of divine appointment, for the interests and good order of human society; (b) that magistrates are to be prayed for, conscientiously honored and obeyed; (c) except only in things opposed to the will of our Lord Jesus Christ; (d) who is the only Lord of the conscience, and the coming Prince of the Kings of the earth.

XVIII. OF THE RESURRECTION, RETURN OF CHRIST AND RELATED EVENTS

We believe in and accept the sacred Scriptures upon these subjects at their face and full value.
(a) The Bodily Resurrection
    Mt. 26:6-7; Lk. 24:39; Jn. 20:27; I Cor. 15:4; Mk. 16:6; Lk. 24:2,4-6.
(b) The Ascension
    Acts 1:9,11; Lk. 24:51; Mk. 16:19; Rev. 3:21; Heb. 8:1; Heb. 12:2.
(c) The High Priesthood
    Heb. 8:6; I Tim. 2:5; I Jn. 2:1; Heb. 2:17; Heb. 5:9-10.
(d) The Second Coming
    Jn. 14:3; Acts 1:11; I Thess. 4:16; Mt. 24:27; Mt. 25:13; Jas. 5:8; Mt. 24:42; Heb. 9:28.
(e) The Resurrection of the Righteous Dead
    I Thess. 4:16; I Cor. 15:42-44; I Cor. 15:52.
(f) The Change of the Living in Christ
    I Cor. 15:51-53; I Thess. 4:17; Phil. 3:20-21.
(g) On the Throne of David
    Lk. 1:32; Is. 9:6-7; Acts 2:29-30.
(h) His Reign on Earth
    I Cor. 15:25; Is. 32:1; Is. 11:4-5; Ps. 72:8; Rev. 20:1-4; Rev. 20:6.

J. *Statements of Faith of the Southern Baptist Convention, 1925 and 1963*

At a meeting of the Southern Baptist Convention in 1919, J. F. Love of Virginia offered a resolution, which was adopted, that a committee of five messengers be appointed to prepare greetings of the Convention to the people of "like precious faith" scattered abroad in all nations. The War had but recently been concluded, and Southern Baptists wished to restore communications with the worldwide Baptist fellowship. The greetings committee appointed was composed of E. Y. Mullins, L. R. Scarborough, J. B. Gambrell, Z. T. Cody, and William Ellyson. The greetings, prepared largely by E. Y. Mullins, took the form of a statement of faith and were sent out following the 1919 meeting. The statement was not a complete system of doctrine, for it lacked, for example, a section on eschatology, and it did not pretend to be an official declaration.

When the Convention met in 1920, a resolution was passed which made reference to "the widespread interest created by the sending out of a statement of their (Southern Baptists') faith," and called for the appointment of Doctors Gambrell and Mullins as messengers to visit Baptists "as far as possible" all over the world "to convey greetings, good wishes, love and affection of Southern Baptists."

By 1923, however a new issue had been injected into the Convention, the controversy over evolutionary theory, and especially the teaching of evolution in the schools. The concluding portion of President Mullins' address, dealing with science and religion, was seized upon by the anti-evolutionists, who urged its approval as the belief of the body. This was quickly done. Resolutions were offered in later sessions referring more specifically to the teaching of evolution, but these were rejected "on the ground of interference beyond the province of the Convention."[39] Persistent agitation and efforts at passing a dogmatic statement on the subject continued in 1924 and at length were responsible for the presentation of a supplementary recommendation by the Resolutions Committee that a committee be appointed to consider the advisability of issuing another statement of the Baptist faith and message. After the recommendation passed, E. Y. Mullins, L. R. Scarborough, C. P. Stealey, W. J. McGlothlin, S. M. Brown, E. C. Dargan, and R. H. Pitt were named

---

[39] *Annual of the Southern Baptist Convention*, 1923, 62.

to serve as the members of the committee.

An enlargement of the Statement of Principles of 1919 was undertaken by the committee, and the New Hampshire Confession actually served as the basis of the new document. Ten additional sections concerning the resurrection, the return of the Lord, religious liberty, peace and war, education, social service, co-operation, evangelism and missions, stewardship, and the Kingdom of God were prepared. Articles 12 and 16 of the New Hampshire Confession were deleted, and the wording of Articles 7, 9, and 18 was considerably changed. The committee, on presenting the new Confession, first offered a lengthy preface, to indicate the traditional uses which Baptists have made of confessions of faith and the possible values to be seen in this Confession. An effort to amend Article 3 failed. The proposed amendment of C. P. Stealey of Oklahoma said:

> We believe man came into the world by direct creation of God, and not by evolution. This creative act was separate and distinct from any other work of God and was not conditioned upon antecedent changes in previously created forms of life.[40]

Obviously, the Confession was intended only as a general expression of the faith of Southern Baptists, and it has never been looked upon as authoritative or binding. It reflects the comparative uniformity of theological outlook in the South; Northern Baptists at the same time were both unwilling to publish a general confession and unable to agree on one. The Sunday School Board of the Southern Convention has steadily published the Confession in pamphlet form, under the title *Baptist Faith and Message,* prefacing the document with a historical statement concerning the origin of the Confession.

The Sunday School Board of the National Baptist Convention, U.S.A., published in 1929 *The Baptist Standard Church Directory and Busy Pastor's Guide.* It was prepared by L. G. Jordan, Secretary of Foreign Missions of the National Baptist Convention, with the assistance of A. M. Townsend and E. W. D. Isaac. Included in it (pp. 38-55) were Articles of Faith, "recommended for adoption by all Baptist churches at the time of their organization," taken from the New Hampshire Confession and the Southern Baptist Convention declaration. These Articles of Faith are the only confession known to represent American Negro Baptists. They retain Articles xii and

---

[40] *Annual, S.B.C.,* 1924, 76.

xvi of the New Hampshire Confession, omitted in the *Baptist Faith and Message,* but they also include articles from the Southern Baptist Convention document on Christian Education, Social Service, Stewardship, and evangelism and missions. On the other hand, the Southern Baptist Convention articles on Religious Liberty, Peace and War, Co-operation, and the Kingdom are omitted. Minor verbal changes appear throughout the Articles.[41]

When tensions over hermeneutics, especially involving the Convention's seminaries, arose around 1960, the Southern Convention adopted a recommendation in 1962 "that the president of this Convention be requested to call a meeting of the men now serving as presidents of the various state conventions . . . to present to the Convention in Kansas City some similar statement [to the 1925 document] which shall serve as information to the churches, and which may serve as guidelines to the various agencies of the Southern Baptist Convention."

The "Committee on Baptist Faith and Message" reported to the 1963 Convention on its work. It recommended anew the 1925 "statement of the historic Baptist conception of the nature and function of confessions of faith" as follows:

"(1) That they constitute a consensus of opinion of some Baptist body, large or small, for the general instruction and guidance of our own people and others concerning those articles of the Christian faith which are most surely held among us. They are not intended to add anything to the simple conditions of salvation revealed in the New Testament, viz., repentance towards God and faith in Jesus Christ as Saviour and Lord.

"(2) That we do not regard them as complete statements of our faith, having any quality of finality or infallibility. As in the past so in the future, Baptists should hold themselves free to revise their statements of faith as may seem to them wise and expedient at any time.

"(3) That any group of Baptists, large or small, have the inherent right to draw up for themselves and publish to the world a confession of their faith whenever they may think it advisable to do so.

"(4) That the sole authority for faith and practice among Baptists is the Scriptures of the Old and New Testaments. Confessions are only guides in interpretation, having no authority over the conscience.

---

[41] Pages 71-76

"(5) That they are statements of religious convictions, drawn from the Scriptures, and are not to be used to hamper freedom of thought or investigation in other realms of life."

Then the Committee asserted that it had "sought to build upon the structure of the 1925 Statement, keeping in mind the 'certain needs' of our generation." The Convention adopted the new Statement.

The 1963 Statement as printed in the 1963 *Annual of the Southern Baptist Convention*,[42] omitting the Scripture references, is as follows:

I. THE SCRIPTURES

The Holy Bible was written by men divinely inspired and is the record of God's revelation of Himself to man. It is a perfect treasure of divine instruction. It has God for its author, salvation for its end, and truth, without any mixture of error, for its matter. It reveals the principles by which God judges us; and therefore is, and will remain to the end of the world, the true center of Christian union, and the supreme standard by which all human conduct, creeds, and religious opinions should be tried. The criterion by which the Bible is to be interpreted is Jesus Christ.

II. GOD

There is one and only one living and true God. He is an intelligent, spiritual, and personal Being, the Creator, Redeemer, Preserver, and Ruler of the universe. God is infinite in holiness and all other perfections. To him we owe the highest love, reverence, and obedience. The eternal God reveals Himself to us as Father, Son, and Holy Spirit, with distinct personal attributes, but without division of nature, essence, or being.

1. God the Father

God as Father reigns with providential care over His universe, His creatures, and the flow of the stream of human history according to the purposes of His grace. He is all powerful, all loving, and all wise. God is Father in truth to those who become children of God through faith in Jesus Christ. He is fatherly in his attitude toward all men.

---

[42] Pages 270-281

2. God the Son

Christ is the eternal Son of God. In His incarnation as Jesus Christ He was conceived of the Holy Spirit and born of the virgin Mary. Jesus perfectly revealed and did the will of God, taking upon Himself the demands and necessities of human nature and identifying Himself completely with mankind yet without sin. He honored the divine law by His personal obedience, and in His death on the cross He made provision for the redemption of men from sin. He was raised from the dead with a glorified body and appeared to His disciples as the person who was with them before His crucifixion. He ascended into heaven and is now exalted at the right hand of God where He is the One Mediator, partaking of the nature of God and of man, and in whose Person is effected the reconciliation between God and man. He will return in power and glory to judge the world and to consummate His redemptive mission. He now dwells in all believers as the living and ever present Lord.

3. God the Holy Spirit

The Holy Spirit is the Spirit of God. He inspired holy men of old to write the Scriptures. Through illumination He enables men to understand truth. He exalts Christ. He convicts of sin, of righteousness and of judgment. He calls men to the Saviour, and effects regeneration. He cultivates Christian character, comforts believers, and bestows the spiritual gifts by which they serve God through His church. He seals the believer unto the day of final redemption. His presence in the Christian is the assurance of God to bring the believer into the fulness of the stature of Christ. He enlightens and empowers the believer and the church in worship, evangelism, and service.

III. MAN

Man was created by the special act of God, in His own image, and is the crowning work of His creation. In the beginning man was innocent of sin and was endowed by his Creator with freedom of choice. By his free choice man sinned against God and brought sin into the human race. Through the temptation of Satan man transgressed the command of God, and fell from his original innocence;

whereby his posterity inherit a nature and an environment inclined toward sin, and as soon as they are capable of moral action become transgressors and are under condemnation. Only the grace of God can bring man into His holy fellowship and enable man to fulfil the creative purpose of God. The sacredness of human personality is evident in that God created man in His own image, and in that Christ died for man; therefore every man possesses dignity and is worthy of respect and Christian love.

IV. SALVATION

Salvation involves the redemption of the whole man, and is offered freely to all who accept Jesus Christ as Lord and Saviour, who by His own blood obtained eternal redemption for the believer. In its broadest sense salvation includes regeneration, sanctification, and glorification.

1. Regeneration, or the new birth, is a work of God's grace whereby believers become new creatures in Christ Jesus. It is a change of heart wrought by the Holy Spirit through conviction of sin, to which the sinner responds in repentance toward God and faith in the Lord Jesus Christ.

Repentance and faith are inseparable experiences of grace. Repentance is a genuine turning from sin toward God. Faith is the acceptance of Jesus Christ and commitment of the entire personality to Him as Lord and Saviour. Justification is God's gracious and full acquittal upon principles of His righteousness of all sinners who repent and believe in Christ. Justification brings the believer into a relationship of peace and favor with God.

2. Sanctification is the experience, beginning in regeneration, by which the believer is set apart to God's purposes, and is enabled to progress toward moral and spiritual perfection through the presence and power of the Holy Spirit dwelling in him. Growth in grace should continue throughout the regenerate person's life.

3. Glorification is the culmination of salvation and is the final blessed and abiding state of the redeemed.

V. GOD'S PURPOSE OF GRACE

Election is the gracious purpose of God, according to which He regenerates, sanctifies, and glorifies sinners. It is consistent with the free agency of man and comprehends all the means in connection with the end. It is a glorious display of God's sovereign goodness, and is infinitely wise, holy, and unchangeable. It excludes boasting and promotes humility.

All true believers endure to the end. Those whom God has accepted in Christ, and sanctified by His Spirit, will never fall away from the state of grace, but shall persevere to the end. Believers may fall into sin through neglect and temptation, whereby they grieve the Spirit, impair their graces and comforts, bring reproach on the cause of Christ, and temporal judgments on themselves, yet they shall be kept by the power of God through faith unto salvation.

VI. THE CHURCH

A New Testament church of the Lord Jesus Christ is a local body of baptized believers who are associated by covenant in the faith and fellowship of the gospel, observing the two ordinances of Christ, committed to His teachings, exercising the gifts, rights, and privileges invested in them by His Word, and seeking to extend the gospel to the ends of the earth.

This church is an autonomous body, operating through democratic processes under the Lordship of Jesus Christ. In such a congregation, members are equally responsible. Its Scriptural officers are pastors and deacons.

The New Testament speaks also of the church as the body of Christ which includes all of the redeemed of all the ages.

VII. BAPTISM AND THE LORD'S SUPPER

Christian baptism is the immersion of a believer in water in the name of the Father, the Son, and the Holy Spirit. It is an act of obedience symbolizing the believer's faith in a crucified, buried, and risen Saviour, the believer's death to sin, the burial of the old life, and the resurrection to walk in newness of life in Christ Jesus. It is a testimony to his faith in the final resurrection of the dead. Being a church ordinance, it is prerequisite to the privileges of church membership and to the Lord's Supper.

The Lord's Supper is a symbolic act of obedience whereby members of the church, through partaking of the bread and the fruit of the vine, memorialize the death of the Redeemer and anticipate His second coming.

VIII. THE LORD'S DAY

The first day of the week is the Lord's Day. It is a Christian institution for regular observance. It commemorates the resurrection of Christ from the dead and should be employed in exercises of worship and spiritual devotion, both public and private, and by refraining from worldly amusements, and resting from secular employments, work of necessity and mercy only being excepted.

IX. THE KINGDOM

The kingdom of God includes both His general sovereignty over the universe and His particular kingship over men who willfully acknowledge Him as King. Particularly the kingdom is the realm of salvation into which men enter by trustful, childlike commitment to Jesus Christ. Christians ought to pray and to labor that the kingdom may come and God's will be done on earth. The full consummation of the kingdom awaits the return of Jesus Christ and the end of this age.

X. LAST THINGS

God, in His own time and in His own way, will bring the world to its appropriate end. According to His promise, Jesus Christ will return personally and visibly in glory to the earth; the dead will be raised; and Christ will judge all men in righteousness. The unrighteous will be consigned to hell, the place of everlasting punishment. The righteous in their resurrected and glorified bodies will receive their reward and will dwell forever in heaven with the Lord.

XI. EVANGELISM AND MISSIONS

It is the duty and privilege of every follower of Christ and of every church of the Lord Jesus Christ to endeavor to make disciples of all nations. The new birth of man's spirit by God's Holy Spirit means the birth of love for others. Missionary effort on the part of all rests thus upon a spiritual necessity of the regenerate life, and is expressly and repeatedly commanded in the teachings of Christ. It is the duty of every child of God to seek constantly to win the lost to Christ by personal effort and by all other methods in harmony with the gospel of Christ.

XII. EDUCATION

The cause of education in the kingdom of Christ is co-ordinate with the causes of missions and general benevolence and should receive along with these the liberal support of the churches. An adequate system of Christian schools is necessary to a complete spiritual program for Christ's people.

In Christian education there should be a proper balance between academic freedom and academic responsibility. Freedom in any orderly relationship of human life is always limited and never absolute. The freedom of a teacher in a Christian school, college, or seminary is limited by the pre-eminence of Jesus Christ, by the authoritative nature of the Scriptures, and by the distinct purpose for which the school exists.

XIII. STEWARDSHIP

God is the source of all blessings, temporal and spiritual; all that we have and are we owe to Him. Christians have a spiritual debtorship to the whole world, a holy trusteeship in the gospel, and a binding stewardship in their possessions. They are therefore under obligation to serve Him with their time, talents, and material possessions; and should recognize all these as entrusted to them to use for the glory of God and for helping others. According to the Scriptures, Christians should contribute of their means cheerfully, regularly, systematically, proportionately, and liberally for the advancement of the Redeemer's cause on earth.

XIV. CO-OPERATION

Christ's people should, as occasion requires, organize such associations and conventions as may best secure co-operation for the great objects of the kingdom of God. Such organizations have no authority over one another or over the churches. They are voluntary and advisory bodies designed to elicit, combine, and direct the energies of our people in the most effective manner. Members of New Testament churches should co-operate with one another in carrying forward the missionary, educational, and benevolent ministries for the extension of Christ's kingdom. Christian unity in the New Testament sense is spiritual harmony and voluntary co-operation for common ends by various groups of Christ's people. Co-operation is desirable between the various Christian denominations, when the end to be attained is itself justified, and when such co-operation involves no violation of conscience or compromise of loyalty to Christ and his Word as revealed in the New Testament.

XV. THE CHRISTIAN AND THE SOCIAL ORDER

Every Christian is under obligation to seek to make the will of Christ supreme in his own life and in human society. Means and methods used for the improvement of society and the establishment of righteousness among men can be truly and permanently helpful only when they are rooted in the regeneration of the individual by the saving grace of God in Christ Jesus. The Christian should oppose in the spirit of Christ every form of greed, selfishness, and vice. He should work to provide for the orphaned, the needy, the aged, the helpless, and the sick. Every Christian should seek to bring industry, government, and society as a whole under the sway of the principles of righteousness, truth, and brotherly love. In order to promote these ends Christians should be ready to work with all men of good will in any good cause, always being careful to act in the spirit of love without compromising their loyalty to Christ and his truth.

XVI. PEACE AND WAR

It is the duty of Christians to seek peace with all men on principles of righteousness. In accordance with the spirit and teachings of Christ they should do all in their power to put an end to war.

The true remedy for the war spirit is the gospel of our Lord. The supreme need of the world is the acceptance of His teachings in all the affairs of men and nations, and the practical application of His law of love.

XVII. RELIGIOUS LIBERTY

God alone is Lord of the conscience, and He has left it free from the doctrines and commandments of men which are contrary to His Word or not contained in it. Church and state should be separate. The state owes to every church protection and full freedom in the pursuit of its spiritual ends. In providing for such freedom no ecclesiastical group or denomination should be favored by the state more than others. Civil government being ordained of God, it is the duty of Christians to render loyal obedience thereto in all things not contrary to the revealed will of God. The church should not resort to the civil power to carry on its work. The gospel of Christ contemplates spiritual means alone for the pursuit of its ends. The state has no right to impose penalties for religious opinions of any kind. The state has no right to impose taxes for the support of any form of religion. A free church in a free state is the Christian ideal, and this implies the right of free and unhindered access to God on the part of all men and the right to form and propagate opinions in the sphere of religion without interference by the civil power.

6

Confessions of Other Nationalities

DURING THE NINETEENTH CENTURY Baptist churches began to appear in a number of lands besides England and America. These churches were usually propagated directly or indirectly from the English-speaking countries, though in some cases they had independent beginnings. In principal areas of English and American Baptist missionary activity, the new churches usually followed the doctrinal and practical standards of the English-speaking missionaries, and so they were slow to draw up new confessions of faith. On the Continent of Europe, however, Baptists drew up independent confessions of considerable weight early in their history. The most significant confessions drawn up in lands other than Great Britain and the United States of America are given here.

A. *Confession of Faith of the Alliance of Evangelical-Freechurch Congregations (Germany), 1944*

The Anabaptists of the Reformation era in Germany were crushed and scattered by persecution. Modern German Baptists claim no direct descent from these people, but sprang rather from the labors of Johann Gerhard Oncken (1800-1884), who had associations with Great Britain and America. When an agent in Germany of the British-sponsored "Continental Society," Oncken was converted to Baptist views through his study of the Scriptures. He was baptized in 1834, and the first Baptist church of Germany was organized in his house in Hamburg in April of that year.

In spite of persecution, the Baptist movement grew rapidly in that country. It was characterized by evangelistic ardor and vigorous leadership. Julius Kobner, a Danish Jew, and G. W. Lehmann of

Berlin, who particularly assisted Oncken, were among those members who were men of marked ability. Oncken himself is known as "Father of the German Baptists." J. H. Rushbrooke suggests "Father of the Continental Baptists" as a larger title for him, because Oncken traveled over many parts of central, eastern, and northern Europe planting Baptist churches.[1]

In 1837 Oncken and Kobner prepared a confession of faith for apologetic purposes which was accepted by the Hamburg Church and presented by it to the government of Hamburg. When a copy was submitted to the Berlin Church, Lehmann, the Berlin pastor, altered and enlarged the Confession, which then was adopted by the Berlin fellowship. The Hamburg community, however, would not accept the Lehmann emendation for a period of nine years. At length, in 1845 a compromise statement of fifteen articles was wrought out during a visit of Lehmann to Hamburg.[2] Kobner gave literary finish to the document and provided Scripture references. This Confession, first printed in 1847, was approved by all the churches in the same year. It was adopted also as the basis of the "Union of Associated Churches of Baptized Christians in Germany and Denmark" upon organization of that body in 1849. A revision of the Confession was undertaken in 1906, but the original Confession continued to be published.[3]

Pressure of the Nazi regime upon several evangelical groups (sects) which lacked national organization caused these groups to seek union with the Baptists by 1940. In that year the Federation of the Free-church Christians (a union of Darbyites and Open Brethren[4]) and the Elim fellowship (which emphasizes the doctrines of the Holy Spirit and of spiritual gifts) joined with the Baptists in forming the Federation of Evangelical Free-church Congregations.[5] Dr. Hans Luckey of the Baptists and Pastor Erich Sauer of the Open Brethren were commissioned in 1943-44 to draw up a Confession for the Federation. A thorough revision of the Baptist Confession of 1847 was made. Two articles on the Word of God were greatly condensed, and the article on "Election to Salvation" was omitted. The new Confession was considerably shorter than the old.

---

[1] *The Baptist Movement on the Continent of Europe,* 17.

[2] McGlothlin, *op. cit.,* 331-332.

[3] McGlothlin offers a translation of the thirteenth edition (of 1908), 333-354.

[4] Commonly referred to in America as Plymouth Brethren.

[5] Franks, *European Baptists Today,* 38.

Since the Second World War some of the Darbyites have withdrawn from the Federation. The Baptists of Germany, who numbered approximately 100,000 in 1950, continue to acknowledge the following Confession[6]:

CONFESSION OF FAITH OF THE ALLIANCE OF EVANGELICAL-FREECHURCH CONGREGATIONS

ARTICLE 1

CONCERNING GOD AND HIS REVELATION

We believe in God, the *one* Lord in heaven and on earth, who as the Creator of all things visible and invisible has created us in His image and who as the governor of the world rules our life according to His counsel and will.

We believe in Jesus Christ, the Son of the living God, who died for us all on the Cross and rose from the grave, in order that He might save us from sin and death and bestow upon us a new life through the Spirit.

We believe that the Holy Spirit is the bearer and mediator of divine life. God does indeed witness to men in the creation and in conscience, but God's Word is given to us in order that we, illuminated by God's Spirit, may know and receive salvation in Christ.

Holy Scripture is therefore to us a true witness of divine revelation and the norm for faith and conduct.

ARTICLE 2

CONCERNING GOD'S CREATURE

We believe that all men come from God and must appear again before God. For God as the Creator is both origin and goal of every creature. He shapes for us the body, the soul, and the spirit, that we may be like Him.

Our natural life, therefore, is subject to the laws of God. And we fulfill our divine destiny only to the extent that we walk in God's orders and honor the Creator in the creature. We do, for this reason, affirm human culture as far as it corresponds to God's will.

ARTICLE 3

CONCERNING SIN

We believe that mankind since the fall of the first man stands under the judgment of God and has become the prey of death.

---

[6] Indebtedness is acknowledged to Dr. Hans Luckey, who provided a copy of *Glaubensbekenntnis des Bundes Evangelisch-Freikirchlicher Gemeinden.* Dr. W. A. Mueller has kindly made the translation into English. The Scripture references have been omitted.

Separated from God and His life, we are dead in our sins and fulfill the will of the flesh. Therefore our conscience condemns us and judges us to be guilty before God. And we remain under the verdict of God's condemnation, if we do not participate in Christ's redemption and if we are not saved.

ARTICLE 4
CONCERNING REDEMPTION

We believe that Jesus Christ, the Son of God, is the redeemer of the whole world. What was impossible for human kind in its alienation from God, that God did in His love through the sinless man Jesus Christ; He sent Him to the earth, in order that he should die for us a sacrificial death on Calvary and bring to us as the Risen One of the Easter morning the victory of imperishable life.

Therefore man is not justified before God through his own merits, but through faith in the living Christ who forgives us our sins, receives us into His living fellowship and who will lead the anxious creature into the freedom of the children of God.

ARTICLE 5
CONCERNING REGENERATION AND SANCTIFICATION

We believe that God wills that all men be saved. Therefore He commands that every man repent. He who submits to God's judgment and acknowledges the salvation that is in Christ, comes to the assurance that all his sins are forgiven him and is being born again to newness of life out of God. This deep transformation in the will and innermost being of the believer is a work of the Holy Spirit and signifies the beginning of the second, the new creation of God.

We furthermore believe that all who are born of the Spirit and who are sanctified in the Spirit, are in need of daily sanctification. The gift of the new life must issue in the walk in the Spirit, and faith must be followed by the deed. Only thus are we being changed into the image of Christ by continuous growth through God's Spirit and under God's Word.

ARTICLE 6
CONCERNING THE CHURCH AS GOD'S CREATION AND ORDER

We believe that Christ is the invisible head of His body, the Church. All who receive the new life from God He makes members of His body, in order that they grow with one another and for one another, each according to his vocation in the *one* body. The Church of the Lord, therefore, belongs to the new creation of God and this

Church is not already in being where God's Word is proclaimed and heard but only there where men press on to newness of life and find their way to the fellowship of the children of God.

We believe that the totality of all the redeemed belong to the body of Christ. Saved and called by the *one* Lord, we are not merely to confess the unity of the children of God with our mouths, but realize it in fact in order that the *one* Christ in the Church may be made manifest to the world and that the gathering power of the Spirit may be revealed in us.

We believe that the Lord of the Church has also given definite orders for our cooperative fellowship.

We are convinced that the inward vitality of the individual is indispensable and his personal responsibility toward God is inviolable. But at the same time we are convinced that according to apostolic order the member is to fit into the body, that is, that the individual is to bow under the fellowship. This order is also valid for the individual congregation as a member of the fellowship.

But in order that the edification of the Church become possible, Christ has ordained beyond the cooperation of the individual member evangelists, pastors, teachers, preachers, elders and deacons for special ministries of the Church. They act as the Spirit of God leads them and as the order of the Church allows.

We believe that the Church is constrained to deny fellowship to those who persist in sin or who continue in turning away from the Lord, but to grant fellowship to those who repent.

ARTICLE 7
CONCERNING BAPTISM

We believe that the baptism which Christ has ordained should be given to those who have come to believe in the Lord Jesus and who desire in obedience towards Him to witness to their faith before many witnesses. According to primitive Christian example the baptismal candidate is buried in the watery grave of baptism, because he is being baptized into the death of Christ. Then he is raised again because he will have a full share in Christ's resurrection. Baptism, therefore, is a gracious pledge of God to the believer that because he has thus died with the Crucified unto sin, he is also permitted to walk with the Risen One in newness of life.

In baptism we pledge ourselves to the Lord and confess our faith in Him. Hence, the testing in our conduct cannot be absent from our lives. And we baptize publicly before the congregation, because it takes notice both of our conduct and our confession.

ARTICLE 8

CONCERNING THE LORD'S SUPPER

We believe that the Lord Jesus has left to His Church the Lord's Supper as a sacred heritage in order that we celebrate it again and again, remembering the Crucified and have fellowship with Him who for our salvation gave His body and who called the Church into the new covenant in His blood.

We furthermore believe that the fellowship of the body of Christ is particularly represented when we eat of the *one* bread and the *one* cup. Therefore only those may partake of the table of the Lord who attest in faith and conduct that they have received the forgiveness of their sins and have been baptized in the *one* Spirit and into the *one* body.

ARTICLE 9

CONCERNING THE NATURAL ORDERS

We believe that God with His creation has also given us certain natural orders which we must fulfill in obedience to His Word.

We believe that it was the gracious will of the Creator to give us a day of rest and that we should follow the example of the apostolic churches by celebrating the first day of the week on which our Lord rose from the dead as the day of the Lord in order that we might cultivate fellowship under God's Word and work for the Kingdom of God.

We furthermore believe that *marriage* has been ordained of God so that man and wife may fulfill the will of the Creator in bodily and spiritual fellowship by bringing forth children and helping each other in the struggles of life. We consider monogamous marriage to be a divine order. According to God's Word the adulterer has no part in the Kingdom of God.

We believe that the *family* and *people* are natural orders of God which we are not only to accept but which we are to shape according to God's intentions and in whose interest we ought to labor in order that the man of God be healthy in body and soul and fit for every good work.

We believe that the *state* is divinely ordered and that we must serve it with all seriousness. For service to our people is also service before God. We pray for the magistracy that they may justly use the power entrusted to it for the protection of law and the punishment of evildoers. We also swear allegiance to the state, engage in war service, since the magistrate according to God's Word, does not bear the sword in vain. Our faith does not keep us from occupying civil office.

ARTICLE 10
CONCERNING THE CONSUMMATION OF THE WORLD

We believe that our Lord Christ will fulfill His Word and that He will return on the day of revelation in order that He might complete the work of world redemption and to help mankind to achieve the promised goal.

The Lord of the Church will gather the host of the redeemed about Him in order that they might share in His glory and power. Those who have fallen asleep in Christ will rise with a transformed body. Those who belong to the Lord and are still alive at His coming, will be transformed and moved into His presence.

But the world moves towards the judgment. The dead will rise again and will appear before the judge at the right hand of God. The just will enter into eternal life, the unjust will be damned. Even Satan will be condemned, and death will be done away. All trouble and sorrow of earth will end.

At last a new heaven and a new earth will crown the work of the new creation. Righteousness and peace will rule in all eternity. For God will be all and in all.

B. *The Confession of Faith of the Swedish Baptists, 1861*

Swedish Baptists comprise one of the most vigorous and progressive Baptist bodies of Europe. Their first church was organized near Gothenburg in 1848. Baptists were harassed by persecution until after 1860, but their position was somewhat relieved by assistance from America. The first conference of Swedish Baptists was held in 1857. Growth was rapid, and by 1920 the Baptist Union included 61,000 members. However, the Pentecostal movement came to Sweden early in the twentieth century and soon drew heavily upon the Baptist fellowship. The Baptist Union membership numbered approximately 40,000 in 1955. In addition, a strong independent Baptist group, which had been influenced by Pentecostalism, supported the Orebro Mission Society, with headquarters at Orebro.[7] These independent churches seem to be moving into closer relations with the Union.

There is a record of a Confession of Faith prepared by a country church in 1868 in a successful effort to obtain legalization from the

---

[7] Franks, *op. cit.*, 74-75.

government.[8] This Confession was never adopted elsewhere, and the church it represented soon died. The Confession, however, was long regarded by civil and ecclesiastical authorities as the representative Baptist Confession, since no other confession was presented as the basis for legalization.

Shortly before 1861 a Confession was drawn up and adopted by the First Baptist Church of Stockholm. It was presented at the Conference of Swedish Baptist Churches held in Stockholm on June 23-28, 1861, and the Conference adopted it. This Confession is still acknowledged by the Union as "The Confession of Faith of the Swedish Baptists." The translation of Rev. Eric Ruden, Executive Secretary of the Union, follows:

SWEDISH BAPTIST CONFESSION OF FAITH

1. We believe that the Holy Scriptures of both the Old and the New Testament (the commonly so-called Apocryphal Books excepted) are inspired by God and constitute the one perfect rule for our Christian faith and practice.

2. We believe that there is one only living and true God—who is a Spirit infinite in all perfections—; who has revealed Himself in three equal persons, the Father, the Son, and the Holy Ghost.

3. We believe that the first man Adam was created holy, in the image of God, but fell by voluntary transgression of the law of God into a state of sin and death; and that in consequence of his fall all his natural posterity have inherited his corruption, are void of all will to turn to God, and without power perfectly to keep His law, and therefore they are guilty before the wrath of God and condemned to eternal punishment.

4. We believe that our Lord Jesus Christ in his one person united true Godhead and true manhood, that he through his perfect obedience before the law of God and through his atoning death has opened for all a way to redemption and salvation from this lost state, and that every one who from his heart believes in him shall become a partaker of this redemption and salvation without any merit or worthiness of his own.

5. We believe that the gospel—viz. the glad tidings of the salvation which is acquired through Christ—ought to be preached to the whole world; that every one who hears the gospel is under obligation to repent— viz. with a sincere .grief before God to confess and abandon his sins, and at the same time to believe in Christ as his

---

[8] McGlothlin, *op. cit.*, 365.

only and all-sufficient Saviour, and that whosoever may refuse to do so will incur upon himself a worse condemnation.

6. We believe that saving faith is a gift from God and entirely a fruit of the working of the Holy Spirit through the word; that all who are to be saved have been given by the Father to the Son and were chosen in him for salvation and sonship before the foundation of this world was laid; and that we ought with utmost diligence to seek to obtain assurance of our own election.

7. We believe that the law of God has for its end to be: 1) a restraint for the ungodly to restrain them from performing all the evil purpose of their heart; 2) a schoolmaster to bring sinners to Christ, inasmuch as it sets before them the just claims of God and his wrath over sin, shows them their inability to fulfil these claims, and thus awakens in them the need of grace and forgiveness of sin; 3) a rule for the walk of believers to be followed in the spirit of the new covenant; and that, therefore, with these ends in view the law ought to be inculcated in all.

8. We believe that baptism ought to be administered only to such as have personally by a trustworthy confession given evidence of possessing a living faith in Christ; that it is properly administered only through the immersion of the whole person in water; and that it should precede admittance into the fellowship of the church and participation in the Lord's supper.

9. We believe that a true Christian church is a union of believing and baptized Christians, who have covenanted to strive to keep all that Christ has commanded, to sustain public worship, under the guidance of the Holy Spirit to choose among themselves shepherds or overseers, and deacons, to administer baptism and the Lord's supper, to practice Christian church-discipline, to promote godliness and brotherly love, and to contribute to the general spread of the gospel;—also that every such church is an independent body, free in its relation to other Christian churches and acknowledging Christ only as its head.

10. We believe that the first day of the week was kept holy by the apostolic churches as the Lord's day, instead of the Jewish Sabbath, and that we specially on this day are together for common worship and to exercise ourselves in godliness.

11. We believe that civil government is ordained by God, and regard it our duty to honor and pray for the King and the magistracy and in all things to obey the laws of the land, unless they plainly are in conflict with the law of Christ.

12. We believe that this world is to come to an end; that our

Lord Jesus Christ will again appear on the earth on the last day, wake up the dead from their graves, and execute a general judgment in which all wicked men will be irrevocably condemned to eternal punishment, while all believing and righteous men will be solemnly established in their possession of the kingdom which was prepared for them from the beginning of the world.

C. *Confession of Faith and Ecclesiastical Principles of the Evangelical Association of French-speaking Baptist Churches, 1879 and 1924*

The first formal organization of a Baptist church in France seems to have occurred in 1835 at Douai, though a small group of believers who later became a church in the village of Nomain in northern France held meetings from around 1815. The Nomain group arose following the discovery of a Bible in a corner of a farmer's house, but the Douai church was formed under the leadership of an American Baptist Missionary.[9] By 1851 two regional groupings of churches were arranged, in the north the Association Franco-Belge and in the south the Association Franco-Suisse.

The first French Baptist Confession was drawn up by the American missionary, Erasmus Willard, and published at Douai in 1848. With the assistance of some French brethren, Willard prepared a second Confession a few years later. Six French preachers, led by A. Ramseyer and H. Andru, produced a third Confession in 1879. This was the first independently prepared Confession of French Baptists and it was published at Chauny. A second edition was printed in Paris in 1895, having the title, *Confession of Faith and Ecclesiastical Principles of the Evangelical Churches called Baptist*. This edition omitted the last section of the first edition entitled "Of the Congregation."[10] In this form the Confession has continued in use among many French churches. McGlothlin included a translation of the first edition of the Confession in his *Baptist Confessions of Faith* (355-364).

An association of churches was formed in 1923 in southern France in protest against supposed theological liberalism in French Baptist circles. This movement soon claimed most of the churches of the Association Franco-Suisse. Under the leadership of Robert DuBarry

---

[9] Franks, *op. cit.*, 32-33.
[10] McGlothlin, *op. cit.*, 354.

of Nimes, the Association Evangelique[11] has undertaken a vigorous expansion of its ministry into French-speaking Switzerland and Belgium as well as northern France. On November 3, 1924, at the annual conference of the Association at Lyon, a Confession of Faith was adopted by the group. A condensation of the Confession of 1879, it has continued in use to the present. Pastor F. J. Waecker of Bienne, President of the Swiss Association of French-speaking Baptist Churches, has provided a copy of the Confession and Dr. W. A. Mueller's translation into English follows (omitting Scripture references):

CONFESSION OF FAITH AND ECCLESIASTICAL PRINCIPLES OF THE EVANGELICAL ASSOCIATION OF FRENCH-SPEAKING BAPTIST CHURCHES

First Part

Doctrines

1. CONCERNING THE TRUE GOD:

We worship one only God in three persons, Father, Son and Holy Spirit, creator of all things, eternal, infinite, immutable, omnipotent, omniscient, perfectly wise, holy, righteous and good, to whom are due, to the highest degree, obedience, trust, gratitude, love and praise.

2. CONCERNING THE HOLY SCRIPTURES:

We believe that the canonical writings of the Old and the New Testaments are the Word of God and constitute the only and infallible rule of faith and Christian life and the only touchstone by which every doctrine, every tradition and every religious and ecclesiastical system as well as every method of Christian action are to be tested.

We believe that the Holy Scripture is a providential document and that the Holy Spirit presided in sovereign manner at its origin and at the formation of the biblical story. We believe that He has Himself assured therein the perfect teaching and the entire historic truth, despite the imperfection of the human instruments who, by His divine inspiration and under His control, have contributed toward communicating to us the divine oracles.

---

[11] The full name of the body is Association Evangélique des Eglises Baptistes de Langue Française. The other major Baptist body in France today is known as the French Baptist Federation.

We believe that the Holy Scriptures reveal to us all that we must know in the spiritual realm. We believe that they need not be modified or completed by any other revelation in the course of the present dispensation.

3. CONCERNING MAN, THE FALL AND THE CONSEQUENCES OF THE FALL:

We believe that man, who is personally and directly responsible to God, is called to determine himself freely and definitely his eternal destiny down here on earth, by the spiritual position which he shall have taken during his earthly life and in the clearness of the lights that have been accessible to him.

We believe that the fall of man has been provoked and that the rebellion of mankind is being maintained by the intervention of a fallen angel, called Satan, who, having become the adversary of the Eternal long before the creation of man, and having involved in his revolt angels whom he has made his instruments, is destined, together with them, to torments without end through the assured triumph of the Son of God.

We believe that our first parents were created innocent, but having wilfully disobeyed their creator, they lost their primitive estate and incurred the just judgment of God. All their descendants, enveloped in this judgment and inheriting their fallen nature, are inclined towards evil. We believe that all those who like them shall have consciously transgressed God's laws, are justly exposed to an eternal punishment.

4. CONCERNING JESUS CHRIST AND HIS WORK:

We believe that Jesus Christ, the Word made flesh, the only mediator between God and men, is from all eternity the unique Son of God.

We believe that Jesus, conceived by the power of the Holy Spirit and born of a virgin, was just as truly man as he was truly God and after having been tempted in all things like we are, He remained perfectly holy.

We believe that by voluntarily abasing Himself the Son of God manifested in the realm of truth the same perfection as in the realm of goodness and that He never erred, neither in His acts nor in His teachings.

We believe that Jesus Christ of His own free will suffered and that He died on the Cross, suffering there in order to satisfy the divine justice, the penalty which is due to sinners, and presenting to the Father for all whom He has purchased by His blood the merits of His perfect life.

We believe that Jesus Christ rose bodily from the grave and ascended in glory to heaven where He intercedes for His own. We also believe that He will return bodily to take His own with Him and in order to establish His glorious reign. We believe that He will be the judge of the quick and the dead.

5. CONCERNING THE SALVATION THROUGH JESUS CHRIST:

We believe that in order to be saved man must, under the action of the Holy Spirit, repent of his sins and claim for himself, through faith, the expiatory faith of Jesus Christ and of His infinite merits. The sinner, thus justified, regenerated and sanctified by grace, has eternal life which involves the entire redemption of spirit, soul, and body.

6. CONCERNING THE HOLY SPIRIT AND HIS WORK IN CHRISTIAN LIFE:

We believe that the Holy Spirit, a divine person, applies to the heart the truths of Holy Writ with which He cannot be in disagreement. He produces in those who are elected according to the purpose of God the Christian life in its principle and its effects. He enables them to make progress in it and to persevere until the end.

We believe that the Holy Spirit is given to each child of God as the earnest and seal of his eternal heritage. He reveals and communicates the glorious riches of Christ. Every prayer and every work, in order to be truly Christian, must result from His action. He alone can assure to the believer the communion with his God and with his brethren.

7. CONCERNING BAPTISM:

We believe that immersion is for the regenerated man the divinely chosen symbol of the purification of his sins, of his burial and resurrection with Christ. We believe that, according to the order of Christ, the immersion of believers is perpetually obligatory and that, according to the apostolic practice, admission to the local church necessarily implies it.

8. CONCERNING THE LORD'S SUPPER:

We believe that the Supper, instituted by our Lord Jesus Christ, for the commemoration and proclamation of His atoning death on the Cross ought to be observed in and under the control of local churches until He comes again. We believe that bread and wine are symbols of the body and the blood given and shed by our Saviour and by participating in them Christians testify that they are one body with Jesus Christ. We believe that by this participation they likewise proclaim their firm assurance of His return in glory of their divine Saviour and Master.

9. CONCERNING THE RESURRECTION AND THE FINAL JUDGMENT:

We believe that all the dead shall be resurrected, both the just and the unjust. We believe in the final judgment. We believe that the rebellious will consciously suffer the eternal punishment that they shall have merited, and, by virtue of the grace which they shall have accepted by faith, the redeemed shall enjoy eternal glory.

Second Part
Ecclesiastical Principles

1. CONCERNING THE LOCAL CHURCH:

We believe that the local church constituted, according to the Word of God, is an assembly of believers, managing its own affairs, and separated from the state, receiving no subsidy from the latter, and, being completely independent in religious matters from any and every authority save that of Jesus Christ, the only Head of the universal Church which is His body.

We believe that, conforming to the practice of the apostles, it is indispensable that all those who compose a local church have accepted the evangelical message, that they have manifested their regeneration by a Christian walk of life, and that they have testified to their faith by being baptized.

Attachment to the local church creates among the newly baptized and its members a union of mutual obligations. By proclaiming through baptism his faith in the evangelical truths, the candidate takes upon himself the obligation to practice these truths in full harmony with the church.

The members of the local church ought, in the common interest, to exercise the gifts which they have received from God.

The admission of new members is declared by the local assembly itself. In the case of candidates coming from other groups of regularly baptized believers the presentation of a letter of recommendation from such a group is sufficient for admission.

We believe that the local church, a pillar and buttress of the truth within the environment wherein its vocation is being realized, has as its mission to accomplish by its witness, through teaching and by the service it shares, all the tasks which the Lord has left in the charge of Christian local fellowships. It is incumbent upon such a local congregation, in responsible manner, to declare the Gospel, maintain sound doctrine, to control the celebration of Christian ordinances, to establish and realize its program of action, to acknowledge the ministries and to exercise discipline.

2. CONCERNING MINISTRIES:

We believe that all those who officially fulfill a ministry within the local church ought to have been called by the latter, after it has been established that they possess the qualifications required by the Word of God for their charge, which they must discharge in a spirit of wisdom and love.

The Scriptures establish no distinction in rank or authority between bishops (overseers), as pastors and elders. The pastors or elders are particularly charged to watch over the teaching and the spiritual health of the local church. In a general sense, it is their mission to preside over its religious meetings, its public functions and deliberations, whose execution it is incumbent on them to assure. They ought never to dominate over the church of God, but they ought to make themselves examples of the flock by watching over the souls of men as having to give an account of them before God.

In addition to pastors or elders, the local church may have other responsible servants, for example deacons and deaconesses whose role it is to assist the pastors or elders in their ministry, by assuming especial responsibility for everything that relates to the material interests of the congregation.

With relation to their attributes and their individual conduct, the members entrusted with a ministry are, just like the other members, subject to the control and the discipline of the local church which sovereignly determines the particular charge of each member.

3. CONCERNING DISCIPLINE:

We believe that the local church possesses, conforming to the evangelical teaching, the power to exclude from its bosom, after having solemnly warned them, all those of its members whose profession is belied by their conduct, or who without reasonable cause abandon the holy assemblies, and who persistently show that they have no interest in the different needs of the church or who reject the brotherly exhortations which are addressed to them.

The member who has been thus excluded and deprived of all his rights in the church may however continue to benefit of the good will and the spiritual solicitude of those who have had the pain of separating themselves from him. He may, moreover, at his own request, be readmitted to the local church, if his testimony and his conduct demonstrate that he has again become pious and faithful.

D. *Doctrinal Basis of the New Zealand Baptist Union, 1882*

The first New Zealand Baptist church was organized at Nelson in 1851. The Baptist Union of that country came into being in 1882, when the following Doctrinal Basis was adopted:[12]

> The doctrinal basis of the Union shall be the Articles of Faith set forth in the First Schedule to the Baptist Union Incorporation Act 1923 as follows:
>
> (1) The inspiration of the Bible and its authority in all matters of faith and practice.
>
> (2) The true humanity and Deity of the Lord Jesus Christ.
>
> (3) The atonement of our Lord on the Cross for the sin of the world.
>
> (4) Salvation by faith in Christ alone.
>
> (5) Membership in the Christian Church for the regenerate.
>
> (6) The immersion of believers as the only scriptural form of baptism.
>
> Subject to its acceptance of the foregoing Articles of Faith every church in membership with the Union shall have liberty to interpret and administer the laws of Christ and to govern its own affairs.

E. *Doctrinal Basis of the Baptist Union of Victoria, Australia, 1888*

Baptist beginnings in Australia date from 1831, the first church having been formed in Sidney in 1836. The organization of the early churches was soon followed by the formation of district associations, and the associations gradually were gathered into six State Unions. The State Unions formed the Baptist Union of Australia in 1926.

The largest single unit of the national Union today is the Baptist Union of Victoria, established in 1858. In 1888, in connection with its becoming an incorporated body under the laws of the State, this Union adopted the following Doctrinal Basis. The Basis has continued to be used in legal statements and for guidance of the Union.

---

[12] Provided by Rev. Ayson Clifford, Auckland, N. Z.

DOCTRINAL BASIS OF THE BAPTIST UNION OF VICTORIA[13]

1. The Divine inspiration and supreme authority of the Scriptures or the Old and New Testaments.

2. The existence of One God in Three Persons—the Father, the Son, and the Holy Ghost.

3. The Deity and Incarnation of the Lord Jesus Christ, who is the Son of God, the Second Person in the Holy Trinity.

4. The fallen, sinful, and lost estate of all mankind.

5. The salvation of men from the penal consequences and the power of sin through the perfect obedience of the Lord Jesus Christ, His atoning death, His resurrection from the dead, His ascension to the right hand of the Father, and His unchanging Priesthood.

6. The immediate work of the Holy Spirit in the regeneration of men, in their sanctification, and in their preservation to the Heavenly Kingdom of the Lord Jesus Christ.

7. The necessity, in order to salvation, of repentance towards God, and of faith in the Lord Jesus Christ.

8. The resurrection of the dead, and the final judgment of all men by the Lord Jesus Christ.

9. The two ordinances of the Lord Jesus Christ, namely, Baptism and the Lord's Supper, which are of perpetual obligation: Baptism being the immersion of believers upon the profession of their faith in the Lord Jesus Christ, and a symbol of the fellowship of the regenerate in His death, burial and resurrection; the Lord's Supper being a memorial, until He come, of the sacrifice of the body and blood of the Lord Jesus Christ.

The following also appears annually in the constitution:

PRINCIPLES AND IDEALS OF THE BAPTIST FAITH

Whilst holding many phases of Christian Truth, in common with other Denominations, Baptists place a distinctive emphasis upon the following fundamental principles of the Christian Faith, as revealed in the New Testament:—

1. THE CHILD IN THE KINGDOM

(a) Baptists believe that infants are God's little ones, whether

---

[13] From *Constitution of Baptist Union of Victoria*, supplied by Rev. G. H. Blackburn, Hon. Secretary of the Baptist Union of Australia, Surrey Hills, Vic.

BB

children of Christian or non-Christian parents, and accept without modification the word of the Lord, "Of such is the Kingdom of Heaven." This Christian view of the child makes the external act of "Infant Baptism" unnecessary.

(b) Baptists approve of the presentation of children to God by parents, if thereby they solemnly undertake to train them in the nurture and admonition of the Lord, in the home and in the Church.

2. THE SIGNIFICANCE OF CONVERSION

(a) To all who at the stage of personal responsibility, ignore God's law, and wander as prodigals from the Father's Home, Baptists preach the gospel of the Father's love, and the message of the Cross, as the Way of Life. Conversion is acceptance of Jesus Christ as Saviour and Lord.

(b) This acceptance of Christ is a personal and deliberate act, involving the assent of the mind, the decisions of the will, and the love of the heart.

(c) This avowal of allegiance to Christ implies a constant endeavour to live a life worthy of, and well-pleasing to Him in all things.

3. THE CHURCH—A SPIRITUAL SOCIETY

(a) Baptists hold that the Church, as established by the Lord Jesus Christ should consist of persons who have personally and intelligently accepted Him as Saviour and Lord, and pledged themselves to discipleship and service in the kingdom of God.

4. THE LORDSHIP OF CHRIST IN THE CHURCH

(a) Baptists hold and teach that Jesus Christ alone is the Head of the Church, and that without any human intervention or ritualistic ceremony.

(b) Therefore, He is the sole authority in all matters of faith and conduct, in the life both of the Church and of the individual.

(c) This involves liberty of thought and of conscience, and the right of the believer and the Church, freed from any ecclesiastical or other external authority, to interpret His mind.

5. THE STANDARD OF BELIEF

(a) Believing that the voice of the Church is subordinate to the voice of Christ, and that the mind of the Master is the standard of Christian belief, Baptists do not subscribe to any formal Church Creed lest it hamper the development of Christian thought.

(b) Further, in their interpretation of the Lord's farewell declaration, "When He, the Spirit of Truth, is come, He will guide you into all Truth," Baptists accept the principle that God has yet "more light and truth to break forth from His Word."

(c) Therefore, Baptists claim the personal privilege, and accept the Christian responsibility of courageously thinking God's thoughts after Him, under the guidance and inspiration of the Spirit of Truth.

6. THE MINISTRY OF LEADERSHIP

(a) In adopting the Congregational Principles of Church government, with no formal creed, with no external authority, and no defined ecclesiastical polity, and each member having equal rights and responsibilities the Baptist Church is largely dependent on the reality and vigor of the spiritual life of its individual members.

(b) This spiritual life is generated by the understanding and inspiration of Christ's ideals, and by the creation and maintenance of a spiritual atmosphere, in which all that is unworthy dies, and in which Christian life becomes healthy and aggressive.

(c) The Baptist minister accepts his office from the Lord of the Church, and while he is a "servant of the Church," the Church is not his master. He is the spiritual leader in the life and ministry of the Church.

(d) Associated with the minister in the spiritual oversight of the Church are men and women chosen for their Christian gifts and graces, who are called to be examples to the members of the Church, in conduct, zeal, self-denial and generosity.

(e) Church officers are appointed as spiritual leaders to work in sympathetic cooperation with the minister and Church members.

(f) The periodic Church Business Meeting is the centre of the Church's Christian activities, and is the seat of authority in the management of Church business.

7. THE CHRISTIAN SIGNIFICANCE OF BAPTISM

(a) Christian Baptism, by which is meant the immersion of believers as instituted by our Lord, is a personal, public confession of the believer's identification with Christ, and also a means of grace to the Christian.

(b) Baptism is an outward act which symbolizes, but does not effect regeneration, and salvation is not dependent on it.

(c) Baptism is a glorious privilege and a personal responsibility, and is a help to the believer in reminding him of his spiritual union with Christ in His death, burial and resurrection.

8. THE FELLOWSHIP OF THE LORD'S SUPPER

(a) To Baptists the Church is not so much an organization as a fellowship, effective only as there is spiritual association with the Head of the Church.

(b) The Lord's Supper is a service of spiritual fellowship whereby, through remembrance of His Life and Death, believers may experience in supreme degree the reality and influence of His Presence.

(c) It is an opportunity of entering into close fellowship with the Lord in the Holy of Holies, where there is a re-kindling of love and a re-consecration of life to His service.

9. THE CHURCH AND THE KINGDOM

Baptists recognize their responsibility to strive for the establishment of the Kingdom of God in the World, and teach that membership in the Church implies service and sacrifice. This involves a stewardship of time, talents and money, which aims at being worthy of the Son of God who loved and served mankind, even unto death.

F. *A Confession of the Baptist Convention of Ontario and Quebec, 1925*

The main bodies of Canadian Baptists have adopted no official confessions of faith. Several small groups, however, in connection with the Fundamentalist-Modernist controversy of the period 1920-1930, adopted creedal statements based essentially on the Confession of the Baptist Bible Union. Two of these groups represented Fundamentalist secessions from the Ontario and Quebec Convention and from the Baptist Union of Western Canada.

In this same controversy the Baptist Convention of Ontario and Quebec in its educational session of October, 1925, drew up an abbreviated Confession which, however, was never intended to be official or binding. The Confession was intended, rather, to demonstrate that Baptists who remained faithful to McMaster University (the storm center of the controversy) were not disloyal to the essentials of the faith. It was never adopted as a pattern which local churches were to follow, nor was it binding on the Convention or associations. It is purposely vague on numerous issues. The statement reads as follows:[14]

_____

[14] Copied from *Proceedings of the Educational Session of the Baptist Convention of Ontario and Quebec,* October, 1925, pp. 9 f., by Professor Dana Albaugh of McMaster University, Hamilton, Ontario.

The regular Baptist Denomination, whereby is intended Regular Baptist churches exclusively composed of persons who have been baptised in a personal profession of their faith in Christ holding and maintaining *substantially* the following doctrines that is to say

The Divine Inspiration of the Scriptures of the Old and New Testaments and their absolute supremacy and sufficiency in matters of faith and practice,

The existence of one living and true God sustaining the personal relations of Father, Son and Holy Spirit, the same in essence and equal in attributes

The total and universal depravity of mankind

The election and effectual calling of all God's people

The atoning efficacy of the death of Christ

The free justification of believers in Him by His imputed righteousness

The preservation unto eternal life of the Saints

The necessity and efficacy of the Spirit in regeneration and sanctification

The resurrection of the dead both just and unjust

The general judgment

The everlasting happiness of the righteous and the everlasting misery of the wicked

Immersion in the name of the Father, the Son and the Holy Spirit, *the only* gospel baptism

That parties so baptised are alone entitled to communion at the Lord's Table

and that a Gospel Church is a Body of baptised believers voluntarily associated together for the service of God.

G. *In Other Lands*

Brazilian Baptists, one of the largest and most vigorous of the younger Baptist groups, have long acknowledged the New Hampshire Confession of Faith. About 1950, however, they appointed a committee to study the possibility of drawing up a new confession, a document of Brazilian provenience. Later the entire matter was tabled pending further study.

Several national Baptist Unions have brief Basic Statements instead of confessions of faith. Pastor T. Jansma of Arnhem, Secretary of the Union of Baptist Churches in the Netherlands, has supplied a translation of the Basic Statement of the Netherlands Union as follows:

> The churches forming the Union, live out of the revelation of God as this has come to them through the Bible, while their members in obedience to the Holy Scriptures confess to have accepted as their Saviour and Lord Jesus Christ, the son of God, the head of the church and the Lord of the world, and having [have] been baptized upon this confession.

Many of the smaller branches of Baptists have confessions of faith which were prepared in the nineteenth and twentieth centuries. It is not possible to include in this work confessional documents of all these groups, whose separate status rests upon theological, ecclesiological, ethnic, or cultural distinctions.

H. *Russian Baptist Confessions*

The Baptist movement appeared in Russia late in the eighteenth century, resulting from a spiritual awakening among newly freed peasants, German Mennonite migrations into Russia, and distribution of vernacular Scriptures in Russia by the British and Foreign Bible Society. Several movements united in the Russian Baptist Union in 1884. A separate group centered in learned circles in the north, led by Ivan S. Prokhanov, and, preferring the name "Evangelicals," joined with the Baptist Union in the period of World War II to form the "Union of Evangelical Christians and Baptists." Later the name was changed to "Union of Evangelical Christian-Baptists."

It appears that each of the four unions which have combined to form the All-Union Conference formerly acknowledged a confession of faith of its own. Churches of the Russian Baptist Union had long acknowledged the German Baptist Confession of Oucken. The Mennonites had their confession. The Union of Christians of Evangelical Faith (Pentecostals) had theirs. The Evangelical Christian Brotherhood preferred the confession written by Prokhanov. Also, in 1913, I. V. Kargel produced a document entitled "Concise Evangelical Christian Doctrine," which was widely used among both Baptists and Evangelical Christians.

The Prokhanov confession, entitled "Religious Doctrine of the Evangelical Christians," is of peculiar interest. Its clear and detailed outline of doctrinal position shows indubitably the identity of its confessors with the Baptist movement. Because the confession occupies some sixty pages, it cannot be given here in full. Articles dealing with the doctrine of the Church are given below, their translation having been done by Stephen P. Kopestonsky.

CHAPTER XIII
THE CHURCH OF CHRIST

In saving mankind, God founded for Himself a Church.* His Word teaches us that there are:

1) the invisible, universal Church;
2) the visible or local church, and
3) the family church [house chapel].

1) *The universal Church* is a gathering of redeemed (repented, converted, regenerated) souls of all ages, of all peoples [nations], of all local churches (congregations) or family churches (Christian families) on the earth, as well as in heaven, i.e., in all the universe (Ephesians 1:22-23; 3:10; 5:24-25; Colossians 1:18; Hebrews 12:23).

The universal Church is the Kingdom of God, the kingdom of the souls redeemed by Christ, over whom God reigns spiritually (Isaiah 62:12; Colossians 1:13; Luke 22:29; 1 Thessalonians 2:12; Daniel 3:33).

2) *The local church* is a gathering, community or congregation of regenerated souls, united by one faith (one confession), one love and hope, which finds itself in one locality (Matthew 18:17; Acts 14:23; 1 Corinthians 1:2; 1 Thessalonians 2:14). The purpose of the local church is to declare the Kingdom of Christ to its members and to propagate it to the world (Acts 16:5; Revelation 3:2; 3:9; Mark 16:15).

3) *The family church* is a gathering of redeemed souls belonging to one household or family (1 Corinthians 16:19; Romans 16:4; Colossians 4:15).

There may be many local churches. They may differ in their organization and their order and even in their understanding of

* "Ecclesia"—gathering.

certain parts of Holy Scripture, but this does not prevent them from belonging to Christ alone, from praying for each other and even from working together where it is possible, if only they hold fast to the freedom which is in Christ (Romans 14:4-8; 10:12).

Belonging to the universal (invisible) Church does not free a person from the obligation of belonging to a local church, because only through the local church can he fulfill his obligations towards his brothers and sisters in Christ (Hebrews 10:25; Matthew 18:17).

We believe that even though the eternal truths of Christianity remain unchanged for any local church, nevertheless, in the matter of explaining and applying these truths to life—and also in the matter of organization and order—every local church should aspire in every way to perfect itself (Ephesians 4:11-16; Philippians 3:14-15).

MEMBERS ENTERING AND LEAVING THE CHURCH

God established only one condition for the entering into membership of the universal (invisible) Church of Christ: faith, repentance, regeneration and rebirth from above (Revelation 7:9, 14; Hebrews 12:23; John 3:3; 1 Peter 1:3-4).

There is only one category of membership in the Church of Christ: all are equal before God (Matthew 20:25-28; 23:8).

Only those persons can leave the membership of the universal Church who fall away from Christ or those who are bound on earth by a decree of the local church (Hebrews 6:4-7; Matthew 18:17-18).		Equal woth of all believers

The selfsame condition was placed by God on those desiring membership in the local church: faith, repentance, regeneration and rebirth, about which fact a person must witness before the church and before God by an oral confession of faith (Romans 10:9-10; Acts 19:2-5; 1 Timothy 6:12) and through visible baptism by water (Acts 2:41) and further—through joint fulfillment in church of the Lord's Supper (Acts 2:42). All this taken together is the highest expression of the communion of the faithful with one another and with Christ (1 Corinthians 10:17).

Members of the local church cut themselves off from the church when they:

1) renounce the faith (Luke 8:13);
2) perpetrate a sin against a brother (Matthew 18:15-18) or

3) against the Church and God
(2 Thessalonians 3:14-15).

1) In the case of the falling away from the faith the Church acts as did Christ—it prays for those who have fallen away, never displaying any force (John 6:67).

2) In the case of a sin against a brother Christ teaches that if the sinning brother repents, his brothers should forgive him (Matthew 18:21-35); but if he does not repent, they should admonish him, first alone, and then in the presence of two or three brothers (Matthew 18:15-16). In the event of his refusal to accept the exhortation, they should tell the church, which affirms the expulsion or excommunication of the transgressing and unrepentant member (Matthew 18:17-18).

3) In the case of a common sin (against the Church or the Lord) the Word of God teaches that those seeing this should pray for the transgressor and admonish him with the purpose of correcting him; only in the event of his refusal to accept the admonition should the church subject such a person to excommunication, but even then the church should not consider him an enemy, but should teach him as a brother (1 John 5:16; Galatians 6:1; James 5:19-20; 1 Timothy 1:3-5; Hebrews 10:25; 2 Thessalonians 3:6-15; 2 Timothy 4:2; 1 Corinthians 5:3-5; Titus 2:15; 1 Thessalonians 5:11).

The purpose of admonition is love from a pure heart; the purpose of expulsion is not vengeance, but a means to correct the erring brother (Galatians 6:1) and to safeguard the Church from the infection of spiritual corruption (Matthew 18:7-9; 2 Timothy 2:16-19).

CHAPTER XIV
THE ORDINANCES OF THE CHURCH

(Two commandments of God for visible execution)
God in His great wisdom gave the Church two ordinances:

A—Baptism
B—The Lord's Supper.

A. BAPTISM. The Word of God teaches us about two forms of baptism: 1) spiritual and 2) by water.

1) *Spiritual Baptism* is referred to in two ways:

a) baptism by the Holy Spirit and fire (Matthew 3:11; John 1:33; 1 Corinthians 12:13) and

b) baptism in the death of Christ (Mark 10:39; Matthew 20:21-22; Romans 6:3-4; Colossians 2:12).

a) Baptism by the Holy Spirit is the first acceptance of the Holy Spirit (Acts 1:5-8); and since it signifies by itself the beginning of a new person, it is accompanied by rebirth from above, communication of gifts, etc.

b) Baptism in the death of Christ is the change in the soul of man when he, likening himself to Christ, dies by his sins and rises by his righteousness (the old man dies, the new man is born, i.e., rebirth proceeds from above).

2) *Baptism by water.* The Greek word "baptizma" in the New Testament, referring to baptism, means "immersion" (Mark 1:5-9; Matthew 3:16; Acts 8:38-39).

Christ Himself commanded that baptism be performed (Matthew 28:19; Mark 16:16); it was accepted by the Apostles (Acts 2:38) and the Church (Romans 6:3-5; Colossians 2:11-12; 1 Peter 3:21).

Baptism by water is an external indication of the prior fulfillment in the soul of the baptism by the Holy Spirit or the death of sin and the resurrection of righteousness (Romans 6:3-4).

For this reason baptism by water has its meaning only then, when it is performed over those who consciously believe in Christ, have repented, are regenerated and have been reborn from above, i.e., those who have received spiritual baptism (Matthew 28:19; Acts 2:41; Matthew 3:1-2, 6; Acts 2:38; 8:12; 10:47; 18:8; 19:5; Galatians 3:26-27; Mark 16:16).

On the basis of this, before performing baptism by water, the Church has the right and duty to convince itself that the person seeking baptism by water experienced rebirth from above and consciously desires to fulfill the commandment of the Lord (Acts 8:37).

Baptism for children, who cannot consciously believe or consciously experience death for sin and resurrection for righteousness, has no meaning, the more so because they inherit the Kingdom of God independently of faith or repentance (Matthew 18:1-4).

B. THE LORD'S SUPPER. The Lord's Supper* was instituted by the Lord Jesus Christ in the last hours of His earthly life (Luke 22:19-20; 1 Corinthians 11:23-24). The Lord's Supper signifies:

---

* "Eucharist"—thanksgiving.

1) the death of Christ for our sins, which the faithful remember and declare (1 Corinthians 11:26);

2) our spiritual communion with Jesus Christ (1 Corinthians 10:16);

3) the permanent dependence of the believer in his spiritual life on the crucified but living Saviour, with whom he is conjoined (John 6:53);

4) the participation of the believer in the death of Christ (i.e., his death to sin and resurrection to righteousness) (Romans 8:10; Philippians 3:10);

5) the bond of the faithful with Christ, their Head (1 Corinthians 10:17);

6) future joy in the attainment of the Kingdom of God (Luke 22:18; Mark 14:25).

In their time, the Apostles and the churches performed the Lord's Supper daily or weekly (Acts 2:46; 20:7; 1 Corinthians 11:23-24; 1 Corinthians 10:16). It should be performed in the gathering of the faithful (Acts 20:7; 1 Corinthians 11:18, 20, 33-34).

Only the following may participate in the Lord's Supper:

1) those who believe and are reborn;

2) those who witnessed death with Christ through baptism by water (Matthew 28:19-20; Acts 2:41-46; 22:16) and who lead a Christian way of life (1 Corinthians 11:29).

CHAPTER XV
ORGANIZATION OF THE LOCAL CHURCH

By the will of God every (local) church should have an organization and order (1 Corinthians 14:33, 40).

Every church has as its only Head Jesus Christ (Ephesians 1:22) and is administered by His Word and through the guidance of the Holy Spirit (2 Peter 1:19-21; Luke 12:12; Revelation 2:7; Romans 8:14) through prayer and communion at gatherings (Matthew 18:19-20; 1 Corinthians 5:4; Acts 1:15, 23, 26; 2:44-45; 4:23-32; 6:1-6; 14:27; 15:2, 22, 28; Romans 12:16; 1 Peter 3:8).

The church elects from among its members teachers or preceptors to carry out current work (Ephesians 4:11-12; Acts 1:20-26). In the Apostolic Church, these were of two main categories:

1) presbyters,* called in other parts of the Holy Scriptures—pastors, bishops** (I Thessalonians 5:12; Hebrews 13:7, 17, 24) ;

2) deacons.***

The number of these and others in any church was not established, but in all circumstances mentioned in the Holy Scriptures there were more than one of each in every church (Acts 14:23; 20:17, James 5:14; Acts 15:6; 1 Peter 5:2).

Presbyters (bishops, pastors) and deacons are ordained by God through sending down upon them corresponding gifts and zeal, which are evaluated in the eyes of the church. The church, recognizing these gifts, elects them for service.

The duties of the presbyters: to enlighten members of the church in the proper doctrines and to expose those who resist (Titus 1:9; 1 Timothy 3:1-5) ; to support the weak (Acts 20:35) ; to guard and shepherd the church of God (Acts 20:28), not lording over the inheritance of God, but by giving an example to the flock (1 Peter 5:2-3), watching over it as a nurse tenderly watches over children (1 Thessalonians 2:7; 1 Titus 5:17; Acts 8:26-40).

Sermons or the performance of church ordinances do not constitute the exclusive prerogative of presbyters or deacons (1 Corinthians 3:6; 1:14-17).

The duties of the deacons: to watch over the matters of charity (Acts 6:1-4) ; they should be learned in the Word and should conduct discourses (Acts 6:9-10). By their individual qualities, they should satisfy the demands of the Word of God (1 Timothy 3:8-13).

There may be deaconesses in the church (Romans 16:1) and other elected ministers: teachers (1 Corinthians 12:29; Romans 12:7), exhorters, distributors (Romans 12:8), etc.

Ministers, dedicating all their time to the church, may receive their maintenance from her (Matthew 10:10; Luke 22:35).

Members of the church may be elected and sent out to preach as missionaries and should be supported by the church (1 Corinthians 9:14).

Ordination of presbyters and deacons: We understand this in the same sense as the ordination through healing, the sending out for ser-

---

* "presbytery"—elders.
** "episcopy"—overseers.
*** "diakony"—ministers.

vice into a far country, etc., i.e., as a special kind of solemn prayer (Acts 28:8; Mark 6:5; Acts 9:17; 13:3; 19:6; Mark 16:18). It can be performed in conjunction with the church by every believing Christian who has faith and the seal of the Holy Spirit, as in healing, and does not depend on any succession.

The Church Council: Presbyters, deacons and other ministers elected by the church may have, with the agreement of the church, special conferences, constituting, if this is necessary, a permanent council which considers questions before they are presented to the whole church (Acts 15:6, compare verse 22; Philippians 1:1).

It is also the obligation of the Council to care for the progress of the church (Ephesians 4:11-16; Colossians 1:9-10; Acts 9:28-31; 14:22; 16:4-5).

Only the church, and no one inside or outside of it, has the right to elect its ministers, and the church cannot yield this right to any one.

Relationship of Churches Among Themselves

Every church stands directly before its Head—the Lord. It gives account only to Him and is responsible before Him alone. It can recognize no other head or leader over itself, neither in the form of civil authority, nor in the form of influence or domination of any other church, community, or institution.

On the other hand, no church should forget about the existence of other churches; it should pray for them, supporting "the unity of spirit in the bond of peace" with all. It should aspire to cooperate and give as much help as is possible to other churches.

With such aspirations, agreements are possible between churches for definite purposes, particular union, etc.

But, by the existence of such unions, a church should not forget about its full independence; it should not seek for itself leadership of unions or other churches, but should remember that it has sufficient leadership in the Word of God and in the Holy Spirit. On the other hand, a church should never aspire to dominate over other churches, or interfere in their internal affairs, or to influence the election of ministers in other churches.

Together with this, a church should never forget that the highest wish of their Head is that they attain "unity in spirit in the bond of peace."

CHAPTER XVI
RELATIONSHIP WITH THE GOVERNMENT

We believe that the Church of Christ, in contrast to the Government, is a kingdom not of this world (John 18:36). The life of the Church and the life of the Government are heterogeneous (1 Corinthians 2:6-7). The Church, acknowledging Christ as its only Head, by its very essence cannot permit itself to be dominated by a temporal authority, nor can it act in the same spirit and deportment (Luke 12:13-14; Matthew 20:20-28). Therefore the Church and Government should be independent of each other (Matthew 22:21).

But in matters where the Church and Government are contiguous, such as education (schools, recording of marriages, births, etc.), individual members of the church as well as the churches themselves should fully submit to all governmental laws which do not contradict the Word of God.

We believe that "no authority can exist without the permission of God; the existing authorities have been established by him, so that anyone who resists the authorities sets himself in opposition to what God has ordained, and those who oppose him will bring down judgment upon themselves. The man who does right has nothing to fear from the magistrates, as the wrongdoer has. If you want to have no fear of the authorities, do right, and they will commend you for it, for they are God's agents to do you good. But if you do wrong you may well be afraid, for they do not carry swords for nothing. They are God's servants, to execute his wrath upon wrongdoers" (Romans 13:1-4).

Therefore "you must obey them, not only to escape God's wrath, but as a matter of principle, just as you pay your taxes; they are God's ministers, devoting themselves to this service. Pay them all what is due them—tribute to the man entitled to receive it, taxes to the man entitled to receive them, respect to the man entitled to it, and honor to the man entitled to it" (Romans 13:5-7).

We recognize military duty as a poll-tax, but we have communion with those who think otherwise on this question.

We acknowedge as a holy obligation to offer prayers, entreaties, petitions and thanksgivings for all mankind, for all governments and for all who are in authority, "so that we may live tranquil, quiet lives, with perfect piety and probity. It is right to do this, and it pleases God our Savior, who wants all men to be saved and to come to know the truth" (1 Timothy 2:1-4).

We also recognize another of our obligations—to declare the truth before all peoples and kings (Luke 13:32; Acts 9:15; Matthew 14:1-4), and by the example of love and prayer to lessen any existing evils in national or community life, cooperating for the triumph of good (Romans 12:17), freedom (1 Corinthians 7:21), justice (Philippians 4:8), safeguarding peace with all (Hebrews 12:14).

Loving our own people and being ready to lay down our lives for their welfare (Romans 9:1-4), we cannot, in the name of this love, hate any other people (Luke 10:25-37).

We believe that the peculiarities of peoples should serve for the eventual good of all mankind and should not serve as a reason for disputes and wars. We believe that when the Spirit of Christ, who taught us to love our enemies, penetrates the conscience of nations, then "mercy and truth are met together; righteousness and peace have kissed each other" (Psalm 85:10).

We believe in the triumph of the idea of peace; the day will come when people "shall beat their swords into plowshares, and their spears into pruninghooks: nation shall not lift up sword against nation, neither shall they learn war any more" (Isaiah 2:4). We consider it our obligation to cooperate for the coming of this time with our prayers and lives (by word and deed) (James 3:18; Ephesians 6:15).

CHAPTER XVII
ABOUT THE CHRISTIAN FAMILY

We believe that the family and its foundation—marriage—were ordained by God himself (Genesis 2:18, 24).

Marriage is a holy union between man and woman for their mutual help and support, for the continuation of the human race, and for their journey through life in love and fidelity until death parts them (Genesis 2:18; 1 Corinthians 7:33; 1 Peter 3:1-7; Ephesians 5:22-33).

A Christian marriage is of two kinds: 1) spiritual (moral) and 2) physical.

Those who reject the physical side of marriage fall into error and sin (1 Timothy 4:3); those who reject the spiritual (moral) side make the union a carnal cohabitation.

So that a marriage might have a spiritual basis, it is necessary that it be performed before God, in the Lord, trusting in him, who alone unites for eternity. So that no one can break the unity of marriage, prayers are offered to God, asking his blessing for the union (Matthew 19:6), that husband and wife remain steadfast believers, regenerated by the Spirit, and that they have renewed hearts (1 Corinthians 7:39).

The Word of God also recognizes as efficacious a marriage performed between people who are unregenerated and does not deprive them of its blessing. If one party to such a marriage is an unbeliever, the other should not leave the unbelieving party, but should pray so that the Lord would also lead that party to salvation (1 Corinthians 7:12-16).

The Word of God does not forbid a believer to enter into marriage, but only that it be in the Lord (1 Corinthians 7:39; 1 Corinthians 7:10-11).

The Word of God permits divorce only because of adultery (Matthew 5:32; Matthew 19:6).

Domination in marriage from either side should not exist (1 Corinthians 7:3-5; 1 Peter 3:7).

A Christian couple should look upon children as a most precious gift of God; it is their duty to protect their children from temptations, spiritual harm and to lead them on the path to salvation.

Parents can safeguard the souls of their children for salvation only by:

1) giving them a Christian upbringing, by tutoring and educating them in the Lord, and mostly by

2) personal example, remembering the great responsibility they carry if "these little ones" are seduced (Matthew 18:6-7; Colossians 3:21).

For the Christian the proper rearing of children is more important than any form of community activity. Children should obey their parents because justice demands this (Ephesians 6:1-2; Colossians 3:20).

The All-Union Conference of Evangelical Christian-Baptists adopted no confession of faith, but it approved constitutions in 1944, 1948, and 1960, and a "Statute of the Union" in 1963. Section IV of the "Statute" concerns "Local Churches." Its articles[15] are as follows:

19.

The parish church of Evangelical Christian-Baptists is an association of the faithful of Evangelical Baptist confession, who have voluntarily come together for joint service to God and for ministering to their ecclesiastical needs.

The goals of the parish church of ECB are:

a) Preaching the Gospel (Acts 20:24);

b) Educating the faithful to achieve sanctity, Christian goodness, and to observe in their life all that Christ commanded (Matthew 28:20; 1 Timothy 2:1-4);

c) Fostering and consolidating Christian love and unity among the faithful, in conformity with Christ's prayer (John 17:21-23).

20.

To carry out these tasks the parish churches of AUCECB conduct services preaching the Gospel, offering prayers, administering Baptism, bread-breaking, performing wedding, burial, and other church rituals. Services are conducted to musical accompaniment and involve general and choir singing.

21.

Services in churches of Evangelical Christian-Baptists are held on Sundays, also on weekdays, as decided by the church, and on Christian holidays: Christmas, New Year, Christ's Baptism, Purification, Annunciation, Easter, Ascension, Trinity, Transfiguration, the Festival of the Harvest, and Unity Day.

22.

Bread-breaking in local churches (communities and groups) of Evangelical Christian-Baptists is held as the church deems necessary, usually on the first Sunday of each month.

23.

Evangelical Christian-Baptist churches conduct their services

[15] *Documents of Moscow 1966 All-Union Conference of Evangelical Christian-Baptists,* pp. 58-62.

in special buildings made available by the state for free use by the church or in premises rented from the local authorities or private individuals.

24.

a) Membership in a parish church can be conferred on one who has come to believe in Christ as his personal Saviour, who has experienced revival from the Word of God and the Holy Spirit, who has come of age, and has undergone water baptism in faith;

b) Each member of the church engages zealously in the life of the church, serves God according to his vocation, enjoys the right of electing and being elected for service, and is responsible before God and the church for his spiritual state (1 Peter 2:5, 9; Galatians 6:1-2).

25.

a) Each believer who desires to join the parish church through water baptism in faith, notifies the presbyter of his intention and undergoes the relevant spiritual probation.

26.

Each church affiliated with the Union of ECB retains its independence and autonomy; its own general meeting decides all the major internal church questions, such as electing and reelecting church officials, admission and excommunication, and other important problems put before the church by the church council.

27.

For day-to-day service and management of the temporal activities, the church elects:

a) For presbyterian service—a presbyter, who is the chief person responsible for church meetings and the spiritual education of church members and who officiates at church rituals, as well as deacons and preachers, who take part together with the presbyter in religious services and in fulfilling church rites.

The presbyter and the church council may appoint other church members to take part in sermons at church meetings.

NOTE: Church rites may be administered by the appointment of the presbyter and church council, by deacons, church council members, and preachers.

b) For general control of the community and for dealing with organizational, economic, and financial affairs, etc., as well as for external representation of the church in these matters—the executive body, the church council.

   c) To manage the collection and spending of the money and to take care of the community property—the Auditing Commission.

   d) The presbyter, church council, and auditing commission present reports to the church at least once a year.

28.

   a) Choir members, leaders, and musicians must all be believers.

   b) Besides the regent, the presbyter of the church is also the spiritual guardian of the choir.

29.

   a) The means of the parish church are derived from voluntary donations, which go into the community treasury (2 Corinthians 9:7).

   b) The church money is spent to maintain prayer houses, for the upkeep of the church ministers, for deductions to AYCECB treasury and to the treasuries of the republican and regional protopresbyter, as well as for other needs of the church.

   c) A treasury account book is kept in each church.

   d) Each church has an inventory book, where all church property is registered property received from the state by agreement, as well as property purchased or donated.

   e) Finances and property are audited by a three-man auditing commission, elected by the church.

30.

The church may have its own seal and stamp.
(Approved by the All-Union Conference of Evangelical Christian-Baptists in Moscow on Wednesday, October 5, 1966).

I. *In Conclusion*

On the basis of this survey, it is obvious that Baptists have continuously sought to formulate and articulate their faith by means of brief doctrinal summaries. These confessions represent the sincere desire of many Baptist communities to set forth their interpretations of the Scriptures regarding Christian belief and practice. No single confession has yet appeared which would be acceptable to all Baptists. On the other hand, all Baptist confessions demonstrate enough of essential agreement to procure for their proponents an acknowledgment of membership in the Baptist family. In every instance, they bespeak the theological and biblical awareness, the freedom, and the sense of responsibility of the movement through succeeding generations.

It is inevitable that other confessions will be prepared and used in various groups in years to come, as men try to put into clear words their understanding of the teachings of the Scriptures.

Index